THE
SHURLEY METHOD

ENGLISH MADE EASY

Student Book

Level 7

By
Brenda Shurley
Ruth Wetsell
Teddie Faye Raines

Shurley Instructional Materials, Inc., Cabot, Arkansas

06-15
ISBN 978-1-881940-20-3 (Level 7 Shurley Method Student Book – Softcover)

Printed in the United States of America by RR Donnelley, Owensville, MO.

For additional information or to place an order, write to: Shurley Instructional Materials, Inc.
366 SIM Drive
Cabot, AR 72023

1 2 3 4 5 6 7 8   15 14 11 08 07 06 04 95

TABLE OF CONTENTS

Chapter

TABLE OF CONTENTS CONTINUED

TABLE OF CONTENTS CONTINUED

TABLE OF CONTENTS CONTINUED

CHAPTER 1 LESSON 1 PRETEST

Exercise 1: Identify the part of speech or the sentence job of each word. Write the abbreviation above the word.

1. Several plump robins /searched diligently (for juicy worms) (in my back yard.)

2. (For my birthday) my generous parents /gave me the most important item on my list.

3. Quickly, Jocelyn and her little brother /led the five horses (into the barn)

4. Four very excited fans /were irate (after the referee's call)

5. Can that history teacher /make this class interesting (to his students?)

6. My two cousins (in El Paso) are students (at Coronado High School)

7. (After an exciting election) John Conner /named Sarah Warren chairman (of the committee)

Exercise 2: Identify each pronoun as indefinite or personal (**I,P**) and as singular or plural (**S, P**). Underline your choices.

8. we (I or **P**) (**S** or P)   10. everybody (**I** or P) (**S** or P)   12. she (I or **P**) (**S** or P)   14. both (**I** or P) (S or P)

9. each (**I** or P) (**S** or P)   11. they   (I or **P**) (S or **P**)   13. either (**I** or P) (**S** or P)   15. it   (I or **P**) (**S** or P)

Exercise 3: Identify each verb as regular or irregular and put **R** or **I** in the blank. Then write the past tense form.

16. cook R cooked   17. swim I swam   18. break I broke

Exercise 4: Fill in the helping verb chart and name the four principal parts of a verb.

19. Write the names of the four principal parts:

Future Tense	Present Perfect		Past Perfect	Future Perfect	Progressive Form		Emphatic Form	
2 verbs	Singular-1	Plural-1	1 verb	3 verbs	Singular -5	Plural - 4	Singular-2	Plural-2
will/shall	has	have	Had	will/shall + have	am, is, are be, been	are, were be, been	does did	do did

Exercise 5: Correct the errors in the following paragraph. Replace each word underlined once with a synonym and each word underlined twice with an antonym. Use this error guide: **Capitals: 27 Homonyms: 6 End Marks: 7 Commas: 4 Semicolons: 1 Subject-Verb Agreement: 4 Apostrophes: 2 Synonym: 3 Antonym: 1 Spelling: 2**

during march, my whole family enjoy watching the n c a a division 1 national men's basketball tournament, we each choose the too teams we think will make the finals, susan and dad always picks u c l a as one of there teams, last year some of the games was in kansas, city kansas which is near our home, sense the games was so close, we went two one session and saw for excellent games, my dream is to play collage basketball however i am to short, i guess ill just have to consintrate on growing

CHAPTER 1 LESSON 1

Study Skills

Good management skills come from good organizational skills, and organizational skills are the foundation for good study skills. You must learn to manage your time, your materials, and your work environment. Good study skills do not just happen. It takes time, determination, and practicing certain guidelines to get organized. The Study Skills chapter will concentrate on the guidelines you need for success in developing good study habits. Follow them carefully until they become habits that will help you for a lifetime.

Everyone has the same twenty-four hours, but everyone does not use his/her twenty-four hours in the same way. In order to get the most for your time, it is important to set goals. Goals will keep you pointed in the direction you want to go, will focus your time, and will keep you on track. With a list of goals, you can check your progress. Long-term goals are what you want to accomplish in your life, your education, and your career. Short-term goals will help you plan things to do over the next school year, and guidelines will give you specific things to do each day to help you achieve your goals. Write down two long term goals and three short-term goals. Discuss these goals with your teacher, counselor, or parents. You can add more as you think of them. Take time to evaluate your goals at the end of every month to see if there are any adjustments you wish to make. Goals change as your needs change and as your abilities grow.

One of the first steps in good organization is learning how to make and follow a daily schedule or routine. Below is a set of guidelines to help you establish a daily schedule to follow at home and school. These guidelines will be one of the keys to your being successful in school with the least amount of wasted effort.

Beginning Setup Plan for School
You should use this plan to keep things in order!

1. Have separate color-coded pocket folders for each subject.
2. Put unfinished work in the left-hand side and finished work in the right-hand side of each subject folder.
3. Put notes to study, graded tests, and study guides in the brads so you will have them to study for nine weeks or semester tests.
4. Have a trash folder to put all paper to be thrown away. If it doesn't belong in a folder, throw it away!
5. Have a paper folder to store extra clean sheets of paper. Keep it full at all times.
6. Have an assignment folder to be reviewed every day. (This is a very important folder. It must go home every night!)

    Do these things and put them in your assignment folder:
    A. Keep a monthly calendar of homework assignments, test dates, report-due dates, project-due dates, meeting times, after-school activities, dates and times, review dates, etc.
    B. Keep a grade sheet to record the grades received in each class. (You might also consider keeping your grades on the inside cover of each subject folder. However you keep your grades, just remember to keep up with them accurately, even if you have to ask for your grades at the end of every week. Your grades are your business, so keep up with them!)
    C. Make a list every day of the things you want to do so that you can keep track of what you finish and what you do not finish. Move the unfinished items to your new list the next day. (Yes, making this list takes some time, but it's your road map to success. You will always know at a glance what you set out to accomplish and what still needs to be done.)

7. Organize your locker, get rid of unnecessary papers, keep locker trips to a minimum. (There should be **no loose papers** in your locker!)
8. Keep all necessary school supplies in a handy, heavy-duty Ziploc bag or a pencil bag.

CHAPTER 1 LESSON 1

Study Plan for School
You should check this plan every day!

1. Attend class regularly after eating breakfast to start your day.
2. Schoolwork is your job -- make it an important part of your daily life.
3. Develop the "I'm-willing-to-do-what-it-takes-to-get-the-job-done" attitude.
4. Work with your teachers and parents to correct any attitudes or habits that keep you from learning.
5. Make the effort to listen, ask questions if you don't understand, and answer questions if asked.
6. Write it down! Write it down! Write it down! Make taking notes in class a habit. Then, put them in the correct folder.
7. Ask about make-up work and turn it in on time.
8. Turn your daily assignments in on time.
9. Check your assignment folder every day. Know what is on your calendar. Remember to record everything on your calendar so you won't get behind!
10. Concentrate on the job at hand. If you don't waste time, you will have a chance to finish your work. Keep your eyes on your work and keep your pencil moving. Don't give yourself a chance to stop working by breaking your concentration. Every time your eyes leave your paper to look around, you lose working time.
11. Do what is important first! Assignments that are due first should be completed first.
12. Think before you leave school! Check your assignment folder and decide what you need to take home. Put books and folders you will need in a book bag so you won't forget them.

Study Plan for Home
Stick to this plan every evening!

1. Schedule a time to study. Think about your family's routine and decide on a good study time. Stick to your schedule.
2. Study where you can concentrate. Sorry! No TV or telephone while you study! (Get your studying job finished and then watch TV or talk on the telephone, if you must. Remember, TV does not get you ahead in life--Education will!)
3. Make a personal decision to concentrate 100 percent on completing your homework assignments. You will get more accomplished in less time with 100 percent concentration than if you give 25 percent of your concentration for a longer period of time.
4. Check your assignment folder every day. Get control of your life!
5. Have a special place to keep homework. When your homework is finished, put it in your bookbag right then, and you will always have it ready to take to school, no matter how hassled your morning is.
6. Use your home study time to get your assignments done or to review for a test. Don't wait until the last minute to study for a test. Study a little every night so that you won't overload the night before. (And, of course, you'll probably have company the night before the big test! That's why you don't wait until the last minute to study – take charge!)
7. If possible, set a weekly meeting time to discuss your progress with your parents. If it is not possible, meet with yourself. You need to discuss your progress and problems. See which study skill you did not follow. Figure out what to do to "fix" them, and try again! You'll get better with practice.
8. You are old enough to help yourself! Remember, school is your business, your job, and your responsibility.

CHAPTER 1 LESSON 1
Student Progress Chart

School is your job. Make it your business to know your progress. The progress chart below is designed for you to record and graph your grades in each subject so you can see your progress. You will know from day to day how you are doing in every subject. You will see from your progress chart if you need to do extra studying in a particular subject.

Write the month and each day's date in the appropriate boxes. Write your percentage grade in the box beside the corresponding letter grade. Your chart will record up to twenty grades.

Student Progress Chart
You should chart your grades with colored pencils.

Month:

Day:																					
English	1	2	3	4	5	6	7	8	9	10	11	12	13	14	15	16	17	18	19	20	Average
A																					
B																					
C																					
D																					
F																					

Day:																					
Math	1	2	3	4	5	6	7	8	9	10	11	12	13	14	15	16	17	18	19	20	Average
A																					
B																					
C																					
D																					
F																					

Day:																					
Science	1	2	3	4	5	6	7	8	9	10	11	12	13	14	15	16	17	18	19	20	Average
A																					
B																					
C																					
D																					
F																					

Day:																					
History	1	2	3	4	5	6	7	8	9	10	11	12	13	14	15	16	17	18	19	20	Average
A																					
B																					
C																					
D																					
F																					

Other:

CHAPTER 1 LESSON 1

The first pages of this book discuss some of the ways for you to manage your time, your materials, and your work environment by making and following a daily schedule, or routine. Now, you will use the *Daily Lesson Record* below to record your assignments and grades. This daily lesson record will help you remember what you do in class, when assignments or projects are due, and what weekly grades you make in each subject.

Daily Lesson Record					
Teacher:		Class:	Period:	For the Week of:	
Class Activity	Monday	Tuesday	Wednesday	Thursday	Friday
Book Page Nos.					
Class Worksheet					
Test					
Homework					
Project					
Project Due Date					
Library, Film, Etc.					
Grades Made					
Work Not Turned In					
Incomplete Work					

Daily Lesson Record					
Teacher:		Class:	Period:	For the Week of:	
Class Activity	Monday	Tuesday	Wednesday	Thursday	Friday
Book Page Nos.					
Class Worksheet					
Test					
Homework					
Project					
Project Due Date					
Library, Film, Etc.					
Grades Made					
Work Not Turned In					
Incomplete Work					

CHAPTER 1 LESSON 2

A/An Choice

1. Use the word **_a_** when the next word begins with a consonant sound. (Example: a round mirror)
2. Use the word **_an_** when the next word begins with a vowel sound.   (Example: an oval mirror)

Guided Practice: Write **_a_** or **_an_** in the blanks.

1. The teacher gave __an__ oral test.
2. The teacher gave __a__ written test.

3. He is __a__ very good artist.
4. He is __an__ artist of landscapes.

Synonyms, Antonyms, and Homonyms

Synonyms are words that have the same, or almost the same, meaning. (boat, ship / quick, fast / raise, lift / flat, level)

Antonyms are words that have opposite meanings. (dry, wet / weary, fresh / wild, tame / cold, hot)

Homonyms are words which sound the same but have different meanings and different spellings.

Guided Practice: Identify each pair of words as synonyms or antonyms by putting parentheses ( ) around **_syn_** or **_ant_**.

5. earlier, prior	(syn) ant	7. calamity, disaster	(syn) ant	9. integrity, honesty	(syn) ant
6. numerous, few	syn (ant)	8. gallant, cowardly	syn (ant)	10. enmity, hostility	(syn) ant

Homonym Chart		
1. **capital** - upper part, main	11. **lead** - metal	21. **their** - belonging to them
2. **capitol** - statehouse	12. **led** - guided	22. **there** - in that place
3. **coarse** - rough	13. **no** - not so	23. **they're** - they are
4. **course** - route	14. **know** - to understand	24. **threw** - did throw
5. **council** - assembly	15. **right** - correct	25. **through** - from end to end
6. **counsel** - advice	16. **write** - to form letters	26. **to** - toward (a preposition)
7. **forth** - forward	17. **principle** - a truth/rule/law	27. **too** - denoting excess
8. **fourth** - ordinal number	18. **principal** - chief/head person	28. **two** - a couple
9. **its** - possessive pronoun	19. **stationary** - motionless	29. **your** - belonging to you
10. **it's** - it is	20. **stationery** - paper	30. **you're** - you are

Guided Practice: Underline the correct homonym.
11. Jason was a member of the student (council, counsel).
12. Mrs. Green gave her math class extra (council, counsel) about their semester test.
13. We saw the (capitol, capital) building during our trip to Columbus, Ohio.
14. I (know, no) that there are (know, no) seats left in the stadium.

Guided Practice: **Editing Paragraph**
Find each error and write the correction above it. Replace words underlined once with a synonym and words underlined twice with an antonym. **Editing Guide: Homonyms: 9 Synonyms: 4 Antonyms: 2 A/An: 2 Misspelled Words: 2 Missing Words: 1**

Our smart hiking guide lead us to an coarse area of grass. Their we saw too quail perfecting they're nest of eggs. We left them alone and began to search for your large tent. Our short coarse took us threw a swampy area and across an stationary bridge. You're tent was the forth one we found at bottom of the shallow ditch.

Student Book

CHAPTER 1 LESSON 2 SKILL TEST

Exercise 1: Write *a* or *an* in the blanks.

1. We heard __an__ amazing story!
2. We heard __a__ story that amazed us!
3. __an__ ice fairy was the main character.
4. __a__ fairy was the main character.

5. It was __an__ exciting evening.
6. They had __a__ lovely evening.
7. __an__ oriole built __an__ outstanding nest.
8. __a__ pair of orioles built __a__ sturdy nest.

Exercise 2: Identify each pair of words as synonyms (syn) or antonyms (ant) by putting parentheses ( ) around *syn* or *ant*.

9. model, copy	(syn) ant	
10. ancient, modern	syn (ant)	
11. feeble, frail	(syn) ant	
12. deprive, enrich	syn (ant)	
13. robust, strong	(syn) ant	
14. taunt, harass	(syn) ant	
15. sincere, dishonest	syn (ant)	
16. seize, surrender	syn (ant)	
17. relish, enjoy	(syn) ant	
18. quiver, vibrate	(syn) ant	
19. heterogeneous, unlike	(syn) ant	?
20. brawny, weak	syn (ant)	

Exercise 3: Underline the correct homonym.

21. (Their, There, They're) new car is red.
22. (Its, It's) a great ball game!
23. (Your, You're) free to go.
24. Our guide (lead, led) us to safety.

25. (Their, They're) going with us to the game.
26. This pink (stationary, stationery) is pretty.
27. Place the punch bowl (their, there) on the table.
28. The band was (stationary, stationery) during the song.

29. The high school band marched (fourth, forth) onto the field.
30. Several of the (principals, principles) of management were discussed at our meeting.
31. The cautious marines quietly slipped (threw, through) the enemy lines.
32. Jake used my father's old wrench to repair the (led, lead) pipe.
33. The teacher asked for the (right, write) answer to the essay question.
34. A very talented musical group won (their, there) first trophy yesterday.
35. Dad asked for a (course, coarse) grade of sandpaper at the hardware store.
36. The frightened rabbit stood (stationary, stationery) as the car approached.
37. The starting quarterback (threw, through) a pass for the winning touchdown!
38. The soldiers trained for battle on a grueling obstacle (coarse, course).
39. All of the club members (no, know) the date of their next meeting.

Exercise 4:   **Editing Paragraph**

Find each error and write the correction above it. Replace words underlined once with a synonym and words underlined twice with an antonym. **Editing Guide: Homonyms: 7 Synonyms: 5 Antonyms: 1 A/An: 1 Misspelled Words: 5 Missing Words: 1**

The ~~kindergardeners~~ (kindergartners) had to decide which of the ~~to~~ (two) paths ~~lead~~ (led) back to ~~there knew~~ (their new) school. They didn't ~~no~~ (know) which one to ~~pick~~ (choose). ~~Finaly~~ (Finally) their principal came ~~too they're rescue~~ (to their rescue). The ~~little~~ (young) boys ~~went~~ (walked) ~~meekly~~ back with ~~principle~~ (the principal). He gave them ~~a~~ (an) extra cool glass of ~~water~~ (H_2O) while they sat ~~inside~~ (outside) his ~~ofice~~ (office) and missed ~~playtime~~ (recess).

100%

CHAPTER 1 LESSON 3 APPLICATION TEST

Exercise 1: Write *a* or *an* in the blanks.

1. We studied about __an__ ancient tribe of Indians.
2. We studied about __a__ tribe of Indians from South America.
3. Each child enjoyed __an__ orange carrot for a snack.
4. The rabbit ate __a__ carrot for his lunch.

Exercise 2: Identify each pair of words as synonyms (syn) or antonyms (ant) by putting parentheses ( ) around *syn* or *ant*.

5. suspect, distrust	(syn) ant	9. expense, income	syn (ant)	13. melancholy, gloomy	(syn) ant
6. foolish, prudent	syn (ant)	10. quaint, ordinary	syn (ant)	14. entertain, annoy	syn (ant)
7. question, doubt	(syn) ant	11. saw, spied	(syn) ant	15. costly, worthless	syn (ant)
8. soothe, pacify	(syn) ant	12. error, blunder	(syn) ant	16. hasten, delay	syn (ant)

Exercise 3: Underline the correct homonym.

17. The racing (course, coarse) was five miles long.
18. The (capital, capitol) of Idaho is Boise.
19. My grandmother wrote her letters on beautiful (stationery, stationary).
20. The (course, coarse) gravel was dumped on the side of the road.
21. The (capital, capitol) building in Arkansas is beautiful.
22. The cat was (stationery, stationary) a moment before she pounced on the mouse.
23. (They're, Their) cousin sent them five tickets to the game.
24. The baby was (to, too) noisy to be taken to the library.
25. The city (counsel, council) met to vote on the water proposal.
26. (Your, You're) allowed to write this report in ink.

Exercise 4: **Editing Paragraph**

Find each error and write the correction above it. Replace words underlined once with a synonym and words underlined twice with an antonym. **Editing Guide: Homonyms: 7 ✓ Synonyms: 5 ✓ Antonyms: 2 ✓ A/An: 2 ✓ Misspelled Words: 7 ✓ Missing Words: 1 ✓**

Yesterday I <u>went</u> to my brother's basketball game. First I <u>walked</u> <u>quickly</u> <u>threw</u> an metal <u>detecter</u> on
[walked] [mosied slowly through] [a] [detector]

my way to the <u>bleechers</u>. I <u>sat</u> on the <u>forth</u> row. The <u>cherleaders</u> <u>lead</u> the <u>large</u> crowd in wild cheers for
[bleachers] [Perched] [fourth] [cheerleaders led] [colossal]

each team. The <u>principles</u> of each school <u>yelled</u> louder than anyone. The <u>too</u> teams were <u>unevenly</u>
[Principals] [howled] [two] [evenly]

matched, and this game ended in a tie. No one was <u>two</u> disapointed, and each team left court amid an
[too] [the] [a]

<u>thundous applase</u> from <u>there fathful</u> fans.
[thunderous applause] [their faithful]

CHAPTER 1 LESSON 4

What is Journal Writing?

Journal Writing is a written record of your personal thoughts and feelings about things or people that are important to you. Recording your thoughts in a journal is a good way to remember how you felt about what was happening in your life at a particular time. You can record your dreams, memories, feelings, and experiences. You can ask questions and answer some of them. It can be fun to go back later and read what you have written because it can show how you have grown on the inside and changed in different areas of your life. A journal can also be an excellent place to look for future writing topics, creative stories, poems, etc. Writing in a journal is an easy and enjoyable way to practice your writing skills without worrying about a writing grade.

What Do I Write About?

Journals are personal, but sometimes it helps to have ideas to get you started. Remember, in a journal, you do not have to stick to one topic. Write about someone or something in school. Write about what you did last weekend or on vacation. Write about what you hope to do this week or on your next vacation. Write about home, school, friends, enemies, hobbies, special talents (yours or someone else's), present and future hopes and fears. Write about what is wrong in your world and what you would do to "fix" it. Write about the good things and the bad things in your world. If you think about a past event and want to write an opinion about it now, put it in your journal. If you want to give your opinion about a present or future event that could have an impact on your life or the way you see things, put it in your journal. If something bothers you, record it in your journal. If something interests you, record it. If you just want to record something that doesn't seem important at all, write it in your journal. After all, it is your journal!

How Do I Get Started Writing in My Personal Journal?

You need to put a journal-entry heading on the title line of your paper with the day's date. Example:
Journal Entry for September 3, 20____.
Skip the next line and begin your entry. You might write a paragraph, a whole page, or several pages. Except for the journal-entry title with the date, no particular organizational style is required for journal writing. You decide how best to organize and express your thoughts. Feel free to include sketches, diagrams, lists, etc., if they will help you remember your thoughts about a topic or an event.

You will also need a spiral notebook, a pen,* a quiet place, and at least 5-10 minutes of uninterrupted writing time.

*(Use a pen if possible. Pencils have lead points that break and erasers, both of which slow down your thoughts. Any drawings you might include do not have to be masterpieces--stick figures will do nicely.)

Journal Writing Assignment: Make an entry in your journal. Follow the instructions on journal entries above.

CHAPTER 1 LESSON 5

The Five Parts of a Correct Sentence

A sentence is a group of words that has a **subject** and **verb**, expresses a **complete thought**, begins with a **capital letter**, and ends with an **end mark**.

There are four kinds of sentences. The chart below will help you recognize and write each kind. Notice that every sentence begins with a capital letter and ends with a punctuation (end) mark.

The Four Kinds of Sentences and the End Mark Flow	
1. A **declarative** sentence makes a statement. It is labeled with a **D**. Example: I walked my dog yesterday. (Period, statement, declarative sentence)	3. An **interrogative** sentence asks a question. It is labeled with an **Int**. Example: Do you live here? (Question mark, question, interrogative sentence)
2. An **imperative** sentence gives a command. It is labeled with an **Imp**. Example: Close the door. (Period, command, imperative sentence)	4. An **exclamatory** sentence expresses strong feeling. It is labeled with an **E**. Example: The field is on fire! (Exclamation point, strong feeling, exclamatory sentence)

Guided Practice: Read each sentence, recite the end mark flow, and put the end mark where it belongs.

1. Mr. Butler is a very good computer programmer . D
2. Do you want ice cream with your chocolate cake ? I
3. What an exciting movie that was . E
4. Place the magazines on this table before you leave , Imp
5. I went camping in the mountains this summer . D
6. The two race cars crashed in the final turn . E

Writing Assignment

Write two each of the four kinds of sentences. Write **D**, **Imp**, **Int**, or **E** at the end of each sentence. Circle the beginning capital letter and the end mark at the end of each sentence.

CHAPTER 1 LESSON 5

How Good Are You?

Anyone who becomes really good in an area that requires skill does so through practice. Basics must be mastered and then practiced daily to become an automatic reflex so that the mind or body does not have to think how to do them. Athletes, musicians, dancers, and typists are examples of people who spend time practicing the basics over and over until they can do them without careless mistakes.

The practice you do day after day in English is no different from the practice an athlete does day after day in his profession. The athlete's training is plain hard work with no frills, but it is necessary if the athlete is going to do well. He must practice the basics so often that the basics become second nature, and he can do them without thinking. Then he is free to concentrate all his energy toward learning more difficult skills.

Likewise, as an English student, some of your training is just plain hard work with no frills, but it is necessary if you are going to do well. You must practice the basic grammar skills so often that they are second nature and can be done with few mistakes. Then you are free to concentrate all your energy on advanced English skills, writing, and editing. The end result of good English and communication skills is the opportunity to advance in any job area, the opportunity to win the academic respect of others, and the opportunity to excel beyond your wildest expectations.

The Four Types of Writing

Writing is like using your muscles - you need to write often to make your writing vibrant, flexible, and powerful. The more you write, the better you get. As you progress through the year, you will learn four types of writing: expository, narrative, descriptive, and persuasive. The type you use will depend upon your topic and purpose for writing. A brief definition for each type of writing is given below.

1. An **expository** paragraph gives facts, directions, explains ideas, or defines words. It is often used for writing assignments. Any time you write expository paragraphs, you should focus on making your meaning clear and understandable. Your reader must be able to understand exactly what you mean.

2. A **descriptive** paragraph gives a single, clear picture of a person, place, thing, or idea. A descriptive paragraph will usually start with an overall impression. Then to support the overall impression and to make a description clear and vivid, you must add strong sensory details, including sight, sound, smell, touch, and taste words. A clear organization of these details makes a descriptive paragraph effective.

3. A **narrative** paragraph is simply the telling of a story. A narrative gives the details of an event or experience in the order that they happened. It will have a beginning, a middle, and an end. Narrative writing will be developed through the use of these story elements: main idea, setting, characters, plot, and ending.

4. A **persuasive** paragraph expresses an opinion and tries to convince the reader that this opinion is correct. Persuading someone to agree with you requires careful thinking and planning. You must make the issue clear and present facts and reasons that give strong support to your opinion. You are encouraging your audience to take a certain action or to feel the way you do.

CHAPTER 2 LESSON 1

The Question and Answer Flow and Classifying Sentences

In order to understand how to write and improve sentences, you must understand how all the parts of a sentence work together. You will learn how to use the information in the definition jingles and a series of questions that will help you identify the parts of a sentence. The questions you ask and the answers you get are called the **Question and Answer Flow**. You will use the Question and Answer Flow to find the name of the function of each word in a sentence. Then you will write an abbreviation above each word. This method of analyzing a sentence is called **classifying** because you classify, or tell, what each word in a sentence is called.

Nouns and Verbs

A **noun** names a person, place, thing, or idea. A noun is labeled according to its function, or job, in a sentence. (subject noun - **SN**, object of the preposition noun - **OP**, etc.)

The **verb** tells what is being said about the subject. The verb tells what the subject does or shows a state of being. The verb of a sentence is labeled with a **V**.

Adverbs and Adjectives

Adverb Definition: An adverb modifies a verb, adjective, or another adverb. Adverbs are labeled **Adv**.
Adverb Questions: How? When? Where? Why? Under what condition? To what degree?

Adjective Definition: An adjective modifies a noun or pronoun. Adjectives are labeled **Adj**.
Adjective Questions: What kind? Which one? How many?

Article Adjective

Article Adjectives are the three most commonly-used adjectives: *a, an,* and *the*. They are sometimes called noun markers because they tell that a noun is close by. These article adjectives must be memorized because there are no questions in the Question and Answer Flow to find the article adjectives. Article adjectives are labeled with an **A**.

Pattern 1 (SN V P1)

The pattern of a sentence is the order of the main parts of the sentence. **Pattern 1** has only two main parts: the subject and the verb. Adjectives and adverbs add information to sentences, but they are not part of a sentence pattern. A Pattern 1 sentence is labeled *SN V P1*.

Complete Subject and Complete Predicate

The **complete subject** is the subject and all the words that modify the subject. The complete subject starts at the beginning of the sentence and usually includes every word up to the verb of the sentence. A vertical line in front of the verb divides the complete subject from the complete predicate.

The **complete predicate** is the verb and all the words which modify the verb. The complete predicate usually starts with the verb and includes every word after the verb. A vertical line in front of the verb divides the complete predicate from the rest of the sentence.

CHAPTER 2 LESSON 1 CONTINUED

Introductory Sentences

You will learn new concepts by classifying a set of Introductory Sentences provided by your teacher. The Question and Answer Flow for one of the Introductory Sentences will always be written out for you in a Question and Answer Flow example like the one below.

Question and Answer Flow Example

Question and Answer Flow for Sentence 12: The small tropical monkey chattered noisily.

1. What chattered noisily? monkey - SN
2. What is being said about monkey?
   monkey chattered - V
3. Chattered how? noisily - Adv
4. What kind of monkey? tropical - Adj
5. What kind of monkey? small - Adj

6. The - A (article adjective)
7. Subject Noun Verb Pattern 1 Check
8. Period, statement, declarative sentence
9. Go back to the verb - divide the complete
   subject from the complete predicate.

Classified Sentence:

<pre>
                                   A   Adj   Adj   SN   V   Adv
              SN V   The small tropical monkey / chattered noisily. D
              ——————
                P1
</pre>

Definitions

Oral Skill Builder Check

A Skill Builder Check is an oral review of certain skills. Your teacher will ask oral questions about each of the five sentences classified together. Oral skill builder checks are designed to make sure you keep **your** skills sharp and automatic.

Noun Check

Even though a noun is only one part of speech, a noun can do many jobs or perform many functions in a sentence. As you learn about each noun job, you will be responsible for finding nouns that perform that job function. The first noun job you have learned is that a noun can function as the subject of a sentence. In a noun check, you will identify all nouns by drawing a circle around them.

Singular and Plural Nouns

A **singular noun** does not normally end in an *s* or *es* and means only one.

A **plural noun** usually ends in an *s* or *es* and means more than one.

Common and Proper Nouns

A **common noun** is a noun that names ANY person, place, or thing. A common noun is not capitalized because it does not name a special person, place, or thing.

A **proper noun** is a noun that names a special, or particular, person, place, or thing. Proper nouns are always capitalized no matter where they are located in a sentence.

Simple Subject and Simple Predicate

The **simple subject** is another name for the subject noun or subject pronoun. The simple subject is just the subject, without all the words that modify the subject.

The **simple predicate** is another name for the verb. The simple predicate is just the verb, without all the rest of the words in the predicate.

CHAPTER 2 LESSON 2

Practice Sentences

You will review the new concepts introduced in the Introductory Sentences by classifying a set of Practice Sentences provided by your teacher. As you classify the Practice Sentences, notice how knowledge of the Question and Answer Flow allows you to analyze and identify all the parts of a sentence easily and accurately. A Question and Answer Flow example from the first set of Practice Sentences is written out for you below.

Question and Answer Flow Example

Question and Answer Flow for Sentence 5: A very hungry alligator lurked dangerously below.

1. What lurked dangerously below? alligator - SN
2. What is being said about alligator? alligator lurked - V
3. Lurked where? below - Adv
4. Lurked how? dangerously - Adv
5. What kind of alligator? hungry - Adj

6. How hungry? very - Adv
7. A - A (article adjective)
8. Subject Noun Verb Pattern 1 Check
9. Period, statement, declarative sentence
10. Go back to the verb - divide the complete subject from the complete predicate.

Classified Sentence:

    A Adv Adj   SN   V   Adv   Adv
SN V
P1   A very hungry alligator / lurked dangerously below. **D**

Guided Practice: Capitalization and Punctuation for Sentences and Paragraphs

Write the capitalization corrections and rule numbers above the word. Write the punctuation corrections and rule numbers below the word. Use the Capitalization and Punctuation Rules on the next pages and use the Editing Guide to know how many errors to correct.

was c. s. lewis, author of the silver chair, born on november 29, 1898, in belfast, ireland ?

Editing Guide for Practice Sentence: Capitals: 10   Commas: 5   Periods: 2   Underlining: 1   End Marks: 1

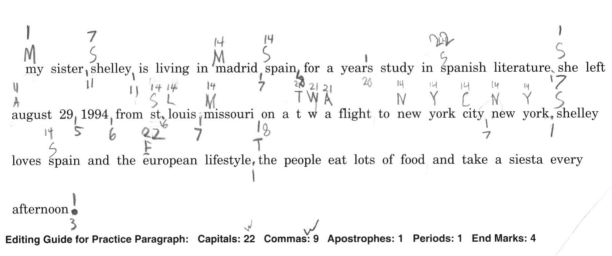

my sister, shelley, is living in madrid, spain, for a years study in spanish literature, she left august 29, 1994, from st. louis, missouri on a t w a flight to new york city, new york, shelley loves spain and the european lifestyle, the people eat lots of food and take a siesta every afternoon.

Editing Guide for Practice Paragraph: Capitals: 22   Commas: 9   Apostrophes: 1   Periods: 1   End Marks: 4

CHAPTER 2 LESSON 2 CAPITALIZATION RULES

SECTION 1: CAPITALIZE THE FIRST WORD

1. The first word of a sentence. (He likes to take a nap.)
2. The first word in the greeting and closing of letters. (Dear, Yours truly)
3. The first and last word and important words in titles of literary works.
   (books, songs, short stories, poems, articles, movie titles, magazines)
   (*Note: Conjunctions, articles, and prepositions with fewer than five letters are not capitalized unless they are the first or last word.*)
4. The first word of a direct quotation. (Dad said, "We are going home.")
5. The first word in each line of a topic outline.

SECTION 2: CAPITALIZE NAMES, INITIALS, AND TITLES OF PEOPLE

6. The pronoun I. (May I go with you?)
7. The names and nicknames of people. (Sam, Joe, Jones, Slim, Shorty)
8. Family names when used in place of, or with, the person's name.
   (Grandmother, Auntie, Uncle Joe, Mother - Do NOT capitalize <u>my mother</u>.)
9. Titles used with, or in place of, people's names.
   (Mr., Ms., Miss, Dr. Smith, Doctor, Captain, President, Sir)
10. People's initials. (J.D., C. Smith)

SECTION 3: CAPITALIZE NAMES OF TIME

11. The days of the week and months of the year. (Monday, July)
12. The names of holidays. (Christmas, Thanksgiving, Easter)
13. The names of historical events, periods, laws, documents, conflicts, and distinguished awards. (Civil War, Middle Ages, Medal of Honor)

SECTION 4: CAPITALIZE NAMES OF PLACES

14. The names and abbreviations of cities, towns, counties, states, countries, and nations.
    (Dallas, Texas, Fulton County, Africa, America, USA, AR, TX)
15. The names of avenues, streets, roads, highways, routes, and post-office boxes.
    (Main Street, Jones Road, Highway 89, Rt. 1, Box 2, P.O. Box 45)
16. The names of lakes, rivers, oceans, mountain ranges, deserts, parks, stars, planets, and constellations. (Beaver Lake, Rocky Mountains, Venus)
17. The names of schools and specific school courses.
    (Walker Elementary School, Mathematics II)
18. North, south, east, and west when they refer to sections of the country.
    (up North, live in the East, out West)

SECTION 5: CAPITALIZE NAMES OF OTHER NOUNS AND PROPER ADJECTIVES

19. The names of pets. (Spot, Tweety Bird, etc.)
20. The names of products. (Campbell's soup, Kelly's chili, Ford cars, etc.)
21. The names of companies, buildings, stores, ships, planes, space ships.
    (Empire State Building, Titanic, IBM, The Big Tire Co.)
22. Proper adjectives. (the English language, Italian restaurant, French test)
23. The names of clubs, organizations, or groups. (Lion's Club, Jaycees, Beatles)
24. The names of political parties, religious preferences, nationalities, and races.
    (Democratic party, Republican, Jewish synagogue, American)

CHAPTER 2 LESSON 2 PUNCTUATION RULES

SECTION 6: END MARK PUNCTUATION

1. Use a (.) for the end punctuation of a sentence that makes a statement.
   (Mom baked us a cake.)

2. Use a (?) for the end punctuation of a sentence that asks a question.
   (Are you going to town?)

3. Use an (!) for the end punctuation of a sentence that expresses strong feeling.
   (That bee stung me!)

4. Use a (.) for the end punctuation of a sentence that gives a command or makes a request.
   (Close the door.)

SECTION 7: COMMAS TO SEPARATE TIME WORDS

5. Use a comma between the day of the week and the month. (Friday, July 23)
   Use a comma between the day and year. (July 23, 1986)

6. Use a comma to separate the year from the rest of the sentence when the year follows the month or the month and the day.
   (We spent July 23, 1985, with Mom. We spent May, 1986, with Dad.)

SECTION 8: COMMAS TO SEPARATE PLACE WORDS

7. Use a comma to separate the city from the state or country.
   (I will go to Dallas, Texas. He is from Paris, France.)

8. Use a comma to separate the state or country from the rest of the sentence when the name of the state or country follows the name of a city.
   (We flew to Dallas, Texas, in June. We flew to Paris, France, in July.)

SECTION 9: COMMAS TO MAKE MEANINGS CLEAR

9. Use a comma to separate words or phrases in a series.
   (We had soup, crackers, and milk.)

10. Use commas to separate introductory words such as *Yes, Well, Oh,* and *No* from the rest of a sentence.
    (Oh, I didn't know that.)

11. Use commas to set off most appositives. (An appositive is a word, phrase, title, or degree used directly after another word or name to rename it.)
    (Sue, the girl next door, likes to draw.)

    One-word appositives can be written two different ways: *(1) My brother, Tim, is riding in the horse* show. *(2) My brother Tim is riding in the horse show.* Your assignments will usually require one-word appositives to be set off with commas.

12. Use commas to separate a noun of direct address (the name of a person directly spoken to) from the rest of the sentence.
    (Mom, do I really have to go?)

SECTION 10: PUNCTUATION IN GREETINGS AND CLOSINGS OF LETTERS

13. Use a comma (,) after the salutation (greeting) of a friendly letter. (Dear Sam,)

14. Use a comma (,) after the closing of any letter. (Yours truly,)

15. Use a colon (:) after the salutation (greeting) of a business letter. (Dear Sir:)

CHAPTER 2 LESSON 2 PUNCTUATION RULES

SECTION 11: PERIODS

16. Use a period after most abbreviations or titles that are accepted in formal writing. (Mr., Ms., Dr., Capt., St., Ave., St. Louis) **(Note: These abbreviations cannot be used by themselves. They must always be used with a proper noun.)**

   In the abbreviations of many well-known organizations or words, periods are not required. (USA, GM, TWA, GTE, AT&T, TV, AM, FM, GI, etc.) Use only one period after an abbreviation at the end of a statement. Do not put an extra period for the end mark punctuation.

17. Use a period after initials. A person's initials should not be separated from the name. (C. Smith, D.J. Brewton, Thomas A. Jones)

18. Place a period after Roman numerals, Arabic numbers, and letters of the alphabet in an outline. (II., IV., 5., 25., A., B.)

SECTION 12: APOSTROPHES

19. Form a contraction by using an apostrophe in place of a letter or letters that have been left out. (I'll, he's, isn't, wasn't, can't)

20. Form the possessive of singular and plural nouns by using an apostrophe. (boy's ball, boys' ball, children's ball)

21. Form the plurals of letters, symbols, numbers, and signs with the apostrophe plus *s* ('s). (9's, B's, b's)

SECTION 13: UNDERLINING

22. Use underlining or italics for titles of books, magazines, works of art, ships, newspapers, motion pictures, etc. (A famous movie is <u>Gone With the Wind</u>. Our newspaper is the <u>Cabot Star Herald</u>. <u>Titanic</u>, <u>Charlotte's Web</u>)

SECTION 14: QUOTATION MARKS

23. Use quotation marks to set off the titles of songs, short stories, short poems, articles, essays, short plays, and book chapters.
   (*Do you like to sing the song "America" in music class?*)

24. The words that tell who is speaking are the explanatory words. Do not set explanatory words off with quotation marks. (Fred said, "I'm here.") (Fred said is explanatory and is not set off with quotations.)

25. Quotation marks are used at the beginning and end of the person's words to separate what the person actually said from the rest of the sentence. Since the quotation tells what is being said, it will always have quotation marks around it.

26. A new paragraph is used to indicate each change of speaker.

27. When a speaker's speech is longer than one paragraph, quotation marks are used at the beginning of each paragraph and at the end of the last paragraph of that speaker's speech.

28. Use single quotation marks to enclose a quotation within a quotation.
   "My teddy bear says 'I love you' four different ways," said little Amy.

29. Use a period at the end of explanatory words that come at the end of a sentence.

30. Use a comma to separate a direct quotation from the explanatory words.

CHAPTER 2 LESSON 2 SKILL TEST

Exercise 1: Classify this sentence.

1. SN V P1 | Three dangerous lions / raced rapidly away! E

Exercise 2: Use the Editing Guide below each sentence to know how many capitalization and punctuation errors to correct. Write the capitalization corrections and rule numbers **above** each word. Write the punctuation corrections and rule numbers **below** each word. Use the capitalization and punctuation rule pages to get the correct rule numbers.

1. no john you cant hike up temple mountain and camp at silver lake with james billy and larry.

Editing Guide: Capitals: 9 Commas: 4 Apostrophes: 1 End Marks: 1

2. aunt sue, my moms sister, visited hoover dam in nevada on march 31, 1993 during easter vacation

Editing Guide: Capitals: 7 Commas: 4 Apostrophes: 1 End Marks: 1

3. last july i went to an italian restaurant with joe my australian friend and ordered a caesar salad.

Editing Guide: Capitals: 7 Commas: 2 End Marks: 1

Exercise 3:   **Editing Paragraph**

Find each error and correct it. Write the capitalization corrections **above** each word. Write the punctuation corrections **below** each word. Use the capitalization and punctuation rule pages to review the rules. (Do not write the rule numbers.)

Editing Guide: Capitals: 23 Commas: 9 End Marks: 7

san francisco is a city with lots of personality clanging cable cars carry visitors up and down the

steep hilly and narrow streets tourists wait in lines to take their cars down lombard street the curviest

street in america visitors to the pier can tour a world war II submarine watch the sea lions playing from

the seal rock cafe or enjoy a performance by a street musician the nearby island of alcatraz offers a tour

of the prison that once housed al capone the gangster chinatown known for its pagodas and exotic

shops sits right in the middle of downtown san francisco yes san francisco is an interesting place to see

CHAPTER 2 LESSON 3 APPLICATION TEST

Exercise 1: Classify each sentence.

1. _____ A dangerous copperhead slithered silently nearby!

2. _____ The very funny comedian laughed quite often.

3. _____ The five weary hikers trudged home slowly yesterday.

Exercise 2: Write the capitalization corrections and rule numbers above each word. Write the punctuation corrections and rule numbers below each word. Use the Editing Guide to know how many errors to correct.

4. linda my uncles brother b.j. sims has taught history at cleveland high school in copper springs texas since september 5 1985 and is the author of the well-known book called war between the states

Editing Guide: Capitals: 14   Commas: 7   Periods: 2   Apostrophes: 1   Underlining: 1   End Marks: 1

5. grandpa rice tina and susan traveled to washington d.c. to visit bob k. sparkman last july mr. sparkman took them to see the lincoln memorial and the potomac river they visited mount vernon the home of george washington

Editing Guide: Capitals: 22   Commas: 5   Periods: 4   End Marks: 3

Exercise 3: **Editing Paragraph**

Find each error and write the correction above it. Replace words underlined once with a synonym and words underlined twice with an antonym. **Editing Guide: Homonyms: 18 Synonyms: 3 Antonyms: 1 A/An: 1 Misspelled Words: 2 Capitals: 12 End Marks: 8**

jan and jill had fun yesterday they're goverment class went to the new capital building to watch the general counsel right laws a tour guide lead there class threw an tunnel too an extra big room where the counsel met to men were debating the principals of seatbelt safety one man got two excited and through his stationary all over the floor the other man charged fourth with glee to pick it up the principle speaker had to tell the excited men to stop there coarse behavier and to act write jan and jill saw everything from the forth row of seats

CHAPTER 2 LESSON 4

Check Time and Journal Writing Time
Journal Writing Assignment: Make an entry in your journal. (Start with your heading and date.)

CHAPTER 2 LESSON 5

Practice Sentence

A **Practice Sentence** is a sentence that is written following certain sentence pattern labels (**A Adj SN V Adv**, etc.). The difficulty level of the sentence labels will increase as your ability increases. To write a Practice Sentence, you will follow the labels given to you in your assignment or by your teacher. You must think of words that fit the labels and that make sense.

Writing Practice Sentences will develop a firm knowledge of how sentences are structured. You will always be able to use this knowledge whenever you write sentences and paragraphs for any subject.

Sample Practice Sentence						
Labels:	A	Adj	Adj	SN	V	Adv	Adv
Practice:	**A**	**large**	**docile**	**monkey**	**walked**	**happily**	**around.**

Improved Sentence

An **Improved Sentence** is a sentence made from the Practice Sentence that is improved through the use of synonym changes, antonym changes, or complete word changes. Writing Improved Sentences will help you mentally to make better word choices as you write because your writing vocabulary increases.

Sample Improved Sentences						
Labels:	A	Adj	Adj	SN	V	Adv	Adv
Practice:	A	large	docile	monkey	walked	happily	around.
Improved:	**An**	**enormous**	**obnoxious**	**gorilla**	**limped**	**painfully**	**around.**
	(change)	(synonym)	(antonym)	(synonym)	(synonym)	(change)	(same)

Guided Practice Assignment:

1. Write one **Practice Sentence** following these labels. **A Adj Adj SN V Adv Adv**

2. Write an **Improved Sentence** for the Practice Sentence. Make at least two synonym changes, one antonym change, and your choice of complete word changes.

CHAPTER 2 LESSON 5

Point of view refers to the writer's use of personal pronouns to determine who is telling a story or event. There are commonly two points of view used in literature and writing: first person point of view and third person point of view. Second person point of view is used to name the person or thing spoken to and can be used with either first person point of view or third person point of view.

Point of View

First Person Point of View uses the first person pronouns *I, we, me, us, my, our, mine,* and *ours* to name the speaker. If any of the first person pronouns are used in a writing, the writing is automatically considered first person writing, even though second and third person pronouns may also be used. First person shows that you (the writer) are speaking, and that you (the writer) are personally involved in what is happening.

First Person Sample Paragraph:

   I heard the phone ringing, but **I** was taking a shower and could not get out fast enough. So, **I** yelled to **my** sister Marie to answer it. **I** didn't know that **she** was outside and couldn't hear the phone. When the phone kept ringing, **I** grabbed a towel, jumped out of the shower, and raced to answer it. Unfortunately, **my** little brother was chasing **our** dog down the hall, and **we** collided.

Second Person Point of View uses the second person pronouns *you, your, yours* to name the person or thing spoken to. Very few stories, paragraphs, or essays are written in second person. Usually, second person point of view is used in giving directions. Therefore, the second person point of view examples used below are sentences of direction instead of a paragraph.

Second Person Sample Sentences

1. Ben, will you please shut the door? 2. You go to Main Street and turn left. 3. You girls need to play outside.

Third Person Point of View uses the third person pronouns *he, his, him, she, her, hers, it, its, their, theirs, them* to name the person or thing spoken about. Except for dialogue and direct quotations, you may <u>not</u> use the first person pronouns *I, we, us, me, my, mine,*and *ours* because using any first person pronouns automatically puts a writing in a first person point of view. Third person means that you (the writer) must write as if you are watching the events take place. Third person shows that you are writing about another person, thing, or event.

Third Person Sample Paragraph

   Bill heard the phone ringing, but **he** was taking a shower and could not get out fast enough. So, **he** yelled to **his** sister Marie to answer **it**. **He** didn't know that **she** was outside and couldn't hear the phone. When the phone kept ringing, Bill grabbed a towel, jumped out of the shower, and raced to answer **it**. Unfortunately, **his** little brother was chasing **their** dog down the hall, and **they** collided.

The scared pretty Gisela licks super incescantly.
The courageous cute Chloe spits quite incescantly

CHAPTER 2 LESSON 5

Guided Practice: Read the paragraphs below and discuss whether they were written in the first person or third person point of view. Then rewrite each paragraph and change the point of view.

Paragraph 1

Joe had just finished reading the book, *The Brooklyn Bridge: They Said It Couldn't Be Built* by Judith St. George. He was surprised that he had even read the book since he had never been fascinated with history. But the history of the Brooklyn Bridge intrigued him once he started. He was amazed to learn that the real story behind the Brooklyn Bridge revolved around the lives of John Roebling, the father, who dreamed and planned the bridge, and Washington Roebling, the son, who built the bridge despite all the tragedy associated with it. After reading about the Brooklyn Bridge, Joe decided that reading about history wasn't that bad after all.

Paragraph 2

I had always wanted to be on the swim team. When I finally got my chance to try out, I was so excited that I couldn't stand it. The try-out list was long, and it took months, sometimes years, to get a chance to try out! For days, I walked around bragging about how I was going to make the team. On the day of the try-outs, I was there in my new bathing suit. Imagine my embarrassment when I found out that I was trying out with six-year-olds! On my application, I had forgotten to put a one in front of the six for sixteen!

How to Narrow a Topic

Sometimes, when you choose a topic for writing, the topic covers too much information for you to write about. This means your topic is too **broad**. When your topic is too broad, you need to **narrow** your topic. To **narrow** the topic means to reduce or limit your topic to only one aspect of your topic.

Suppose your topic is **Cars**. This topic is too broad because there are too many different areas relating to cars. Since the topic is so broad, it could cover hundreds of pages. Therefore, you need to limit the topic to tell only **one thing** about cars.

A logical narrowed topic might be **The Responsibilities of Owning a Car**. Although you have narrowed your topic, it still covers a great deal of information. Therefore, you limit, or restrict it further. The final narrowed topic could be **Cleaning a Car**.

Now the topic is narrowed so that there is still enough material to write about, but it is focused on one specific area of the topic.

Guided Practice: Narrow these three topics: **Horses, School,** and **History.**

CHAPTER 3 LESSON 1

Preposition and Object of the Preposition

A **preposition** is a joining word. It joins a noun or a pronoun to the rest of the sentence. To know whether a word is a preposition, say the preposition word and ask *What* or *Whom*. If the answer is a noun or pronoun, then the word is a preposition. Prepositions are labeled with a *P*.

An **object of the preposition** is a noun or pronoun after the preposition in a sentence. An object of the preposition is labeled with an *OP*.

Knowing the Difference Between Prepositions and Adverbs

A word can be a preposition or an adverb, depending on how it is used in a sentence. For example, the word *down* can be an adverb or a preposition. How do you decide if the word *down* is an adverb or a preposition? If *down* is used alone, with no noun after it, it is an adverb. If *down* has a noun after it that answers the question *what* or *whom*, then *down* is a preposition, and the noun after *down* is an object of the preposition.

Adv
In the sample sentence, *John fell **down***, the word *down* is an adverb because it does not have a noun after it.

P   noun (OP)
In the sample sentence, *John fell **down the stairs***, the word *down* is a preposition because it has the noun *stairs* (the object of the preposition) after it. It is said in the Question and Answer Flow like this:

down - P   (Say: *down - preposition*)
down what? stairs - OP   (Say: *down what? stairs - object of the preposition*)

Prepositional Phrase

A **prepositional phrase** starts with the preposition and ends with the object of the preposition. It includes any modifiers between the preposition and object of the preposition. A prepositional phrase adds meaning to a sentence and can be located anywhere in the sentence.

Prepositional phrases are identified in the Question and Answer Flow after you say the word *check*. Now when you say *check*, you are looking for prepositional phrases in the sentence. If you find a prepositional phrase, you will read the whole prepositional phrase and put parentheses around it. If there is more than one prepositional phrase in a sentence, read all prepositional phrases during this check time. For example, after you classify the sentence ***Joe went to town***, you will now say "Subject Noun Verb Pattern 1 - Check: (to town) - prepositional phrase."

A Preposition's Relationship to Its Object

For example, a preposition might tell the relationship an ant has to a tree: The ant can be (in the tree), (on the tree), (about the tree), (over the tree), (under the tree), (up the tree), (down the tree), (of the tree), etc.

Note: A preposition will tell what the relationship of its object is to the word the phrase modifies.

CHAPTER 3 LESSON 1

Definitions

Adverb Exception

Most adverbs which modify the verb are located <u>after</u> the verb; therefore, they are located in the predicate part of the sentence. Since the verb usually starts the predicate, these adverbs are part of the predicate. An **adverb exception** occurs when you have an adverb immediately <u>before</u> the verb that modifies the verb. As a result, the predicate will now start with the adverb that is immediately before the verb. (The student / *quickly stepped inside the classroom*.)

In the Question and Answer Flow, say *"Go back to the verb - divide the complete subject from the complete predicate."* Then ask, *"Is there an adverb exception?"* If there is not an adverb before the verb, you say *"No."* If there is an adverb before the verb you say *"Yes - change the line."* To show the adverb exception, simply erase your slash mark and put it in front of the adverb that is immediately before the verb. (The dog swiftly / *retreated*.) (The dog / <u>swiftly retreated</u>.)

Natural and Inverted Word Order in Sentences

A sentence that is in a **natural order** has all subject parts first and all predicate parts last. A sentence that is in an **inverted order** will have predicate words in the complete subject. There are three types of predicate words that are sometimes found in the complete subject:

1. A prepositional phrase at the beginning of a sentence will modify the verb.
    (Example: <u>After</u> <u>lunch</u> <u>we</u> / <u>went home</u>.)

2. A helping verb at the beginning of a sentence will always be part of the verb.
    (Example: <u>Are</u> <u>you</u> / <u>going to the concert</u>?)

3. An adverb at the beginning of the sentence will modify the verb.

    (Example: <u>Yesterday</u> <u>we</u> / <u>went to my grandfather's house</u>.)

In the Question and Answer Flow, say, *"Is there an adverb exception?"* Then you ask, *"Is this sentence in a natural or inverted order?"* If there are no predicate words in the complete subject, then you say, *"Natural - No change."* If there are predicate words in the complete subject, then you say, *"Inverted - Underline the subject parts once and the predicate parts twice."* To show the inverted order, draw one line under the subject parts and two lines under the predicate parts.

Question and Answer Flow Example

Question and Answer Flow for Sentence 5: Today the band members worked very hard on the competition music.	
1. Who worked very hard on the competition music? members - SN	10. The - A
2. What is being said about members? members worked - V	11. Worked when? today - Adv
3. Worked how? hard - Adv	12. Subject Noun Verb Pattern 1 Check
4. How hard? very - Adv	13. (On the competition music) - Prepositional phrase
5. On - P	14. Period, statement, declarative sentence
6. On what? music - OP	15. Go back to the verb - divide the complete subject from the complete predicate.
7. What kind of music? competition - Adj	16. Is there an adverb exception? No.
8. The - A	17. Is this sentence in a natural or inverted order? Inverted - underline the subject parts once and the predicate parts twice.
9. What kind of members? band - Adj	

Classified Sentence:

	Adv	A	Adj	SN	V	Adv	Adv	P	A	Adj	OP
SN V	Today	the	band	members	/ worked	very	hard	(on	the	competition	music.) D
P1											

CHAPTER 3 LESSON 1

Assignment:
1. Write two **Practice Sentences** following these labels:

   1. **A Adj SN V Adv P A Adj OP**   2. **P A OP A Adj SN V Adv P A Adj OP**

2. Write an **Improved Sentence** from one of the two Practice Sentences. Make at least two synonym changes, one antonym change, and your choice of complete word changes.

CHAPTER 3 LESSON 2

Practice Sentences

You will review the new concepts introduced in the introductory sentences by classifying a set of Practice Sentences with your teacher. As you classify the Practice Sentences, notice how knowledge of the Question and Answer Flow allows you to analyze and identify all the parts of a sentence easily and accurately.

Written Noun Job Check

Nouns have many jobs in a sentence: subject noun, object of the preposition, direct object, indirect object,
possessive noun, predicate noun, and object complement. To find nouns, go to their jobs in a sentence and list the noun and the noun job. Then identify whether the noun is singular or plural and common or proper.

Guided Practice: Use the classified sentence below to complete the noun job table.

```
                         P  A  OP    SN    V     Adv  P  A  Adj  OP
              SN  V   (In the morning) Ben / groped sleepily (for the coffee cups.)  D
              P1
```

List the Noun Used	List the Noun Job	Singular or Plural	Common or Proper
1. Morning	2. OP	3. S	4. C
5. Ben	6. SN	7. S	8. P
9. cups	10. OP	11. P	12. C

Using Definitions and Jingles

Definitions and jingles give you the extra information you need to understand the parts of a sentence. Use the information from the definitions and jingles you have learned to help you do the guided practice exercises below.

Guided Practice: Match the definition to the answer.

  C 1. article adjectives   A. SN, OP
  A 2. name two noun jobs   B. antonyms
  D 3. all subject parts   C. a, an, the
  B 4. opposite meanings   D. complete subject

Guided Practice: Answer the questions below.

   5. What does a preposition do? *connects a noun to the rest sentence*

   6. Write a prepositional phrase with two modifiers. *On the slippery wet roof*

   7. What is the Q & A Flow for a declarative sentence? *statement declarative sentence*

CHAPTER 3 LESSON 2 SKILL TEST

Exercise 1: Match the definitions. Write the correct letter beside each numbered concept.

D 1. noun
B 2. subject noun question (person)
E 3. subject noun question (thing)
C 4. verb question
A 5. adverb modifies
I 6. adjective modifies
M 7. article adjective can be called
L 8. punctuation for declarative
K 9. adverb that comes right before the verb
G 10. exclamatory sentence
J 11. punctuation for exclamatory sentence
F 12. all the predicate parts
O 13. all the subject parts
H 14. sentence with predicate words in the complete subject
N 15. word that usually starts the complete predicate

A. verb, adjective, or adverb
B. who?
C. what is being said about?
D. person, place, thing
E. what?
F. complete predicate
G. shows strong feeling
H. inverted order
I. noun or pronoun
J. exclamation point
K. adverb exception
L. period
M. noun marker
N. verb
O. complete subject

Exercise 2: Fill in the blank: Write the answer for each question.

16. What is the Question and Answer Flow for an exclamatory sentence? *Exclamatory, ! strong feeling*
17. What word tells what the subject does? *a verb*
18. What are the three article adjectives? *a an the*
19. What are all the parts in the predicate of a sentence called? *complete predicate*
20. What are the adjective questions? *What kind, which one, how many*
21. Name two noun jobs. *SN, OP*

Exercise 3: Classify each sentence and then complete the noun job table.

22. _SN V P1_ SN V P A adj OP P A adj OP D
The spoiled Doberman/begs (for dog biscuits)(during the dinner meal.) D

List the Noun Used	List the Noun Job	Singular or Plural	Common or Proper
23. Doberman	24. SN	25. S	26. P
27. biscuits	28. OP	29. P	30. C
31. meal	32. OP	33. S	34. C

35. _SN V P1_ SN V adv P A OP P OP D
Aunt Sara/stood silently (by the shore)(of Windy Lake) D

List the Noun Used	List the Noun Job	Singular or Plural	Common or Proper
36. Aunt Sara	37. SN	38. S	39. P
40. shore	41. OP	42. S	43. C
44. Windy Lake	45. OP	46. S	47. C

CHAPTER 3 LESSON 3 APPLICATION TEST

Exercise 1: Classify each sentence.

1. SN V P / Yesterday the confident debater / spoke clearly to the audience during the competition. D

2. SN V P / The famous dancers / bowed gracefully to Sara from the dance floor. D

3. SN V P / During the summer months vegetables / grow in abundance in the valleys of California. D

Directions: Complete the noun job table. Use Sentence 3.

List the Noun Used	List the Noun Job	Singular or Plural	Common or Proper
4. vegetables	5. SN	6. P	7. C
8. months	9. OP	10. P	11. C
12. abundance	13. OP	14. S	15. C
16. valleys	17. OP	18. P	19. C
20. California	21. OP	22. S	23. P

Exercise 2: Match the definitions. Write the correct letter or letters beside each numbered concept.

F   24. all the predicate parts
I   25. all the subject parts
DRX 26. adjective questions
GWU 27. adverb questions
E   28. declarative sentence
H   29. predicate words in the subject
M   30. simple predicate
A   31. simple subject
L   32. words with the same meaning
K   33. words opposite in meaning
TVQBN 34. five parts of a sentence
C   35. words pronounced the same
       but are different in meaning

A. subject noun
B. subject
C. homonyms
D. what kind
E. statement
F. complete predicate
G. how
H. inverted order
I. complete subject
J. noun
K. antonyms
L. synonyms

M. verb
N. verb
O. preposition
P. adverb
Q. sense
R. which one
S. adjective
T. capital letter
U. where
V. end mark
W. when
X. how many

Exercise 3: Write a prepositional phrase with two modifiers.

36. in the scary dark house.

Exercise 4:   **Editing Paragraph**

Find each error and write the correction above it. Replace each word underlined once with a synonym. **Editing Guide:**
Homonyms: 4 Synonyms: 4 A/An: 1 Misspelled Words: 2 Capitals: 20 Commas: 2 Periods: 3 End Marks: 5 Underlining: 1
Apostrophes: 1

all students at conway high school must read a tale of two cities by charles dickens in there

high school english class. the english teacher mr. c.r. green, shows his class how too right an good

report on this book, then the principle chooses the best report, the winner will repersent the

school in an national compition. its good fun.

CHAPTER 3 LESSON 4

Check Time and Journal Writing Time
Journal Writing Assignment: Make an entry in your journal. (Start with your heading and date.)

Word Analogies

This is an analogy question: **puppy:dog::kitten: _____ .**
It is read like this: **puppy is to dog as kitten is to _____ .**

Analogy is a kind of reasoning based on comparison. An analogy compares two pairs of words and shows how the pairs of words are alike. An analogy has two parts. In the first part of the analogy, you are given two words. You must decide how these two words relate to each other.

1. foal:horse (A foal is a baby horse.)
2. glove:hand (A glove goes on a hand.)
3. fear:confidence (Fear is the opposite of confidence.)

In the second part of the analogy, you are given only one of the two words. Since you must supply the missing word, you must think about how the first pair of words is related so that you can choose only the word that relates the second pair in the same way.

Step 1: Look closely at the first pair of words.
Step 2: Decide how they are related.
Step 3: Look at how the second pair of words should relate.   The comparison should be similar.
Step 4: Choose a word that relates the second pair in the same way.

Guided Practice: Choose the correct missing word and put the letter in the blank.
1. foal:horse::kitten: _cat_ (Just as a foal **is a baby** horse, a kitten **is a baby** _____ .)
2. glove:hand:: _____ :foot   (Just as a glove **goes on** a hand, a _____ **goes on** a foot.)
3. fear:confidence::hate: ____ (Just as fear **is the opposite of** confidence, hate **is the opposite of** ___.)

Word Analogy Exercise: Choose the correct missing word and put the letter in the blank.
1. foal:horse::kitten:__C____   a. playful   b. fur   c. cat   d. paw
2. glove:hand:: __d.__ :foot   a. leather   b. laces   c. toe   d. shoe
3. fear:confidence::hate:__b.__ a. surprise   b. love   c. worry   d. dislike

Setting Up Writing Folders

In Chapter 1 you learned that there are four types of writing: expository, narrative, descriptive, and persuasive. As you begin to study each kind of writing in detail, you will be given writing assignments. Each writing assignment will be placed in three writing folders as you progress through the different stages of the writing process. Now you will set up your writing folders and label them according to the directions below.

1. You will need 3 different-colored pocket folders for writing. (Check with your teacher for the colors.)
2. Label the first folder *Rough Draft Folder*. This folder will be used to keep all unedited writings.
3. Label the second folder *Final Writing Folder*. This folder will be used to keep all edited papers that are ready to be graded. Your teacher can call for a final paper to be turned in any time after it is placed in the Final Writing Folder.
4. Label the third folder *Graded Writing Folder*. After your teacher grades a writing assignment from the Final Writing Folder, you will place it in the last folder of the writing process, the Graded Writing Folder. Papers placed in the Graded Writing Folder can be selected for further editing and rewriting for the purpose of publishing. (Your teacher will tell you what to do with your published papers.)

CHAPTER 3 LESSON 5

Review Narrowing the Topic

The lesson on narrowing the topic taught you several things. First, you must limit your topic to only one thing about your topic. You may then need to narrow it again. Always check your narrowed topic to see if it has been narrowed enough. Does it still cover too much information to write about? For example, the topic for your first writing assignment is **Winter**. But this topic is too broad. It must now be narrowed to tell only one thing about the topic. A logical narrowed topic is **Winter Activities.** However, this topic still covers too much information to write about; therefore, it must be narrowed again to limit the number of winter activities. The final narrowed topic is **Winter Activities That I Enjoy**. Now the topic is narrowed so that there is enough to write about, but not too much.

Expository Paragraph Writing

Our first type of writing is EXPOSITORY writing, or EXPOSITION. The purpose of expository writing is to inform, to give facts, to give directions, to explain, or to define. Expository writing is the discussion or telling of ideas. Any time you write expository paragraphs, you should focus on making your meaning clear and understandable. Your reader must be able to understand exactly what you mean.

Expository writing may be organized in different ways. One of the most common ways to write exposition is to use a **three-point paragraph format.** The three-point paragraph format is a way of organizing the sentences in your expository paragraph that will help make your meaning clear and understandable. Now you will learn how to write a three-point expository paragraph by following the directions below.

Steps in Writing the Three-Point Expository Paragraph

NARROWING THE TOPIC

- Read the broad topic: **Winter**
- Decide on a logical narrowed topic: **Winter Activities**
- If needed, narrow the topic again: **Winter Activities That I Enjoy**
- Writing Topic: **Winter Activities That I Enjoy**

ENUMERATE THE TOPIC

- Select and list three points to enumerate about the topic. **(1. sledding   2. ice skating   3. skiing)**

WRITING THE INTRODUCTION AND TITLE

1. Sentence #1 - Topic Sentence:
   Write the topic sentence by using the words in your topic and adding either an exact number word (three, four, etc.) or a general number word (several, many, some, numerous, etc.) that tells how many points you will mention. This must be a complete sentence, and it should be indented.
   (When the weather gets cold, there are several winter activities that I enjoy.)

2. Sentence #2 - Three Point Sentence:
   Write a complete sentence listing your three points in the order you will present them in your paragraph. **(My three favorites are sledding, ice skating, and skiing.)**

- The Title - Look at the writing topic and Sentences #1-2 in the introduction. Decide if you want to leave the topic as your title or if you want to write a different phrase to tell what your paragraph is about. Capitalize the first, last, and important words in your title. **(Winter Activities That I Enjoy)**

CHAPTER 3 LESSON 5

Steps in Writing the Three-Point Expository Paragraph, Continued

WRITING THE BODY

3. <u>Sentence #3 - First Point</u>:
   Write a sentence stating your first point.
   (The first winter activity that I enjoy is sledding.)

4. <u>Sentence #4 - Supporting Sentence</u>:
   Write a sentence that gives more information about your first point.
   (All the kids in our town go sledding down a long hill near my house.)

5. <u>Sentence #5 - Second Point</u>:
   Write a sentence stating your second point.
   (The second winter activity that I enjoy is ice skating.)

6. <u>Sentence #6 - Supporting Sentence</u>:
   Write a sentence that gives more information about your second point.
   (Each winter my cousins and I can hardly wait for my uncle's pond to freeze over so we can go ice skating.)

7. <u>Sentence #7 - Third Point</u>:
   Write a sentence stating your third point.
   (The third winter activity that I enjoy is skiing.)

8. <u>Sentence #8 - Supporting Sentence</u>:
   Write a sentence that gives more information about your third point.
   (Every winter I go to the mountains in Colorado on a ski trip with a youth group.)

WRITING THE CONCLUSION

9. <u>Sentence #9 - Concluding Sentence</u>:
   Write a concluding (final) sentence that summarizes your paragraph. Read the topic sentence again and then rewrite it, using some of the same words to say the same thing in a different way. (Adding an extra thought about the topic will make it easier to restate the topic sentence.)
   (I do not always get involved in as many winter activities as I would like, but the three that I enjoy most are sledding, ice skating, and skiing.)

SAMPLE PARAGRAPH

Winter Activities That I Enjoy

   When the weather gets cold, there are several winter activities that I enjoy. My three favorites are sledding, ice skating, and skiing. The first winter activity that I enjoy is sledding. All the kids in our town go sledding down a long hill near my house. The second winter activity that I enjoy is skating. Each winter my cousins and I can hardly wait for my uncle's pond to freeze over so we can go ice skating. The third winter activity that I enjoy is skiing. Every winter I go to the mountains in Colorado on a ski trip with a youth group. I do not always get involved in as many winter activities as I would like, but the three that I enjoy most are sledding, ice skating, and skiing.

CHAPTER 3 LESSON 5

The Three-Point Expository Paragraph Outline

I. Title
II. Paragraph
   A. Topic sentence
   B. A three-point sentence
   C. A **first** point sentence
   D. A **supporting** sentence for the first point
   E. A **second** point sentence
   F. A **supporting** sentence for the second point
   G. A **third** point sentence
   H. A **supporting** sentence for the third point
   I. A concluding sentence

Writing Assignment

Use the Expository Steps and Paragraph Outline in this lesson to do the writing assignment below. After you finish writing your paragraph, underline the topic sentence, the first point sentence, second point sentence, third point sentence, and concluding sentence. Circle the capital letter and end mark at the beginning and end of each sentence. Put your finished writing in your Rough Draft Folder.

Writing Assignment #1: Three-Point Expository Paragraph in First Person
(Remember, first person is the point of view in writing that uses the personal pronouns *I, me, my, mine, we, us, our,* and *ours*. Also remember that this expository writing uses the three-point pattern.)

Topic: Weekend Activities
Logical narrowed topic: Things I Like to Do on the Weekend
Writing topic: Things I Like to Do on the Weekend

Before you start your writing assignment, read and discuss the *Rough Draft Guidelines* below. You will use these guidelines for every writing assignment.

Rough Draft Guidelines

1. Label your writing assignment in the top right hand corner of your page with the following information:
   A. Your Name
   B. The Writing Assignment Number (Example: WA#1, WA#2, etc.)
   C. Type of Writing (Examples: 3-Point Expository Paragraph, etc.)
   D. Put the title of the writing on the top of the first line
2. Think about the topic which you are assigned.
3. Think about the type of writing assigned, which is the purpose for the writing.
   (Is your writing intended to explain, persuade, describe, or narrate?)
4. Think about the writing format, which is the organizational plan you are expected to use.
   (Is your assignment a paragraph, a 3-paragraph essay, a 5-paragraph essay, or a letter?)
5. Write your rough draft in pencil.
6. Skip every other line on your rough draft. This will give you room to edit.
7. Have the supplies you need handy.
   (Do you have pencils, paper, and the writing steps at your fingertips?)
8. Use your writing time wisely.
   (Begin work quickly and concentrate on your assignment until it is finished.)
9. Place your completed writing assignment in your Rough Draft Folder to be edited at a later time.

CHAPTER 4 LESSON 1

Pronoun

A pronoun takes the place of a noun. A pronoun may stand for a person, place, thing, or idea and can stand in place of any noun in a sentence. Frequently used pronouns should be memorized.

Subject Pronoun

1. A **subject pronoun** takes the place of a noun that is used as the subject of a sentence.
2. These are subject pronouns: *I, we, he, she, it, they*, and *you*.
3. To find a subject pronoun, ask the question *who* or *what* to get the subject.
4. Label a subject pronoun with an *SP*.

Understood Subject Pronoun

1. A sentence has an **understood subject** when someone gives a command or makes a request and leaves the subject unwritten or unspoken. This understood subject will always be the pronoun *you*.
2. The understood subject pronoun *you* is always written in parentheses at the beginning of the sentence with the label *SP* above it.

Object Pronouns

1. If a pronoun does any job that has the word *object* in it, that pronoun is an object pronoun. Object pronouns can be used as objects of the prepositions, direct objects, or indirect objects. (These jobs all have the word *objects* in them.)
2. These are the object pronouns: *me, us, him, her, it, them*, and *you*.
3. An object pronoun does not have a special label. An object pronoun keeps its **OP, DO,** or **IO** label to tell its job.

Question and Answer Flow Example

Question and Answer Flow for Sentence 5: Run to the window for a closer look at the President!	
1. Who run to the window for a closer look at the President? (You) - Understood subject pronoun	12. The - A
2. What is being said about you? you run - V	13. Subject Noun, Verb, Pattern 1, Check
3. To - P	14. (To the window) - prepositional phrase
4. To what? window - OP	15. (For a closer look) - prepositional phrase
5. The - A	16. (At the President) - prepositional phrase
6. For - P	17. Exclamation point, strong feeling, exclamatory sentence.
7. For what? look - OP	18. Go back to the verb - divide the complete subject from the complete predicate.
8. What kind of look? closer - Adj	19. Is there an adverb exception? No.
9. A - A	20. Is this sentence in a natural or inverted order? Natural - no change.
10. At - P	
11. At whom? President - OP	

Classified Sentence:

```
                          SP    V   P  A  OP      P  A  Adj  OP    P  A    OP
          SN  V          (You) / Run (to the window) (for a closer look) (at the President!)  E
          P1
```

Assignment

1. Write two **Practice Sentences** following these labels:
   1. **SP V Adv P A Adj OP**   2. **(SP) V Adv P A OP**
2. Write an **Improved Sentence** from Practice Sentence 1. Make at least two synonym changes, one antonym change, and your choice of complete word changes.

CHAPTER 4 LESSON 1

Writing Assignment

Use the Expository Steps, Paragraph Outline, and Rough Draft Guidelines in Chapter 3 to do the writing assignment below. After you finish writing your paragraph, underline the topic sentence, the first point sentence, second point sentence, third point sentence, and concluding sentence. Circle the capital letter and end mark at the beginning and end of each sentence. Put your paragraph in your Rough Draft folder.

Writing Assignment #2: Three-Point Expository Paragraph in Third Person
(Remember, third person is the point of view in writing that uses the personal pronouns *he, his, him, she, her, hers, it its, their, theirs, them*, and this expository writing uses the three-point pattern.)

Topic: Occupations
Logical narrowed topic: The Dangers of Being a _____
Writing topic: The Dangers of Being a _____ (Choose an occupation)

CHAPTER 4 LESSON 2

Practice Sentences

You will review the new concepts introduced in the introductory sentences by classifying a set of Practice Sentences with your teacher. As you classify the Practice Sentences, notice how knowledge of the Question and Answer Flow allows you to analyze and identify all the parts of a sentence easily.

Subject-Verb Agreement Rule Box
1. A singular subject must use a singular verb or a singular verb form: *is, was, has, does, or verbs ending with* **s** *or* **es**.
2. A plural subject must use a plural verb or a plural verb form: *are, were, do, have, or verbs without* **s** *or* **es** *endings.* (A plural verb form without **s** or **es** endings is called a *plain form*).
3. The subject **YOU** is considered plural. Always use a plural verb or a plural verb form (see the plural verb list above).

Guided Practice: Underline the subject once and the correct verb twice. Put the correct rule number (1,2,3) in the blank.

___1___ 1. Jamie (type, <u>types</u>) quickly on her typewriter.
___2___ 2. My cousins will (<u>help</u>, helps) in my garden this summer.
___2___ 3. Those parrots (is, <u>are</u>) talking to each other!
___3___ 4. You (was, <u>were</u>) the favorite act in our show!

Guided Practice: **Editing Paragraph**
Underline each verb that has an error in subject-verb agreement. Then write the correction above it. Use the Editing Guide to know how many errors to correct. **Editing Guide: Subject-Verb Agreement: 6**

     are
Charlotte and David <u>is</u> my cousins from Tuscon, Arizona. They are very nice people. David is a fifth

                    packs
grade teacher with a special hobby. He likes to ride his mountain bike on long trips. He <u>pack</u> camping

   spends   *sells*
gear and <u>spend</u> a couple of weeks on his bike touring the countryside. Charlotte <u>sell</u> cosmetics at a

                  has
department store in Tuscon. She likes to collect antiques. She <u>have</u> a house full of them! Charlotte

   are
and David <u>is</u> interesting people!

ok
-10

CHAPTER 4 LESSON 2 SKILL TEST

Subject-Verb Agreement Rule Box
1. A singular subject must use a singular verb or a singular verb form: *is, was, has, does, or verbs ending with* **s** *or* **es**.
2. A plural subject must use a plural verb or a plural verb form: *are, were, do, have, or verbs without* **s** *or* **es** *endings*. (A plural verb form without **s** or **es** endings is called a *plain form*).
3. The subject **YOU** is considered plural. Always use a plural verb or a plural verb form (see the plural verb list above).

Exercise 1: Underline the subject noun once and the correct verb twice. Put the verb rule number (1, 2, 3) in the blank.

2	1. Cody and Mike (trade, trades) baseball cards often.
1	2. My mountain bike (race, races) better than anyone else's!
2	3. Those cowboys (is, are) practicing for the rodeo tonight.
1	4. One row of seats (is, are) still completely vacant.
2	5. Five stamps from the post office (was, were) placed on the letters.
3	6. You (was, were) playing your trumpet too loudly.
2	7. The icicles on our roof (has, have) melted this morning.
2	8. My new shoes (has, have) dark brown shoelaces.
2	9. The leaves of the bush (does, do) not change colors in the fall.
3	10. You (does, do) not need to use a straw in your drink.
2	11. Spotted owls (live, lives) in the forests of Oregon and California.
3	12. You (win, wins) a gold medal in the skating competition.
2	13. Two sacks of money (was, were) found in the parking lot!
2	14. Joe and John (is, are) floating in a canoe on the river this weekend.
3	15. You (was, were) late for your appointment two days in a row.

Exercise 2: Answer the questions below.

16. Name the seven subject pronouns. I, we, he, she, It they, you

17. Name the understood subject pronoun. you

18. How do you label and mark the understood subject pronoun? SP (you)

19. What is an imperative sentence? a command

20. What is the Question and Answer Flow for an imperative sentence? period, command, Imperative sentence

21. Name the seven object pronouns. me, you, them, us, him her it

Exercise 3: Editing Paragraph
Underline each verb that has an error in subject-verb agreement. Then write the correction above it. Use the Editing Guide to know how many errors to correct. **Editing Guide: Subject-Verb Agreement: 7**

    Our family <u>have</u> [has] a hard time teaching my dad to stay out of the refrigerator at night. He <u>do</u> [does] not

know we <u>is</u> [are] watching him sneak late night snacks. Mom <u>try</u> [tries] to sleep with one eye open so she can

catch him getting up. Our dog, Arf, <u>help</u> [helps] Mom keep an eye on Dad. Arf <u>growl</u> [growls] at Dad when he <u>try</u> [tries]

to leave the bedroom.

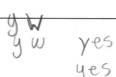 

(handwritten margin: y W / y w yes / yes)

CHAPTER 4 LESSON 3 APPLICATION TEST

Exercise 1: Classify each sentence.

1. <u>SN V P1</u> *adv* *SP*/V *P A OP* / *P A OP* / *P adj OP* / *P OP* Yesterday he/spoke to the students about the location of ancient tribes of Indians. D

2. <u>SN V P1</u> *(you) SN* V / *P A adj OP* / *P A adj OP* / *P A OP* Look at the world map on the south wall in the public library. Imp

3. <u>SN V P1</u> *adj SN* V / *P A OP* / *P adj OP* / *P A OP* / *P A adj OP* Gigantic trees/stand on a carpet of green grass at the edge of the thick forest. D

Directions: Complete the noun job table. Use Sentence 3.

List the Noun Used		List the Noun Job		Singular or Plural		Common or Proper	
4. trees		5. SN		6. P		7. C	
8. carpet		9. OP		10. S		11. C	
12. grass		13. OP		14. S		15. C	
16. edge		17. OP		18. S		19. C	
20. forest		21. OP		22. S		23. C	

Subject-Verb Agreement Rule Box
1. A singular subject must use a singular verb or a singular verb form: *is, was, has, does, or verbs ending with* **s** *or* **es**.
2. A plural subject must use a plural verb or a plural verb form: *are, were, do, have, or verbs without* **s** *or* **es** *endings*. (A plural verb form without **s** or **es** endings is called a *plain form*).
3. The subject **YOU** is considered plural. Always use a plural verb or a plural verb form (see the plural verb list above).

Exercise 2: Underline the subject noun once and the correct verb twice. Put the verb rule number (1, 2, 3) in the blank.

____1____ 24. <u>Cindy</u> (wash, <u>washes</u>) all the dirty clothes on Monday.

____2____ 25. <u>Kelly</u> and <u>Steven</u> (<u>ride</u>, rides) their new bikes everywhere!

____2____ 26. Those <u>ducks</u> (is, <u>are</u>) eating our grass seed.

____1____ 27. The <u>book</u> about dolphins (<u>is</u>, are) on the book shelf.

____2____ 28. <u>Robert</u> and <u>Tommy</u> (was, <u>were</u>) shopping at the bicycle shop.

____2____ 29. <u>They</u> (was, <u>were</u>) nervous about their math test.

____1____ 30 The band <u>instructor</u> (<u>has</u>, have) several beginning students in his class.

____2____ 31. The <u>children</u> (has, <u>have</u>) enough free time to play outside.

____1____ 32. <u>She</u> (do, <u>does</u>) eat vegetables for every meal.

____2____ 33. Several <u>lamps</u> (<u>do</u>, does) not burn brightly at all.

Exercise 3:   **Editing Paragraph**

Find each error and write the correction. Replace each word underlined once with a synonym and each word underlined twice with an antonym. Use the Editing Guide to help you. **Editing Guide: Homonyms: 3 Synonyms: 2 Antonyms: 2 A/An: 1 Misspelled Words: 2 Capitals: 6 Apostrophes: 1 Subject-Verb Agreement: 5 End Marks: 6**

S   *live*   *giant* several geese <u>lives</u> in the <u>tiny</u> pond in front of our house. twice a day they leave the pond and follow

their   *to*   *has a*   *walks* there leader up the hill too our neighborhood. one goose have an broken foot and walk along behind the

T   *waddle*   *Patiently*   *injured* others. they <u>walk</u> around slowly and patently looking for food and waiting for the <u>hurt</u> one to catch up.

T *honk*   *get too*   T   *loud neighborhood* they <u>honks</u> and fuss if children gets two close. its fun watching the geese visit our <u>quiet neighborhood</u>.

CHAPTER 4 LESSON 4

Check Time, Journal Writing Time, and Analogy Time
Journal Writing Assignment: Make an entry in your journal. (Start with your heading and date.)

Remember that an analogy compares two pairs of words and shows how the pairs of words are alike. An analogy has two parts. Remember to follow these steps to decide how the pairs of words are compared.

Step 1: Look closely at the first pair of words.
Step 2: Decide how they are related.
Step 3: Look at how the second pair of words should relate.   The comparison should be similar.
Step 4: Choose a word that relates the second pair in the same way.

Word Analogy Exercise: Choose the correct missing word and put the letter in the blank.

1. drop:rain::__d__:snow   a. cold   b. winter   c. ice   d. flake
2. ocean:water::beach:__b__   a. water   b. sand   c. shells   d. people
3. Santa:sleigh::witch:__c__   a. cat   b. hat   c. broom   d. pumpkin

CHAPTER 4 LESSON 5

Writing Assignment

Use the Expository Steps, Paragraph Outline, and Rough Draft Guidelines in Chapter 3 to do the writing assignment below. After you have finished writing your paragraph, put it in your Rough Draft folder.

Writing Assignment #3: Three-Point Expository Paragraph in First Person
Topic: Food
Logical narrowed topic: Eating Places
Writing topic: My Three Favorite Eating Places

Editing Time

Read and discuss the *Guidelines for Editing Rough Drafts* and the *Guidelines for Writing Final Papers* below and the *Editing Checklist* on the next page. Use these guidelines to edit Writing Assignment #3. Staple the final paper to the rough draft and put both in the Final Writing Folder until your teacher calls for them. You will use these guidelines every time you edit a writing assignment.

Guidelines for Editing Rough Drafts

1. Write the correct heading on your paper, and start the editing process by editing your own paper.

2. Exchange papers with your editing partner. (Your teacher will assign editing partners.)

3. Use the Editing Checklist on the next page to edit the writing assignment.

4. Circle errors and write the correction above each error.

5. Edit neatly with a pencil. Do not make unnecessary marks or comments.

6. Exchange back and do a final edit on your own paper.

7. Place edited rough draft in Rough Draft Folder.

Guidelines For Writing Final Papers

1. Write the correct heading on your paper.

2. Write your final paper in ink.

3. Single space your final paper.

4. Write your final paper neatly.

5. Staple the final paper to the rough draft and put both in the Final Writing Folder.

6. Keep your final paper and rough draft in the Final Writing Folder until your teacher calls for them.

7. After papers are graded and returned, place the graded writing in your Graded Writing Folder.

CHAPTER 4 LESSON 5

Use the Editing Checklist below to check your rough draft. The sentence-by-sentence check guides you as you edit for grammar, mechanics, usage, and sentence structure mistakes. The paragraph, rough draft, and final paper checks give you a review of the specific directions you are to follow for each part of your assignment.

EDITING CHECKLIST

Sentence-by-Sentence Check: Usage and Mechanics (5 points each / 35 total)

_____ 1. Check for complete sentences: subject, verb, complete sense, capital letter, and end mark.
_____ 2. Check for words that are left out and check for words or ideas that are repeated (except for a concluding sentence that summarizes, or paraphrases, the topic sentence).
_____ 3. Check all words for capitalization mistakes.
_____ 4. Check for all punctuation mistakes, which include 5 areas: (commas, periods, apostrophes, quotation marks, underlining.)
_____ 5. Check for subject-verb agreement mistakes.
_____ 6. Check for problems in usage (pronoun usage, double negatives, a/an choices, etc.).
_____ 7. Check for misspelled words.

Sentence-by-Sentence Check: Style and Sentence Structure (5 points each / 25 total)

_____ 8. Check for sentence variety. Do not begin all sentences with the same word.
_____ 9. Check for too many simple sentences. Use simple, compound, and complex sentences.
_____ 10. Check for run-on sentences: two sentences connected with a conjunction and no comma.
_____ 11. Check for a comma splice: two sentences connected with a comma and no conjunction.
_____ 12. Check for correct punctuation of complex sentences: use a comma after the first sentence only if it is dependent or cannot stand alone.

Paragraph Check (6 points each / 30 total)

_____ 13. Check to see that each paragraph is indented.
_____ 14. Check each paragraph for a topic sentence.
_____ 15. Check each sentence to make sure it supports the topic of the paragraph.
_____ 16. Check the content for interest and creativity.
_____ 17. Check the type and format of writing assigned.

Rough Draft (1 point each / 5 total)

_____ 18. Have you written the correct heading on your paper?
_____ 19. Have you written your rough draft in pencil?
_____ 20. Have you skipped every other line?
_____ 21. Have you circled every error and have you written corrections above each error?
_____ 22. Have you place your edited rough draft in your Rough Draft Folder?

Final Paper (1 point each / 5 total)

_____ 23. Have you written the correct heading on your paper?
_____ 24. Have you written your final paper in ink?
_____ 25. Have you singled spaced your final paper?
_____ 26. Have you written your final paper neatly?
_____ 27. Have you stapled your final paper to your rough draft and put them in the Final Folder?

CHAPTER 5 LESSON 1

Possessive Pronouns

1. A pronoun takes the place of a noun.
2. A possessive pronoun has two jobs: to show ownership and to modify like an adjective.
3. These are the possessive pronouns: *my, our, his, her, its, their,* and *your.*
4. To find possessive pronouns, ask the question *whose* and then say the pronoun. (Whose hat? His - **PPA**)
5. Label a possessive pronoun with a **PPA** (*possessive pronoun adjective*)*.*

Possessive Nouns

1. A noun is the name of a person, place, or thing.
2. A possessive noun has two jobs: to show ownership and to modify like an adjective.
3. A possessive noun will always have an *apostrophe s ('s)* or an *s apostrophe (s')* after it. The apostrophe makes a noun possessive.
4. Label a possessive noun with a **PNA** (*possessive noun adjective*).
5. To find the possessive noun, ask the question *whose* and then say the noun. (Whose hat? Bill's **PNA**)

Question and Answer Flow Example

Question and Answer Flow for Sentence 5: For several hours he worked steadily on his brother's motorcycle.	
1. Who worked steadily on his brother's motorcycle? he - SP	10. How many hours? several - Adj
2. What is being said about he? he worked - V	11. Subject Verb Pattern 1 Check
3. Worked how? steadily - Adv	12. (for several hours) - Prepositional Phrase
4. On - P	13. (on his brother's motorcycle) - Prepositional Phrase
5. On what? motorcycle - OP	14. Period, statement, declarative sentence
6. Whose motorcycle? brother's - PNA	15. Go back to the verb - divide the complete subject from the complete predicate.
7. Whose brother's? his - PPA	16. Is there an adverb exception? No
8. For - P	17. Is this sentence in a natural or inverted order? Inverted - Underline the subject parts once and the predicate parts twice.
9. For what? hours - OP	

Classified Sentence:

```
                        P    Adj    OP    SP    V    Adv    P  PPA  PNA      OP
         SN V        (For several hours) he / worked steadily (on his brother's motorcycle.) D
         P1
```

Assignment

1. Write one **Practice Sentence** following these labels: **PPA PNA SN V Adv P PPA OP**
2. Write an **Improved Sentence** from the practice sentence. Make at least two synonym changes, one antonym change, and your choice of complete word changes.

Writing Assignment

Use the Expository Steps, Paragraph Outline, and Rough Draft Guidelines in Chapter 3 to do the writing assignment below. After you have finished writing your paragraph, put it in your Rough Draft folder.

Writing Assignment #4: Three-Point Expository Paragraph in First Person

Topic: Vacations
Logical narrowed topic: Places to Visit
Writing topic: Three Places I Would Like to Visit

CHAPTER 5 LESSON 2

Study the following explanations in the boxes below to help you determine whether to use a singular or a plural verb in the special cases of subject-verb agreement.

Box 1: Agreement Rules for Collective Nouns

Collective Nouns refer to a number of people or things that make up one group.
1. **Singular Collective Nouns:** When the entire group acts as one unit and is not divided in action, thought, or effort (united action, all together), use a singular verb.
   Example: The **crew works** well together. (united action for a united result, all together)
2. **Plural Collective Nouns:** When the individuals that make up the group act separately, one-by-one, and are divided in action, thought, or effort (separate actions for separate results, one by one), use a plural verb. Example: The **crew were** reading in their bunks. (separate actions, one by one)
   Common Collective Nouns: class, family, team, group, flock, band, audience, club, committee, crew, school, majority, army, choir, chorus, convoy, crowd, faculty, jury, herd, gang, mob, faculty

---

Guided Practice: In the guided practice exercises below, underline the subject once. In the **Sp Case** column, write the special case rule number of the subject from each rule box. In the **S/P** column, write **S** if the subject is singular or **P** if the subject is plural. Then underline the verb twice that agrees with the special subject.

Sp Case	S/P
1	S
1	S
2	P

Guided Practice 1:

1. The pit <u>crew</u> (keep, <u>keeps</u>) the race car in good condition.
2. The <u>crowd</u> (cheer, <u>cheers</u>) for its team at every football game.
3. The <u>crowd</u> (<u>scatter</u>, scatters) in different directions during the explosion.

Box 2: Agreement Rules for Nouns Singular in Meaning but Plural in Form and Nouns Ending in *-ics*

3. **Nouns Singular in Meaning but Plural in Form**: Only a few nouns are plural in form but are singular in meaning: *news, series, mumps, measles*. These nouns end in *s* as most plural nouns do, but they do not stand for more than one thing. Therefore, they are used with a singular verb.
   The **news *is*** on TV at six o'clock.   The **measles *is*** going around.
4. **Plural *ics* nouns**: Most nouns that end in *ics* are plural. If the nouns ending in *ics* are preceded by an article, a possessive pronoun, or a plural modifier, they will be plural and will use a plural verb.
   His politics are bold. **The ethics** of the group **were** high.
5. **Singular *ics* nouns:** Nouns that end in *ics* are singular only when they are used as one unit of thought or one unit of study (a school subject, a science, or a general practice.) Singular *ics* nouns usually do not have modifiers in front. Singular *ics* nouns will use a singular verb.
   Politics *is* everyone's business. **Civics is** the study of government.

Sp Case	S/P
5	S
4	P
3	S

Guided Practice 2:

4. <u>Politics</u> (<u>is</u>, are) an interesting career opportunity.
5. His <u>politics</u> (is, <u>are</u>) known throughout the world.
6. <u>Mumps</u> (<u>is</u>, are) usually a childhood disease.

Box 3: Agreement Rule for Titles or Names of Countries

6. **Titles or Names of Countries** refer to a single thing and are used with a singular verb.
   The United States *has* a base in our country.   ***The Brave Bulls*** is the title of a motion picture

Sp Case	S/P
6	S
6	S

Guided Practice 3:

7. "<u>Three Blind Mice</u>" (<u>is</u>, are) a favorite nursery rhyme among children.
8. The <u>Netherlands</u> (participate, <u>participates</u>) in the Olympic games.

CHAPTER 5 LESSON 2

Box 4: Agreement Rules for Words of Amount or Time
7. **Words of amount and time:** Words or phrases that tell amounts of money, time, or measurement will usually use a singular verb.
Five cents *is* in my hand.   **Eight hours *is*** a workday.   **Three yards *is*** sufficient.
8. **Amount or time with plural object of the prepositon:** When a prepositional phrase with a plural object falls between an amount (or time) and the verb, the verb becomes plural.
Fifty pounds of oranges ***have*** arrived.   *BUT*   **Fifty pounds** of sugar ***has*** arrived.
Three-fourths of the books ***are*** new.   *BUT*   **Three-fourths** of the job ***is*** finished.
Exception: <u>**Three** of the nickels ***are*** in his hand.</u>   *BUT*   <u>**One** of the nickels ***is*** in his hand.</u>

Sp Case	S/P
7	S
8	S
8	P
8	S
7	S

Guided Practice 4:

9. One hundred <u>dollars</u> (<u>is</u>, are) your weekly salary.
10. Twenty <u>minutes</u> of studying (<u>is</u>, are) not enough.
11. Twenty <u>pounds</u> of apples (has, <u>have</u>) been unloaded.
12. <u>One</u> of the new tables (<u>has</u>, have) scratches on the top.
13. Two thousand <u>pounds</u> (seem, <u>seems</u>) extremely heavy to me.

Box 5: Agreement Rules for Compound Subjects
9. ***And* Compound:** Whenever two or more subjects are connected by ***and***, use a plural verb.
John *and* Sara *are* coming.   The new **cars *and* trucks *are*** on display.
10. ***Or, Nor* Compound:** Whenever compound subjects are connected by ***or*** or ***nor***, make the verb agree with the subject closer to it.
John *or* Sara *is* coming. **John *or* the boys *are*** coming. The **boys *or* John *is*** coming.

Sp Case	S/P
9	P
10	S
10	P
10	S

Guided Practice 5:

14. <u>Skippy</u> and <u>Jake</u> (<u>like</u>, likes) a special kind of dog food.
15. Either <u>Janet</u> or <u>Susan</u> always (eat, <u>eats</u>) this kind of cake for dessert.
16. Neither the tigers nor the <u>lions</u> (is, <u>are</u>) in their cages!
17. Neither the <u>doctor</u> nor the <u>nurse</u> (<u>is</u>, are) able to come to the phone.

Box 6: Agreement Rules for Subjects Following the Verb
11. **Inverted sentences:** In totally inverted sentences, the complete predicate comes before the complete subject. To be sure which verb to use, find the subject by rearranging the sentence into the usual subject-before-predicate order. Decide whether the subject is singular or plural and then choose the verb that agrees.
Where <u>**were**</u> the tiny <u>**rabbits**</u>?   There <u>**was**</u> a tiny <u>**rabbit**</u>.   Who <u>**was**</u> the <u>**inventor**</u> of the telephone?
(The tiny <u>rabbits</u> <u>were</u> where?)   (A tiny <u>rabbit</u> <u>was</u> there.)   (The <u>inventor</u> of the telephone <u>was</u> who?)

Sp Case	S/P
11	P
11	S
11	S

Guided Practice 6:

18. Who (was, <u>were</u>) the new <u>students</u> today?
19. There (<u>was</u>, were) a new <u>student</u> in our room.
20. Behind a hidden panel (<u>was</u>, were) a secret <u>door</u>.

CHAPTER 5 LESSON 2 SKILL TEST

Subject-Verb Agreement Rules for Special Cases
1. Singular collective nouns (united action, all together) 2. Plural collective nouns (separate actions, one by one) 3. Nouns singular in meaning but plural in form 4. Plural *ics* nouns 5. Singular *ics* nouns 6. Titles or names of countries 7. Words of amount and time 8. Amount or time with plural object of the preposition 9. *And* compound 10. *Or, Nor* compound 11. Inverted sentence

Exercise 1: Underline the subject once. In the **Sp Case** column, write the special case rule number of the subject from the box above. In the **S/P** column, write **S** if the subject is singular or **P** if the subject is plural. Then underline the verb twice that agrees with the special subject.

Sp Case	S/P	
1	S	1. The band (was, were) playing beautifully.
2	P	2. The band (was, were) running away in all directions.
10	S	3. Either private cars or a chartered bus (is, are) taking us there.
10	P	4. Either a chartered bus or private cars (is, are) taking us there.
7	S	5. The fifteen minutes (seem, seems) more like fifteen hours!
1	S	6. The enthusiastic audience (clap, claps) wildly for the singer.
6	S.	7. *The Three Musketeers* (is, are) a book that has been made into a movie.
10	P	8. Neither the chairs nor the tables (has, have) arrived.
5	S	9. Athletics (produce, produces) healthy, fit young people.
7	S	10. Eight weeks never (seem, seems) long enough for our summer vacation.
3	S	11. The mumps (is, are) widespread in our community.
10	S	12. Neither the principal nor the teacher (is, are) able to come to the phone.
1	S	13. The entire group (believe, believes) in hard work.
2	S	14. The class (disagree, disagrees) on a theme for the dance.
9	P	15. Jack and Jill (is, are) going up the hill.
3	S	16. The news (is, are) on a local channel.
1	S	17. The army of ants (march, marches) busily along the sidewalk.
11	S	18. There (is, are) a large area of new homes.
5	S	19. Politics in a business office (is, are) dangerous.
4	P	20. My sister's politics (seem, seems) to change every year.
2	P	21. The jury (was, were) in hot disagreement.
6	S	22. The United Nations (is, are) sending a team to the Middle East.
8	P	23. Twenty pounds of apples (was, were) sent to us.
1	S	24. Our family (spend, spends) time together every Sunday afternoon.
7	S	25. Five tons (is, are) the average weight of most elephants.

Exercise 2: Answer the questions below.

26. Name the seven possessive pronouns.
My our, his her, its their your

27. What do possessive pronouns and possessive nouns show?
ownership

28. What punctuation mark does a possessive noun always have?
an apostraphe

29. What is the question you ask in the Question and Answer Flow to find possessive words?
whose

30. Name the seven subject pronouns.
I we, he she, it you, they

Student Book

CHAPTER 5 LESSON 3 APPLICATION TEST

Exercise 1: Classify each sentence.

1. <u>SN V P1</u> Yesterday the dog's teeth snapped viciously at the intruder's leg!

2. <u>SN V P1</u> During study hall we reviewed quickly for our big math test.

3. <u>SN V P1</u> The thieves' fingerprints were on Mr. Bank's desk in his office.

Directions: Complete the noun job table. Use Sentence 3.

List the Noun Used	List the Noun Job	Singular or Plural	Common or Proper
4. thieves'	5. PNA	6. P	7. C
8. fingerprints	9. SN	10. P	11. C
12. desk	13. OP	14. S	15. C
16. Mr. Banks	17. PNA	18. S	19. P
20. office	21. OP	22. S	23. C

Exercise 2: Underline the subject noun once. In the **S/P** column, write **S** if the subject is singular or **P** if the subject is plural. Underline the correct verb twice to agree with the subject.

S/P	
S	24. The whole <u>class</u> (practice, <u>practices</u>) hard every day on its play.
S	25. <u>Mathematics</u> (<u>is</u>, are) a required course every year at our school.
S	26. <u>Mumps</u> (<u>is</u>, are) sometimes a very painful illness.
S	27. *Two Gentlemen of Verona* (<u>is</u>, are) one of Shakespeare's early comedies.
S	28. <u>The Netherlands</u> (<u>is</u>, are) a land of plentiful water and beautiful flowers.
S	29. One hundred <u>pounds</u> (<u>is</u>, are) the average weight of the young swim team.
S	30. Two <u>weeks</u> never (seem, <u>seems</u>) long enough for our vacation.
P	31. Neither <u>Jack</u> nor the <u>boys</u> (<u>like</u>, likes) Italian food.
S	32. Where (<u>is</u>, are) the <u>box</u> for these ornaments?

Exercise 3:   **Editing Paragraph**

Find each error and write the correction. Replace each word underlined once with a synonym. Use the Editing Guide to know how many errors to correct. **Editing Guide: Capitals: 24 Homonyms: 4 Subject-Verb Agreement: 8 <u>Synonyms</u>: 2 Apostrophes: 2 Periods: 3 Misspelled Words: 4 End Marks: 13**

the united states have good doctors for animals. doctors for animals is called veternarians. i like working for a veternarian. every tuesday i work at dr. bensons veterinery clinic. dr. benson lets me feed and exercise the animals. usually i takes care of the dogs and cats. ben and adam is my favorite dogs. their always glad to see me because they no I feed them and let them out of there cages. three hours are all i work. three-fourths of my job is great. i only have one problem. dr. bensons parrot get on my nerves. he talk to mush.

CHAPTER 5 LESSON 4

Check Time, Journal Writing Time, and Analogy Time
Journal Writing Assignment: Make an entry in your journal. (Start with your heading and date.)

Word Analogy Exercise: Choose the correct missing word and put the letter in the blank.
1. hear:here:: _C_ :their   a. wear   b. that   c. there   d. pronoun
2. Czar:Russia::Pharoah: _A_ a. Egypt   b. Japan   c. emperor   d. Israel
3. hop:frog::slither: _C_   a. worm   b. snail   c. snake   d. lily pad

CHAPTER 5 LESSON 5

The Study of the Essay

The essay is an easy and fun form of writing. The **essay** is a written discussion of one idea and is made up of several paragraphs. It might be interesting to know that the word *essay* comes from the French word *Essai*, meaning "a trial" or "a try." Many students consider essay writing a real "trial." However, with the Shurley Method, you will find essay writing quite easy and even pleasant.

To make essay writing easier, you will first learn how to develop a three-paragraph expository essay using the three-point format. The three-point format is a way of organizing your expository essay that will help make your meaning clear and understandable.

The essay has four parts: 1. Title 2. Introduction 3. Body 4. Conclusion. All these parts, except the title, will always be written in that order. Although the title will be the first item appearing at the top of your essay, you will not write the title until you have written the introduction. In a three-paragraph expository essay, there will be three paragraphs, no more and no fewer. The introduction forms the first paragraph, the body forms the second paragraph, and the conclusion forms the third paragraph of the essay.

As you are learning to write a three paragraph essay, it will help to remember the outline for the three-point paragraph that you have already learned. Look at the outlines below. Compare and discuss the differences in the paragraph and essay. Compare the number of sentences and differences in the introduction and conclusion.

Outline of a Three-Point Paragraph	Outline of a Three-Paragraph Essay
I. Title	I. Title
II. Paragraph (9 sentences)	II. Paragraph 1 - Introduction (3 sentences)
A. Topic sentence	A. Topic and general number sentence
B. A three-point sentence	B. Extra information about the topic sentence
C. A **first point** sentence	C. Enumeration sentence
D. A **supporting** sentence for the first point	III. Paragraph 2 - Body (6-9 sentences)
E. A **second point** sentence	A. **First point** sentence
F. A **supporting** sentence for the second point	B. One or two **supporting** sentences for the first point
G. A **third point** sentence	C. **Second point** sentence
H. A **supporting** sentence for the third point	D. One or two **supporting** sentences for the second point
I. A concluding sentence	E. **Third point** sentence
	F. One or two **supporting** sentences for the third point
	IV. Paragraph 3 - Conclusion (2 sentences)
	A. Concluding general statement
	B. Concluding summary sentence

CHAPTER 5 LESSON 5

Now you will learn how to write each sentence and paragraph in the three-paragraph expository essay by following the steps below.

Steps for Writing a Three-Paragraph Expository Essay

NARROWING THE TOPIC

♦ Read the broad topic: **Winter**
♦ Decide on a logical narrowed topic: **Winter Activities**
♦ If needed, narrow the topic again: **Winter Activities That I Enjoy**
♦ Writing Topic: **Winter Activities That I Enjoy**

ENUMERATE THE TOPIC

♦ Select three points to enumerate about the topic. **(1. sledding   2. ice skating   3. skiing)**

WRITING THE INTRODUCTION AND TITLE

1. Sentence #1 - Topic Sentence
   Write the topic sentence by using the words in your topic and adding a general number word, such as *several, many, some*, or *numerous*, instead of the exact number of points you will discuss.
   (When the weather gets cold, there are several winter activities that I enjoy.)

2. Sentence #2 - Extra Information about the topic sentence
   This sentence can clarify, explain, define, or just be an additional, interesting comment about the topic sentence. If you need another sentence to complete your information, write an extra sentence here. If you write an extra sentence, your introductory paragraph will have four sentences in it instead of three sentences. **(Although some of these activities are not available here in my community, I am still able to do the ones I enjoy the most.)**

3. Sentence #3 - Enumeration sentence
   This sentence will list the three points to be discussed in the order that you will present them in the Body of your paper. You can list the points with or without the specific number in front.
   (I love to go sledding, ice skating, and skiing.) or **(My three favorites are sledding, ice skating, and skiing.)**

♦ The Title - Since there are many possibilities for titles, look at the topic and the three points listed about the topic. Use some of the words in the topic and write a phrase to tell what your paragraph is about. Your title can be short or long. Capitalize the first, last, and important words in your title.
   (Winter Fun)

WRITING THE BODY

4. Sentence #4 - First Point - Write a sentence stating your first point.
   (The first winter activity that I enjoy is sledding.)

5. Sentence #5 - Supporting Sentence(s) - Write one or two sentences that give more information about your first point. **(All the kids in our town go sledding down a long hill near my house.)**

6. Sentence #6 - Second Point - Write a sentence stating your second point.
   (The second winter activity that I enjoy is ice skating.)

CHAPTER 5 LESSON 5

Steps for Writing a Three-Paragraph Expository Essay, Continued

7. <u>Sentence #7 - Supporting Sentence(s)</u> - Write one or two sentences that give more information about your second point. **(Each winter my cousins and I can hardly wait for my uncle's pond to freeze over so we can go ice skating.)**

8. <u>Sentence #8 - Third Point</u> - Write a sentence stating your third point. **(The third winter activity that I enjoy is skiing.)**

9. <u>Sentence #9 - Supporting Sentence(s)</u> - Write one or two sentences that give more information about your third point. **(Every winter I go to the mountains in Colorado on a ski trip with a youth group.)**

WRITING THE CONCLUSION

10. <u>Sentence #10 - Concluding General Statement</u> - Read the topic sentence again and then rewrite it using some of the same words to say the same thing in a different way.
(There are many winter activities that provide fun during cold weather.)

11. <u>Sentence #11 - Concluding Summary (Final) Sentence</u> - Read the enumeration sentence again and then rewrite it using some of the same words to say the same thing in a different way.
(I do not always get involved in as many winter activities as I would like, but the three that I enjoy most are sledding, ice skating, and skiing.)

SAMPLE THREE-PARAGRAPH ESSAY
Winter Fun

When the weather gets cold, there are several winter activities that I enjoy. Although some of these activities are not available here in my community, I am still able to do the ones I enjoy the most. My three favorites are sledding, ice skating, and skiing.

The first winter activity that I enjoy is sledding. All the kids in our town go sledding down a long hill near my house. The second winter activity that I enjoy is ice skating. Each winter my cousins and I can hardly wait for my uncle's pond to freeze over so we can go ice skating. The third winter activity that I enjoy is skiing. Every winter I go to the mountains in Colorado on a ski trip with a youth group.

There are many winter activities that provide fun during cold weather. I do not always get involved in as many winter activities as I would like, but the three that I enjoy most are sledding, ice skating, and skiing.

Writing Assignment
Use the three-paragraph essay steps and the essay outline to do the writing assignment below. After you finish writing your essay, circle the capital letter and end mark at the beginning and end of each sentence. Indent each paragraph. Put your essay in your Rough Draft Folder.

Writing Assignment #5: Three-Paragraph Expository Essay in First Person
Topic: Entertainment
Logical narrowed topic: Movies (or TV Shows)
Writing topic: My Three Favorite Movies (or TV Shows)

CHAPTER 6 LESSON 1

Helping Verb, *Not*-Adverb, and Question Verb

Helping verb - When there are two or more verbs, the verbs in front are known as the helping verbs, and the last verb is the main verb. Helping verbs are also called **auxiliary** verbs. The main verb and helping verbs together are called a **verb phrase**. When directions are given to underline the verb, the helping verb and the main verb are both underlined because they are both part of the verb phrase. Helping verbs are labeled with *HV*. (Example: Mosquitoes **have been buzzing** around my head.)

Not **Adverb** - The helping verb can be split from the main verb by the adverb *NOT*. The word *NOT* is always an adverb telling how. Most negative words are adverbs telling how or to what extent. (Example: We *are* **not** *going* home.)

Question Verb - When the helping verb is placed before the subject, the sentence is usually a question. When the sentence is a question, the helping verb will be at the beginning of the sentence. The subject will always come between the helping verb and the main verb. Check a question by making a statement. (Example: **Are** you **going** home? You **are going** home.)

Question and Answer Flow Example

Question and Answer Flow for Sentence 4: Did Cinderella ride to the ball in an orange pumpkin coach?	
1. Who did ride to the ball in an orange pumpkin coach? Cinderella - SN	10. What kind of coach? orange - Adj
2. What is being said about Cinderella? Cinderella did ride - V	11. An - A
	12. Subject Noun, Verb, Pattern 1 Check
3. Did - HV	13. (To the ball) - Prepositional phrase
4. To - P	14. (In an orange pumpkin coach) - Prepositional phrase
5. To what? ball - OP	15. Question mark, question, interrogative sentence
6. The - A	16. Go back to the verb - divide the complete subject from the complete predicate.
7. In - P	17. Is there an adverb exception? No.
8. In what? coach - OP	18. Is this sentence in a natural or inverted order? Inverted - underline the subject parts once and the predicate parts twice.
9. What kind of coach? pumpkin - Adj	

Classified Sentence:

```
                        HV   SN        V  P  A OP  P A  Adj   Adj   OP
          SN  V         Did Cinderella / ride (to the ball) (in an orange pumpkin coach?) Int
          P1
```

Assignment:

1. Write one **Practice Sentence** following these labels. **HV A Adj SN V P OP Adv**

2. Write an **Improved Sentence** from the practice sentence. Make at least two synonym changes, one antonym change, and your choice of complete word changes.

Writing Assignment

Use the three-paragraph essay steps and the essay outline to do the writing assignment below. Remember to indent each paragraph. Put your essay in your Rough Draft folder.

Writing Assignment #6: Three-Paragraph Expository Essay in First Person

Topic: Friends
Logical narrowed topic: Best Friends
Writing topic: Qualities I Want in a Best Friend

CHAPTER 6 LESSON 2

Making Nouns Possessive

To learn how to form possessive nouns that show ownership, first you must decide if the noun is singular or plural before you add the apostrophe. After you know whether it is singular or plural, you can use three rules to tell you how to make the noun possessive. Follow the directions given for each part of the guided practice below. Make sure you use the rule box for *Making Nouns Possessive* to help you complete the practice exercises below.

Making Nouns Possessive		
Decide if the noun you want to make possessive is singular or plural before you add the apostrophe. Follow these rules.		
1. For a singular noun - add (**'s**) boy's	2. For a plural noun that ends in *s* - add (**'**) boys'	3. For a plural noun that does not end in *s* - add (**'s**) men's

Guided Practice: Use the rule box *Making Nouns Possessive* to complete each exercise below. For Practice 1, underline each noun to be made possessive and write singular or plural (**S-P**), the rule number, and the possessive form.   For Practice 2, write each noun as singular possessive and then as plural possessive.

Practice 1				Practice 2		
Nouns	**S-P**	**Rule**	**Possessive Form**	**Nouns**	**Singular Poss**	**Plural Poss**
1. baby tooth	S	1	baby's	6. boss	boss's	bosses'
2. Browns seats	P	2	Browns'	7. bicycle	bycicle's	bycicles'
3. singer voice	S	1	singer's	8. woman	woman's	women's
4. children toys	P	3	children's	9. wife	wife's	wive's
5. deer food	S or P	1 or 3	deer's	10. box	box's	boxes'

Guided Practice: For Practice 3 and Practice 4, rewrite each phrase and use a possessive noun.

Practice 3		Practice 4	
11. the coat of Ted	Ted's coat	13. the noise of the city	city's noise
12. the jobs of the men	Men's jobs	14. the plans of the coaches	choaches' plans

Guided Practice: **Editing for Possessive Nouns**

In the Editing Paragraph below, underline the seven nouns that need an apostrophe. Then rewrite each noun, adding the correct punctuation to make the noun possessive.

     Kathy's
    Kathy skates hung silently on a hook in her locker. The <u>team</u> first game was tomorrow, but her <u>feet</u> ^*team's*   ^*feet's*

                                 coach's   *Kathy's*
blisters were killing her! Soon the <u>coach</u> speech had Kathy wanting to play again. As Kathy feet slid into

                                    girls'
her skates, she winced at the pain. The other <u>girl</u> moans and groans told her they had the same

                                         coach's
problem. No one felt like laughing until they heard the <u>coach</u> moans and groans as he tried to get his

blistered feet into his skates, too.

CHAPTER 6 LESSON 2 SKILL TEST

Exercise 1: Use the rule box *Making Nouns Possessive* to complete the exercise below. For Test 1, underline each noun to be made possessive and write singular or plural **(S-P)**, the rule number, and the possessive form. For Test 2, write each noun as singular possessive and then as plural possessive. For Test 3 and Test 4, rewrite each phrase and use a possessive noun.

Making Nouns Possessive		
Decide if the noun you want to make possessive is singular or plural before you add the apostrophe. Follow these rules.		
1. For a singular noun - add (**'s**) boy's	2. For a plural noun that ends in **s** - add (**'**) boys'	3. For a plural noun that does not end in **s** - add (**'s**) men's

Test 1				Test 2		
Nouns	S-P	Rule	Possessive Form	Nouns	Singular Poss	Plural Poss
1. eagle wings	S	1	eagle's	16. clock	clock's	clocks'
2. boots laces	P	2	boots'	17. scientist	scientist's	scientists'
3. geese feathers	P	3	geese's	18. child	child's	children's
4. horse bridle	S	1	horse's	19. pony	pony's	ponies'
5. flutes notes	P	2	flutes'	20. mouse	mouse's	mice's
6. mice trap	P	3	mice's	21. dish	dish's	dishes'
7. bus windows	S	1	bus's	22. baby	baby's	babies'
8. glasses rims	P	2	glasses'	23. man	man's	men's
9. fish tank	S	1	fish's	24. driver	driver's	drivers'
10. tomato seeds	S	1	tomato's	25. teacher	teacher's	teachers'
11. oxen hooves	P	3	oxen's	26. coach	coach's	coaches'
12. tiger stripes	S	1	tiger's	27. Kelly	Kelly's	Kellys'
13. mirrors frames	P	2	mirrors'	28. tooth	tooth's	teeth's
14. game score	S	1	game's	29. leaf	leaf's	leaves'
15. ladies shoes	P	2	ladies'	30. crowd	crowd's	crowds'
Test 3				Test 4		
31. the bibs of the babies	babies' bibs			35. the bikes of the boys	boys' bikes	
32. the ties of the men	men's ties			36. the bikes of the boy	boy's bikes	
33. the pizza of the girls	girls' pizza			37. the claws of the bear	bear's claws	
34. the store of Amy	Amy's store			38. the speed of the jets	jets' speed	

Exercise 2: Answer each question below.

39. What part of speech is the word NOT? adv

40. Write the punctuation for an interrogative sentence. ?

41. What punctuation is used for possessive nouns? an apostrophe [']

42. What are the two jobs of the possessive noun? ownership, and modifies like an adjective

43. List the 8 *be* verbs. am, is, are, was, were, be, being, been

44. List the 15 other helping verbs. has, have, had, does, do, did, might, must, may, can, could, would, should, shall, will

Exercise 3: Underline all the nouns that need an apostrophe. Write the correct possessive form. **Possessive nouns: 6**

Our schools musical production is coming soon! The choirs songs are beginning to sound wonderful.

All the choir members hard work is paying off. The bands music sounds beautiful, too. The bands

director is especially pleased with his students performance in practice and in competition.

CHAPTER 6 LESSON 3 APPLICATION TEST

Exercise 1: Classify each sentence.

1. _SN V P1_ The entry words in a dictionary are arranged in alphabetical order.

2. _SN V P1_ The buried treasure of Captain Kidd was never found by the sailors.

3. _SN V P1_ Are the twins going to the fair with you tonight?

Directions: Complete the noun job table. Use Sentence 2.

List the Noun Used	List the Noun Job	Singular or Plural	Common or Proper
4. treasure	5. SN	6. S	7. C
8. Cp. Kidd	9. OP	10. S	11. P
12. sailors	13. OP	14. P	15. C

Exercise 2: Use the rule box *Making Nouns Possessive* to complete each exercise below. For Test 1, underline each noun to be made possessive and write singular or plural (**S-P**), the rule number, and the possessive form. For Test 2, write each noun as singular possessive and then as plural possessive. For Test 3 and Test 4, rewrite each phrase and use a possessive noun.

Making Nouns Possessive					
Decide if the noun you want to make possessive is singular or plural before you add the apostrophe. Follow these rules.					
1. For a singular noun - add (**'s**) boy's		2. For a plural noun that ends in **s** - add (**'**) boys'		3. For a plural noun that does not end in **s** - add (**'s**) men's	

Test 1				Test 2		
Nouns	**S-P**	**Rule**	**Possessive Form**	**Nouns**	**Singular Poss**	**Plural Poss**
16. shirts sleeves	P	2	shirts'	21. party	party's	parties'
17. women voices	P	3	women's	22. radio	radios'	radios'
18. James room	S	1	james's	23. calf	calfs'	calves'
19. sheep pen	S P	1 3	sheep's	24. ox	ox's	oxen's
20. pianos keys	P	2	pianos'	25. bus	bus's	buses'

Test 3		Test 4	
26. the tails of dogs	dogs' tails	30. the spikes of the boot	boot's spikes
27. the traps of the mice	mice's traps	31. the limbs of the trees	trees' limbs
28. house of the Smiths	Smiths' house	32. the pages of the book	book's pages
29. the hair of Susie	Susie's hair	33. the pets of children	children's pets

Exercise 3:   **Editing Paragraph**

Find each error and write the correction. Replace each word underlined once with a synonym. Use the Editing Guide to help you. **Editing Guide: Homonyms:1 Synonyms: 4 Capitals: 21 Subject-Verb Agreement: 4 Misspelled Words: 5 Commas: 8 Apostrophes: 4 Underline: 1 End Marks: 5**

the sluggers our towns little league baseball team travel to omaha nebraska for their big

championship tornament on labor day weekend the players baseball shoes is donated by sams shoe store

in topeka kansas for this event all the parents is going to the final game on satuday to suport the

sluggers there hometown newspaper the kansas sun write big articles about the girls trip every thusday

the team likes it

CHAPTER 6 LESSON 4

Check Time and Journal Writing Time

Journal Writing Assignment: Make an entry in your journal. (Start with your heading and date.)

Figures of Speech

When you write a sentence that means exactly what you say, you are using literal language.

> **Literal Language:** Since the wind was blowing hard, I ran down the street and into my house.

When you write a sentence that makes imaginative comparisons that cannot be taken literally, you are using figurative language.

> **Figurative Language**: Since the wind was blowing 90-mile-an-hour blasts down my neck, I flew down the street and into my house.

Figurative language is used most often in creative writing. It uses what are called "figures of speech." Three of these figures of speech are *simile, metaphor*, and *personification*.

A **simile** is a figure of speech that compares two things by using the words *like* or *as*. Since the two things that are compared ordinarily have nothing in common, the image portrayed is vivid. Look at the examples of similes below. What two things are being compared?

> Ramona stood as still **as** a statue when the hornet buzzed angrily around her head.
> (*Ramona* and *statue* are being compared to emphasize how still Ramona stood.)

> Monica's heart fluttered **like** a lace curtain in wind.
> (*Heart* and *curtain* are being compared to emphasize how her heart fluttered.)

A **metaphor** is a figure of speech that compares two things by saying that something **is** something else. Metaphors do not use the words *like* or *as*. Look at the example of a metaphor below. What two things are being compared?

> By her bedtime, the grumpy little *girl* was a *bear*.
> (*Girl* and *bear* are compared to emphasize how grumpy the little girl was.)

> The road snaked its way down into the canyon.
> (The *road is* compared to a *snake* to emphasize its winding curves.)

Personification is a figure of speech that compares two things by giving something nonhuman, human qualities. Look at the example of personification below. What two things are being compared?

> Blindfolded, Andrea walked right into the arms of a grapevine.
> (The *grapevine's limbs* are compared to a *human's arms*.)

> The sunflowers craned their necks to face the sun.
> (The *craning sunflowers' stems* are compared to *a human neck that turns*.)

Exercise 1: Use the information above to help you complete the exercises below. Identify which figure of speech is being used in the sentences. Write the labels **S** for simile, **M** for metaphor, and **P** for personification.

_____ 1. The climbers sensed the anger brewing in the clouds.

_____ 2. Life is a vapor.

_____ 3. She ignored all warnings and appeared as carefree as a butterfly.

_____ 4. Whenever Josh was around, she became an angel.

_____ 5. Milton was tempted by the three apple dumplings sunning themselves on the picnic table.

_____ 6. Moving like a sloth, the old woman gathered her gardening tools.

CHAPTER 6 LESSON 5

You have already learned how to write a three-paragraph essay. Now you will learn how to write a five-paragraph essay. In a five-paragraph expository essay, there will be five paragraphs, no more and no fewer. The introduction forms the first paragraph, the body forms the second, third, and fourth paragraphs, and the conclusion forms the fifth paragraph of the essay.

As you are learning to write a five-paragraph essay, it will help you to remember the outline for the three-paragraph essay that you have already learned. Look at the two outlines below. Compare and discuss the differences in the three-paragraph essay and the five-paragraph essay. Notice that the introduction and conclusion are the same for both essays. Also notice that the body of the five-paragraph essay has three paragraphs. Each point and its supporting sentences will be a separate paragraph in the body of the five-paragraph essay.

Outline of a 3-Paragraph Essay	Outline of a 5-Paragraph Essay
I. Title	I. Title
II. Paragraph 1 - Introduction (3 sentences) A. Topic and general number sentence B. Extra information about the topic sentence C. Enumeration sentence	II. Paragraph 1 - Introduction (3 sentences) A. Topic and general number sentence B. Extra information about the topic sentence C. Enumeration sentence

III. Paragraph 2 - Body   (6-9 sentences)
A. **First point** sentence
B. One or two **supporting** sentences
    for the first point
C. **Second point** sentence
D. One or two **supporting** sentence
    for the second point
E. **Third point** sentence
F. One or two **supporting** sentences
    for the third point
	III. Paragraph 2 - First Point Body (3-4 sentences)
	A. **First point** sentence
	B. Two or three **supporting** sentences for the first point
	
	IV. Paragraph 3 - Second Point Body (3-4 sentences)
	A. **Second point** sentence
	B. Two or three **supporting** sentences for the second
	    point
	
	V. Paragraph 4 - Third Point Body (3-4 sentences)
	A. **Third point** sentence
	B. Two or three **supporting** sentences for the third point

IV. Paragraph 3 - Conclusion   (2 sentences)
A. Concluding general statement
B. Concluding summary sentence
	VI. Paragraph 5 - Conclusion (2 sentences)
	A. Concluding general statement
	    (Restatement of the topic sentence)
	B. Concluding summary sentence
	    (Restatement of the enumeration sentence)

Now you will learn how to write each sentence and paragraph in the five-paragraph expository essay by following the steps below.

Steps in Writing a Five-Paragraph Expository Essay

NARROWING THE TOPIC

- ♦ Read the broad topic: **Winter**
- ♦ Decide on a logical narrowed topic: **Winter Activities**
- ♦ If needed, narrow the topic again: **Winter Activities That I Enjoy**
- ♦ Writing Topic: **Winter Activities That I Enjoy**

CHAPTER 6 LESSON 5

Steps in Writing a Five-Paragraph Expository Essay, Continued

ENUMERATE THE TOPIC

♦ Select the points to enumerate about the topic. **(1. sledding   2. ice skating   3. skiing)**

WRITING THE INTRODUCTION AND TITLE

1. Sentence #1 - Topic Sentence
   Write the topic sentence by using the words in your topic and adding a general number word, such as *several, many, some*, or *numerous*, instead of the exact number of points you will discuss.
   (When the weather gets cold, there are several winter activities that I enjoy.)

2. Sentence #2 - Extra Information about the topic sentence
   This sentence can clarify, explain, define, or just be an extra, interesting comment about the topic sentence. If you need another sentence to complete your information, write an extra sentence here. If you write an extra sentence, your introductory paragraph will have four sentences in it instead of three sentences, and that is okay. **(Although some of these activities are not available here in my community, I am still able to do the ones I enjoy the most.)**

3. Sentence #3 - Enumeration sentence
   This sentence will list the three points to be discussed in the order that you will present them in the Body of your paper. You can list the points with or without the specific number in front.
   (I love to go sledding, ice skating, and skiing.) or **(My three favorites are sledding, ice skating, and skiing.)**

♦ The Title - Since there are many possibilities for titles, look at the topic and the three points listed about the topic. Use some of the words in the topic and write a phrase to tell what your paragraph is about. Your title can be short or long. Capitalize the first, last, and important words in your title.
   (Winter Fun Begins with the Letter S̲)

WRITING THE BODY

4. Sentence #4 - First Point - Write a sentence stating your first point.
   (The first winter activity that I enjoy is sledding.)

5. Sentences #5 - #7 - Supporting Sentences - Write two or three sentences that give more information about your first point. **(There is a long hill behind my house that glazes over every time it snows.) (People from all over town gather there, and we all go sledding.) (It's great to feel the rush of excitement as several sleds push off to race to the bottom.)**

6. Sentence #8 - Second Point - Write a sentence stating your second point.
   (The second winter activity that I enjoy is skating.)

7. Sentences #9 -#11 - Supporting Sentences - Write two or three sentences that give more information about your second point. **(If the weather gets cold enough, my uncle's pond freezes over and is thick enough to support skaters.) (My cousins and I love to skate on that pond.) (We are not professionals, but we have lots of fun making figure 8's and doing our version of the triple axle.)**

CHAPTER 6 LESSON 5

Steps in Writing a Five-Paragraph Expository Essay, Continued

8. <u>Sentence #12 - Third Point</u> - Write a sentence stating your third point.
(The third winter activity that I enjoy is skiing.)

9. <u>Sentences #13 - #15 - Supporting Sentences</u> - Write two or three sentences that give more information about your third point. **(Although there are no mountains nearby on which I can ski, there is almost always a ski trip with a youth group.) (On a ski trip, I get a chance to try out all kinds of slopes from "easy" to "dangerous.") (If I don't "wipe out" on a tree, I have a wonderful time skiing.)**

WRITING THE CONCLUSION

10. <u>Sentence #16 - Concluding General Statement</u> - Read the topic sentence again and then rewrite it using some of the same words to say the same thing in a different way.
(There are many winter activities that provide fun during cold weather.)

11. <u>Sentence #17 - Concluding Summary (Final) Sentence</u> - Read the enumeration sentence again and then rewrite it, using some of the same words to say the same thing in a different way.
(I do not always get involved in as many winter activities as I would like, but the three that I enjoy most are sledding, ice skating, and skiing.)

SAMPLE FIVE-PARAGRAPH ESSAY

Winter Fun Begins with the Letter <u>S</u>

When the weather gets cold, there are several winter activities that I enjoy. Although some of these activities are not available here in my community, I am still able to do the ones I enjoy the most. My three favorites are sledding, ice skating, and skiing.

The first winter activity that I enjoy is sledding. There is a long hill behind my house that glazes over every time it snows. People from all over town gather there, and we all go sledding. It's great to feel the rush of excitement as several sleds push off to race to the bottom.

The second winter activity I have fun doing is ice skating. If the weather gets cold enough, my uncle's pond freezes over and is thick enough to support skaters. My cousins and I love to skate on that pond. We are not professionals, but we have lots of fun making figure 8's and doing our version of the triple axle.

The third winter activity I enjoy is skiing. Although there are no mountains nearby on which I can ski, there is almost always a ski trip with a youth group. On a ski trip, I get a chance to try out all kinds of slopes from "easy" to "dangerous." If I don't "wipe out" on a tree, I have a wonderful time skiing.

There are many winter activities that provide fun during cold weather. I do not always get involved in as many of these activities as I would like, but the three that I enjoy most are sledding, ice skating, and skiing.

CHAPTER 6 LESSON 5

Writing Assignment

Choose one of the topics below and write a five-paragraph essay. Use the five-paragraph essay steps and the essay outline to do the writing assignment. Circle the capital letter and end mark at the beginning and end of each sentence. Indent each paragraph. Put your essay in your Rough Draft folder.

Writing Assignment #7: Five-Paragraph Expository Essay in First Person
Topic: My Life
Logical narrowed topic: Things That Have Happened to Me
Writing topic: Hilarious Things That Have Happened to Me Or
Writing topic: Serious Things That Have Happened to Me

Editing Time

Use the *Guidelines for Editing Rough Drafts* and the *Guidelines for Writing Final Papers* and the *Editing Checklist* in Chapter 4, Lesson 5, to edit Writing Assignment #7. Staple the final paper to the rough draft and put both in the Final Writing Folder until your teacher calls for them.

CHAPTER 7 LESSON 1

Conjunction

A **conjunction** is a word that joins words or groups of words together. The three most common conjunctions are *and, or,* and *but*. The conjunctions *and, or,* and *but* are used so often that they should be memorized. There are no questions to ask to find a conjunction. Conjunctions are labeled with a **C**.

Compound Parts

When words or groups of words in a sentence are joined with a conjunction, the parts that are joined are called **compound parts**. The label *C* is written in front of the regular labels for the compound parts. Example: **CSN** for compound subject noun or **CV** for compound verb.

Interjection

An **interjection** is one or more words used to express mild or strong emotion. Interjections are usually located at the beginning of a sentence and are separated from the rest of the sentence with a punctuation mark. Mild interjections are followed by a comma or period; strong interjections are followed by an exclamation point. Example: **Oh! Well, Wow! Hey! Yes,**

Interjections are not to be considered when you are deciding whether a sentence is declarative, interrogative, exclamatory, or imperative. There are no questions to find interjections. Interjections are named and then labeled with the abbreviation **I** above them.

Question and Answer Flow Example

Question and Answer Flow for Sentence 5: Whew! The mountain climbers gasped and panted in the thin air yesterday.	
1. Who gasped and panted in the thin air yesterday? climbers - SN	10. The - A
2. What is being said about climbers? climbers gasped and panted - CV, CV	11. Whew - I (interjection)
3. In - P	12. Subject Noun, Verb, Pattern 1 Check
4. In what? air - OP	13. (In the thin air) - Prepositional phrase
5. What kind of air? thin - Adj	14. Period, statement, declarative sentence
6. The - A	15. Go back to the verb - divide the complete subject from the complete predicate.
7. Gasped and panted when? yesterday - Adv	16. Is there an adverb exception? No.
8. And - C (conjunction)	17. Is this sentence in a natural or inverted order? Natural - no change.
9. What kind of climbers? mountain - Adj	

Classified Sentence:

```
                              I    A    Adj     SN      CV    C   CV    P  A  Adj OP    Adv
       SN  V          Whew! The mountain climbers / gasped and panted (in the thin air) yesterday.  D
       P1
```

Assignment:

1. Write one **Practice Sentence** following these labels. **I A Adj Adj SN CV C CV P A Adj OP Adv**

2. Write an **Improved Sentence** from the practice sentence using synonyms, antonyms, and complete word changes.

CHAPTER 7 LESSON 1

A Descriptive Paragraph

An artist paints a picture on canvas with paint. A descriptive writer paints a picture on paper with words. Both the artist and writer must carefully select what he will include in his picture. Descriptive writing **shows** the reader what is being described. It does not just **tell** him about it.

Even though you can use description in expository, narrative, and persuasive writing, sometimes you are asked to write simply description. Then you must know that a **descriptive paragraph** gives a detailed picture of a person, place, thing, or idea.

A descriptive paragraph will usually start with an overall impression of what you are describing. That will be your topic sentence. Then you will add supporting sentences that give details about the topic. To make a description clear and vivid, these "detail" sentences should include as much information as possible about how the topic looks, sounds, feels, or tastes. The sensory details that you include will depend on what you are describing. Since all the senses are not significant in all situations, the following guidelines on descriptive writing will give you the types of details that you should consider when you are describing certain topics.

Guidelines for Descriptive Writing

1. **When describing people,** it will be helpful to notice these types of details: appearance, walk, voice, manner, gestures, personality traits, any special incident related to the person being described, and any striking details that will help make that person stand out in your mind.

2. **When describing places or things,** it will be helpful to notice these types of details: the physical features of a place or thing (color, texture, smell, shape, size, age), any unusual features, any special incident related to the place or thing being described, and whether or not the place or thing is special to you.

3. **When describing nature,** it will be helpful to notice these types of details: the special features of the season, the sights, smells, sounds, colors, animals, insects, birds, and any special incident related to the scene being described.

4. **When describing an incident or an event,** it will be helpful to notice these types of details: the order in which the events take place, any specific facts that will keep the story moving from a beginning to an ending, the answers to any of the *who, what, when, where, why,* and *how* questions that the reader needs to know, and especially the details that will create a clear picture, such as how things look, sound, smell, feel, etc.

CHAPTER 7 LESSON 1

Study the sample steps for writing a descriptive paragraph below.

Sample Steps in Writing a Descriptive Paragraph

NARROWING THE TOPIC

♦ Read the broad topic: **Places**
♦ Decide on a logical narrowed topic: **Favorite Places**
♦ Writing Topic: **My Favorite Place**

♦ <u>The Title</u> - Since there are many possibilities for titles, decide if you want to leave the topic as your title or if you want to write a different phrase to tell what your paragraph is about. **(My Home Away from Home)**

1. Sentence #1 - Write a topic sentence that that tells what you are describing.
    (My grandparents' house in the little town of Greenbrier is a special place to me.)

2. Sentence #2 - Write a sentence that tells why you have chosen this topic.
    (Because I spend so much of my time there, their house is "home" to me.)

3. Sentence #3 - Write a sentence that gives a visual description of your topic.
    (The house is an old three-bedroom, one-bath country house with a huge screened front porch.)

4. Sentence #4 - Write another sentence that gives more visual details about your topic.
    (It is surrounded by hickory, evergreen, and fruit trees, and it is made of wood covered with gray siding.)

5. Sentence #5 - Write a sentence that tells a special feature about the topic.
    (I love to sit in the old white wooden swing on the porch and listen as the mockingbirds have their early morning fuss with Grandmother's ancient cat.)

6. Sentence #6 - Write a sentence that tells more about your topic.
    (As I sit there, I can feel the pleasant morning breeze that tickles the leaves of the hickory tree.)

7. Sentence#7 - If you need more description, write another sentence that describes your topic.

8. Sentence #8 - Write a concluding (final) sentence that summarizes your paragraph. Read the topic sentence again and then rewrite it using some of the same words to say the same thing in a different way. **(I have always loved to visit my grandparents' house, a place of very special memories.)**

SAMPLE DESCRIPTIVE PARAGRAPH

My Home Away from Home

My grandparents' house in the little town of Greenbrier is a special place to me. Because I spend so much of my time there, their house is "home" to me. The house is an old three-bedroom, one-bath country house with a huge screened front porch. It is surrounded by hickory, evergreen, and fruit trees, and it is made of wood covered with gray siding. I love to sit in the old white wooden swing on the porch and listen as the mockingbirds have their early morning fuss with Grandmother's ancient cat. As I sit there, I can feel the pleasant morning breeze that tickles the leaves of the hickory tree. I have always loved to visit my grandparents' house, a place of very special memories.

CHAPTER 7 LESSON 1

The Descriptive Paragraph Outline Guide

I. Title

II. Paragraph

    A. Topic sentence that tells what you are describing

    B. Sentence that tells why you have chosen this topic

    C. Sentence that gives a visual description of your topic

    D. Sentence that gives another visual description of your topic

    E. Sentence that tells a special feature about the topic

    F. Sentence that tells more about your topic

    G. Sentence that tells more about your topic (optional)

    H. A concluding sentence that restates your topic sentence

Writing Assignment

Use the guidelines, sample steps, and the outline guide for descriptive writing to do the writing assignment below. After you finish writing your paragraph, circle the capital letter at the beginning of each sentence and the end mark at the end of each sentence. Put your paragraph in your Rough Draft Folder.

Writing Assignment #8: Descriptive Paragraph in First Person

Topic: Places

Logical narrowed topic: Favorite Places

Writing Topic: **My Favorite Place**

CHAPTER 7 LESSON 2

Double Negatives

Double means TWO, and negative means NOT. We have a **double negative** when two negative words are in the same sentence. Most negative words begin with the letter *n*. Other negative words do not begin with the letter *n* but are negative in meaning. There are also some prefixes that give words a negative meaning.

Look at the charts below for a list of commonly used negative words and negative prefixes.

Negative Words That Begin With *N*			Other Negative Words	Negative Prefixes
neither	nobody	not (n't)	barely	dis
never	none	nothing	hardly	non
no	no one	nowhere	scarcely	un

Rules for Correcting Double Negatives

A sentence with a double negative is not correct. There are three ways to correct a double negative:

1. **Change** one of the negatives to a positive:
   Wrong: Ginger **couldn't** find **nothing**.   Right: Ginger **couldn't** find **anything**.

2. **Take out** the negative part of a contraction:
   Wrong: Ginger **couldn't** find **nothing**.   Right: Ginger **could** find **nothing**.

3. **Remove** one of the negative words:
   Wrong: Ginger **didn't** say **nothing**.   Right: Ginger **said nothing**.

Look at the chart below for a list of how to change negative words to positive words.

Changing Negative Words to Positive Words		
1. Change *no* or *none* to *any*.	4. Change *nothing* to *anything*.	7. Change *neither* to *either*.
2. Change *nobody* to *anybody*.	5. Change *nowhere* to *anywhere*.	8. Remove the *n't* from a
3. Change *no one* to *anyone*.	6. Change *never* to *ever*.	contraction.

Guided Practice: Write *any* or *no* to correctly complete the sentences.

1. Daisy didn't have *any* hay to eat.
2. Daisy had *no* hay to eat.
3. The regional band could play *no* marches in the competition.
4. The regional band couldn't play *any* marches in the competition.

Guided Practice: Underline the negative words in each sentence. Then on notebook paper, write two ways to correct each double negative. Put the rule number at the end of each correction.

1. I hope we don't have no homework over the weekend.
2. We can't hardly wait for summer vacation.
3. Don't never leave the keys in the car.
4. There isn't no more cake.
5. He hasn't done nothing about his toothache.

CHAPTER 7 LESSON 2

Using Adjectives and Adverbs in Making Comparisons

Adjectives and adverbs have three forms, or degrees, which we use in making comparisons. These forms, called degrees of comparison, are simple (sometimes called positive), comparative, and superlative. The comparative and superlative forms of the adjective and adverb not only describe an item, but they also give you the ability to compare one item with others.

Rules for Making Regular Adjectives and Adverbs in the Comparative and Superlative Forms	
The **Simple (or Positive) Form** is used when no comparison is made. There are no rules for the simple form.	
The **Comparative Form** is used to compare **TWO** people, places, or things. There are 3 rules for this form.	The **Superlative Form** is used to compare **THREE** or more people, places, or things. There are 3 rules for this form.
Rule 1. Use *-er* with most 1- or 2-syllable words.	**Rule 1.** Use *-est* with most 1- or 2-syllable words.
Rule 2. Use *more* with most *-ly* and *-ful* words or whenever the *-er* sounds awkward.	**Rule 2.** Use *most* with most *-ly* and *-ful* words or whenever the *-est* sounds awkward.
Rule 3. Use *more* for all words with 3 or more syllables.	**Rule 3.** Use *most* for all words with 3 or more syllables.
Simple (or Positive) fast, nervous	**Comparative** faster, more nervous	**Superlative** fastest, most nervous

Some irregular adjectives and adverbs don't use the basic rules and have to be memorized.

Irregular Adjectives and Adverbs Have No Rule Numbers and Have to be Memorized

Simple Adjective	Comparative	Superlative	Simple Adverb	Comparative	Superlative
1. good	better	best	1. well	better	best
2. bad, ill	worse	worst	2. badly	worse	worst
3. little (amount)	less or lesser	least	3. little	less	least
4. much, many	more	most	4. much	more	most

Sentence Examples

1. Maria spoke good English.
2. Maria spoke better English than Roberto.
3. Maria spoke the best English of all the other students.

1. Gus played well today.
2. Gus played better than Joe today.
3. Gus played best of all.

Guided Practice: Write the different forms and rule numbers for these adjectives or adverbs. For irregular forms write *Irr* in the rule box.

Simple Adjective/Adverb	Rule	Comparative Form	Rule	Superlative Form
1. tall	1	taller	1	tallest
2. comfortable	3	more comfortable	3	most comfortable
3. eager	2	more eager	2	most eager
4. boldly	2	more boldly	2	most boldly
5. good	Irr	better	Irr	best

Guided Practice: Write the correct form of the adjective or adverb in parentheses in the blank to complete each sentence.

6. He read the lesson *carefully* . (carefully)
7. I am *taller* than my brother. (tall)
8. I am the *tallest* one in my family. (tall)
9. She was *prettier* than my sister. (pretty)
10. She read the story *better* than Sue. (good)
11. Of all the girls, she was the *most eager* to go. (eager)

CHAPTER 7 LESSON 2 SKILL TEST

Exercise 1: Write *any*, *no*, or *none* to correctly complete each sentence.

1. Susie couldn't find __any__ pencils.
2. Susie could find __no__ pencil to do her work.
3. Susie did __none__ of the things on the list.
4. Jason hasn't __any__ pencils to do his work.
5. Anne had __no__ paper plates for the picnic.
6. We could find __none__ of the lost coins.

Exercise 2: Underline the negative words in the sentences below. On a sheet of notebook paper, write two ways to correct each double negative.

7. Rhonda hasn't never driven our car.   *has ever*
   Rhonda has never driven our car.
   Rhonda hasn't ever driven our car.
8. Nick didn't talk to no one on the telephone.
   Nick talked to no one on the telephone.
   Nick didn't talk to anyone on the telephone.
9. Our car wasn't going nowhere with that flat!   *was anywhere*
   Our car was going nowhere with that flat.
   Our car wasn't going anywhere with that flat.
10. This shortwave radio isn't doing us no good.   *is*
    This shortwave radio is doing us no good.
    This shortwave radio isn't doing us any good.
11. I don't have no excuse.   *any*
    I don't have any excuse.
    I have no excuse.
12. We couldn't get nothing out of the burning house.   *could anything*
    We could get nothing out of the burning house.
    We couldn't get anything out of the burning house.

Exercise 3: Write the different forms and rule numbers for these adjectives or adverbs. For irregular forms write **Irr** in the rule box.

Comparative Rules: Rule 1. -er Rule 2. use **more** with -ly or -ful or awkward words Rule 3. use **more** for 3 or more syllable words
Superlative Rules: Rule 1. -est Rule 2. use **most** with -ly or -ful or awkward words Rule 3. use **most** for 3 or more syllable words

Simple Adjective/Adverb	Rule	Comparative Form	Rule	Superlative Form
13. sharp	14. 1	15. sharper	16. 1	17. sharpest
18. smoothly	19. 2	20. more smoothly	21. 2	22. most smoothly
23. busy	24. 1	25. busier	26. 1	27. busiest
28. fast	29. 1	30. faster	31. 1	32. fastest
33. beautiful	34. 3	35. more beautiful	36. 3	37. most beautiful
38. early	39. 1	40. earlier	41. 1	42. earliest
43. good	44. Irr	45. better	46. Irr	47. best
48. little	49. Irr	50. less	51. Irr	52. least

Exercise 4: Write the correct form of the adjective or adverb in parentheses in the blank to complete each sentence.

53. James drew the __straightest__ lines of all the students. (straight)

54. Our swim team did __better__ than the opposing team. (well)

55. Joe was a __better__ reader than my sister. (good)

56. Jeanne is the __most careful__ of the two hairdressers. (careful)

57. He was the __most frequently__ decorated war hero of all. (frequently)

Exercise 5: Answer these definition questions.

58. Name the three main conjunctions. __and, but, or__
59. Words that are joined with a conjunction are called __compounds__.
60. Name two interjections. __Oh!, Wow!__

CHAPTER 7 LESSON 3 APPLICATION TEST

Exercise 1: Classify each sentence.

1. *SN V P1* Ducks and whales do not breathe (under water.) D

2. *SN V P1* The sick children (at the hospital) clapped and shouted (with delight) (at the funny clowns.) D

3. *SN V P1* A young boy and his sisters stopped and shopped (at the new grocery store.) D

Directions: Complete the noun job table. Use Sentence 2.

List the Noun Used	List the Noun Job	Singular or Plural	Common or Proper
4. children	5. SN	6. P	7. C
8. hospital	9. OP	10. S	11. C
12. delight	13. OP	14. S	15. C
16. clowns	17. OP	18. P	19. C

Exercise 2: Underline the negative words and write two ways to correct each double negative.

20. My aunt hasn't spent none of her extra money.
21. My aunt hasn't spent any of her extra money.
22. My aunt has spent none of her extra money.

23. I don't want nothing from the store.
24. I want nothing from the store.
25. I don't want anything from the store.

Exercise 3: Write the correct form of the adjective or adverb in parentheses in the blank to complete each sentence.

26. Today my taco salad was _bigger_ than it was yesterday. (big)
27. These math problems are the _easiest_ I've ever done. (easy)
28. He had the _most responsibility_ of all the doctors. (responsibility)
29. The two girls worked _well_ together. (well)
30. Janice worked _better_ than Jill did. (well)

Exercise 4: **Editing Paragraph**

Find each error and write the correction. Replace each word underlined once with a synonym. Use the Editing Guide to help you. **Editing Guide:** Homonyms: 3 Synonyms: 3 A/An: 3 Misspelled Words: 3 Capitals: 26 Subject-Verb Agreement: 1 Commas: 2 Apostrophes: 1 Periods: 9 Double Negatives: 1 End Marks: 4

i was surprised when mom bought an ibm computer from b, j, evans because my mom dont no nothing about computers. mr, evans sent an expert, mr, p, c, sims, to help my mom get started, mr, sims spent to hours with mom and her computer, the next day mr, sims and mr, evans brough mom a new typewriter with an big red ribon and picked up there ibm computer,

---

© SHURLEY INSTRUCTIONAL MATERIALS, INC.

CHAPTER 7 LESSON 4

Check Time, Journal Writing Time, and Analogy Time
Journal Writing Assignment: Make an entry in your journal. (Start with your heading and date.)

Word Analogy Exercise: Choose the correct missing word and put the letter in the blank.

1. content:calm::anxious: __d__	a. smile	b. patient	c. lazy	d. agitated
2. ears:Mickey Mouse:: __C__ :Pinocchio	a. black	b. big	c. nose	d. pretend
3. electricity:light bulb::gasoline: __b__	a. fuel	b. car	c. solar	d. diesel

Story Elements: Main Idea, Setting, Character, and Plot

Short stories have certain characteristics that make them different from other types of writing. You will study five characteristics known as Story Elements. These Story Elements are main idea, setting, characters, plot, and ending. You will always use the five Story Elements: main idea, setting, characters, plot, and ending to make a Story Elements Outline. This outline will help keep your writing focused and help you choose details and events that support the main idea of your story. Before you begin every story writing assignment, you will complete a Story Element Outline like the one below.

Story Elements Outline

  I. Main idea
       (Tell the problem or situation that needs a solution.)
 II. Setting
       (Tell when and where the story takes place, either clearly stated or implied.)
III. Character
       (Tell whom or what the story is about.)
IV. Plot
       (Tell what the characters in the story do and what happens to them.)
 V. Ending
       (Use a strong ending that will bring the story to a close.)

Assignment

Copy the five Story Elements on your notebook paper in outline form. Listen for the Story Elements as your teacher reads a short story. Write down each Story Element answer to complete your outline. Discuss your completed outline with your class.

CHAPTER 7 LESSON 5

Narrative Writing

Narrative writing is simply the telling of a story. When you compose stories, you are actually writing what professional writers call narratives, or short stories. Short stories have certain characteristics that make them different from other types of writing. Five of these characteristics were discussed earlier when you learned these Story Elements: main idea, setting, characters, plot, and ending. Your narrative writing skills will be developed through the use of the story elements. A narrative also gives the details of an event or experience in the order that they happened. Narrative writing will have a beginning, a middle, and an end.

CHAPTER 7 LESSON 5

A story starter is a type of narrative writing. You are given either first lines or whole paragraphs that begin a story for you. You will use your experience and imagination to finish the story.

Writing Assignment

Choose one of the following story starters and then use the Writing Steps for Narrative Story Starters in the box below to finish writing your short story. Put your finished writing in your Rough Draft folder.

Writing Assignment #9: Narrative Writing Using a Story Starter in First Person

Story Starter 1 Carl Williams slowly backed farther into the shadows.
Story Starter 2 The sun beat down on the hikers as they slowly climbed higher.
Story Starter 3 It was a rainy, stormy night for the Annual Seventh-Grade Play.

Writing Steps for Narrative Story Starters

1. Make a Story Elements Outline after you have selected the story starter for your narrative writing assignment.
2. Check your Story Elements Outline as you write your story to make sure you keep your writing focused on the main idea and to help you choose details and events that support the main idea.
3. Think about what is already happening in the story and then use your imagination to write about what happens next.
4. Continue telling the story in the order that you want the events to happen. Remember to keep your details and events focused on the main idea of the story.
5. Look over what has happened in the story and decide on an ending that makes sense.
6. The title in a personal narrative is usually written after the story is finished. Go back and read the story that you have written and think of a title that will tell what your story is about.

Share Time

Share your Assignment #9, Narrative Writing using Story Starters, with your class.
Your teacher will tell you if you will be sharing in small groups or with the whole class. Your teacher will also tell you what to do with your audience response sheet after the stories have been read. Remember to be courteous to other students as you listen to their stories.

Share Time Guidelines	
Reader Preparation	**Audience Response**
1. Have your paper ready to read when called upon.	1. Pay attention and listen attentively.
2. Write the title of your story on the board.	2. After each reader finishes reading his/her story, the
3. Stand with your feet flat on the floor and your shoulders straight. Do not shift your weight as you stand.	audience (students) will write a brief response to the reader's story using the guidelines below.
4. Hold your paper about chin high to help you project your voice to your audience.	1. Title of the story.
5. Make sure you do not read too fast.	2. Main idea (what character had to do to solve problem)
6. Read in a clear voice that can be heard so that your audience does not have to strain to hear you.	3. Setting (time and place of story)
7. Change your voice tone for different characters or for different parts of the story.	4. Main character
	5. Favorite part of the story
	6. Liked or disliked the ending because...

CHAPTER 8 LESSON 1 SKILL TEST A

Exercise 1: Match the definitions. Write the correct letter beside each concept in the first column.

P	1. all the predicate parts	A.	inverted order
R	2. all the subject parts	B.	homonyms
M	3. adjective questions	C.	person, place, or thing
W	4. adverb questions	D.	subject noun or subject pronoun
J	5. declarative sentence	E.	verb, adjective, or another adverb
A	6. predicate words in the subject	F.	noun markers
U	7. simple predicate	G.	a, an, the
D	8. simple subject	H.	who
B	9. words pronounced the same but different in meaning	I.	subject, verb, end mark, capital letter, complete sense
Q	10. words opposite in meaning	J.	statement
Y	11. words with the same meaning	K.	period
I	12. the 5 parts of a sentence	L.	noun or a pronoun
C	13. noun	M.	what kind, which one, how many
H	14. subject noun question (person)	N.	period, statement, declarative sentence
S	15. subject noun question (animal, place, thing)	O.	strong feeling
V	16. verb	P.	complete predicate
X	17. verb question	Q.	antonyms
E	18. what the adverb modifies	R.	complete subject
L	19. what the adjective modifies	S.	what
G	20. 3 article adjectives	T.	exclamation point
F	21. article adjectives can be called	U.	verb
K	22. punctuation for declarative sentence	V.	tells what the subject does
N	23. Q & A Flow for declarative sentence	W.	how, when, where
O	24. exclamatory sentence shows	X.	what is being said about the subject
T	25. punctuation for exclamatory sentence	Y.	synonyms

Exercise 2 Write 30 prepositions in the blanks below.

1.	aboard	11.	before	21.	during
2.	about	12.	behind	22.	except
3.	above	13.	below	23.	for
4.	across	14.	beneath	24.	from
5.	after	15.	beside	25.	in
6.	against	16.	between	26.	inside
7.	along	17.	beyond	27.	into
8.	among	18.	but	28.	like
9.	around	19.	by	29.	near
10.	at	20.	down	30.	of, off

CHAPTER 8 LESSON 1

Writing Assignment

Use the guidelines, sample steps, and the outline guide for descriptive writing in Chapter 7 to do the writing assignment below. After you finish writing your pargraph, circle the capital letter at the beginning of each sentence and the end mark at the end of each sentence. Put your paragraph in your Rough Draft Folder.

Writing Assignment #10: Descriptive Paragraph in First Person

Topic: People
Logical narrowed topic: Important People
Writing topic: **An Important Person in My Life**

Editing Time

Use the *Guidelines for Editing Rough Drafts and for Writing Final Papers* and the *Editing Checklist* in Chapter 4, Lesson 5, to edit Writing Assignment #10. Staple the final paper to the rough draft and put both in the Final Writing Folder until your teacher calls for them.

CHAPTER 8 LESSON 2

You should feel comfortable using a variety of sentences in your writing. You should also be skilled in constructing long or short sentences that are simple, compound, or complex. This basic knowledge of different kinds of sentence structure is necessary for you to become a confident and effective writer.

THE SIMPLE SENTENCE

1. A complete sentence must have a subject, a verb, and state a complete thought.
2. A simple sentence is complete sentence.
3. Adjectives, adverbs, and prepositional phrases add greater meaning, more life, and more color to simple sentences, but they are not necessary for a sentence to be a complete sentence.
4. The abbreviation for a simple sentence is the letter *S*. (Example: The fresh apple tasted good for a snack. **S**)

THE SENTENCE FRAGMENT

1. A fragment is a group of words that may not have a subject.
2. A fragment is a group of words that may not have a verb.
3. A fragment is a group of words that does not complete a thought.
4. Sentence fragments should not be punctuated as complete sentences.
5. The abbreviation for a fragment is the letter *F*. (Example: For a snack in the afternoon **F**)

THE SIMPLE SENTENCE WITH COMPOUND PARTS

1. A simple sentence may have compound parts, such as a compound subject or a compound verb, even though it expresses only one complete thought.
2. The abbreviation for a simple sentence with compound parts is *SCS* (simple, compound subject) or *SCV* (simple, compound verb), etc.
   (Examples: 1. Sara's mom and dad worked in the yard. (**SCS**)   2. Sara's dad raked and burned the leaves in the yard. (**SCV**)

CHAPTER 8 LESSON 2

Guided Practice: Identify each kind of sentence by writing its abbreviations on the line (**S, F, SCS, SCV**).

1. _SCS_ Pepperoni and sausage taste great on a pizza.
2. _S_ The dog eyed the stranger suspiciously.
3. _F_ The wild mares and stallions in the canyon.
4. _SCV_ The ophthalmologist checks eyes and does surgery.

Guided Practice: Underline the missing part of the sentence in parentheses. Discuss how to add the needed parts.

1. Under the porch in the back yard   (subject part, predicate part, <u>both the subject and predicate</u>)
2. Screeched and squealed on the concrete   (<u>subject part</u>, <u>predicate part</u>, both the subject and predicate)

THE COMPOUND SENTENCE

1. A compound sentence is two complete sentences joined together correctly.

2. <u>The first way to join two sentences</u> and make a compound sentence is to use <u>a comma and a conjunction</u>. The formula for you to follow will always be given at the end of the sentence. The formula gives the abbreviation of the compound sentence and lists the conjunction to use (**CD, but**). Remember to place the comma BEFORE the conjunction.
   Example: The mosquito flew around my **head, but** I ignored it. (**CD, but**)

3. The second way to join two sentences and make a compound sentence is to use <u>a semicolon and a connective (conjunctive) adverb</u>. The formula to follow is given at the end of the sentence. The formula gives the abbreviation of the compound sentence and lists the connective adverb to use (**CD; however,**). Remember to place a semicolon BEFORE the connective adverb and a comma AFTER the connective adverb. (This method is particularly useful when you are working with longer sentences.)   **Example:** The mosquito flew around my **head; however,** I ignored it. (**CD; however,**)

4. <u>The third way to join two sentences</u> and make a compound sentence is to use <u>a semicolon only</u>. The formula to follow is given at the end of the sentence and lists the semicolon after the abbreviation of the compound sentence (**CD;**). Remember, there is no conjunction or connective adverb when the semicolon is used alone. (This method is usually used with short sentences that are closely related in thought.)   **Example:** The mosquito flew around my **head;** I ignored it. (**CD;**)

5. Compound sentences should be closely related in thought and importance.
   <u>Correct:</u>   The mosquito flew around my head, but I ignored it.
   <u>Incorrect:</u>   The mosquito flew around my head, but I failed my math test today.

WHEN A COMPOUND SENTENCE IS NOT JOINED TOGETHER CORRECTLY, YOU HAVE A COMMA SPLICE OR A RUN-ON SENTENCE.

1. **A comma splice** is two or more sentences incorrectly connected with a comma and no conjunction.
   Incorrect: The mosquito flew around my **head, I** ignored it.

2. To correct a comma splice, put a conjunction (*and, or, but*) after the comma.
   Correct: The mosquito flew around my **head, but I** ignored it.

3. **A run-on sentence** is two or more sentences written together as one sentence, or two or more sentences written with a conjunction and no comma.
   <u>Incorrect:</u> The mosquito flew around my **head I** ignored it.
   <u>Incorrect:</u> The mosquito flew around my **head but** I ignored it.

4. To correct a run-on sentence:
   1. Put a comma and a conjunction between the two complete thoughts.
   2. Put a semicolon and a connective adverb between the two complete thoughts.
   3. Put a semicolon between the two complete thoughts.
      <u>Correct:</u> The mosquito flew around my **head, but I** ignored it.
      <u>Correct:</u> The mosquito flew around my **head; however, I** ignored it.
      <u>Correct:</u> The mosquito flew around my **head; I** ignored it.

CHAPTER 8 LESSON 2

COORDINATE CONJUNCTIONS

You have already learned that conjunctions join words or groups of words together, and the three most common conjunctions are *and, or*, and *but*. Since there are different kinds of conjunctions, you will now learn the name of conjunctions that join. Conjunctions that join are called **coordinate conjunctions, or coordinating conjunctions**. Coordinate conjunctions join things of equal importance, like compound subjects, compound verbs, or compound sentences. The conjunctions *and, but, or, nor,* and *yet* are coordinate conjunctions. They join together words, phrases, or sentences that have equal importance. Sometimes, the word *so* is used as a coordinate conjunction. You will know to use *so* as a coordinate conjunction if it means as a result. Do not use *so* as a coordinate conjunction if you can substitute "so that" as you read the sentence.

Examples: We have a new **car, so** we are happy. We arrived early **so (that)** we could get a good seat.

The coordinate conjunctions and some of the connective adverbs are listed in the chart below to help make it easy for you to use them.

Coordinate Conjunction and Connective Adverb Chart				
Type of Conj / Adv	More Information	Contrast/Choice	Alternative	As a result
Coordinate Conjunction	,and ,nor	,but ,yet	,or	,so
Connective Adverbs	;moreover, ;furthermore, ;besides, ;also, ;likewise;	;however, ;nevertheless,	;otherwise,	;therefore, ;hence, ;thus, ;consequently, ;accordingly,

 Guided Practice: Put a slash to separate the two complete thoughts in each run-on sentence. Correct the run-on sentences or fragments as indicated by the labels in parentheses at the end of each sentence.

1. Katie enjoyed the movie ,but she didn't like the popcorn. (**CD, but**)
2. The young man tried not to laugh ;however, he could not conceal his glee. (**CD; however,**)
3. She swam At the lake during the afternoon. (**S**)
4. The teenager was buying new clothes and she bought new shoes ,too. (**S**)
5. Amanda is at the track meet and Amy is at the track meet. (**SCS**)
6. Jason ran in the 200-meter race and threw the discus. (**SCV**)
7. I love band , we perform at every football game. (**CD;**)

 Guided Practice: Identify each kind of sentence by writing the abbreviation in the blank (**S, F, SCS, SCV, CD**).

_CD_ 8. My brother raced toward the bus, but he missed it anyway.
_SS_ 9. I march in the band. My brother sings in the choir.
_CD_ 10. We rode a roller coaster at the fair; we did not ride the Ferris wheel.
SCS 11. Gail and Danny drove down the dirt roads.
_F_ 12. The funny little bear cubs beside their mother.
SCV 13. The cook fried eggs and bacon and toasted bread for our breakfast.

Guided Practice: Use the 2 complete thoughts in bold print below to write each kind of sentence listed below (14-19).

oraly

Dan chopped down the tree   he used it for firewood

14. SCV
15. CD; consequently,

16. CD, and
17. CD; furthermore,

18. CD;
19. CD, so

CHAPTER 8 LESSON 2 SKILL TEST B

Exercise 1: In the parentheses at the end of each sentence, underline the part you will have to add to make a complete sentence. On a sheet of notebook paper, write complete sentences by adding the parts needed.

1. under the porch in the backyard   (subject part, predicate part, <u>both the subject and predicate</u>)
2. screeched and squealed on the concrete   (subject part, predicate part, <u>both the subject and predicate</u>)
3. before the final buzzer sounded   (subject part, predicate part, <u>both the subject and predicate</u>)
4. soared high above the trees   (<u>subject part</u>, predicate part, both the subject and predicate)
5. the soft white feather from the baby owl   (subject part, <u>predicate part</u>, both the subject and predicate)

Exercise 2: Put a slash to separate each run-on sentence. Then on your <u>notebook paper</u>, correct the run-on sentences as indicated by the labels in parentheses at the end of each sentence.

6. Lindsay is going to space camp in May/her class is going, too. (**SCS**)
7. Katie enjoyed the movie/she didn't like the restaurant. (**CD, but**)
8. Payton was frightened by the zoo animals/he wanted to see them again. (**CD, yet**)
9. Dean grows vegetables in his garden/he shares them with his friends. (**CD;**)
10. I didn't need any more books/I bought one anyway. (**CD; however**)
11. Ashley's grandma hid eggs in the front yard/Ashley's grandpa hid eggs in the front yard, too. (**SCS**)
12. The blue paint spilled on the floor/the blue paint splashed on the carpet. (**SCV**)

Exercise 3: Identify each kind of sentence by writing the abbreviation in the blank. (**S, F, SCS, SCV, CD**).

SCV 13. My grandmother does cross-stitch and makes quilts as a hobby.
_CD_ 14. Karen owns a stable, and she gives riding lessons on weekends.
SCS 15. New Orleans and Miami are important coastal cities in America.
_S,S_ 16. Coffee bushes grow well in shade. Corn does not grow well in shade.
_CD_ 17. We rented two movies, but we only watched one of them.
_F_ 18. The Indians of the forests of North America.
_CD;_ 19. Ice cream is a solid; buttermilk is a liquid.
_S_ 20. Dan found fishing worms under rocks and logs.

Exercise 4: Use the 2 complete thoughts in bold print to write the kind of sentence listed below.

the pioneer men built log cabins / the pioneer women made clothing

21. (S, S) The pioneer men built log cabins. The pioneer women made

22. (CD, and) The pioneer men built log cabins, and the pioneer women made clothing.

23. (CD;) The pioneer men built log cabins; the pioneer women made clothing.

24. (SCS and CV) The pioneer men and women built log cabins and made clothing.

25. (CD; however,) The pioneer men built log cabins; however, the pioneer women made clothing.

Exercise 5: Write three compound sentences using these labels to guide you: (CD, conj) (CD; connective adverb) (CD;)

CHAPTER 8 LESSON 3 APPLICATION TEST A

Exercise 1: Classify each sentence

1. SN V P1 (During the summer) clumps (of weeds) grow (in abundance) along the river's edge. D

2. SN V P1 Jason and Justin grinned broadly and waited patiently for the final scene (of the play.) D

3. SN V P1 That amazing football player was not sent (to the sidelines) (for the entire season.) D

Directions: Complete the noun job table. Use Sentence 2.

List the Noun Used		List the Noun Job	Singular or Plural	Common or Proper
4. Jason	5. CSN		6. S	7. P
8. Justin	9. CSN		10. S	11. P
12. scene	13. OP		14. S	15. C
16. play	17. OP		18. S	19. C

Exercise 2: Identify each kind of sentence by writing the abbreviation in the blank (**S, F, SCS, SCV, CD**).

SCV 20. We ate biscuits and drank juice for our breakfast.

F   21. In the car on the way to Florida for summer vacation.

S   22. My dad jogged down the street and up the hill.

CD 23. The flashlight needed batteries, so Dad bought some at the store.

SCS 24. Monarch butterflies and honeybees search for nectar.

S, S 25. Apples are growing on the trees. Pumpkins are growing on the vine.

CD 26. We persisted in our search; our efforts were rewarded.

Exercise 3: Use the 2 complete thoughts in bold print to write each kind of sentence listed below.

Ron painted the boat / he replaced the sails

27. (SCV) Ron painted the boat and replaced the sails.

28. (CD, and) Ron painted the boat, and he replaced the sails.

29. (CD;) Ron painted the boat; he replaced the sails.

30. (CD; likewise,) Ron painted the boat; likewise, he replaced the sails.

Exercise 4:   **Editing Paragraph**

Find each error and write the correction. Replace each word underlined once with a synonym and each word underlined twice with an antonym. Use the Editing Guide to help you. **Editing Guide:** Synonyms: 1 Antonyms: 1 A/An: 1 Misspelled Words: 1 Capitals: 20 Subject-Verb Agreement: 4 Commas: 1 Underline: 1 Periods: 3 End Marks: 3

the new jersey football team rides down main street and turns south on capital avenue. mayor davis greets them with a frown and introduces them to an young reporter from the daily news. then the mayor introduces the athletic director and mr. b. j. wise the football coach of the university of new jersey wildcats.

CHAPTER 8 LESSON 3 APPLICATION TEST B

Exercise 1: Match the definitions. Write the correct letter beside each concept in the first column.

W	1. Q&A Flow for exclamatory sentence
H	2. word that starts the complete predicate
T	3. adverb that comes right before the verb
X	4. preposition
M	5. name of noun/pronoun after a preposition
O	6. the 7 subject pronouns
S	7. understood subject pronoun
Q	8. imperative sentence
R	9. punctuation for imperative sentence
N	10. Q&A Flow for imperative sentence
U	11. the 7 object pronouns
E	12. 2 noun jobs
T	13. the 7 possessive pronouns
G	14. possessive noun
D	15. punctuation mark for possessive noun
V	16. the possessive question
B	17. verbs in front of a main verb
J	18. part of speech for *NOT*
F	19. interrogative sentence
A	20. punctuation for interrogative sentence
Y	21. Q & A Flow for interrogative sentence
P	22. 3 main conjunctions
L	23. compound
C	24. interjection
K	25. part of speech for a possessive noun

A. question mark
B. helping verbs
C. one- or two-word exclamation
D. apostrophe
E. subject noun, object of the preposition
F. question sentence
G. nouns showing ownership
H. verb
I. my, our, his, her, its, their, your
J. adverb
K. adjective
L. two or more words joined by a conjunction
M. object of the preposition
N. period, command, imperative sentence
O. I, we, he, she, it, they, you,
P. and, but, or
Q. command
R. period
S. you
T. adverb exception
U. me, us, him, her, it, them, you
V. whose
W. exclamation point, strong feeling, exclamatory sentence
X. connects a noun or a pronoun to the rest of the sentence
Y. question mark, question, interrogative sentence

Exercise 2: Write the 8 forms of the verb *be* in the blanks below.

26. am	28. is	30. are	32. was
27. were	29. be	31. being	33. been

Exercise 3: Write the 15 other helping verbs in the blanks below.

34. has	39. did	44. could
35. have	40. might	45. would
36. had	41. must	46. should
37. do	42. may	47. shall
38. does	43. can	48. will

CHAPTER 8 LESSON 4

Check Time, Journal Writing Time, and Analogy Time
Journal Writing Assignment: Make an entry in your journal. (Start with your heading and date.)

Word Analogy Exercise: Choose the correct missing word and put the letter in the blank.

1. hat:head::coat: __c__   a. scarf   b. boots   c. body   d. hand
2. cat:fur:: __d__ :feather   a. black   b. skin   c. dog   d. bird
3. reading:letters::math: __d__ a. add   b. words   c. five   d. numbers

---

CHAPTER 8 LESSON 5

Personal Narrative

You learned that **Narrative** writing is simply the telling of a story. A narrative can be a story that is made up. Another type of narrative writing is a personal narrative. A **personal narrative** is written in first person and tells a story about something that has personally happened to you, the writer. Because you are the writer of the narration, you are called the narrator.

The same Story Elements that made your narrative writing so effective will now be used for the personal narrative as well. Likewise, a personal narrative gives the details of an event or experience that happened to you in the order that they happened. Your personal narrative will have a beginning, a middle, and an end.

Assignment
Copy the five Story Elements on your notebook paper in outline form. Listen for the Story Elements as your teacher reads a personal narrative. Write down each Story Element answer to complete your outline. Discuss your completed outline the your class.

Story Elements Outline

I. Main idea
   (Tell the problem or situation that needs a solution.)
II. Setting
   (Tell when and where the story takes place, either clearly stated or implied.)
III. Character
   (Tell whom or what the story is about.)
IV. Plot
   (Tell what the characters in the story do and what happens to them.)
V. Ending
   (Use a strong ending that will bring the story to a close.)

CHAPTER 8 LESSON 5

Writing Assignment

Think about something that has happened to you that you can narrate (tell the story of). Since it will be written in first person, you will be one of the characters. Will there be any more characters? What will the main idea be? What will the setting be? What will the plot be? How will your narrative end? Only you can answer these questions. Now, using the *Writing Steps for a Personal Narrative* in the box below, write your own personal narrative. Put your finished writing in your Rough Draft folder.

Writing Assignment #11: Personal Narrative in First Person

Writing Steps for a Personal Narrative

1. Make a Story Elements Outline after you have read the personal narrative writing assignment.

2. Check your Story Elements Outline as you write your story to make sure you keep your writing focused on the main idea and to help you choose details and events that support the main idea.

3. Think about what happened in the story and then tell the story in the order that the events happened. Remember to keep your details and events focused on the main idea of the story. (Write 7-10 sentences to tell the story in one paragraph.)

4. Write one or two concluding sentences that express your feelings about the event you have just narrated.

5. The title in a personal narrative is usually written after the story is finished. Go back and read the story that you have written and think of a title that will tell what your story is about.

Editing Time

Use the *Guidelines for Editing Rough Drafts and for Writing Final Papers* and the *Editing Checklist* in Chapter 4, Lesson 5, to edit Writing Assignment #11. Staple the final paper to the rough draft and put both in the Final Writing Folder until your teacher calls for them.

CHAPTER 9 LESSON 1 SKILL TEST A

Exercise 1: Write the correct answer to each definition question in the blanks below.

1. What does a noun name? _a person, place, thing, idea_

2. What question do you ask to find the subject noun if the sentence is about a person? _who_

3. What question do you ask to find the subject if the sentence is not about a person? _what_

4. What word tells what the subject does or what the subject is? _verb_

5. What question do you ask in the Q & A Flow to find the verb? _what is being said about_ _noun (subject)_

6. What does an adverb modify? _verb, adjective, adverb_

7. What are the adverb questions? _how, when, where, why, under what_ _condition, to what degree_   3 more

8. What does an adjective modify? _noun, pronoun_

9. What are the adjective questions? _What kind, which one, how many_

10. What are the three article adjectives? _a, an, the_

11. What is a declarative sentence? _statement_

12. What is an exclamatory sentence? _strong feeling_

13. What word usually starts the complete predicate? _verb_

14. What are all the parts in the subject of a sentence called? _complete subject_

15. What are all the parts in the predicate of a sentence called? _complete predicate_

16. What is an adverb exception? _an adverb before the verb that_ _modifies the verb_

17. What is a preposition? _connects a noun or a pronoun to the rest of the_ _sentence._

18. What is an object of the preposition? _name of a Noun/pronoun after a preposition_

19. Name the 7 subject pronouns. _I you he she it we they_

Writing Assignment

Use the descriptive writing steps and the descriptive outline in Chapter 7 to do the writing assignment below. After you have finished writing your paragraph, put it in your Rough Draft Folder.

Writing Assignment #12: Descriptive Paragraph in First Person
Topic: Freedom
Logical narrowed topic: What Freedom Means to Me
Writing Topic: What Freedom Means to Me
Or Choose: What Freedom Means to My Family

CHAPTER 9 LESSON 2

THE COMPLEX SENTENCE

1. A complex sentence is made by joining an independent sentence and a subordinate sentence together correctly.

2. An **independent sentence** has a subject and a verb and expresses a complete thought. It can stand alone as a simple sentence because it is independent.
   Independent sentence: We were on the lake.

3. A **subordinate sentence** has a subject and a verb, but it does not express a complete thought by itself. A subordinate sentence always begins with a joining word called a subordinate conjunction. It is the subordinate conjunction that makes a sentence dependent upon an independent sentence to complete its meaning.   **Subordinate sentence:** When the storm began.

4. To join the sentences, a formula to follow is given at the end of each sentence. The formula gives the abbreviation of the complex sentence, lists the subordinate conjunction to use, and indicates whether to put the subordinate conjunction with the first sentence by a number one or with the second sentence by a number two **(CX, when, 1)** or **(CX, when, 2)**.

5. If the subordinate sentence comes before the independent sentence, a comma is required at the end of the subordinate sentence.
   Subordinate sentence first: When the storm began, we were on the lake. (CX, when, 1)

6. If the independent sentence comes before the subordinate sentence, a comma is normally not required at the end of the independent sentence.
   Independent sentence first: We were on the lake when the storm began. (CX, when, 2)

7. Any independent sentence can be made subordinate (dependent) by simply adding a subordinate conjunction to the beginning of that sentence.
   Subordinate sentence: (**When** we were on the lake) (**If** we were on the lake) (**Before** we were on the lake)

SUBORDINATE CONJUNCTIONS

Another kind of conjunction is the subordinate conjunction. A subordinate conjunction always introduces a subordinate sentence. Since there are many subordinate conjunctions, only a few of the most common subordinate conjunctions are provided for you in the chart below.

A SUBORDINATE CONJUNCTION CHART					
after	because	except	so that	though	when
although	before	if	than	unless	where
as; as soon as	even though	since	that	until	while

Guided Practice 1 and 2:

1. Put a slash to separate each sentence. Rewrite and correct the run-on sentences as indicated by the labels in parentheses.

1. Danny fed our new puppy/she slept peacefully. (CX, when, 1)
2. Danny fed our new puppy/she slept peacefully. (CX, so that, 2)
3. Our team will not win/we do not practice every day. (CX, if, 2)
4. The ship sailed/everyone went home. (CX, after, 1)

2. Identify each kind of sentence by writing the abbreviation in the blank (**S, F, SCS, SCV, CD, CX**).

5. _CX_ The campers sang after they ate.
6. _SCS_ Cowboys and cattle traveled on this trail.
7. _CD_ The land was flat, but it had some trees.
8. _SCV_ We walked and jogged around the track.

Guided Practice 3 and 4:

3. Use the 2 complete thoughts in bold print to write each kind of sentence listed below.

   I heard a crash   I ran to the window
9. (CX, after, 1)
10. (CX, as, 2)
11. (CD, and)
12. (SCV)
13. (CD; therefore,)
14. (CX, as soon as, 1)

4. Make these fragments into complex sentences.

15. whenever our team scores 3 points
16. because the door was left open
17. at the bottom of the squeaky stairs
18. hundreds of tiny spiders

CHAPTER 9 LESSON 2 SKILL TEST B

Exercise 1: In the parentheses at the end of each sentence, underline the part you will have to add to make a complete sentence. On a sheet of notebook paper, write complete sentences by adding the parts needed.

1. because Charles locked the door   (subject part, predicate part, both the subject and predicate)
2. while Susan took a nap   (subject part, predicate part, both the subject and predicate)
3. at the computer desk in her office   (subject part, predicate part, both the subject and predicate)
4. unless our group works hard on this project (subject part, predicate part, both the subject and predicate)
5. watered the seeds and watched them grow   (subject part, predicate part, both the subject and predicate)

Exercise 2: Put a slash to separate each run-on sentence. Then on your notebook paper, correct the run-on sentences as indicated by the labels in parentheses at the end of each sentence.

6. The couple sat in the front/they could see their son. (**CX,** where, 2)
7. My car is small/we can all crowd into it. (**CX,** although, 1)
8. The math student was confused/he did not ask questions. (**CD;** however, 2)
9. The small child did not understand/he could not have more candy. (**CX,** why, 2)
10. The dance troupe danced to classical music/they sang beautiful songs. (**SCV**)
11. You are kind to others/they will think highly of you. (**CX,** if, 1)
12. The young man sold his furniture/he moved to a new state. (**SCV**)

Exercise 3: Identify each kind of sentence by writing the abbreviation in the blank (**S, F, SCS, SCV, CD, CX**).

_CX_ 13. After we swam for several hours, we were ready for a big meal.
_S_ 14. The vet gave Bingo a shot and some antibiotic pills.
_CD_ 15. Pamela took notes on her topic, and she wrote her essay last night.
_CX_ 16. Where my group sits in the library, I must sit.
_F_ 17. Though you are captain of the team.
SCV 18. The dictionary gives definitions and offers pronunciations of words.
_CX_ 19. Brown bats were living in the cave that we explored.
_CX_ 20. Even though I try to avoid illness, the flu bug always finds me.

Exercise 4: Use the 2 complete thoughts in bold print to write each kind of sentence listed below.

the buzzer sounds / the game is over

21. (CX, if, 1) _If the buzzer sounds, the game is over._

22. (CX, when, 2) _The buzzer sounds when the game is over._

23. (CD, and) _The buzzer sounds, and the game is over._

24. (CX, as soon as, 1) _As soon as the buzzer sounds, the game is over._

25. (S, S) _The buzzer sounds. The game is over._

Exercise 5: Write two complex sentences.

When I ride my horse, she is happy.
When Wrem was born, I want to see her.

CHAPTER 9 LESSON 3 APPLICATION TEST A

Exercise 1: Classify each sentence.

1. _SN V P1_ Yesterday the hungry wolves / were howling (outside the horses' corral) (by our house.)

2. _SN V P1_ Do comets / travel (around the sun) (in egg-shaped paths?) Int.

3. _SN V P1_ My brother and his friends / are flying (to Louisiana) tomorrow (for the soccer tournament.)

Directions: Complete the noun job table. Use Sentence 1.

List the Noun Used	List the Noun Job	Singular or Plural	Common or Proper
4. wolves	5. SN	6. P	7. C
8. horses'	9. PNA	10. P	11. C
12. corral	13. OP	14. S	15. C
16. house	17. OP	18. S	19. C

Exercise 2: Identify each kind of sentence by writing the abbreviation in the blank (**S, F, SCS, SCV, CD, CX**).

_CX_ 20. The mischievous toddler giggled whenever he saw his mother.

_CX_ 21. Because the morning fog was thick, we drove to Grandpa's in the afternoon.

_S_ 22. Mom bought a quilt and some jelly at the fair.

_CD_ 23. The men worked hard for their boss; therefore, they received an extra bonus.

_F_ 24. Unless we buy our fireworks today.

_CX_ 25. We think of the South when we think of cotton.

_F_ 26. Since you spent an hour in the library.

Exercise 3: Use the 2 complete thoughts in bold print to write each kind of sentence listed below.

Tom is a skilled mechanic / he has opened his own repair shop

27. (CX, because, 1) Because Tom is a skilled mechanic, he has opened his own repa

28. (CD, and) Tom is a skilled mechanic, and he has opened his own repair sho

29. (SCV) Tom is a skilled mechanic and has opened his own repair shop.

Exercise 4:   **Editing Paragraph**
Find each error and write the correction. Use the Editing Guide to help you. **Editing Guide: Homonyms:1 A/An: 1 Misspelled Words: 4 Capitals: 19 Subject-Verb Agreement: 4 Commas: 7 Periods: 4 End Marks: 3**

dr, j, d, park, an former investigater for the department of justice, now teach sience, world

history I, and spanish at liberty high school in brooklyn, new york, since dr, park have degrees in

several study areas, he is qualifed too do many diferent jobs, however, he likes teaching best

because he loves helping kids learn,

CHAPTER 9 LESSON 3 APPLICATION TEST B

Exercise 1: Write the correct answer to each definition question in the blanks below.

1. Name two noun jobs. _Subject and object of the preposition_

2. Name the understood subject pronoun. _you_

3. What is an imperative sentence? _a command_

4. What is the punctuation mark used at the end of an imperative sentence? _(.!)_

5. Name the 7 object pronouns. _me, us, him, her, it, them, you_

6. Name the 7 possessive pronouns. _my, our, his, her, its, their, your_

7. What does a possessive noun show? _ownership_

8. What one punctuation mark does a possessive noun always have? _an apostrophe_

9. What 2 jobs does a possessive noun have? _noun, adj._

10. What question do you ask to find possessive words? _whose_

11. Where are helping verbs found? _before the verb_

12. Name the 8 forms of the be verb. _am, is, are, was, were, be, being, been_

13. What part of speech is the word NOT? _an adverb_

14. What is an interrogative sentence? _a question_

15. What is the punctuation mark used at the end of an interrogative sentence? _question mark_

16. Name the three main conjunctions. _and, but, or_

17. What are 2 subjects or 2 verbs called? _compound_

18. What is a 1- or 2-word exclamation called? _interjection_

19. What is a natural sentence order? _SN V_

20. What is an inverted order? _part of the predicate comes before the subject_

21. Show 3 ways to join a CD sentence. _; however, ; but ;_

22. Name the 2 sentences found in a CX sentence. _subordinate, independent_

23. What are the names of the two kinds of sentences that are joined by coordinate conjunctions and subordinate conjunctions? _CD, CX_

CHAPTER 9 LESSON 4

Check Time, Journal Writing Time, and Analogy Time
Journal Writing Assignment: Make an entry in your journal. (Start with your heading and date.)

Word Analogy Exercise: Choose the correct missing word and put the letter in the blank.

1. narrative:story::contemplate: ___a___   a. ~~think~~   b. swim   c. sleep   d. library
2. dog:poodle:: ___c___ :daisy   a. name   b. rose   ~~c. flower~~ d. kennel
3. elephant:mouse::large: ___d___   a. trunk   b. cheese   c. rat   ~~d. small~~

CHAPTER 9 LESSON 5

Personification in Narrative Writing

Personification is what we call a figure of speech in which a writer gives human features to something that is not human. You have probably noticed statements such as "The sun smiled down on us as we prepared for the picnic." Notice how the writer has given the sun the ability to "smile." Obviously, the sun does not actually "smile," but when a writer gives the sun a human feature or characteristic, he is using what we call *personification*. The very spelling of the word *personification* indicates that we are "PERSON-izing" something that is a thing, not a person.

Personification is often used in narrative writing. It is part of what we call "figurative language," or language that is not taken literally. In other words, in the example above, we realize that the sun does not actually "smile," but when we read that the sun "smiled" down on us, we get the feeling that it was a great day for a picnic and that a pleasant and happy feeling surrounded the picnic. In this case the non-human thing that is personified plays only a small role in the story. In some stories, however, a non-human thing can be a main character.

For your narrative writing assignment, you will be using personification. In your writing you will assume the role (take the part) of some non-human thing and write as if that thing is speaking. (In addition to talking, you may want your non-human character to perform other human-like actions, such as running, crying, sleeping, etc.) Use this sample story with personification to guide you.

Example: Excuse me, did you stub your toe on me? Stop yelling like that! Down here, down here! Yes, I'm a rock; what did you expect? Ouch! Hurts, doesn't it? Kicking me deliberately wasn't very smart. I sometimes wonder about you humans.

Story Elements Outline
I. Main Idea
II. Setting
III. Character
IV. Plot
V. Ending

CHAPTER 9 LESSON 5

Writing Assignment

Choose one of the following situations and then use the writing steps for personification below to write your short story. Put your finished writing in your Rough Draft Folder.

Writing Assignment #13: Narrative Writing with Personification in First Person

Situation 1: You are the magic lamp of Aladdin. Discuss how you feel about everything that has happened to you.

Situation 2: You are a long, red worm. You keep being attacked by a large robin. Discuss your terrible predicament and your plans.

Situation 3: You are a football (basketball, dancing shoes, musical instrument, etc.) at a junior high school practice. Your coach (teacher) and everyone on the team have worked hard, but the upcoming competition is tough. Discuss what you see and hear and how you feel at the last practice before the big event.

Writing Steps for Using Personification

1. Make a Story Elements Outline after you have read and selected the personification situation for your narrative writing assignment. (See the previous page for a Story Element Outline.)
2. Check your Story Elements Outline as you write the story to make sure you keep your writing focused on the main idea.
3. Assume the role of the non-human character in your selection.
4. Begin to write as if the non-human character is talking.
5. Your non-human character can be talking to someone else or just to himself or herself.
6. Have your non-human character discuss whatever the personification selection calls for.
7. Continue telling the story in the order that you want the events to happen.
8. Look over what has happened in the story and decide on an ending that makes sense.
9. The title in a narrative is usually written after the story is finished. Go back and read the story that you have written and think of a title that will tell what your story is about.

Share Time

Share your Assignment #13, Narrative Writing using Personification, with the class.
Your teacher will tell you if you will be sharing in small groups or with the whole class. Your teacher will also tell you what to do with your audience response sheet after the stories have been read. Remember to be courteous to other students as you listen to their stories.

Share Time Guidelines	
Reader Preparation	**Audience Response**
1. Have your paper ready to read when called upon.	1. Pay attention and listen attentively.
2. Write the title of your story on the board.	2. After each reader finishes reading his/her story, the audience (students) will write a brief response to the reader's story using the guidelines below.
3. Stand with your feet flat on the floor and your shoulders straight. Do not shift your weight as you stand.	1. Title of the story.
4. Hold your paper about chin high to help you project your voice to your audience.	2. Main idea (what character had to do to solve problem)
5. Make sure you do not read too fast.	3. Setting (time and place of story)
6. Read in a clear voice that can be heard so that your audience does not have to strain to hear you.	4. Main character
7. Change your voice tone for different characters or for different parts of the story.	5. Favorite part of the story
	6. Liked or disliked the ending because...

CHAPTER 10 LESSON 1

Introducing Sentence Pattern 2 and Reviewing Sentence Pattern 1

Earlier you learned that nouns can have different jobs, or functions, in a sentence. You have studied two of these jobs already: A noun can be a subject or an object of a preposition. You must remember, however, that a noun used as a subject is a basic part of a sentence pattern (like **SN V**). But a noun that is used as an object of a preposition is not a basic part of a sentence pattern.

You will now study how nouns function in different sentence patterns. The first pattern, **Pattern 1**, has a ***Noun Verb*** for the basic sentence pattern and is written **N V**. However, notice that when you write Pattern 1 in the Shurley Method, you write **SN V** because you name the job of each basic part as well, which is *Subject Noun / Verb*. You will also add the pattern number to each pattern to make it easier to identify. Therefore, the **first pattern** in the Shurley Method is *subject noun / verb / Pattern 1*, and it is written as **SN V P1**.

In the new sentence pattern, **Pattern 2**, there are two nouns in the basic sentence pattern: **N V N.** The first noun is a subject noun and is still written as **SN**. The second noun will always come after the verb (as its position in the pattern indicates) and is required to complete the meaning of the sentence. This second noun is called a direct object and is written with the abbreviation **DO**. Any time there is a direct object in a sentence pattern, the verb is transitive and is written as **V-t** to indicate that it is used with a direct object noun. The **second pattern** in the Shurley Method is *subject noun / verb-transitive / direct object / Pattern 2,* and it is written as **SN V-t DO P2.**

Direct Object and Verb-transitive

1. A **direct object** is a noun or pronoun after the verb that completes the meaning of the sentence.

2. A **direct object** is labeled as **DO**.

3. To find the **direct object**, ask WHAT or WHOM after the verb.

4. A **direct object** must be verified to mean someone or something different from the subject noun.

5. A **verb-transitive** is an action verb with a direct object after it and is labeled V-t. (Whatever receives the action of a transitive verb is the direct object.)

Sample Sentence for the exact words to say to find the direct object and verb-transitive.

1. Dad builds a house.
2. Who builds a house? Dad - SN
3. What is being said about Dad? Dad builds - V
4. Dad builds what? house - verify the noun
5. Does house mean the same thing as Dad? No.
6. House - DO *(Say: House - direct object.)*
7. Builds - V-t *(Say: Builds - verb-transitive.)*
8. A - A
9. SN V-t DO P2 Check
   (Say: Subject Noun, Verb-transitive, Direct Object, Pattern 2, Check.)

10. Check the verb: verb-transitive.
11. Check again for prepositional phrases.
12. No prepositional phrases.
13. Period, statement, declarative sentence
14. Go back to the verb - divide the complete subject from the complete predicate.
15. Is there an adverb exception? No.
16. Is this sentence in a natural or inverted order? Natural - no change.

The Question and Answer Flow for Sentence 5 on page 83 has also been provided as an example for you.

CHAPTER 10 LESSON 1

Question and Answer Flow Example

Question and Answer Flow for Sentence 5: California's valleys always require irrigation for their crops.

1. What require irrigation for their crops? valleys - SN
2. What is being said about valleys? valleys require - V
3. Valleys require what? irrigation - verify the noun
4. Does irrigation mean the same thing as valleys? No.
5. Irrigation - DO
6. Require - V-t
7. Require how (to what extent)? always - Adv
8. For - P
9. For what? crops - OP
10. Whose crops? their - PPA
11. Whose valley? California's - PNA
12. SN V-t DO P2 Check
13. Check the verb: verb-transitive.
14. Check again for prepositional phrases.
15. (For their crops) - Prepositional phrase
16. Period, statement, Declarative sentence
17. Go back to the verb - divide the complete subject from the complete predicate.
18. Is there an adverb exception? Yes - Change the line.
19. Is this sentence in a natural or inverted order? Natural - no change

Classified Sentence:

	PNA	SN	Adv	V-t	DO	P	PPA	OP

SN V-t
DO P2   California's valleys / always require irrigation (for their crops). **D**

Assignment

1. Write one **Practice Sentence** following these labels:
   A Adj Adj CSN C CSN V-t A DO P PPA OP

2. Write an **Improved Sentence** from the practice sentence. Make at least two synonym changes, one antonym change, and your choice of complete word changes.

CHAPTER 10 LESSON 2

Improving Short, Choppy Sentences

Well-written simple sentences are easy to understand because they contain one main thought and are clear and direct. Sometimes, however, simple sentences cannot adequately express an idea. Using too many short, choppy sentences can make your writing boring and difficult to read. Read the paragraph below. The writer of this paragraph has used several sentences that are too short. The result is that the paragraph sounds choppy, and the sentences do not flow together.

Sample Paragraph with Short, Choppy Sentences

I had worked for hours decorating the gym with balloons. My friends had worked for hours decorating the gym with balloons. Our brothers broke all the red balloons. We were angry with the boys. We were upset with the boys. The boys apologized. We turned our backs. We walked away. Finally, the boys redecorated the gym with balloons. We were happy once again.

To correct short, choppy sentences, you must learn how to combine the related information, or ideas, to form longer sentences. Combining sentences involves putting two or more sentences together as a single sentence. Being able to choose different kinds of sentences and patterns helps you to express ideas as clearly as possible and to achieve variety in your paragraph.

At first, you will be given a Sentence Guide for every two sentences to help you learn different ways to combine sentences. A Sentence Guide gives you the sentence abbreviations that you are to follow as you combine short, choppy sentences in a paragraph.

CHAPTER 10 LESSON 2

Discuss the guidelines for combining sentences below. Then, study how the sample paragraph was improved by using the different kinds of sentences suggested by the Sentence Guide. Finally, work through the guided practice exercises for improving paragraphs with short, choppy sentences.

Guidelines for Combining Sentences

1. Combine short, related sentences by using compound subjects.
   Example: María shopped at the market. Larry shopped at the market.
   María and Larry shopped at the market.

2. Combine short, related sentences by using compound verbs.
   Example: Tim copied his paragraph again. Tim corrected his paragraph.
   Tim copied and corrected his paragraph again.

3. Combine short, related sentences by making them into compound sentences.
   Example: The weary travelers rested in the airport terminal. The weary travelers could not sleep.
   The weary travelers rested in the airport terminal, but they could not sleep.

4. Combine short, related sentences by making them into complex sentences.
   Example: The audience applauded. The concert pianist returned to the stage.
   The audience applauded until the concert pianist returned to the stage.

5. You may combine ideas from different sentences into a sentence with compound parts, a compound sentence, or a complex sentence. Be sure you use a connecting word that will make sense when you combine the sentences.
   Example: The children listened carefully. The parents listened carefully. They wanted to find the treasure.
   The children and their parents listened carefully. They wanted to find the treasure.
   The children and their parents listened carefully because they wanted find the treasure.
   The children and their parents listened carefully; they wanted to find the treasure.

Sample Paragraph Improved By Combining Sentences
Study the improved paragraph below. Notice how the sentences have been combined using the guidelines above and this Sentence Guide for every two sentences: (CX, CS-1, After-1), (S, CV), (CX, even though-1, CV-2), (CD, and).   After my friends and I had worked for hours decorating the gym with balloons, our brothers broke all the red balloons. We were angry and upset with the boys. Even though the boys apologized, we turned our backs and walked away. Finally, the boys redecorated the gym with balloons, and we were happy once again.

Guided Practice: Rewrite the two paragraphs below. Correct fragments and improve the short, choppy sentences by using a combination of simple, compound, and complex sentences. Underline <u>simple</u> sentences once, <u>compound</u> sentences twice, and put parentheses around the (complex) sentences. **I. Sentence Guide** for every two sentences: (SCS) (CD, and) (CD, but) (CX, because, 1) **II. Sentence Guide** for every two sentences: (SCS) (CX because, 2)

I.   Forty cows graze on new grass in our pasture. Their calves graze on new grass in our pasture. The front fence keeps the cows off the road. The side fence keeps the cows out of our neighbor's pasture. Dad enjoys taking care of the cows. Mom doesn't enjoy it. Mom is tired of chasing cows that get out of the fences. She frowns every time Dad mentions buying another cow.

II.   Jack went to his room to study. Sara went to her room to study. They closed their doors. They wanted to have some private study time.

Student Book

CHAPTER 10 LESSON 2 SKILL TEST A

Exercise 1: In the parentheses at the end of each sentence, underline the part you will have to add to make a complete sentence. On a sheet of notebook paper, write complete sentences by adding the parts needed.

1. howled and bayed at the moon (<u>subject part</u>, predicate part, both the subject and predicate)
2. the sparkling chandelier with hundreds of crystals (subject part, <u>predicate part</u>, both the subject and predicate)
3. under the hammock next to the maple tree (subject part, predicate part, <u>both the subject and predicate</u>)
4. children of all races and nationalities (subject part, <u>predicate part</u>, both the subject and predicate)

Exercise 2: Put a slash to separate each run-on sentence. Then on the lines provided, correct the run-on sentences as indicated by the labels in parentheses at the end of each sentence.

5. Paratroopers landed on the grass the audience clapped. (**CX, when, 1**)

When paratroopers landed on the grass, the audience clapped.

6. Jeanne drives carefully down the mountain Joseph drives down the mountain. (**SCS**)

Jeanne and Joseph drive carefully down the mountain

7. Laura likes to cook supper she dislikes washing the dishes. (**CD, but**)

Laura likes to cook supper, but she dislikes washing the dishes

8. Dale crawled under the ledge Dale crawled across the fallen tree. (**SCPrep**)

Dale crawled under the ledge and across the fallen tree,

9. We sold 500 pounds of shrimp we did not make enough money. (**CX, although, 1**)

Although we sold 500 pounds of shrimp, we did not make enough money.

10. Huge mosquitoes buzzed in our ears they bit our bare legs. (**SCV**)

Huge mosquitos buzzed in our ears and bit our bare legs.

Exercise 3: Identify the kind of sentence by writing the abbreviations in the blank (**S, F, SCS, SCV, CD, CX**).

_CD_ 11. Scott paints landscapes in art class, but Martin sculpts with clay.
SCV 12. Kirk races motorcycles and flies model airplanes.
_CX_ 13. Randy studied for his exam until Vanessa called him for dinner.
_CD_ 14. Jennifer is having fun at band camp; however, she misses her friends.
_F_ 15. The charming yellow cottage by the sea in the summertime.

Exercise 4: Use the 2 complete thoughts in bold print to write each kind of sentence listed below.

the female rabbit lines her burrow with fur / she keeps her babies warm

16. (CD, and) _The female rabbit lines her burrow with fur, and she keeps her babies warm_

17. (SCV) _The female rabbit lines her burrow with fur and keeps her babies warm_

18. (CD;) _The female rabbit lines her burrow with fur; she keeps her babies warm._

19. (CX, because, 1) _because the female rabbit lines her burrow with fur, she keeps her babies warm,_

CHAPTER 10   LESSON 2   SKILL TEST B

Exercise 1: Rewrite this paragraph. Correct fragments and improve the short, choppy sentences by using a combination of simple, compound, and complex sentences. Underline simple sentences once, compound sentences twice, and put parentheses around the complex sentences. **Sentence Guide for every two sentences: (S CV) (CX, because, 1) (SCS - CD, but) (CX, because, 2)**

Amanda fell out of bed. Amanda broke her arm. Amanda has a cast on her right arm. Amanda doesn't have to do her homework. Amanda's brother is jealous. Amanda's sister is jealous. Amanda's brother and sister would not want to break their arms to get out of homework. Amanda cannot wait to get her cast off. Never minded homework, anyway.

Amanda fell out of bed and broke her arm. (Because Amanda has a cast on her right arm, she doesn't have to do her homework.) Amanda's brother and sister are jealous, but they would not want to break their arms to get out of homework. Amanda cannot wait to get her cast off because she had never minded homework, anyway

Exercise 2: Rewrite this paragraph. Correct fragments and improve the short, choppy sentences by using a combination of simple, compound, and complex sentences. Underline simple sentences once, compound sentences twice, and put parentheses around the complex sentences. **Sentence Guide for every two sentences: (SCS) *(SCOP) (CD, but) (CX, since, 1) (CX, when, 2)** (*SCOP means simple sentence with a compound object of the preposition.)

The tired donkeys plodded along the dusty trail. The hot, sweaty horses plodded along, too. In the heat the exhausted travelers looked for shade trees. The travelers looked for a cool stream. Their eyes searched the desert horizon desperately for shelter from the scorching heat. There was no relief in sight. Nature's lessons were harsh. Second chances were rare. However, the travelers got lucky. Found water and survived.

The tired donkeys and the hot, sweaty horses plodded along the dusty trail. In the heat the exhausted travelers looked for shade trees and a cool stream. Their eyes searched the desert horizon desperately for shelter from the scorching heat, but there was no relief in sight. Since nature's lessons were harsh, second chances were rare. However, the travelers got lucky when they found water and survived.

Exercise 3: On notebook paper, write a paragraph using *dancing* as your topic. Use a combination of simple, compound, and complex sentences throughout the paragraph. Underline simple sentences once, compound sentences twice, and put parentheses around the complex sentences.

CHAPTER 10 LESSON 3 APPLICATION TEST

Exercise 1: Classify each sentence.

1. <u>SN V+ DO</u> Tommy could not finish the crossword puzzle by himself. D

2. <u>SN V+ PO</u> A large wolf can break a sheep's neck with one savage snap! E

3. <u>SN V+DO</u> For breakfast I like ham and eggs with a piece of toast. D

Directions: Complete the noun job table. Use Sentence 2.

List the Noun Used	List the Noun Job	Singular or Plural	Common or Proper
4. wolf	5. SN	6. S	7. C
8. sheep's	9. PNA	10. S	11. C
12. neck	13. DO	14. S	15. C
16. snap	17. OP	18. S	19. C

Exercise 2: Identify the kind of sentence by writing the abbreviations in the blank (**S, F, SCS, SCV, CD, CX**).

F   20. At the beginning of my history class.

CD   21. Our science class gathered plants from the forest; we made terrariums at school.

SCV   22. Jay writes instructions and designs pictures for manuals.

S   23. Joyce planted seeds in her vegetable garden and in her flower garden.

CX   24. Although the worried lady searched frantically for her jewelry, she did not find it.

CX   25. I baked chocolate brownies while Dad washed the car.

Exercise 3: On your notebook paper, rewrite this paragraph. Correct fragments and improve the short, choppy sentences by using a combination of simple, compound, and complex sentences. Underline simple sentences once, compound sentences twice, and put parentheses around the complex sentences.

     Scotty ate two donuts for his breakfast. Levi ate six donuts for his breakfast. Scotty enjoyed his donuts. Levi got a stomach ache. Levi moaned all morning at school. Levi groaned all morning, too. Finally, Levi's teacher had Scotty take Levi to the nurse's office. Scotty told the nurse about the donuts. She understood why Levi had a stomach ache. Promised the nurse that he would never eat so many donuts again. Levi promised Scotty the same thing. Left the office. Unhappy but wiser.

Exercise 4:   **Editing Paragraph**

Find each error and write the correction. Replace each word underlined once with a synonym. Use the Editing Guide to help you. **Editing Guide: Homonyms:5 Synonyms: 3 A/An: 1 Misspelled Words: 3 Capitals: 22 Subject-Verb Agreement: 2 Commas: 5 Apostrophes: 2 Periods: 3 End Marks: 6**

mr. p. t. armstrong, my uncle on my mother's side of the family, was a expert on king arthur. i had herd storys all my life about king arthur. my sisters and i had memorised how each story started, and we actualy learned a lot of history by listening to my uncles stories. king arthur was the strong and noble leader of the knights at camelot, england. these english knights road too the rescue of those in need. king arthur and his nights was called the knights of the round table, and they was known for there courage and goodness.

CHAPTER 10 LESSON 4

Check Time, Journal Writing Time, and Analogy Time
Journal Writing Assignment: Make an entry in your journal. (Start with your heading and date.)

Word Analogy Exercise: Choose the correct missing word and put the letter in the blank.

1. terrarium:plant:: _d_ :fish
2. fiction:tall tale::non-fiction: _B?_
3. grass:green::snow: _C_

	a. squid	b. water	c. rock	d. aquarium
a. myth	b. biography	c. book	d. films
a. black	b. blue	c. white	d. cold

CHAPTER 10 LESSON 5

Narrative Writing - Tall Tales

A **tall tale** is a story that "stretches" people, places, or events into unbelievable proportions. Pecos Bill's roping a tornado is an example of a tall tale. The story of Paul Bunyan, the giant lumberjack, and his blue ox, Babe, is also a tall tale.

A tall tale may take different forms, but every tall tale is a "far-fetched" story that is hard to believe. It usually takes something believable, such as a man fishing and "stretches" the story into an unbelievable tale. Although you know the story is "stretched," you still find it fun to read or hear the tall tale told. Use this sample tall tale to guide you.

THE BIG ONE

Once my friend Garland Kennedy and I were fishing down on the Blue Pie River. It was a pretty slow day for catching fish, and both of us had almost fallen asleep in Garland's little old fishing boat.

All of a sudden something struck my line, pulling the cork completely under. Garland and I woke up fast, and I got a firm grip on my pole. It had to be the biggest fish I had ever hooked!

Suddenly it surfaced, and, to my surprise, it wasn't a fish at all! It was a big, ugly old grandaddy alligator, and he was really angry! Neither I nor the alligator was willing to turn loose, so the battle began.

We each tugged and tugged on our end of the line. Then, that gator began swimming, the fastest I've ever seen a gator swim. And he began pulling our boat with me hanging onto my pole and with Garland laughing like something crazy.

That gator pulled us all the way to Frisbee, ten miles up river, AGAINST the current. And when we got there, he just walked out on the dry land and kept on pulling the boat. He pulled us a good fifty feet uphill to the top of the riverbank, and then he just spit out my bait, turned, gave us a long stare, and crawled down the riverbank into the river.

CHAPTER 10 LESSON 5

Writing Assignment

Choose one of the following situations and then use the writing steps for a tall tale below to write your tall tale. (Put your finished writing in your Rough Draft Folder.)

Writing Assignment #14: Narrative Writing - Tall Tale in Third Person

Situation 1: A field of corn, some extremely hungry crows, a farmer
(How hungry were the crows?)

Situation 2: An alarm clock, Jill (a sound sleeper), Jill's neighborhood friends
(What did Jill's neighbors do to wake her?)

Situation 3: A pet snake, a boy named Pete, assorted objects the snake could (or could not) swallow
(How much can Pete's snake swallow?)

Situation 4: Angie, some bubble gum, a bubble gum contest, a big wind
(Just how big was Angie's bubble?)

Writing Steps for a Tall Tale Narrative

1. Make a Story Elements Outline after you have read and selected the tall tale situation for your narrative writing assignment. (Story Elements: Main idea, Setting, Character, Plot, Ending)
2. Check your Story Elements Outline as you write the story to make sure you keep your writing focused on the main idea.
3. Write a tall tale using the situation you have chosen for your story.
4. "Stretch" the story to make it unbelievable in some way.
5. Have fun with your tall tale so your reader will enjoy it, too.
6. Continue telling the story in the order that you want the events to happen.
7. Look over what has happened in the story and decide on an ending that makes sense.
8. The title in a narrative is usually written after the story is finished. Go back and read the story that you have written and think of a title that will tell what your story is about.

Share Time

Share your Assignment #14 - Narrative Writing - Tall Tale with your class.
Your teacher will tell you if you will be sharing in small groups or with the whole class. Your teacher will also tell you what to do with your audience response sheet after the stories have been read. Remember to be courteous to other students as you listen to their stories.

Share Time Guidelines	
Reader Preparation	**Audience Response**

1. Have your paper ready to read when called upon.
2. Write the title of your story on the board.
3. Stand with your feet flat on the floor and your shoulders straight. Do not shift your weight as you stand.
4. Hold your paper about chin high to help you project your voice to your audience.
5. Make sure you do not read too fast.
6. Read in a clear voice that can be heard so that your audience does not have to strain to hear you.
7. Change your voice tone for different characters or for different parts of the story.
	1. Pay attention and listen attentively.
	2. After each reader finishes reading his/her story, the audience (students) will write a brief response to the reader's story using the guidelines below.
	  1. Title of the story
	  2. Main idea
	    (what character had to do to solve problem)
	  3. Setting (time and place of story)
	  4. Main character
	  5. Favorite part of the story
	  6. Liked or disliked the ending because...

CHAPTER 11 LESSON 1

Recognizing Fact and Opinion

A **fact** is a specific statement which can be looked up, measured, counted, or otherwise proven to be true.   Example: Abraham Lincoln was the sixteenth president of the United States.

An **opinion** is a belief, estimate, judgment, or feeling held by one or more people which cannot be checked or proven to be true.   Example: Abraham Lincoln was probably the best president America has ever had.

There are certain *judgment words* that will help you recognize when a statement is an opinion. These words signal that a writer is expressing an opinion: *hope, seem, best, better, worse, worst, probably, excellent, terrible, should, love, hate, think, believe, feel, etc.*

Guided Practice: Below is a list of statements. In the blank, write *F* if the statement is a fact. Write *O* if the statement is an opinion.

_F_ 1. Our football team has won 10 games this season.

_O_ 2. Everyone should stand while the national anthem is sung.

_F_ 3. My dad paid $16,450 for our new car.

_F_ 4. My dad got the best price for our new car.

Recognizing Propaganda

Propaganda is an organized effort to spread ideas or information that will change the opinions and actions of a group of people. Propaganda usually contains some accurate facts along with exaggerations and untruths. You need to recognize propaganda techniques so that you will not be misled by them.

Common Propaganda Techniques

1. **Loaded Words**: Loaded words are words that appeal to your emotions. Loaded words can give pleasant or unpleasant feelings, like *new, best, exciting, tired, dull, boring, etc.*
    Example: Do the patriotic thing – Vote for Act 99!

2. **Famous People**: This technique uses a famous person to recommend that you do, buy, or believe something.
    Example: Improve your game! Wear the shoes that Michael Morgan wears!

3. **Everybody Does It**: This technique is to make you feel left out if you don't join the crowd.
    Example: Wake up to America's favorite coffee.

4. **Mudslinging**: This technique tells you why competitors are "no good," but does not give facts to support these claims.
    Example: Other oat cereals get soggy before you're done. Try great-tasting Crunchy-O's.

5. **Fact/Opinion**: A fact is followed by a reasonable opinion that appears to be true.
    Example: We've been in business 75 years. That makes us the best!

Guided Practice: In the blank, identify the propaganda technique used in each message by giving the number of the technique listed above.

_1,3,5_ 1. Thousands of concerned citizens have signed our petition. Shouldn't you give your support?

_2_ 2. Play the trumpet Louis Armelia played. Choose Bach!

CHAPTER 11 LESSON 1 SKILL TEST A

Exercise 1: In the blank beside each statement below, write *F* if the statement is a fact or *O* if the statement is an opinion.

_____F_____ 1. Fire needs air in order to burn.

_____O_____ 2. The food in the cafeteria is terrible.

_____O_____ 3. Sally will make a good class president.

_____F_____ 4. Casey scored two touchdowns in the game Friday night.

_____F_____ 5. I go to Washington Junior High School.

_____F_____ 6. George Washington was the first president of the United States.

_____F_____ 7. Kittens are cuter than puppies.

_____O_____ 8. Everyone loves puppies because they're adorable.

_____F_____ 9. We bought new shop equipment yesterday.

_____O_____ 10. This is an excellent school.

_____F_____ 11. The Liberty Bell is in Philadelphia, Pennsylvania.

_____O_____ 12. Nature's Best cereal is the healthiest new cereal on the market today.

_____O_____ 13. Most people hate spinach.

_____O_____ 14. This steak house serves the best food in the state.

_____O_____ 15. Everyone loves to travel.

Exercise 2: In the blanks below, write the number(s) of the propaganda technique(s) used in each message.
(1- Loaded Words,   2- Famous People,   3- Everybody Does It,   4- Mudslinging,   5- Fact/Opinion)

_4,1_____ 1. Are you tired of batteries that don't last? Buy Long Life Batteries the next time you buy.

_5,1_____ 2. Arkansas leads the nation in growing rice. Arkansas rice tastes the best!

_____ 3. A vote for Alice Duncan is a vote for education!

_3,1,5_____ 4. Hundreds of farmers in Michigan rely on *Agriculture Today* to keep them informed about current agricultural issues. Do the smart thing. Subscribe to this informative magazine today!

_3,1,5_____ 5. Six thousand people attended the fund raiser. It was a huge success!

_1,5_____ 6. Public education, health care, taxes, the environment. Governor Johnson cares about the things that are important to you.

_2,5,1_____ 7. Actress Diana Doll uses Silky Smooth Shampoo to keep her hair shiny and beautiful. Don't you want beautiful, healthy hair like Diana Doll?

CHAPTER 11 LESSON 2

Improving Long, Rambling Sentences

Sometimes you may try to avoid writing short, choppy sentences by overusing the conjunctions *and, but,* and *so* to connect many simple sentences together. The result is long, rambling sentences that confuse your reader and make your writing difficult to read. These are also called **run-on** sentences because no end punctuation is used at the end of each sentence. Such rambling sentences are just as irritating and monotonous to read as short, choppy sentences.

Read the paragraph below. The writer of this paragraph has used long, rambling sentences. The result is that the paragraph sounds confusing because the ideas all run together.

Sample Paragraph with Long, Rambling Sentences
Larry liked to play basketball and he would play basketball everyday in the park next to his house but he did not have a team and not having a team really bothered him so he asked all his friends to join him and form a team and then they could all play other teams and maybe they could even get uniforms so that they could play in the city tournament and get recognized as the best team around.

Rambling sentences always interfere with **clarity**, which is the clear expression of ideas. Clarity is a general quality for which all good writers constantly strive. Effective writing is clear, readable, and understandable. The ideas in your writing should be presented clearly so that they can be followed easily. These ideas should be connected and should follow logically from one to another. Follow the directions below to correct paragraphs with long, rambling sentences.

Direction Box for Correcting Paragraphs with Long, Rambling Sentences
1. Identify each thought by putting a slash between each one.
2. Rewrite the paragraph, using the *Guidelines for Combining Sentences* in Chapter 10 to combine related thoughts to make compound, complex, or simple sentences with compound parts. Avoid overusing the conjunctions *and, but,* and *so.*
3. Underline simple sentences once, compound sentences twice, and put parentheses around complex sentences.

Sample Paragraph Improved by Correcting Long, Rambling Sentences

Larry liked to play basketball / and he would play basketball everyday in the park next to his house / but he did not have a team / and not having a team really bothered him / so he asked all his friends to join him and form a team / and then they could all play other teams / and maybe they could even get uniforms / so that they could play in the city tournament and get recognized as the best team around.

Larry liked to play basketball. He would play basketball everyday in the park next to his house, but he did not have a team. (Since not having a team really bothered him, he asked all his friends to join him and form a team.) They could all play other teams, and maybe they could even get uniforms. Then they could play in the city tournament and get recognized as the best team around.

Guided Practice: Follow the directions from the direction box above as you correct the paragraph below.

Steve and I enjoyed going to the movie theater Friday night to watch one of the greatest comedy movies of our time and we laughed very hard and as we stepped out into the brisk night air Steve shoved a dime into my hand and asked me to call his brother to come get him and his reason was classic because he wanted me to call because he wasn't speaking to his brother because they had just had a fight but he didn't have a way home unless his brother came to get him.

CHAPTER 11 LESSON 2 SKILL TEST B

Exercise 1: In the parentheses at the end of each sentence, underline the part you will have to add to make a complete sentence. On a sheet of notebook paper, write complete sentences by adding the parts needed.

1. the apples and oranges in those crates   (subject part, predicate part, both the subject and predicate)
2. swung and missed the buzzing flies   (subject part, predicate part, both the subject and predicate)
3. baked delicious pies and cakes   (subject part, predicate part, both the subject and predicate)
4. if we clean our mess in the kitchen.   (subject part, predicate part, both the subject and predicate)
5. fought and won their battle on the soccer field. (subject part, predicate part, both the subject and predicate)

Exercise 2: Put a slash to separate each run-on sentence. Then on the lines provided, correct the run-on sentences as indicated by the labels in parentheses at the end of each sentence. (CParts means compound parts in the sentence.)

6. The young artist received special paints for his birthday he got a set of brushes, too. (**SCParts**)

_____

7. The snake slithered across the grass it slithered under the woodpile. (**SCParts**)

_____

8. The young artist received special paints for his birthday he got a set of brushes, too. (**CD**, and)

_____

9. The snake slithered across the grass it slithered under the woodpile. (**CX**, after, 1)

_____

10. I cannot run in the race I have warmed up. (**CX**, until, 2)

_____

Exercise 3: Identify the kind of sentence by writing the abbreviations in the blank (**S, F, SCS, SCV, CD, CX**).

_____ 11. Mother's coffee had sugar and cream in it.
_____ 12. I could hear the bass on his radio as he drove down the street.
_____ 13. Mother likes her coffee with sugar and cream in it.
_____ 14. Because I was the most qualified, I was offered the management position in our office.
_____ 15. The big ship beyond the pier and across the waterway.
_____ 16. The farmer planted soybeans, and his neighbor planted milo.

Exercise 4: Use the 2 complete thoughts in bold print to write each kind of sentence listed below.

I read and studied for three hours / I made an A on my test

17. (CX, because, 1) _____

18. (CD; therefore) _____

19. (SCV) _____

20. (CX, before, 2) _____

Exercise 5: Write a simple sentence, a compound sentence, and a complex sentence and identify them with these labels: (**S**) (**CD**) (**CX**). The simple sentence can have compound parts, but you must identify the compound parts in the label: (**SCV**) (**SCS**) (**SCParts**).

CHAPTER 11 LESSON 2 SKILL TEST C

Directions for Exercises 1-2: Identify each thought below by putting a slash between each one. Then rewrite the paragraph. Use the *Guidelines for Combining Sentences* in Chapter 10 to combine related thoughts to make compound, complex, or simple sentences with compound parts. Avoid overusing the conjunctions *and, but*, and *so*. Underline simple sentences once, compound sentences twice, and put parentheses around the complex sentences.

Exercise 1:

My mother is teaching my brother how to cook and my brother's friends are giving him a lot of sympathy because they feel sorry for him slaving away in the kitchen however, my mother is a smart woman she starts my brother's cooking education with fudge, cookies, and cakes and now my brother's friends are asking if they can come over to join him in the kitchen and they have suddenly seen the value of learning to cook and yes, my mother is certainly a wise woman.

_____

_____

_____

_____

_____

_____

_____

Exercise 2:

I went with my big sister, the cowgirl, to the horse show last week to help out and I can't understand why she loves to go to horse shows and rodeos because it was hot and noisy and smelly and I got tired of washing horses brushing horses and riding horses but my sister seemed to enjoy all the dust and confusion and in fact, she talked and laughed with all the cowboys and actually had a great time and I just don't understand girls, especially my sister!

_____

_____

_____

_____

_____

_____

Exercise 3: On a sheet of notebook paper, write a paragraph using *Three Ways to Have a Great Day* as your topic. Underline simple sentences once, compound sentences twice, and put parentheses around the complex sentences.

CHAPTER 11 LESSON 3 APPLICATION TEST

Exercise 1: Classify each sentence.

1. _____ Instantly the aroma of the popcorn filled the room!

2. _____ Dad parked his new car in the parking lot rather carefully before the big meeting.

3. _____ Did your brother borrow our lawnmower yesterday?

Directions: Complete the noun job table. Use Sentence 2.

List the Noun Used	List the Noun Job	Singular or Plural	Common or Proper
4.	5.	6.	7.
8.	9.	10.	11.
12.	13.	14.	15.
16.	17.	18.	19.

Exercise 2: Identify each kind of sentence by writing the abbreviations in the blank (**S, F, SCS, SCV, CD, CX**).

_____ 20. The grouchy man grumbled when he saw the neighborhood dogs in his yard.

_____ 21. Steam rose invitingly from the hot cup of hot chocolate.

_____ 22. An oxygen tank sat dangerously close to the flame, but no one noticed.

_____ 23. The windows rattled and shook from the blast of dynamite.

_____ 24. Until the fire department arrived, the grass fire was out of control.

Exercise 3:   **Editing Paragraph**

Find each error and write the correction. Replace each word underlined once with a synonym. Use the Editing Guide to help you. **Editing Guide: Synonyms: 2 Misspelled Words: 4 Capitals: 28 Periods: 5 Commas: 8 Apostrophes: 1 Quotations: 2 End Marks: 4**

we expect mom and dad to arrive in dallas texas on the fourth of july with dr o g frog the presedent of the univrsity in lily pond england mr frog is staying with us while he is in dallas for the <u>annual</u> amphibians anonymous convention dr frog a man of <u>many</u> talents will provide entertainment at the conventin he will sing the crazy hit song im croaking over you leap frog

Exercise 4: Identify each thought below by putting a slash between each one. Then rewrite the paragraph on a sheet of notebook paper. Correct fragments and improve the long, rambling sentences by using different kinds of sentences. Underline simple sentences once, compound sentences twice, and put parentheses around the complex sentences.

My alarm clock hates me because it will not go off when it should go off and it goes off when it should not go off in the middle of the night my faithful mechanical tormentor rings loud clear and long and then early the next morning there is total silence and I am always late for school and I am blurry-eyed from hearing that alarm all during the night but I have finally found the perfect place for my pesky little alarm clock because I have given it to my pesky little brother because they deserve each other.

CHAPTER 11 LESSON 4

Check Time, Journal Writing Time, Analogy Time, and Figures of Speech Time
Journal Writing Assignment: Make an entry in your journal. (Start with your heading and date.)

Word Analogy Exercise: Choose the correct missing word and put the letter in the blank.

1. seven:eight::two: _____   a. one   b. two   c. three   d. four
2. bacteria:microscope::star: _____   a. lab   b. science   c. meteor   d. telescope
3. umbrella:rain:: _____ sword   a. horse   b. shield   c. army   d. lightning

Figures of Speech Exercise: Identify which figure of speech is being used in the sentences below. Write the labels **S** for simile, **M** for metaphor, and **P** for personification.

____ 1. "Phillip," Leah scolded, "stop stuffing food in your mouth. You are a pig!"

____ 2. The surprised boy ran like a gazelle.

____ 3. The window slammed shut, biting off a piece of flowing ivy.

____ 4. The washing machine has eaten six of my socks.

____ 5. Listen, Sleeping Beauty; you have to stay awake.

____ 6. He's as old as the pyramids.

CHAPTER 11 LESSON 5

Persuasive Writing

Persuasion means getting other people to see things your way. When you write a persuasive paragraph, you choose for your topic something you want to "persuade" people to do or believe. A persuasive paragraph expresses an opinion and tries to convince the reader that this opinion is correct. Persuading someone to agree with you requires careful thinking and planning. As the writer, you must make the issue clear and present facts and reasons that give strong support to your opinion. You are encouraging your audience to take a certain action or to feel the same way you do.

In attempting to persuade anyone to your way of thinking, it is VERY important to consider just who the reader is that you are trying to persuade. Your reader is your audience. When you know who your reader is, you must use persuasive reasoning that will appeal to that reader. Know your reader well enough to use arguments that will appeal to him. You would not use the same kind of argument to persuade your five-year-old sister to tell you where she hid your skates that you would use to persuade the President of the United States to make you a member of his Cabinet.

Knowing more about persuasive writing and using the *Guidelines for Writing a Persuasive Paragraph* will make this type of writing easy and enjoyable.

Guidelines for Writing a Persuasive Paragraph
1. A persuasive paragraph should begin with a clearly stated opinion in the topic sentence.
2. The topic sentence that states the opinion should then be supported by at least three strong reasons.
3. Think of three reasons you want to use to support your opinion and list (enumerate) them.
4. Each reason should be followed by at least two good supporting sentences.
5. Know the audience that you are trying to persuade and always use reasons that will be most convincing to that particular audience.
6. Conclude the paragraph with two sentences that restate your opinion and your position.

CHAPTER 11 LESSON 5

Persuasive Writing

The three-point writing format is one of the best ways to present your persuasive argument because it gives you an organized way of stating your opinion and supporting it. The persuasive writing format is the same as your earlier expository writing format. They both use the three-point organization. The main differences between persuasive and expository writing are your purpose for writing, the content of your paper, and the wording of your sentences.

Remember, persuasive writing states your opinion with supporting facts that try to convince your reader to think or act in a certain way, and expository writing attempts to give an explanation or information to your reader.

Look at the outline below. It is a three-point outline for a persuasive paragraph. Notice how similar it is to the three-point expository format. You will find that the main difference is that the topic sentence is an opinion statement. In addition, all the points and supporting sentences are persuasive in nature and are intended to back up the opinion statement.

The Three-Point Persuasive Paragraph Outline

I. Title
II. Paragraph (13 sentences)
    A. Topic sentence (Opinion statement)
    B. Explanation sentence
    C. **First point** persuasive sentence
    D. Two **supporting** sentences for the first point
    E. **Second point** persuasive sentence
    F. Two **supporting** sentences for the second point
    G. **Third point** persuasive sentence
    H. Two **supporting** sentences for the third point
    I. Concluding summary sentence
    J. Concluding call-for-decision sentence

Follow the persuasive outline and persuasive guidelines as you go through the explanation for writing a persuasive paragraph. Your **Sample Persuasive Paragraph Topic** is **Why Our School Needs a Longer Lunch Break**. You will attempt to persuade the administration in your school that you should have a longer lunch break. You should begin your paragraph with a clearly-stated opinion in the topic sentence; therefore, your first sentence will be your TOPIC SENTENCE. Follow the topic sentence with an explanation sentence. It will explain something about the topic sentence. Then think of three reasons you want to use to support your opinion and list (enumerate) them on the back of your paper. Making a list of your reasons will help keep your writing focused on the points you are trying to make.

The next nine sentences will make up the BODY of your persuasive paragraph. You will write THREE PERSUASIVE SENTENCES. These three sentences will be your THREE POINTS attempting to convince your reader. Following each sentence, you will write TWO SUPPORTING SENTENCES that will back up what each PERSUASIVE SENTENCE states.

There are two sentences in the CONCLUSION of the persuasive paragraph. The first sentence is a CONCLUDING SUMMARY sentence that summarizes your persuasive argument. The second sentence is a CALL FOR DECISION sentence that asks the reader to respond to your argument. There are a total of at least thirteen sentences in your persuasive paragraph.

CHAPTER 11 LESSON 5

Persuasive Paragraph

TOPIC SENTENCE (OPINION STATEMENT)

Our school needs a longer lunch break.

You will write your topic sentence from your topic "Why Our School Needs a Longer Lunch Break." Notice that your persuasive paragraph will be written in first person.

ENUMERATE (LIST) THE REASONS TO SUPPORT YOUR OPINION

1. benefit our health   2. benefit our teachers   3. benefit our students

Think of three reasons you want to use to support your opinion and list (enumerate) them on the back of your paper. Refer to these reasons as you write, to help keep you focused.

EXPLANATION SENTENCE

A five-to-ten minute increase in our present forty-minute lunch break would help all of us.

The second sentence will be an explanation sentence, or a sentence that adds to the reader's understanding of the topic sentence . In this sentence, you will give your explanation in general terms. You will NOT list your three points as you usually do in the other three-point papers you have written.

FIRST POINT PERSUASIVE SENTENCE

First, a longer lunch break would benefit our health.

FIRST POINT SUPPORTING SENTENCES

Medical science has proven that hurried lunches lead to stomach disorders. Adding extra minutes to our lunch break would take away some of the "hurry," and, hopefully, lead to better digestion and better health.

SECOND POINT PERSUASIVE SENTENCE

Next, a longer lunch break would benefit our teachers.

This is your second argument to persuade the reader. Notice that it begins with _next_, which helps the reader follow your organization.

SECOND POINT SUPPORTING SENTENCES

Since teachers often suffer from stress, a few extra minutes would give them additional preparation time. In addition, it could give them a little more R and R (rest and recreation) before facing that next class.

THIRD POINT PERSUASIVE SENTENCE

Finally, a longer lunch break would benefit our students.

This gives your third argument for a longer lunch break. Notice that it begins with _finally_, which lets the reader know you are giving your final argument.

THIRD POINT SUPPORTING SENTENCES

Students, like teachers, need some extra moments to escape stress. Also, they could probably use extra time to cram for an afternoon test.

CHAPTER 11 LESSON 5

Persuasive Paragraph, continued

CONCLUDING SUMMARY SENTENCE

It appears that extra time at lunch would be beneficial to everyone.

The first concluding sentence is simply a summary sentence that will summarize your persuasive argument.

CONCLUDING CALL-FOR-DECISION SENTENCE

Seeing so many benefits, we would be wise to add five to ten minutes to our noon break.

The second concluding sentence is a call-for-decision sentence. It asks the reader to respond to your argument.

SAMPLE PERSUASIVE PARAGRAPH:

Why Our School Needs a Longer Lunch Break

Our school needs a longer lunch break. A five-to-ten minute increase in our present forty-minute lunch break would help all of us. **First, a longer lunch break would benefit our health.** Medical science has proven that hurried lunches lead to stomach disorders. Adding extra minutes to our lunch break would take away some of the "hurry," and, hopefully, lead to better digestion and better health. **Next, a longer break would benefit our teachers.** Since teachers often suffer from stress, a few extra minutes would give them additional preparation time. In addition, it could give them a little more R and R (rest and recreation) before facing that next class. **Finally, a longer lunch break would benefit our students.** Students, like teachers, need some extra moments to escape stress. Also, they could probably use extra time to cram for an afternoon test. **It appears that extra time at lunch would be beneficial to everyone.** Seeing so many benefits, we would be wise to add five to ten minutes to our noon break.

Remember, the persuasive writing format is the same as your earlier expository writing format. They both use the three-point organization. The main differences between persuasive and expository writing are your purposes for writing, the content of your paper, and the wording of your sentences. Persuasive writing tries to convince your reader to think or act a certain way, while expository writing attempts to give an explanation or provide information to your reader.

Writing Assignment

Use the steps and outline of writing a persuasive paragraph to do your writing assignment below. Put your finished writing in your Rough Draft folder.

Writing Assignment #15: Persuasive Paragraph in First Person

Topic: Choose one of these topics for your persuasive paragraph:
1. Why I am for (or against) wearing seat belts
2. Why I am for (or against) smoking (or drinking)
3. Why I need an allowance
4. Why schools need (or do not need) a dress code

CHAPTER 12 LESSON 1

Mixed Patterns 1-2

The sentences that you classify with your teacher will be a mixture of Pattern 1: SN V P1 and Pattern 2: SN V-t DO P2. As you classify these sentences, look carefully at the main parts so you can identify the correct pattern for each sentence.

Transition Words

Words that help writers move from one sentence to the next or from paragraph to paragraph are called **transition words**. They include such expressions as *however, for example, in fact, on the other hand, therefore, etc.* Transition words are most often placed at the **beginning of the sentence** and are always **followed by a comma**. Because they will make your writing so much smoother, you should learn a list of transition words and when to use them. Learning the transition jingle will make transition words fun and easy to remember.

Three-Paragraph Persuasive Essay

Writing a persuasive essay is very easy with the Shurley Method. You will now follow the sample persuasive paragraph in Chapter 11, "Why Our School Needs a Longer Lunch Break," as it is enlarged to a three-paragraph persuasive essay and five-paragraph persuasive essay.

Remember, the persuasive writing format is the same as your earlier expository writing format. They both use the three-point organization. The main differences between persuasive and expository writing are your purposes for writing, the content of your paper, and the wording of your sentences. Persuasive writing tries to convince your reader to think or act a certain way, while expository writing attempts to give an explanation or provide information to your reader.

As you are learning to write a persuasive essay, it will help to review the outline for the persuasive paragraph that you have already learned. Look at the outlines below. Compare and discuss the differences in the single paragraph and the three-paragraph essay. Compare the number of sentences and differences in the introduction and conclusion.

Outline of a Persuasive Paragraph	Outline of a 3-Paragraph Persuasive Essay

I. Title
II. Paragraph (13 sentences)
  A. Topic sentence (opinion statement)
  B. Explanation sentence
  C. **First point** persuasive sentence
  D. Two **supporting** sentences for the first point
  E. **Second point** persuasive sentence
  F. Two **supporting** sentences for the second point
  G. **Third point** persuasive sentence
  H. Two **supporting** sentences for the third point
  I. Concluding summary sentence
  J. Concluding call-for-decision sentence
	I. Title
	II. Paragraph 1 - Introduction (3 sentences)
	  A. Topic sentence (opinion statement)
	  B. Explanation sentence
	  C. Three-point introductory sentence
	III. Paragraph 2 - Body (9 sentences)
	  A. **First point** persuasive sentence
	  B. Two **supporting** sentences for the first point
	  C. **Second point** persuasive sentence
	  D. Two **supporting** sentences for the second point
	  E. **Third point** persuasive sentence
	  F. Two **supporting** sentences for the third point
	IV. Paragraph 3 - Conclusion (3 sentences)
	  A. Concluding number sentence
	  B. Concluding summary sentence
	  C. Concluding call for decision sentence

CHAPTER 12 LESSON 1

The main difference between the persuasive paragraph and the three-paragraph persuasive essay is that the **introduction, body, and conclusion are divided into three paragraphs.** Another difference is that an extra sentence has been added in the **introduction**, and an extra sentence has been added in the **conclusion**.

Look at the example of a three-paragraph persuasive essay below. The sentences in bold type will show you the things that were added to make this a three-paragraph persuasive essay.

Three-Paragraph Persuasive Essay

Only a Few Minutes for Great Benefits

Our school needs a longer lunch break. **In fact,** a five-to-ten minute increase in our present forty-minute lunch break would help all of us. **There are several benefits that could come from these few minutes.**

First, a longer lunch break would benefit our health. Medical science has proven that hurried lunches lead to stomach disorders. Adding extra minutes to our lunch break would take away some of the "hurry," and, hopefully, lead to better digestion and better health. Next, a longer break would benefit our teachers. Since teachers often suffer from stress, a few extra minutes would give them additional preparation time. In addition, it could give them a little more R and R (rest and recreation) before facing that next class. Finally, a longer lunch break would benefit our students. Students, like teachers, need some extra moments to escape stress. Also, they could probably use extra time to cram for an afternoon test.

There are many benefits to a longer lunch break. Extra time at lunch would be beneficial to everyone. In light of all these benefits, we would be wise to add five to ten minutes to our noon break.

A persuasive essay can also be written as a five-paragraph essay. Look at the example of a five-paragraph persuasive essay below. The sentences in bold type will show you the things that were added to make this a five-paragraph persuasive essay. Notice that each point has been put into a separate paragraph and an extra suppporting sentence has been added.

Five-Paragraph Persuasive Essay

Only a Few Minutes for Great Benefits

Our school needs a longer lunch break. In fact, a five-to-ten minute increase in our present forty-minute lunch break would help all of us. There are several benefits that could come from these few minutes.

First, a longer lunch break would benefit our health. Medical science has proven that hurried lunches lead to stomach disorders. Adding extra minutes to our lunch break would take away some of the "hurry," and, hopefully, lead to better digestion and better health. **People who feel good do better work.**

Next, a longer break would benefit our teachers. Since teachers often suffer from stress, a few extra minutes would give them additional preparation time. In addition, it could give them a little more R and R (rest and recreation) before facing that next class. **On the other hand, if they needed to schedule student make-up work, they could do so.**

Finally, a longer lunch break would benefit our students. Students, like teachers, need some extra moments to escape stress. Also, they could probably use extra time to cram for an afternoon test. **They might even settle down quicker after lunch.**

There are many benefits to a longer lunch break. Extra time at lunch would be beneficial to everyone. In light of all these benefits, we would be wise to add five to ten minutes to our noon break.

CHAPTER 12 LESSON 1

As you can see, a basic persuasive paragraph can easily be expanded into either a three-paragraph or five-paragraph essay. The organization of both essays is discussed below.

Introduction

The introduction forms the first paragraph of the three-paragraph and five-paragraph essay. Notice that the words *In fact* have been added to the beginning of the second sentence in the introduction. The transitional words *In fact* are needed to help the sentences "flow together." Three sentences make up the introduction. Notice that the introductory sentences stay the same.

The third sentence in the introduction is called a **three-point introductory sentence**. This is the sentence you will add when writing any persuasive essay. It gives a general or specific number of points (reasons or proofs) that will be mentioned to prove the topic sentence. You will NOT list your three points as you usually do in the other three-point papers you have written.

Body

The second paragraph of a three-paragraph essay is the body. Nine sentences make up the body. Notice that the persuasive and supporting sentences stay the same as in the persuasive paragraph.

The body of a five-paragraph essay has three paragraphs. Each of the three persuasive points forms a new paragraph. Also, notice that each of the three paragraphs has an extra supporting sentence.

Conclusion

The conclusion forms the third paragraph of a three-paragraph essay and the fifth paragraph of a five-paragraph essay. The closing paragraph, or conclusion, should tie all the important points together with a restatement of the main idea and your final comments on it.

The first sentence in the conclusion is called the **concluding number sentence.** To write this sentence, you can refer to the new (third) sentence in the introduction. Using the general or specific number and topic as stated in that introductory sentence, you can write a similar concluding sentence.

Three sentences make up the conclusion. Notice that the concluding sentences stay the same.

Writing Assignment

Use the outline and three-paragraph persuasive essay example to do the writing assignment below. Indent each paragraph. Remember to use some of the transition words you just learned to make the sentences and paragraphs in your essay flow together smoothly. Put your finished writing in your Rough Draft Folder.

Writing Assignment #16: Three-Paragraph Persuasive Essay in First Person

Topic: Choose one of these topics for your persuasive essay:

1. Why I should be principal for the day
2. Why dogs (or cats) make good pets
3. Why I should have good study habits
4. Why I should be interested in politics
5. Why I think schools should offer _____
6. Why I should plan the school lunch menu
7. Why I should run for President

CHAPTER 12 LESSON 2 SKILL TEST

Exercise 1: In the parentheses at the end of each sentence, underline the part you need to add to make a complete sentence. On a sheet of notebook paper, write complete sentences by adding the parts needed.

1. while we sang songs around the campfire   (subject part, predicate part, both the subject and predicate)
2. during the blizzard at the top of the mountain   (subject part, predicate part, both the subject and predicate)
3. a nutritious snack of peanut butter and crackers   (subject part, predicate part, both the subject and predicate)

Exercise 2: Put a slash to separate each run-on sentence. Then on the lines provided, correct the run-on sentences as indicated by the labels in parentheses at the end of each sentence.

4. Buster patiently herds the sheep into the pen he is a good sheepdog. (**CX**, because, 2)

5. Worker ants feed the queen ant they take care of her eggs. (**CD**, and)

6. The beginning skiers learned from their instructor they did not ski down the small slope. (**CX**, until, 1)

Exercise 3: Identify each kind of sentence by writing the abbreviations in the blank (**S, F, SCS, SCV, CD, CX**).

_____ 7. The noisy jalopy sputtered and jerked down the street.
_____ 8. The teacher permitted her class to watch the election returns while they ate their lunch.
_____ 9. We hurried down the aisle; consequently, we found some good seats.

Exercise 4: Use the 2 complete thoughts in bold print to write each kind of sentence listed below.

Mom and Dad jog every morning / they are losing weight

10. (CX, since, 1) _____

11. (CD, so) _____

12. (CD; thus) _____

Exercise 5: Identify each thought below by putting a slash between each one. Then rewrite the paragraph. Use the *Guidelines for Combining Sentences* in Chapter 10 to combine related thoughts to make compound, complex, or simple sentences with compound parts. Avoid overusing the conjunctions *and, but*, and *so*. Underline simple sentences once, compound sentences twice, and put parentheses around the complex sentences.

     The weather is cold today and the weather is damp today and I had big plans today but the weather is not cooperating and this morning I called the weather station to get a weather report and the weatherman predicts rain this afternoon and the weatherman predicts sleet this afternoon and I am so disappointed because I will have to cancel my hiking expedition with my friends and I will probably end up sitting in front of the TV moaning and groaning and that is why I do not want it to rain or sleet today.

Exercise 6: Write a simple sentence, a compound sentence, and a complex sentence and identify them with these labels: (**S**) (**CD**) (**CX**). The simple sentence can have compound parts, but you must identify the compound parts in the label: (**SCV**) (**SCS**) (**SCParts**).

CHAPTER 12 LESSON 3 APPLICATION TEST

Exercise 1: Mixed Patterns 1-2. Classify each sentence.

1. _____ Some mining practices have caused serious environmental problems to our landscape.

2. _____ Write your name in the upper corner of your paper.

3. _____ The young pianist flew to the concert from a small town in Italy.

Directions: Complete the noun job table. Use Sentence 3.

List the Noun Used	List the Noun Job	Singular or Plural	Common or Proper
4.	5.	6.	7.
8.	9.	10.	11.
12.	13.	14.	15.
16.	17.	18.	19.

Exercise 2: Identify each kind of sentence by writing the abbreviations in the blank (**S, F, SCS, SCV, CD, CX**).

_____ 20. Although the trip was long, the travelers were cheerful and excited.

_____ 21. Cody was sleepy, but he would not go to bed.

_____ 22. Ed and Mary owned a small restaurant on the outskirts of town.

_____ 23. The jeweler designed pendants and rings from gold and precious gems.

_____ 24. The audience could not hear because the sound system was turned off.

Exercise 3:   **Editing Paragraph**
Find each error and write the correction. Replace each word underlined once with a synonym. Use the Editing Guide to help you. **Editing Guide: Homonyms: 1 Synonyms: 1 Misspelled Words: 3 Capitals: 23 Subject-Verb Agreement: 1 Periods: 1 Commas: 7 Apostrophes: 2 End Marks: 3**

on monday june 13 i hope too visit johns brother tom c alexander because tom lives near

the alantic ocean in miami florida while i am in florida i hope to visit disneyworld and sea world in

orlando toms family know how to have <u>fun</u> and i am looking foreward to my vacatison with them

Exercise 4: Identify each thought below by putting a slash between each one. Then rewrite the paragraph on notebook paper. Correct fragments and improve long, rambling sentences by using different kinds of sentences. Underline simple sentences once, compound sentences twice, and put parentheses around the complex sentences.

I am a strong, good-looking young man in his junior high prime and I have suddenly realized how

important it is to eat a good nourishing breakfast in the mornings so that I will be able to take an early

morning jog around the block in my muscle shirt and jogging shorts and my mom loves my sudden

interest in health and exercise but she has become suspicious since she realized my early morning jogging

takes me right by the cheerleaders' early-morning practice session. Grins at me now when I fuss over

which running outfit to wear.

CHAPTER 12 LESSON 4

Check Time, Journal Writing Time, and Analogy Time
Journal Writing Assignment: Make an entry in your journal. (Start with your heading and date.)

Word Analogy Exercise: Choose the correct missing word and put the letter in the blank.

1. cold-blooded:amphibian::warm-blooded: _____   a. reptile   b. mammal   c. frog   d. insect
2. war:peace::chaos: _____   a. blitzed   b. intricate   c. calm   d. guns
3. Paris:France:: _____ :England   a. New York   b. Peking   c. London   d. Mexico

CHAPTER 12 LESSON 5

Writing Assignment
Use the sample *Five-Paragraph Persuasive Essay* in Lesson 1 to do the writing assignment below. Indent each paragraph.

Writing Assignment #17: Five-Paragraph Persuasive Essay in First Person

Topic: Choose a different topic from the one you chose for your other persuasive writings.

1. Why I should be principal for the day
2. Why dogs (or cats) make good pets
3. Why I should have good study habits
4. Why I should be interested in politics
5. Why I am for (or against) smoking (or drinking)
6. Why schools need (or do not need) a dress code
7. Why I think schools should offer _____
8. Why I should plan the school lunch menu
9. Why I should run for President
10. Why I am for (or against) wearing seatbelts
11. Why I need an allowance

Editing Time
Use the guidelines for *Editing Rough Drafts and for Writing Final Papers* and the *Editing Checklist* in Chapter 4, Lesson 5, to edit Writing Assignment #17. Staple the final paper to the rough draft and put both in the Final Writing Folder until your teacher calls for them.

CHAPTER 13 LESSON 1

Introducing Sentence Pattern 3 and Reviewing Sentence Pattern 1 and Sentence Pattern 2

Earlier you learned that nouns can have different jobs, or functions, in a sentence. You have studied three of these jobs already: A noun can be a subject, an object of a preposition, or a direct object. You must remember, however, that a noun used as a subject or direct object is a basic part of a sentence pattern (like **SN V** or **SN V-t DO**). But a noun that is used as an object of a preposition is not part of a basic sentence pattern.

In the new sentence pattern, **Pattern 3**, there are three nouns in the basic sentence pattern: **N V N N.** The first noun is a subject noun and is still written as **SN**. The third noun is a direct object and is still written as **DO**. The verb is labeled **V-t** after identifying the direct object. The second noun is called an indirect object and is written with the abbreviation **IO**. The indirect object will *always* come between the verb and direct object. This third pattern in the Shurley Method is *subject noun / verb-transitive / indirect object / direct object / Pattern 3,* and it is written as **SN V-t IO DO P3.**

Indirect Object

1. An **indirect object** is a noun or pronoun.

2. An **indirect object** receives what the direct object names.

3. An **indirect object** is located between the verb-transitive and the direct object.

4. An **indirect object** is labeled as IO.

5. To find the **indirect object**, ask TO WHOM or FOR WHOM after the direct object.

Sample Sentence for the exact words to say to find the indirect object.

1. Dad builds Mom a house.

2. Who builds Mom a house? Dad - SN

3. What is being said about Dad? Dad builds - V

4. Dad builds what? house - verify the noun

5. Does house mean the same thing as Dad? No.

6. House - DO

7. Builds - V-t

8. Dad builds house for whom? Mom - IO
   (*Say: Mom - Indirect object.*)

9. A - A

10. SN V-t IO DO P3 Check
    (*Say: Subject Noun, Verb-Transitive, Indirect Object, Direct Object, Pattern 3 Check.*)

11. Check the verb: verb-transitive.

12. Check again for prepositional phrases.

13. No prepositional phrases.

14. Period, statement, declarative sentence

15. Go back to the verb - divide the complete subject from the complete predicate.

16. Is there an adverb exception? No.

17. Is this sentence in a natural or inverted order? Natural - no change.

The Question and Answer Flow for Sentence 5 on page 107 has also been provided as an example for you.

CHAPTER 13 LESSON 1

Question and Answer Flow Example

Question and Answer Flow for Sentence 5: The restaurant gave me a uniform for my waitress job.

1. What gave me a uniform for my waitress job?
   restaurant - SN
2. What is being said about restaurant?
   restaurant gave - V
3. Restaurant gave what? uniform - verify the noun
4. Does uniform mean the same thing as restaurant?
   No.
5. Uniform - DO
6. Gave - V-t
7. Restaurant gave uniform to whom? me - IO
8. A - A
9. For - P
10. For what? job - OP

11. What kind of job? waitress - Adj
12. Whose job? my - PPA
13. The - A
14. SN V-t IO DO P3 Check
15. Check the verb: verb-transitive.
16. Check again for prepositional phrases.
17. (For my waitress job) - Prepositional phrase
18. Period, statement, declarative sentence
19. Go back to the verb - divide the complete subject
    from the complete predicate.
20. Is there an adverb exception? No.
21. Is this sentence in a natural or inverted order?
    Natural - no change.

Classified Sentence:

$$\text{A} \quad \text{SN} \qquad \text{V-t} \quad \text{IO} \; \text{A} \quad \text{DO} \qquad \text{P PPA Adj} \quad \text{OP}$$

<u>SN V-t</u>   The restaurant / gave me a uniform (for my waitress job.) **D**
IO DO P3

Assignment

1. Write one **Practice Sentence** following these labels:

   A   Adj   Adj   SN   V-t   IO   A   DO   P   PPA   OP

2. Write an **Improved Sentence** from the Practice Sentence. Make at least two synonym changes, one antonym change, and your choice of complete word changes.

Assignment

Identify each thought below by putting a slash between each one. Then rewrite the paragraph on a sheet of notebook paper. Correct fragments and improve the long rambling sentences by using different kinds of sentences. Underline simple sentences once, compound sentences twice, and put parentheses around the complex sentences.

The honey bees are fascinating insects and the organization of their jobs is even more fascinating and the worker bees perform many different jobs and the jobs are determined by the age of the honey bee and the first job of young bees is the job of housecleaning and housecleaning bees are from one to five days old and their chores include cleaning the cells and their chores also include carrying dead bees far away from the hive and then at six to twelve days old, the young bees begin nurse duty the nurse bee makes royal jelly and then feeds it to all the young bee larvae.

CHAPTER 13 LESSON 2

Quotations

Quotations are words spoken by someone, and quotation marks are used to set off the exact words that are spoken. These words set off by quotation marks are usually called a direct quotation. In your writing you will often find it necessary to tell what someone has said, and you will need to know several rules of punctuation in order to write quotations. Read and discuss each set of rules below and complete the practice examples.

QUOTATION RULES FOR BEGINNING QUOTES

1. Pattern "C -quote- (,!?) " <u>explanatory words (.)</u>
   (Quotation marks, capital letter, quote, end punctuation choice, quotation marks closed, explanatory words, period.)

2. Underline **end explanatory words** and use a period at the end.

3. You should have a **beginning quote** – Use quotation marks at the beginning and end of what is said. Then put a comma, question mark, or exclamation point (no period) after the quote but in front of the quotation mark.

4. Capitalize the beginning of the quote and any proper nouns or the pronoun *I*.

5. Punctuate the rest of the sentence by checking for any apostrophes, periods, or commas that may be needed within the sentence.

Guided Practice

Sentence: the dogs and i are going hunting on friday with j b hunt my dad said

1. Pattern: **"C -quote- (,!?) "** <u>explanatory words **(.)**</u>

2. the dogs and i are going hunting on friday with j b hunt **<u>my dad said</u>**(.)

3. **"**the dogs and i are going hunting on friday with j b hunt,**"** <u>my dad said</u>.

4. **"The** dogs and **I** are going hunting on **F**riday with **J B H**unt,**"** <u>my dad said</u>.

5. "The dogs and I are going hunting on Friday with J. B. Hunt," <u>my dad said</u>.

6. **Corrected Sentence:** "The dogs and I are going hunting on Friday with J. B. Hunt," <u>my dad said</u>.

CHAPTER 13 LESSON 2

QUOTATION RULES FOR END QUOTES

1. **Pattern:** <u>C -explanatory words(**,**)</u> "**C** -quote- **(.!?)** "
   (Capital letter, explanatory words, comma, quotation marks, capital letter, quote, end punctuation choice, quotation marks closed)

2. Underline **beginning explanatory words** and use a comma at the end of them.

3. You should have an **end quote** – Use quotation marks at the beginning and end of what is said. Then put a period, question mark, or exclamation point (no comma) after the quote but in front of the quotation mark.

4. Capitalize the first of the explanatory words at the beginning of a sentence, the beginning of the quote, and any proper nouns or the pronoun *I*.

5. Punctuate the rest of the sentence by checking for any apostrophes, periods, or commas that may be needed within the sentence.

Guided Practice

Sentence: my dad said the dogs and i are going hunting on friday with j b hunt

1. Pattern: <u>C -explanatory words(**,**)</u> "**C** -quote- **(.!?)** "
2. **<u>my dad said</u>**(,) the dogs and i are going hunting on friday with j b hunt
3. <u>my dad said</u>, "the dogs and i are going hunting on friday with j b hunt**.** "
4. <u>My dad said</u>, "**T**he dogs and **I** are going hunting on **F**riday with **J B H**unt.
5. <u>My dad said</u>, "The dogs and I are going hunting on Friday with J. B. Hunt."
6. **Corrected Sentence:** <u>My dad said</u>, "The dogs and I are going hunting on Friday with J. B. Hunt."

CHAPTER 13 LESSON 2

QUOTATION RULES FOR SPLIT QUOTES

1. **Pattern:** "**C** -quote- (,) "**c** -explanatory words(,) "**c** -quote- (.!?) "
   (Quotation marks, capital letter, first part of quote, comma, quotation marks, explanatory words, comma, quotation marks again, second part of quote, end punctuation choice, quotation marks.)

2. Underline **middle explanatory words** and use a comma at the end of them.

3. You should have the **first part of a split quote** - Use quotation marks at the beginning and end of the first part of what is said. Then put a comma after the first part of the quote but in front of the quotation mark.

4. You should have the **second part of a split quote** - Use quotation marks at the beginning and end of the second part of what is said. Then put an end mark punctuation (no comma) after the quote but in front of the quotation mark.

5. Capitalize the beginning of the quote and any proper nouns or the pronoun *I*. (Do not capitalize the first word of the second part unless it is a proper noun or the pronoun *I*.)

6. Punctuate the rest of the sentence by checking for any apostrophes, periods, or commas that may be needed within the sentence.

Guided Practice

Sentence: the dogs and i my dad said are going hunting on friday with j b hunt

1. Pattern: "**C** -quote- (,) "**c** -explanatory words(,) "**c** -quote- (.!?) "
2. the dogs and i **my dad said**(,) are going hunting on friday with j b hunt
3. "the dogs and i," <u>my dad said</u>, are going hunting on friday with j b hunt
4. "the dogs and i," <u>my dad said</u>, "are going hunting on friday with j b hunt(.)"
5. "**T**he dogs and **I**," <u>my dad said</u>, "are going hunting on **F**riday with **J B H**unt."
6. "The dogs and I," <u>my dad said</u>, "are going hunting on Friday with J. B. Hunt."
7. **Corrected Sentence:** "The dogs and I," <u>my dad said</u>, "are going hunting on Friday with J. B. Hunt."

Note: When you enclose two successive sentences in quotation marks, you still have two sentences, not a split quote. "The dogs and I are going hunting on Friday," my dad said. "I think they need the exercise."

CHAPTER 13 LESSON 2

Quotations in Dialogue

Conversation, or talking between two or more characters, is called **dialogue**. Dialogue is used to make a story more like real life, but it can also reveal a character's personality as well as move the action of the story forward. **When writing conversation, you must indent and create a new paragraph each time a different character speaks.** Otherwise, all the rules for punctuating quotations in dialogue are the same as the rules for punctuating beginning, end, and split quotations.

Guided Practice for Dialogue: Rewrite the conversation below on notebook paper. Capitalize and punctuate the conversation correctly. (Remember to start a new paragraph for each new speaker.)

i cant believe i have a flat tire in the middle of nowhere toni muttered as she kicked the flat tire in front of her she looked at the scorching sun and she looked up and down the empty highway well i wonder if i have a spare tire with my luck i probably dont toni muttered again as she kicked the flat for a third time my my arent we a little testy today said a jolly little voice behind her as toni turned she caught a quick glimpse of a little elf blinking her eyes quickly toni said very loudly i dont believe in elves ghosts or little people but if you can help me change this tire i ll let you

CHAPTER 13 LESSON 2

OTHER QUOTATION RULES

1. Longer Quotes

A. When a quotation consists of several sentences, put quotation marks only at the beginning and at the end of the whole quotation, not around each sentence in the quotation.

> "The dogs and I are going hunting on Friday with J. B. Hunt. I think they are ready for a good workout. We'll spend three or four hours in the woods behind Blue Lake. If you want to go, we'll see you on Friday!" said my dad as he hung up the phone.

B. When one person has a lengthy quote which is longer than one paragraph, quotation marks are used at the beginning of each paragraph and at the end of the last paragraph of that speaker's quote. Then, when the speaker changes, a new paragraph is started.

> "_____
> _____ (same speaker continues)
> "_____
> _____" (same speaker ends)
> "_____" (new speaker begins and ends)

2. A Quote Within a Quote

Single quotation marks are used to punctuate a quotation within a quotation.

> My mom said, "Did you hear your dad say, 'Finish your homework'?"

3. Quotation Marks to Punctuate Titles

Quotation marks are used to punctuate titles of songs, poems, short stories, chapters of books, articles, TV programs, and short plays. (Capitalize the first word, last word, and every word except for articles, short prepositions, and short conjunctions.)

> I can recite several stanzas of "Paul Revere's Ride."

4. Direct Quotations, Indirect Quotations, and Statements

A. A **direct quotation** occurs when you show exactly what someone says by using quotation marks.

> Direct quotation: Gina said, "I want a cup of hot chocolate."

B. An **indirect quotation** occurs when you simply describe what someone says without using his exact words.

> Indirect quotation: Gina said she wanted a cup of hot chocolate.

C. A **statement** occurs when no speaker is mentioned and no quotation is used.

> Statement: Gina wants a cup of hot chocolate.

CHAPTER 13 LESSON 2 SKILL TEST

Exercise 1: Use the Quotation Rules to help punctuate the quotations below. Underline the explanatory words.

1. taylor shouted hey chad did you see that huge spider that crawled into tinas desk

2. hey chad did you see that huge spider that crawled into tinas desk taylor shouted

3. hey chad taylor shouted did you see that huge spider that crawled into tinas desk

4. hey chad taylor shouted did you see that huge spider that crawled into tinas desk lets warn her

5. the frightened girl said weakly im lost and hungry

6. our ship is beginning to take on water grumbled the captain

7. i have no further questions for this witness said the lawyer

8. my parents are chaperones billy groaned dad says he and mom are even going to dance

9. would you care for any dessert mrs smith the waitress asked politely

10. jake the teacher asked sternly wheres your homework

11. my new shoes hurt my feet whined the little girl to her mother

12. tomorrows lunch our teacher announced will be spaghetti salad and garlic bread

Exercise 2:   **Editing Paragraph**
Find each error and write the correction. Use the Editing Guide to help you. **Editing Guide: Capitals: 41   Commas: 12**
Periods: 6   Apostrophes: 7   Misspelled Words: 4   Quotations: 14   End Marks: 20

chad was desperete he was broke and his job hunting all morning had turned up nothing he needed money to pay for the football-training weekend next month as he checked off the rest of the rejections from his list of job posibilities mr wiser his next door neighbor, drove up in his beat-up farm truck

chad jumped up and ran across the street mr wiser i need an extra job do you have anything i can do to earn some money

mr wiser grinned as he looked at the eager young man standing in front of him well chad i think i might be able to find a few extra things that need to be done on the farm since this is our busyest season ill pick you up in ten minutes tell your mom that you wont be back until about ten tonight

wait chad exclaimed disappointedly to mr wiser i cant work that long the biggest game of the season is playing on tv tonight and id miss it

life is full of tough choices mr wiser told him remember chad you have to work when the work is ready and not when youre ready see you in ten minutes or not at all

as chad crawled wearily out of mr wisers truck at ten oclock he cluched the money he had earned he walked proudly through his front door and announced i have a full-time job for the rest of the summer

CHAPTER 13 LESSON 3 APPLICATION TEST

Exercise 1: Classify each sentence.

1. _____ Tell me the company's address over the phone.

2. _____ Yesterday Sally's brother bought her a motorcycle for her birthday.

3. _____ Tom's friends at work gave him money for his operation.

Directions: Complete the noun job table. Use Sentence 3.

List the Noun Used	List the Noun Job	Singular or Plural	Common or Proper
4.	5.	6.	7.
8.	9.	10.	11.
12.	13.	14.	15.
16.	17.	18.	19.
20.	21.	22.	23.

Exercise 2: Use the Quotation Rules to help punctuate the quotations below. Underline the explanatory words.

24. the agent said jeff you must pay for your ticket in advance

25. jeff you must pay for your ticket in advance the agent said

26. jeff the agent said you must pay for your ticket in advance

27. you must pay for your ticket in advance jeff the agent said you may use your credit card

28. carol whispered i cant find my seat in this dark theater

29. yes we are ready chuckled mom to see your big surprise

30. now where wondered paul out loud have i put my baseball shoes

31. i paid good money for those shoes bellowed dad as andy tromped through the muddy yard then he added sympathetically as he saw andy slip and fall flat on his face on second thought why dont you go take a shower then you can come back and scrape the mud off your clothes and shoes by the way andy don't forget to wash your face

Exercise 3   **Editing Paragraph**

Find each error and write the correction. Replace each word underlined once with a synonym. Use the Editing Guide to help you. **Editing Guide: Synonyms: 1 Misspelled Words: 4 Subject-Verb Agreement: 1 Capitals: 14 Periods: 1 Commas: 6 End Marks: 2 Underlining: 1**

can we get joe t hill author of wild times to come to walton arena in fayetteville arkansas on july 5 1995 to <u>speak</u> to our english department i hope this distingished speaker can come to our college campas because we will also invites the people in the fayetteville comunity and in the surounding areas

CHAPTER 13 LESSON 4

Check Time, Journal Writing Time, and Analogy Time
Journal Writing Assignment: Make an entry in your journal. (Start with your heading and date.)

Word Analogy Exercise: Choose the correct missing word and put the letter in the blank.

1. Lincoln:Civil::Washington: _____   a. war   b. president   c. Vietnam   d. Revolutionary
2. child:tricycle::adult: _____   a. toddler b. car   c. human   d. toys
3. word:sentence:: _____ :essay   a. pencil   b. paragraph   c. paper   d. assignment

CHAPTER 13 LESSON 5

Writing Assignment

Use the outline and sample paragaph for the Five-Paragraph Persuasive Essay in doing the writing assignment below. Indent each paragraph.

Writing Assignment #18: Five-Paragraph Persuasive Essay in First Person

Topic: Choose a different topic from the one you chose for your other persuasive writings.

1. Why I should be principal for the day
2. Why dogs (or cats) make good pets
3. Why I should have good study habits
4. Why I should be interested in politics
5. Why I am for (or against) smoking (or drinking)
6. Why schools need (or do not need) a dress code
7. Why I think schools should offer _____
8. Why I should plan the school lunch menu
9. Why I should run for President
10. Why I am for (or against) wearing seatbelts
11. Why I need an allowance

Editing Time

Use the *Guidelines for Editing Rough Drafts and for Writing Final Papers* and the *Editing Checklist* in Chapter 4, Lesson 5, to edit Writing Assignment #18. Staple the final paper to the rough draft and put both in the Final Writing Folder until your teacher calls for them.

CHAPTER 14 LESSON 1

Writing Conversation from Dictation

Study the paragraphing and punctuation of the following conversation. Prepare to write the conversation correctly as your teacher dictates it to you.

Dictation Box

"My pencil won't stay sharp. It keeps getting dull," Joey whispered to his friend, Sarah. "I think I must be using it too much. What do you think?"

Sarah looked at Joey thoughtfully before she answered. "I think you must be right. And if I were you, I'd sharpen that pencil at least twice during the school year!"

Assignment

Identify each thought below by putting a slash between each one. Then rewrite the paragraph on a sheet of notebook paper. Correct fragments and improve the long rambling sentences by using different kinds of sentences. Underline simple sentences once, compound sentences twice, and put parentheses around the complex sentences.

when a bee is thirteen to fourteen days old and it is strong enough to handle the jobs of a mature bee and mature bees collect nectar and mature bees fan the hive and mature bees make honey the collecting bees gather pollen to make bee bread for the larvae and the collecting bees also collect nectar and they give it to the adult workers in the hive these adult workers are called the fanners these adult workers are also called the house bees they work together to change the nectar into honey.

Writing Assignment

Use the descriptive writing steps and the descriptive outline in Chapter 7, Lesson 1, if you need them for a reference to do the writing assignment below. After you have finished, put your writing in your Rough Draft Folder.

Writing Assignment #19: Descriptive Paragraph in Third Person

Topic: Plants
Logical narrowed topic: Trees
Writing Topic: **A Tree** . . . (In an Ice Storm, At Christmas Time, In the Spring, Autumn, Summer, etc.)
       Or: Describe a Thing of Your Choice. (Make sure your topic is narrowed enough.)

CHAPTER 14 LESSON 2 SKILL TEST

Exercise 1: Use the Quotation Rules to help punctuate the quotations below. Underline the explanatory words.

1. whew sighed the old timer theres a storm blowing in from the north

2. there is a time limit for this test the teacher said calmly you have thirty minutes to complete it

3. oh no my favorite sweater is ruined wailed elaine

4. the travel guide said yes your flight will stop in atlanta and dallas before arriving in memphis

5. wow squealed the girls this water is too cold for swimming

6. maria giggled samson you are the silliest dog ive ever seen

7. sara smith the intercom crackled please report to the information desk immediately

Exercise 2: Edit the conversation below. **Editing Guide: Capitals: 11   End Marks: 6   Quotation Marks: 10   Commas: 8   Apostrophes: 4**

travis come look at my new car shouted sammy

why sammy replied travis this car doesnt look new at all its missing two doors and the top

oh travis sighed sammy dont you know this is a dune buggy hop in and ill take you for a spin

Exercise 3: Edit the conversation below. **Editing Guide: Capitals: 7   End Marks: 3   Commas: 5   Quotation Marks: 8   Apostrophes: 1**

skip the shop called to say your motorcycle is ready said lois to her brother

skip asked did they say how much the repair bill was

yes replied lois but i dont think you want to hear it

Exercise 4: Edit the conversation below. **Editing Guide: Capitals: 14   End Marks: 10   Commas: 7   Quotation Marks: 14   Apostrophes: 2**

hey joey kevin hollered across the fence to his best friend do you know what my big sister

and her friends are having tonight they are having a no make-up no dress-up no boyfriend party

hmm i wonder what the girls would do if their boyfriends suddenly showed up asked joey

well laughed kevin maybe we should invite the boys and find out

this will be great fun exclaimed joey my sister wont even step outside the house without make-up

so i cant wait to see what the girls do when their boyfriends show up and see them without make-up

CHAPTER 14 LESSON 3 APPLICATION TEST

Exercise 1: Classify each sentence.

1. _____ My boss finally gave me a big raise and a big promotion!

2. _____ Cindy and Linda brought me a huge piece of birthday cake and a large cup of punch.

3. _____ Did you send Andy and Larry a singing telegram for their birthday present?

Directions: Complete the noun job table. Use Sentence 3.

List the Noun Used	List the Noun Job	Singular or Plural	Common or Proper
4.	5.	6.	7.
8.	9.	10.	11.
12.	13.	14.	15.
16.	17.	18.	19.

Exercise 2: Edit the story below. Use the Editing Guide to help you. **Editing Guide: Capitals: 20   Commas: 9 Quotations: 20   Apostrophes: 4   End Marks: 15**

mmm whats that wonderful smell exclaimed cindy

that smell happens to be my special homemade chocolate chip cookies replied the cook smugly

spencer my sweet brother wheedled cindy you make the best cookies i cant wait to eat some

wait a minute these cookies are going to cost you said spencer gleefully waving the plate of

chocolate chip cookies under her nose

oh you make me so mad glared cindy all right whatever you think theyre worth

spencer said triumphantly you can have all these cookies if you and mark will take me along

when you go to the movies tonight

well said cindy as she grinned and reached for a cookie thats a small price to pay are you

buying the popcorn

Exercise 3:   **Editing Paragraph**

Find each error and write the correction. Use the Editing Guide to help you. **Editing Guide: Homonyms:1   Capitals: 17 Apostrophes: 1   A/An: 1   Misspelled Words: 1   Subject-Verb Agreement: 1   Commas: 6   Underlining: 2   End Marks: 4**

my sister vonda and her family live in an small suburb north of cheyenne called big lake they

have titled their small two-acre estate the ponderosa because they all love water sports vondas

family keep a little boat at big daddy lake since my sister named there boat the titanic i have

come to the concluion that they have all gone a little overboard on big names for small things

CHAPTER 14 LESSON 4

Check Time, Journal Writing Time, Analogy Time, and Figures of Speech Time
Journal Writing Assignment: Make an entry in your journal. (Start with your heading and date.)

Word Analogy Exercise: Choose the correct missing word and put the letter in the blank.

1. hungry:ravenous::debris:_____   a. starved   b. trash   c. clean   d. contented
2. five:ten::twenty:_____   a. twenty-five   b. twenty-one   c. fifteen   d. numbers
3. moon:earth::_____:sun   a. stars   b. solar   c. planets   d. yellow

Figures of Speech Exercise: Identify which figure of speech is being used in the sentences below. Write the labels **S** for simile, **M** for metaphor, and **P** for personification.

____ 1. The fatherly old oak hovered over the frightened children.

____ 2. Some clouds look as soft as cotton balls.

____ 3. Fred's tiny house was just a shell.

____ 4. The poppies twirled their red skirts in the wind.

____ 5. After Chad's inappropriate remark, Mrs. Frank was a smoldering fire.

____ 6. The three cubs came tumbling down the snowbank like furry avalanches.

CHAPTER 14 LESSON 5

Narrative Writing with Dialogue

A special element that makes narration especially interesting is conversation. Remember from Chapter 13 that another word for conversation is "dialogue." Writers use dialogue, or conversation, in their short stories or novels because it helps move the plot along, and it helps the reader understand the characters better.

Also, remember that narrative writing is simply the telling of a story. A narrative gives the details of an event and has a beginning, middle, and end. Now you will use another Story Element in narrative writing: dialogue. Since there are a few rules of punctuation and paragraphing you need to review, use the following dialogue to discuss the three rules below:

> Marshall whispered to Chris, "I didn't hear anything,"
> as he took a step backwards.
> His friend's only answer was, "Me neither."

Use these general rules as well as the steps for punctuating quotations in Chapter 13 to help you as you write narratives with dialogue:

1. Dialogue is always placed in quotation marks like a direct quotation. This placement will separate dialogue from any explanatory words or other words that develop the plot of the story.
2. Periods, commas, question marks, and exclamation marks that punctuate dialogue always go INSIDE quotation marks.
3. If more than one character is speaking, you must indent and create a new paragraph each time a different character speaks.

CHAPTER 14 LESSON 5

Read the sample narrative with dialogue below. Look for ways the dialogue develops the plot and helps you understand the story characters.

Once Upon a Time . . .There Was a Ferris Wheel

One year ago my family went to the State Fair. My little sister Angie was four years old, and when she became tired, my dad suggested, "Why don't you take your sister to ride the Ferris wheel?"

"Aw, Dad," I complained, "you know that when Angie gets in a bad mood, practically nothing pleases her." But I finally agreed to do it.

Actually it wasn't so bad the first two rounds, and I was beginning to think it was O.K., when all of a sudden, I heard a loud "Bang!" and saw a puff of smoke coming from a telephone pole. I didn't pay much attention to it until a few minutes later when the Ferris wheel ground to a stop, with Angie and me sitting at the very top of the world.

I probably would have thought we were only loading and unloading, except I knew we had only been around twice. Then I figured it out: power failure.

"Linny," Angie whined, wrinkling her forehead and curling up her lip, "I wanna get off."

"Sit still," I said. "We can't get off until the Ferris wheel comes back down."

In about three minutes, she started crying, and in about two more minutes she was screaming and kicking her feet. At first I tried yelling at her, but I saw that wasn't going to work. Suddenly, I had an idea. "Listen," I said desperately, "let me tell you a story!"

"Okay," Angie said in a cheerful voice as she calmed down and leaned her head on my shoulder.

Relieved, I started "Little Red Riding Hood." I finished it and continued with "The Three Little Pigs," "The Three Bears" (all the "littles" and "threes" I could think of), "Cinderella," "Sleeping Beauty," "Beauty and the Beast," "Aladdin," and everything else I had ever seen on Disney.

Anyway, one hour later, after my mouth had dried out and Angie had fallen asleep from boredom, power was restored, and we arrived safe on earth again.

Now, not only do I have a bad feeling about Ferris wheels, but I also never want to even think about another fairy tale as long as I live.

Discussion Points

Dialogue often "shows" instead of "tells" in narratives. Notice how the dialogue does just that in this narrative. In the first paragraph, Linny "shows" by what she replies to her father that she does not really want to take Angie on a Ferris wheel ride.

Dialogue also "shows" what a character is like. It is much better than the writer's "telling" what a character is like. Linny's personal quotations show the reader a great deal about her relationship to her little sister. Her little sister frequently "bugs" her; but Linny can be patient in a tight situation.

CHAPTER 14 LESSON 5

Writing Assignment

Choose one of the following story starters and then use the Writing Steps for Narratives with Dialogue below to finish writing a story with dialogue. Put your finished writing in your Rough Draft folder.

Writing Assignment #20: Narrative Writing Using Dialogue (First or Third Person)

Story Starter 1 As you go to the gorilla cage to check the food and water, you suddenly realize the door is already open, and Mugsy, the gorilla, is gone!

Story Starter 2 Phil and Phlo, the two houseflies, were uncertain where the smell was coming from, but they knew it made them hungry. "Look out!" yelled Phlo as the swatter missed her by inches.

Story Starter 3 Garland tiptoed past his sister's room. He gestured for Tony to follow him. If Gwen should wake up, his mom would insist that he and Tony take her along.

Story Starter 4 Your choice. You make up your own story and your own characters.

Writing Steps for Narratives with Dialogue

1. Make a Story Elements Outline after you have selected the story starter for your narrative writing assignment. (Story Elements: Main idea, Setting, Character, Plot, Ending)

2. Check your Story Elements Outline as you write your story to make sure you keep your writing focused on the main idea and to help you choose details and events that support the main idea.

3. Think about what is already happening in the story and then use your imagination to write about what happens next. **Remember to use dialogue to develop the plot and personalities of the characters.**

4. Continue telling the story in the order that you want the events to happen. Remember to keep your details and events focused on the main idea of the story.

5. Look over what has happened in the story and decide on an ending that makes sense.

6. The title in a narrative is usually written after the story is finished. Go back and read the story that you have written and think of a title that will tell what your story is about.

Share Time

Share your Assignment #20, Narrative Writing Using Dialogue, with your class.
Your teacher will tell you if you will be sharing in small groups or with the whole class. Your teacher will also tell you what to do with your audience response sheet after the stories have been read. Remember to be courteous to other students as you listen to their stories.

Share Time Guidelines	
Reader Preparation	**Audience Response**

1. Have your paper ready to read when called upon.
2. Write the title of your story on the board.
3. Stand with your feet flat on the floor and your shoulders straight. Do not shift your weight as you stand.
4. Hold your paper about chin high to help you project your voice to your audience.
5. Make sure you do not read too fast.
6. Read in a clear voice that can be heard so that your audience does not have to strain to hear you.
7. Change your voice tone for different characters or for different parts of the story.
	1. Pay attention and listen attentively.
	2. After each reader finishes reading his/her story, the audience (students) will write a brief response to the reader's story using the guidelines below.
	  1. Title of the story
	  2. Main idea
	    (what character had to do to solve problem)
	  3. Setting (time and place of story)
	  4. Main character
	  5. Favorite part of the story
	  6. Liked or disliked the ending because...

CHAPTER 15 LESSON 1

Mixed Patterns 1-3

The sentences that you classify with your teacher will be a mixture of Pattern 1: SN V P1, Pattern 2: SN V-t DO P2, and Pattern 3: SN V-t IO DO P3. As you classify these sentences, look carefully at the main parts so you can identify the correct pattern for each sentence.

Writing a Friendly Letter

A letter written to or received from friends or relatives is called a **friendly letter**. Writing a friendly letter is a great way to stay in touch with people you care about and who care about you. Below you will find some tips that will make your friendly letter interesting and enjoyable to read.

Tips for Writing Friendly Letters

Tip #1: Write as if you were talking to the person face-to-face. Share information about yourself and mutual friends. Tell stories, conversations, or jokes. Share photographs, articles, drawings, poems, etc. Avoid saying something about someone else that you'll be sorry for later.

Tip #2: If you are writing a return letter, be sure to answer any questions that were asked. Repeat the question so that your reader will know what you are writing about. (You asked about . . .)

Tip #3: End your letter in a positive way so that your reader will want to write a return letter.

The Five Parts of a Friendly Letter

Now that you know what things to write about, you must learn to put your friendly letter in correct friendly letter form. The friendly letter has five parts:

1. Heading   2. Friendly Greeting or Salutation   3. Body   4. Closing   5. Signature

Look at these five parts of a friendly letter below.

The Parts of a Friendly Letter

1. Heading
1. Box or street address of writer
2. City, state, zip code of writer
3. Date letter was written
4. Placement: upper right hand corner

2. Friendly Greeting or Salutation
1. Begins with *Dear*
2. Names person receiving the letter
3. Has comma after person's name
4. Placement: at left margin, two lines below heading

3. Body
1. Tells reason the letter was written
2. Can have one or more paragraphs
3. Has indented paragraphs
4. Is placed one line after the greeting
5. Skips one line between each paragraph

4. Closing
1. Closes letter with a personal phrase-(Your friend, With love,)
2. Capitalizes only first word
3. Is followed by a comma
4. Is placed two lines below the body
5. Begins just to the right of the middle of the letter

5. Signature
1. Tells who wrote the letter
2. Is usually signed in cursive
3. Uses first name only unless there is a question as to which friend or relative you are
4. Is placed beneath the closing

CHAPTER 15 LESSON 1

Each of the parts of a friendly letter has a specific place it should be written in order for your letter to have correct friendly letter form. Look at the friendly letter example below. Notice each of the five parts, what information is contained in each part, and where each part is placed in the friendly letter.

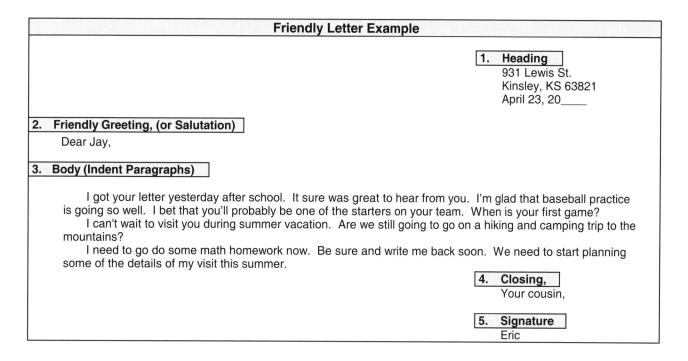

Friendly Letter Example

1. Heading
931 Lewis St.
Kinsley, KS 63821
April 23, 20____

2. Friendly Greeting, (or Salutation)
Dear Jay,

3. Body (Indent Paragraphs)

   I got your letter yesterday after school. It sure was great to hear from you. I'm glad that baseball practice is going so well. I bet that you'll probably be one of the starters on your team. When is your first game?
   I can't wait to visit you during summer vacation. Are we still going to go on a hiking and camping trip to the mountains?
   I need to go do some math homework now. Be sure and write me back soon. We need to start planning some of the details of my visit this summer.

4. Closing,
Your cousin,

5. Signature
Eric

In order to address the envelope of your friendly letter correctly, you must know the parts that go on the envelope and where to write them. Look at the envelope parts and example below. Notice each of the parts, what information is contained in each part, and where each part is placed on the envelope.

Envelope Parts	Friendly Envelope Example

The return address:
1. Name of the person writing the letter
2. Box or street address of the writer
3. City, state, zip code of the writer
 	
The mailing address:
1. Name of the person receiving the letter
2. Street address of the person receiving the letter
3. City, state, zip of the person receiving the letter
	Return Address
	Eric Miller
	931 Lewis Street
	Kinsley, KS 63821 Stamp
	
	       Mailing Address
	       Jay Kingfisher
	       1234 Little Street
	       Pawnee, OK 74058

CHAPTER 15 LESSON 1 SKILL TEST A

Exercise 1: In the numbered boxes below, write the five parts of a friendly letter.

Friendly Letter Parts

1.	2.	4.
Box or street	Dear _____,	Your friend,
City, state, zip code	**3.**	**5.**
Date	_____ _____ _____	Writer's First and/or Last Name

Exercise 2: Draw a line to separate all the parts and sentences of the friendly letter in the box below. Then on notebook paper, use the information from the Friendly Letter Information Box below to write a friendly letter in the correct form. Capitalize and punctuate as needed.

Friendly Letter Information Box

From: maria hernandez 341 southbend road great plains montana 89762 september 30 20____ dear carlos i am looking forward to my first winter in montana i am already wearing a sweater mexico seems so far away but I love it here ill write more later your sister

To: carlos garcia 1527 pablo drive mexico city mexico 99872

Exercise 3: In the numbered boxes below, write the two parts of an envelope used for a friendly letter.

Friendly Envelope Parts

1.	2.
Writer's Name Box or street City, state, zip code	Name of Receiver Box or street City, state, zip code

Exercise 4: On notebook paper, draw an envelope and use the parts in your Friendly Letter Information Box above to help you address the envelope correctly. Also, draw a stamp on your envelope.

Exercise 5: Answer these questions about the friendly letter and envelope you have just completed.

1. Who wrote the letter?
2. Who will receive the letter?
3. When was the letter written?
4. Where does the writer live?
5. What closing did the writer use?
6. What greeting did this writer use?
7. What is another word for greeting?
8. What name is in the mailing address?
9. What name is in the return address?
10. Where does the person receiving the letter live?
11. What is this letter about?
12. Did you draw a stamp on the envelope?
13. What are the five parts of a friendly letter?
14. What is the hardest part for you?

CHAPTER 15 LESSON 2

Writing Conversation from Dictation

Study the paragraphing and punctuation of the following conversation. Prepare to write the conversation correctly as your teacher dictates it to you.

Dictation Box

"Well, we finally made it to DisneyWorld before our kids grew up," said Dad with a tired smile on his face as the bus made its way back to the motel.

"Coming to DisneyWorld for our vacation makes those last two years of overtime worth it, doesn't it?" asked his wife.

Dad grinned broadly as he surveyed his two teenage sons and young daughter. "Yes, it was worth it," he replied thoughtfully. "We get four whole days to see and do things that we could only dream about at home!"

"Hey, Dad! Dave and I want to go to the movies tomorrow instead of DisneyWorld," his thirteen-year-old son announced as they got off the bus. "We've been wanting to see this movie for weeks, and it is just down the street from our motel!"

Writing Assignment

Use the friendly letter situation given below to write a friendly letter. Then draw a friendly letter envelope on the back of your friendly letter and fill in the mailing address and the return address. Remember to draw a stamp and use today's date.

Writing Assignment #21: Friendly Letter

Friendly Letter Situation: You live at #35 Post Oak Lane, Russellville, TN 38976. You are writing your Uncle Harvey Knight, who lives at 200 Berkely Trail, Miles City, Montana 48890. Your uncle has just recently moved to Montana from Tennessee and operates a youth ranch for orphaned children. Tell your uncle what has been going on in Tennessee since he moved. Ask to come and visit and be a ranch hand this summer.

CHAPTER 15 LESSON 3

Types of Business Letters

Sharing information with a friend or relative is not the only reason to write a letter. Sometimes you may need to write a letter to someone you do not know, about something that is not personal in nature. This kind of letter is called a **business letter**. Even if you are not in business, there are several reasons why you may need to write a business letter. Look at the reasons for writing a business letter that are listed below and then read the guidelines that tell you what information to include in each type of business letter.

These are four common reasons to write a business letter:

1. If you need to send for information - letter of inquiry.
2. If you want to order a product - order letter.
3. If you want to express an opinion - letter to an editor or official.
4. If you want to complain about a product - letter of complaint.

Guidelines for Writing Different Types of Business Letters	
Letter of Inquiry	**Order Letter**
1. Ask for information or answers to your questions. 2. Keep the letter short and to the point. 3. Word the letter so that there can be no question as to what it is you need to know.	1. Carefully and clearly describe the product. 2. Keep the letter short and to the point. 3. Include information on how and where the product should be shipped. 4. Include information on how you will pay for the product.
Letter to an Editor or Official	**Letter of Complaint About a Product**
1. Clearly explain the problem or situation. 2. Offer your opinion of the cause and possible solutions. 3. Support your opinions with facts and examples. 4. Suggest ways to change or improve the situation.	1. Carefully and clearly describe the product. 2. Describe the problem and what may have caused it. (Don't spend too much time explaining how unhappy you are.) 3. Explain any action you have already taken to solve the problem. 4. End your letter with the action you would like the company to take to solve the problem.

CHAPTER 15 LESSON 3

Now that you know the different types of business letters, you must learn to put your business letter in correct business letter form. Look at the parts of a business letter and the sample business letter below. Notice each of the six parts, what information is contained in each part, and where each part is placed in the business letter.

The Six Parts of a Business Letter

1. **Heading:** The heading for a business letter includes the writer's complete address and the full date. The heading is placed about an inch from the top of the page.

2. **Inside Address:** The inside address includes the name and complete address of the person and/or company you are writing. Place a person's title after his/her name. Separate the title from the name with a comma. If the title is two or more words, place the title separately on the next line. The inside address is placed two lines below the heading.

3. **Formal Greeting or Salutation:** A formal greeting is placed two lines below the inside address. For a specific person, use a greeting like *Dear Mr.* (last name) or *Ms.* (last name). For a letter addressed to a person by title, use *Dear Sir, Dear Madam*, or *Dear* (Title). For a company or organization, use *Gentlemen, Dear Sirs*, or *Dear* (Company name). Place a colon at the end of a business greeting. (Check the first line of the inside address to determine the right greeting to use.)

4. **Body:** The information in the body of any business letter should be clearly and briefly written. Skip a line between each paragraph. The body of the business letter is placed two lines below the greeting.

5. **Closing:** Use a formal phrase for a business-letter closing (*Very truly, Yours truly, Sincerely*). Place a comma at the end of the closing. The closing is placed two lines below the body.

6. **Signature:** A business letter is ended by signing your name beneath the closing. If you are typing your letter, skip four lines and type your full name. Then, write your signature between the closing and your typed name.

BUSINESS LETTER EXAMPLE

1. HEADING
438 Simmons Street
Oilton, OK 38669
January 17, 20____

2. INSIDE ADDRESS
Ms. Marianne Folsom, Advertising
Sunlight Publishing Company
6220 Yale Blvd.
Glennwood, Mississippi 82505

3. FORMAL GREETING, (OR SALUTATION)
Dear Ms. Folsom:

4. BODY (INDENT PARAGRAPHS)

Please accept my order for a half-page ad in your magazine, Solar Energy Today, to be placed in the fall issue.

I am enclosing a copy of the ad with my application. You may bill me at the address above.

5. FORMAL CLOSING,
Sincerely yours,

6. SIGNATURE
Sam R. Williams

CHAPTER 15 LESSON 3

Envelope for a Business Letter

In order to address the envelope of your business letter correctly, you must know the parts that go on the envelope and where to write them. Look at the envelope parts and example below.

Notice that these parts are similar to the parts of an envelope for a friendly letter. There are two differences in the mailing address for the business envelope:

(1) You must put the name of the person within the company to whom you are writing and his/her title (if you know it) on the first line of the mailing address.

(2) You must put the name of the company on the second line of the mailing address. If you do not know the name of a particular person in the company who would handle your request or problem, you can just choose a department within the company (such as, SALES, SHIPPING, ACCOUNTING, etc.) to write on the first line of your mailing address, or you can leave the first line blank.

Envelope Parts	Business Envelope Example
The return address: 1. Name of the person writing the letter 2. Box or street address of the writer 3. City, state zip code of the writer **The mailing address:** 1. Name of the person receiving the letter 2. Name of the company receiving the letter 3. Street address of the person receiving the letter 4. City, state, zip of the person receiving the letter	**Return Address** stamp Sam R. Williams 438 Simmons Street Oilton, OK 38669 **Mailing Address** Ms. Marianne Folsom, Advertising Sunlight Publishing Company 6220 Yale Blvd. Glennwood, Mississippi 82505

Figures of Speech Time

Figures of Speech Exercise: Identify which figure of speech is being used in the sentences below. Write the labels **S** for simile, **M** for metaphor, and **P** for personification.

____ 1. The little boys marched off like a troop of dwarves.

____ 2. She is a tiger when she gets upset.

____ 3. We watched the dancing raindrops.

____ 4. The metal bridge announced the approach of a visitor.

____ 5. They were as nervous as a flock of turkeys on Thanksgiving.

____ 6. Cherie, you little gremlin, give me back my five dollars.

CHAPTER 15 LESSON 3 SKILL TEST B

Exercise 1: In the numbered boxes below, write the six parts of a business letter.

Business Letter Parts

1.	2.	3.		5.
Box or street City, state, zip code Date	Name of Receiver Name of Company Box or street City, state, zip code	Dear Mr./Ms._____:		Sincerely yours,
		4. _____ _____ _____		**6.** Writer's Full Name

Exercise 2: Draw a line to separate all the parts and sentences of the business letter in the box below. Then on notebook paper, use the information from the Business Letter Information Box to write a business letter in the correct form. Capitalize and punctuate as needed.

Business Letter Information Box

From: janette woods 578 hudson street white cloud michigan 82023 october 1 20____ dear mr hames i would like to order the blue deluxe sleeping bag #568 in your catalog enclosed is my check for $48.95 please send the sleeping bag by ups sincerely yours

To: robert c hames casey hunting supplies 1422 riverdale drive rifle colorado 79987

Exercise 3: In the numbered boxes below, write the two parts of an envelope used for a business letter.

Business Envelope Parts

1.	2.
Writer's Name Box or street City, state, zip code	Name of Receiver Name of Company Box or street City, state, zip code

Exercise 4: On your notebook paper, draw an envelope and use the parts in your Business Letter Information Box to help you address the envelope correctly. Also, draw a stamp on your envelope.

Exercise 5: Answer these questions about the business letter and envelope you have just completed.

1. Who wrote the letter?
2. Who will receive the letter?
3. When was the letter written?
4. Where does the writer live?
5. What closing did the writer use?
6. What greeting did this writer use?
7. What is another word for greeting?
8. What name is in the mailing address?
9. What name is in the return address?
10. Where does the person receiving the letter live?
11. What is this letter about?
12. Did you draw a stamp on the envelope?
13. What are the six parts of a business letter?
14. What is the hardest part for you?

CHAPTER 15 LESSON 4 APPLICATION TEST

Exercise 1: Mixed Patterns 1-3. Classify each sentence.

1. _____ My teacher gave Jamie and Susan a big homework assignment over the holiday weekend.

2. _____ Maria and Lindsey climbed over the wall and sneaked into the concert during spring break.

3. _____ Did you send Victoria a box of candy for her birthday?

Directions: Complete the noun job table. Use Sentence 1.

List the Noun Used	List the Noun Job	Singular or Plural	Common or Proper
4.	5.	6.	7.
8.	9.	10.	11.
12.	13.	14.	15.
16.	17.	18.	19.
20.	21.	22.	23.

Exercise 2: Writing Assignment

Use the business letter situation given below to write a business letter. Then draw a business letter envelope on the back of your business letter and fill in the mailing address and the return address. Put your finished writing in your Rough Draft Folder.

Writing Assignment #22: Business Letter

Business Letter Situation: Read the advertisement below and select one pet you wish to order. Write a business letter, placing your order. Use your own mailing address. You will find all the information you need to order your pet if you read the ad very carefully.

LOVE-A-PET
Unusual Pets for Unusual Persons

Now you can own that VERY SPECIAL
UNUSUAL PET that you've never thought of before!

Select from these favorites
LLAMAS   **$75.00**
COATI MUNDI **$55.00**
WOMBATS   **$45.00**

And now for a limited time only
At the fantastically reduced rate of $7.50
GENUINE PIT VIPERS

Simply send the amount above plus only
$100 for shipping and handling to

LOVE-A-PET
3202 Everglade Trail
Swampland, FL 25000

CHAPTER 15 LESSON 5

You usually write thank-you notes to thank someone for a gift or for doing something nice for you. In either case, a thank-you note should include at least three statements.

1. You should tell the person <u>what</u> you are thanking him/her for.
2. You should tell the person <u>how the gift was used</u> or <u>how it helped</u>.
3. You should tell the person <u>how much you appreciated the gift or action</u>.

For a Gift	
What -	Thank you for... (tell color, kind, and item)
Use -	Tell how the gift is used.
Thanks -	I appreciate your remembering me with this special gift.

For an Action	
What -	Thank you for... (tell action)
Helped -	Tell how the action helped.
Thanks -	I appreciate your thinking of me at this time.

A thank-you note should follow the same form as a friendly letter: heading, greeting, body, closing, and signature.

Example 1:

1519 Lewis Road
London, Ohio 46281
November 30, 20____

Dear Grandma,

Thank you for the warm ski gloves. They arrived just in time for my ski trip! I appreciate your thoughtful gift.

Love always,

Rebecca

Example 2:

1910 Lincoln Street
West Plains, Iowa 60311
March 1, 20____

Dear David,

Thank you for helping with the Coats for Tots Campaign. Our work was a huge success because of people like you. I appreciate your help very much.

Your friend,

Lee

Writing Assignment
Use the steps and examples of the thank-you notes above as you do the writing assignment below. Put your finished writing in your Rough Draft folder.

Writing Assignment #23: Thank-you Note

You are writing a thank you note to your Uncle Kirk for the motorcycle magazines he brought you when you were in the hospital. Use your own address and today's date.

CHAPTER 15 LESSON 5

An invitation should include the following information in any logical order.

1.   What   – Tell what the event or special occasion is.

2.   Who   – Tell whom the event is for.

3.   Where   – Tell where the event will take place.

4.   When   – Tell the date and time of the event.

5.   Whipped cream statement - A polite statement written to make the person feel welcome.

An invitation will sometimes have an R.S.V.P. This is a French expression that means "please respond," and a reply is needed. If a phone number is included, reply by phone. Otherwise, a written reply is expected.

Example for an Invitation	
1. What	– a farewell party
2. Who	– for Mindy Miller
3. Where	– at 1724 Waterway Drive
4. When	– on Saturday, July 1, at 2:00
5. Whipped Cream	– I hope you can come!

An invitation should follow the same form as a friendly letter: heading, greeting, body, closing, and signature. Notice how the five parts of an invitation are used in the written invitation below. They are underlined in the example; however, you would not underline them in an actual invitation.

> 1724 Waterway Drive
> Boston, Florida 44629
> June 15, 20____
>
> Dear Stephanie,
>
>   You are invited to a <u>farewell party</u> for <u>Mindy Miller</u>. She is moving to Ohio. The party will be at <u>2:00 on Saturday, July 1</u>, in our backyard at <u>1724 Waterway Drive</u>. Lots of games and food are planned. <u>We hope to see you there</u>!
>
>   Your friend,
>
>   Lisa Scott

Writing Assignment

Use the steps and example of the invitation above as you do the writing assignment below. Put your finished writing in your Rough Draft folder.

Writing Assignment #24: Invitation

You are writing an invitation to your best friend, inviting him/her to your birthday pizza-fest. The party starts at 6:30 P.M. on (your birthday) at (place of your choosing). (Don't forget your whipped cream statement.) For the heading, use your own address and today's date.

CHAPTER 15 LESSON 5

Writing Assignment

Use the steps and examples of the thank-you notes as you do the writing assignment below. Put your finished writing in your Rough Draft Folder.

Writing Assignment #25 and #26: Thank-you Notes

Using the information in the *Situation Box*, write two thank-you notes on your own notebook paper. Use Situation A for your first thank-you note and Situation B for your second thank-you note. Remember the form of a thank-you note is the same as a friendly letter.

Situation Box	
Thank-you Note, Situation A	**Thank-you Note, Situation B**
A. You are Princess Cinderella Royal Palace, West Wing Imagi, Nation 91111 You are writing a thank-you note to your stepmother: (You supply the reason.) Lady Ima Griper 876 Crosspatch Road Imagi, Nation 91111	B. You are Prince Maximillian (husband of Cinderella) Royal Palace, West Wing Imagi, Nation 91111 You are writing a thank-you note to your employee who successfully searched for and found your bride (the one who lost the glass slipper at the ball): Dooley Trackem Captain of the Guards Gatekeeper's Cottage Royal Road Imagi, Nation 91111

CHAPTER 16 LESSON 1

Sentence Pattern 4

Earlier, you learned that nouns can have different jobs, or functions, in a sentence. You have studied four of these jobs already: A noun can be a subject, an object of a preposition, an indirect object, or a direct object. You must remember, however, that a noun used as an object of a preposition is not a basic part of a sentence pattern.

In the new sentence pattern, **Pattern 4**, there are only two nouns in the basic sentence pattern: **N LV N**. The first noun is a subject noun and is still written as **SN**. The second noun is called a predicate noun and is written with the abbreviation **PrN**.

Notice that in this new pattern, there is a different kind of verb in the basic sentence pattern, the linking verb, and it will always be written with the abbreviation **LV**. A predicate noun will always come after a linking verb. This fourth pattern in the Shurley Method is subject noun / linking verb / predicate noun / Pattern 4, and it is written as **SN LV PrN P4**.

Predicate Noun and Linking Verb

1. A **predicate noun** is a noun or pronoun after the verb that means the same thing as the subject.
2. A **predicate noun** is labeled as *PrN*.
3. To find the **predicate noun**, ask WHAT or WHO after the verb.
4. A **predicate noun** is often called a predicate nominative.
5. A **predicate noun** is always after a linking verb.
6. A **linking verb** links or connects the subject to a predicate noun or a predicate pronoun.

Sample Sentence for the exact words to say to find the linking verb and predicate noun.

1. Dad is an excellent carpenter.
2. Who is an excellent carpenter? Dad - SN
3. What is being said about Dad? Dad is - V
4. Dad is what? carpenter - verify the noun
5. Does carpenter mean the same thing as Dad? Yes.
6. Carpenter - PrN
   (Say: Carpenter - Predicate Noun.)
7. Is - LV *(Say: Is - Linking Verb.)*
8. What kind of carpenter? excellent - Adj
9. An - A
10. SN LV PrN P4 Check *(Say: Subject Noun, Linking Verb, Predicate Noun, Pattern 4, Check.)*
11. Check the verb: linking verb.
12. Check again for prepositional phrases.
13. No prepositional phrases.
14. Period, statement, declarative sentence
15. Go back to the verb - divide the complete subject from the complete predicate.
16. Is there an adverb exception? No.
17. Is this sentence in a natural or inverted order? Natural - no change.

CHAPTER 16 LESSON 1

A question and answer example of Sentence 5 from the Introductory Sentences is written out for you below.

Question and Answer Flow Example

Question and Answer Flow for Sentence 5: My favorite uncle became a successful journalist in the newspaper business.

1. Who became a successful journalist in the newspaper business? uncle - SN
2. What is being said about uncle? uncle became - V
3. Uncle became what? journalist - verify the noun
4. Does journalist mean the same thing as uncle? Yes.
5. Journalist - PrN
6. Became - LV
7. What kind of journalist? successful - Adj
8. A - A
9. In - P
10. In what? business - OP
11. What kind of business? newspaper - Adj
12. The - A
13. What kind of (or which) uncle? favorite - Adj
14. Whose uncle? my - PPA
15. SN LV PrN P4 Check
16. Check the verb: linking verb.
17. Check again for prepositional phrases.
18. (In the newspaper business) - Prepositional phrase
19. Period, statement, Declarative sentence
20. Go back to the verb - divide the complete subject from the complete predicate.
21. Is there an adverb exception? No.
22. Is this sentence in a natural or inverted order? Natural - no change.

Classified Sentence:

```
                      PPA Adj  SN    LV   A   Adj      PrN    P  A   Adj      OP
          SN LV    My favorite uncle / became a successful journalist (in the newspaper business.)  D
          PrN P4
```

Assignment

1. Write one **Practice Sentence** following these labels:

   A   Adj   SN   Prep   A   OP   LV   PPA   PrN

2. Write an **Improved Sentence** from the Practice Sentence. Make at least two synonym changes, one antonym change, and your choice of complete word changes.

Writing Conversation from Dictation

Study the paragraphing and punctuation of the following conversation. Prepare to write the conversation correctly as your teacher dictates it to you.

Dictation Box

"Grandpa! Grandpa!" yelled Donnie. "I got one! I got a big one! It's so big that I can't pull it in! Come help me!"

"I'm on my way, boy! Don't let it get away!" Grandpa said as he slid down the steep bank and hurried to help Donnie.

"Grandpa," Donnie said earnestly, "do you think I could have it mounted?"

"Of course you can have it mounted!" Grandpa said excitedly as Donnie worked hard to bring the big fish in.

Donnie looked mournfully at his grandpa, but his grandpa was smiling as he looked across the lake. Then he said, "Donnie, those big fish are smart. Just when you think you've got them, they give you the slip." Grandpa paused and then added, "But at least you got his boots!"

CHAPTER 16 LESSON 1

Assignment

Identify each thought below by putting a slash between each one. Then rewrite the paragraph on a sheet of notebook paper. Correct fragments and improve the long rambling sentences by using different kinds of sentences. Underline simple sentences once, compound sentences twice, and put parentheses around the complex sentences.

The fanners cool the hive and the fanners help make honey by flapping their wings to produce a strong current of air and the house bees hold drops of nectar on their tongue in front of this air current and the current of air evaporates the water in the nectar until it is the right thickness for honey and then they put the honey in a wax storage cell and then they seal it and the honey stays there until it ripens and then it is used as food for the hive.

CHAPTER 16 LESSON 2

Writing Conversation from Dictation

Study the paragraphing and punctuation of the following conversation. Prepare to write the conversation correctly as your teacher dictates it to you.

Dictation Box

"We're lost. I know we're lost," grumbled Ricky's sister as she followed closely behind. "I thought I hated hiking, but now I know I hate hiking." She stopped long enough to swat another mosquito and then added, "I also hate brothers who get me into messes like this!"

"Now, Melody, don't get discouraged," Ricky said as he tried to calm her. "It's just a two-hour hike, and you promised you'd try to have a good time. Besides, it was your idea, remember!"

Melody glared at her older brother. "I want you to know that it was Mom's idea. She was the one who wouldn't let me go to the concert without you. I just didn't think I would have to hike two miles to get you to take me to the concert!"

CHAPTER 16 LESSON 2

Persuasive Friendly Letter

A **persuasive friendly letter** will have all the parts of a friendly letter in it, and it will also have some of the features of a persuasive essay. Remember, in persuasive writing you must consider the person whom you are trying to persuade.

A friendly persuasive letter is easy to write because it is usually easy to present a "case" for something you already like, want, or believe. In presenting your "case," or giving your reasons, you are presenting what is called the "argument." The following letter is an example of a persuasive friendly letter.

Sample Persuasive Friendly Letter

922 Ocean Drive
Baker, Oregon 52000
July 8, 20____

Dear John,

I'm glad you're coming to town to visit your aunt and uncle for two weeks, and I know you had planned to go swimming at the lake this weekend. Well, I have another idea for you to consider.

If possible, I'd like you to go with me Thursday through Saturday to the mountains upstate. It will be our only opportunity to go while you're here. My parents have arranged for the two of us to have our own cabin for two nights! Remember how you love hiking and swimming? We'll be able to hike all the way to Wymer Peak and swim at Cascade Falls.

Think it over and call me if you can change your plans.

Your friend,

Bill

Notice what Bill has done in the sample letter. He has considered his "audience," John the reader. He has presented his case for going to the mountains and has made his appeal based on two things that he knows John likes: hiking and swimming. Also, he has mentioned the extra persuasive attraction of the boys' having their own cabin for two nights. How can John resist?

Discussion Points

Study the persuasive friendly letter above. Like a short persuasive essay, it has three paragraphs.

The **first paragraph** is the introduction, and it contains two things:
1. A polite statement of greeting.
2. A statement that acknowledges the reader's position.

The **second paragraph** is the body. It contains two things:
1. A statement of the point or points you are trying to persuade your reader to accept.
2. The reasons why your reader should consider your position.

The **third paragraph** is the conclusion. It contains one thing: A request for a response from your reader.

CHAPTER 16 LESSON 2

You are now going to combine your knowledge of persuasive writing and letter writing to write a persuasive letter. Your first letter will be a **persuasive friendly letter**. It will have all the parts of a friendly letter in it; so, you must remember all you have learned about writing a friendly letter. The letter will also have some of the features of a persuasive essay, so you must remember to consider the person whom you are trying to persuade.

Steps for Writing a Persuasive Friendly Letter
1. Follow the friendly letter form.
2. Know that persuasion means getting other people to see things your way.
3. Know that your audience is the person you are trying to persuade.
4. State the point or points you are trying to persuade your audience to accept.
5. Think about what your audience likes or dislikes.
6. Consider the audience's likes or dislikes when choosing the reasons you will use to persuade the audience.
7. Present your reasons by using carefully-chosen words that will influence your audience to consider your request.
8. Ask your audience to respond to your request.
9. Remember that a persuasive letter has an introduction, body, and conclusion, just like the persuasive essay.

Writing Assignment

Use the *Steps for Writing a Persuasive Friendly Letter* and the *Sample Persuasive Friendly Letter* as you do the writing assignment below. Put your finished writing in your Rough Draft folder.

Writing Assignment #27: Use the persuasive friendly letter situation below.

Persuasive Friendly Letter Situation

Your assignment is to write a persuasive friendly letter to one of your friends, persuading her/him to come to your house this weekend and help you prepare a surprise birthday meal for one of your relatives. Be sure to consider your "audience," your friend, the reader. Present your case and make your appeal based on one or two things that you know your friend likes. If you can think of an extra persuasive attraction to help persuade your friend, include it in your letter. Finally, draw and address an envelope for your letter, and don't forget to draw a stamp.

Letter and Envelope Information

To: John Parker, Route 6, Box 47-A, Leeds, Oregon 53333
From: Bill Martin, 922 Midfield Drive, Anderson, Oregon 52000

CHAPTER 16 LESSON 3

Persuasive Business Letter

Your next letter is the persuasive business letter. Follow the form for a business letter. Also, always remember that in any form of persuasive writing, you must consider the person whom you are trying to persuade.

Steps for Writing a Persuasive Business Letter

1. Follow the business letter form.
2. Know that persuasion means getting other people to see things your way.
3. Know that your audience is the person you are trying to persuade.
4. State the point or points you are trying to persuade your audience to accept.
5. Think about what your audience likes or dislikes.
6. Consider the audience's likes or dislikes when choosing the reasons you will use to persuade the audience.
7. Present your reasons by using carefully chosen words that will influence your audience to consider your request.
8. Ask your audience to respond to your request.
9. Remember that a persuasive letter has an introduction, body, and conclusion, just like the persuasive essay.

In the sample letter below, Anne Morris has started her own baby-sitting service, and she wants to persuade parents of small children that she would be a great baby-sitter. You will see how Anne has taken some time considering what parents of small children would like to find in a baby-sitter whom they would hire.

Sample Persuasive Business Letter

755 Sunset Drive
Vista, Utah 84091
June 5, 20____

Mr. and Mrs. Phil Franks
890 Bridgeford Street
Vista, Utah 84091

Dear Mr. and Mrs. Franks:

    I have just started my own baby-sitting service, and I would be happy to baby-sit your children, Mark and Laura, any time you need me.

    I love children and enjoy doing activities with them. I will follow all instructions you give me. Also, I will take my job seriously by watching your children carefully and by not spending time talking on the phone or having friends over to visit.

    I believe you will find me a responsible baby-sitter. I will be glad to supply references of satisfied customers. If you are interested, you may call me at 999-0000. Thank you.

Sincerely,

Anne Morris

CHAPTER 16 LESSON 3

Discussion Points

Look at the persuasive business letter on the previous page. Like a short persuasive essay, it has three paragraphs.

The **first paragraph** is the introduction, and it contains two things. Notice that Anne has put these two things in one sentence. You could put them in either one or two sentences.
1. Introduction to her business (what she wants to sell - in this case, babysitting service).
2. Her desire to serve her customers.

The **second paragraph** is the body. It contains your qualifications (why she is qualified to be their babysitter). Notice that Anne does not make a statement saying she believes she is qualified. She simply gives her qualifications.
1. I love children...
2. I will follow all instructions...
3. I will take my job seriously...

The **third paragraph** is the conclusion. It contains four things.
1. A summary sentence re-stating that she believes herself to be qualified to serve her customers.
2. An offer to supply references. References are names, addresses, and phone numbers of people for whom she has worked before, who will be willing to "put in a good word" for her.
3. Her phone number.
4. Thank you.

CHAPTER 16 LESSON 3 APPLICATION TEST

Exercise 1: Classify each sentence.

1. _____ After sunset the rain became sleet.

2. _____ The best mathematicians in our class are you and Beth.

3. _____ My uncle is a collector of rare art from Japan.

Directions: Complete the noun job table. Use Sentence 3.

List the Noun Used	List the Noun Job	Singular or Plural	Common or Proper
4.	5.	6.	7.
8.	9.	10.	11.
12.	13.	14.	15.
16.	17.	18.	19.

Exercise 2:
You are now going to combine your knowledge of persuasive writing and letter writing to write your second persuasive letter. Your second letter will be a **persuasive business letter**. It will have all the parts of a business letter in it; so, you must remember all you have learned about writing a business letter. The letter will also have some of the features of a persuasive essay; so, you must remember to consider the person whom you are trying to persuade.

Writing Assignment
Use the *Steps for Writing a Persuasive Business Letter* and the *Sample Persuasive Business Letter* as you do the writing assignment below. Put your finished writing in your Rough Draft folder.

Writing Assignment #28: Use the persuasive business letter situation below.

Persuasive Business Letter Situation

Your assignment is to write a persuasive business letter on your own notebook paper. Without using Anne's idea of baby-sitting, come up with an idea for a business of your own. Use your own name and your own street address, city, state, and zip code. Use Ann's letter as a pattern and write a persuasive letter to Mr. Robert Blakemore, 856 Robin Cove. He lives in your hometown, so use your town and state to finish his address. Finally, draw and address an envelope for your letter, and don't forget to draw a stamp.

Letter and Envelope Information
To: Mr. Robert Blakemore, 856 Robin Cove, student's hometown, state, and zip code
From: Student's name, student's street address, student's city, state, and zip code

---

CHAPTER 16 LESSON 4

Main Parts of the Library

You will soon be going to the library to look up information about a topic for a report. In order to make this an easy and fun experience, you will need to know about some of the major sections in the library.

Fiction Section

Fiction books contain stories about people, places, or things that are not true. Fiction books are arranged on the shelves in alphabetical order according to the authors' last names. Since fiction stories are made-up, they cannot be used when you research your report topic.

Non-Fiction Section

Non-Fiction books contain information and stories that are true. You will use the books in this section to help you gather information for your report.

Reference Section

The Reference Section is designed to help you find information on many topics. The Reference Section contains many different kinds of reference books and materials. Some of the ones that you need to know about are listed below.

1. **Dictionary** - The dictionary gives the definition, spelling, and pronunciation of words and tells briefly about famous people and places.

2. **Encyclopedia** - The encyclopedia gives concise, accurate information about persons, places, and events of world-wide interest.

3. **Atlas** - The atlas is primarily a book of maps, but it often contains facts about oceans, lakes, mountains, areas, population, products, and climates of every part of the world.

4. **Almanac** - *The World Almanac* and *Information Please Almanac* are published once a year and contain brief, up-to-date information on a variety of topics.

5. ***The Readers' Guide to Periodical Literature*** - *The Readers' Guide to Periodical Literature* is an index for magazines. It is a monthly booklet that lists the titles of articles, stories, and poems published in all leading magazines. These titles are listed under topics which are arranged alphabetically. The monthly issues of *The Readers' Guide to Periodical Literature* are bound together in a single volume once a year and filed in the library. By using the *Readers' Guide*, a person researching a topic can know which back issues of magazines might contain an article about his topic.

6. **Card Catalog** - The card catalog is a file of cards, arranged alphabetically, and usually placed in the drawers of a cabinet called the card catalog. It is an index to the library. The cards inside the card catalog contain information about every book and nearly all the other materials located in the library. (Sometimes this information is listed on files in a computerized card catalog.)

CHAPTER 16 LESSON 4

Card Catalog

In a card catalog, the cards inside the drawers are in alphabetical order. The labels on the drawers tell which cards are in each drawer. Each of the catalog cards carries the name of a book in the library.

Example Card Catalog

A-Az	Fed-Gus	La-Mz	S	W
=	=	=	=	=
B-Cam	Gut-Iz	N-Pz	T	X-Y
=	=	=	=	=
Can-Fec	J-Kz	Q-Rz	U-V	Z
=	=	=	=	=

Three Kinds of Card Catalog Cards

A book is listed in three ways – by author, by title, and by subject. So the card catalog has three kinds of cards: the **author card**, the **title card**, and the **subject card**. All three kinds of cards are arranged alphabetically by the word or words on the top line.

All three kinds of cards – the author card, the title card, and the subject card - give the name of the book, the name of the author, and the call number of the book. They also give the place and date of publication, the publisher, the number of pages in the book, and other pertinent information.

Author cards have the name of the author of the book on the top line, and author cards are filed alphabetically by the author's last name.

Title cards have the title of the book on the top line, and title cards are filed alphabetically by the first word of the title (except *A, An,* or *The*).

Subject cards will have the subject of the book on the top line, and subject cards are filed alphabetically by the first word of the subject (except *A, An,* or *The*).

Author Card
523.8
Author-<u>Challand, Helen J.</u>
Title   Science Projects & Activities
Ill. by Linda Kimball
Children's Press, Chicago
(c1985) 93p.

Title Card
523.8
Title   <u>Science Projects & Activities</u>
Author-Challand, Helen J.
Ill. by Linda Kimball
Children's Press, Chicago
(c1985) 93p.

Subject Card
523.8
Topic   <u>Science Projects</u>
Author Challand, Helen J.
Title   Science Projects & Activities
Ill. by Linda Kimball
Children's Press, Chicago
(c1985) 93p.

CHAPTER 16 LESSON 4

Finding Nonfiction Books in the Card Catalog and on the Library Shelves

To find out if your library has a certain nonfiction book, look in the card catalog for the title card of that book. If you don't know the title, but do know the author, look for the author card. If you don't know the title or the author, look under the subject of the book. Also, look under the subject if you are interested in finding several books on your topic.

After you find the card for the book you want in the card catalog, you must know how to find the book on the library shelves. Nonfiction books are arranged on the shelves in **numerical order** according to a **call number**.

This numerical order is called the *Dewey Decimal System*, and a **call number** is part of that system. Since the Dewey Decimal System is a numerical system for locating nonfiction books, all nonfiction books are given a call number which will identify where they are located on the shelf. (Be sure to write the call number down on paper before you look for the book on the shelves.)

When you go to the library shelf, look at the call numbers printed on the spines of the books until you find the same number on the book that you copied from the catalog card. All three catalog cards for a book will have the same call number on the top left corner of the cards.

Helpful Note: Individual biographies and autobiographies are arranged on a separate shelf by the last name of the person about whom they are written.

Finding Fiction Books in the Card Catalog and on the Library Shelves

To find out if your library has a certain fiction book, look in the card catalog for the title card of that book. If you don't know the title, but do know the author, look for the author card. If you don't know the title or the author, look under the subject of the book. Also, look under the subject if you are interested in finding several books on your topic. (Sometimes fiction books are not classified by subject like other books. You must then look for the title or author of the book.)

After you find the card for the book you want in the card catalog, you must know how to find the book on the library shelves. Fiction books are arranged on the shelves in **alphabetical order** according to the **authors' last names**; therefore, a fiction book is located by the author's last name.

If you look on the spine of a fiction book, you will see only a letter(s). This is the first letter in the author's last name, and all three catalog cards will have the first letter of the author's last name on the top left corner of each card. (Be sure to write the author's last name and the book title down on paper before you look for the book on the shelves.)

When you go to the library shelf, look at the letter printed on the spines of the books until you find the same letter(s) on the book that you copied from the catalog card. If two authors have the same last name, their books are arranged in alphabetical order according to the authors' first names. If there are two or more books by the same author, they are arranged in alphabetical order by titles.

CHAPTER 16 LESSON 4 SKILL TEST A

Exercise 1: Number your paper from 1 to 7 and write the answer to each question.

1. What would you find by going to *The Readers' Guide to Periodical Literature*?

2. Name the main reference book that gives the definition, spelling, and pronunciation of words.

3. Name the main reference book that is primarily a book of maps.

4. Name the main reference book that is published once a year with a variety of up-to-date information.

5. How are fiction books arranged on the shelves?

6. How are nonfiction books arranged on the shelves?

7. What are the names of the three cards located in the card catalog?

Exercise 2: Number your paper from 8 to 14 and write the title and author of each fiction book below in the correct order to go on the shelves.

8. *Freckle Juice* by Judy Blume
9. *A Taste of Blueberries* by Doris Smith
10. *The Wise Fool* by Paul Galdone
11. *The Arrow of Fire* by Roy Snell
12. *Stone Soup* by Marcia Brown
13. *Good-bye My Island* by Jean Rogers
14. *Dirt Bike Racer* by Matt Christopher

Exercise 3: Number your paper from 15 to 22 and write True or False for each statement.

15. The card catalog is an index to books in the library.
16. The *Readers' Guide to Periodical Literature* is an index to magazines.
17. The title of the book is always the first line on each of the catalog cards.
18. The books in the fiction section are arranged alphabetically by the author's last name.
19. The books in the nonfiction section are arranged numerically by a call number.
20. Biographies are arranged on the shelves according to the author's last name.
21. Fiction and nonfiction books have numbers on their spines to locate them on a shelf.
22. Encyclopedias give concise information about persons, places, and events of world-wide interest.

Exercise 4: For 23-25, draw and label the three catalog cards for this book: 590.6 *Birds of All Kinds* by Walter Ferguson, Golden Press, N.Y., 1959, p.25. (Use the catalog card examples in Lesson 4.)

23. Author Card
24. Title Card
25. Subject Card

CHAPTER 16 LESSON 5

Parts of a Book

Any time you use a nonfiction book to help you with an assignment, it is necessary to understand how to use that book efficiently. Knowing the parts of a book will help you make full use of the special features that are sometimes found in nonfiction books. Below, you will find a brief description of each of the features that could appear in a book.

Parts That Could Be Found in the Front of a Book

1. **Title Page**
   This page has the full title of the book, the author's name, the illustrator's name, the publishing company, and the city where the book was published.

2. **Copyright Page**
   This page is right after the title page and tells the year in which the book was published and who owns the copyright. If the book has an ISBN number (International Standard Book Number), it is listed here.

3. **Preface** (also called **introduction,** or acknowledgement)
   If a book has this page, it will come before the table of contents and will usually tell you briefly why the book was written and what it is about.

4. **Table of Contents**
   This section lists the major divisions of the book by units and chapters and tells their beginning page numbers.

5. **Body**
   This is the main section, or text, of the book.

Parts That Could Be Found in the Back of a Book

1. **Appendix**
   This section gives extra informative material such as maps, charts, tables, diagrams, letters, etc. It is always wise to find out what is in the appendix since it may contain supplementary material that you could otherwise find only by going to the library.

2. **Glossary**
   This section is like a dictionary and gives the meanings of some of the important words in the book.

3. **Bibliography**
   This section gives a list of books used by the author. It could serve as a guide for further reading on a topic.

4. **Index**
   This will probably be your most useful section. The purpose of the index is to help you quickly locate information about the topics in the book. It has an alphabetical list of specific topics and tells on which page(s) that information can be found. It is similar to the table of contents, but it is much more detailed.

CHAPTER 16 LESSON 5 SKILL TEST B

Exercise 1: 1-15: Match each part of a book listed below with the type of information it may give you. Write the appropriate letter in the blank. You may use a letter more than once.

A. Title page	B. Table of contents	C. Copyright page	D. Index	E. Bibliography
F. Preface	G. Appendix	H. Glossary	I. Body	

1. ___ Illustrator's name

2. ___ Books for finding more information

3. ___ Titles of units and chapters

4. ___ Copyright date

5. ___ Publisher's name

6. ___ ISBN number

7. ___ Extra maps in a book

8. ___ Exact page numbers for a particular topic

9. ___ Author's name

10. ___ Text of the book

11. ___ Meanings of important words in the book

12. ___ Reason the book was written

13. ___ Used to locate topics quickly

14. ___ City where the book was published

15. ___ A list of books used by the author as references

Exercise 2: 16-20: Name the five parts found at the front of a book.

16. _____

17. _____

18. _____

19. _____

20. _____

Exercise 3: 21-24: Name the four parts found at the back of a book.

21. _____ 22. _____ 23. _____ 24. _____

CHAPTER 17 LESSON 1

Writing Conversation from Dictation

Study the paragraphing and punctuation of the following conversation. Prepare to write the conversation correctly as your teacher dictates it to you.

Dictation Box

Mom quickly settled the two youngest kids at the table and said, "Hurry up and eat! You're going to be late, and you'll miss the bus."

Then Laura poked her head into the kitchen and announced, "I don't have anything to wear!"

"Go in your pajamas! But you better hurry, or you'll miss the bus!" said Mom as she hustled the little ones into coats and backpacks.

"Why do we have to go to school anyway?" Laura asked as she whizzed past her mother.

"You have to go to school so I can have peace and quiet on my day off," Mom said quietly as she waved good-bye to her children.

Writing Assignment

Writing Assignment #29:

This writing assignment will be a research report. The steps for writing your research report are presented in the rest of this chapter. Your teacher will guide you as you work through each step in this guided writing assignment. All your guided assignments in this chapter will be part of Writing Assignment #29.

CHAPTER 17 LESSON 1

Writing a Report

Now it is time to learn how to write a short report. There are certain things you need to know and certain steps you need to follow in order to make writing a report an easy and interesting learning experience. In this lesson, you will walk through the steps of writing a report from beginning to end. Then, in Chapter 18, you will go through the steps again and actually write a report.

When your teacher assigns a report, your first job is to research, or gather, information about your topic. In doing this research, you learn facts and details about a specific subject that you did not know before. Your second job is to organize these facts and details into a clear, well-written report. By writing a report, you share the information you have learned with others.

There are fourteen easy steps you need to know in order to research a topic and write a report. Read over the fourteen steps below. Then you will go through each step, one at a time. You will be taught how to apply each step in the report-writing process.

---

14 Steps for Researching a Topic and Writing a Report

Step 1: Narrow the topic.

Step 2: Make an outline guide.

Step 3: Select sources by skimming.

Step 4: Make a bibliography card for each source selected.

Step 5: Take notes.

Step 6: Organize note cards.

Step 7: Write a first draft outline.

Step 8: Write a second draft outline.

Step 9: Write a rough draft.

Step 10: Edit the rough draft

Step 11: Write the final outline.

Step 12: Write the final report.

Step 13: Put the final report and all related research work in the correct order.

Step 14: Hand in final report and all related papers.

(Note: Make sure you write everything, except your final outline and report, in pencil.)

Step 1. Narrow the topic.

Use the assigned topic or choose a topic from the list your teacher gives you. Narrow the topic and have your teacher approve your narrowed topic. Sometimes, however, your assigned topic will be narrow enough.

1. Topic: Woodland Plants
2. Narrow: Poisonous Woodland Plants
3. Narrow again: Poison Ivy

CHAPTER 17 LESSON 1

Step 2. Make an outline guide.

The second thing you need to do when beginning the report-writing process is to make an outline guide. An outline guide does not follow an outline format because it is just a guide that will enable you to make an outline more easily when you are ready. An outline guide is simply a numbered list of some of the categories that you may use to group the information you gather about your topic. The categories that you use from your outline guide will become the main topics when you make your outline.

The purpose of an outline guide is to give the writer a way to organize information that will be gathered about a topic. Making an outline guide before you start taking notes will save you a lot of work because it will keep you focused on what to read and will help you be selective in the type of notes you take. Your outline guide must be flexible because it will usually go through many changes as you determine the direction of your report.

Guided Assignment: Make an outline guide.

1. Your narrowed topic is **Poison Ivy**.
2. Look over the topic categories in the *Main Point Outline Guide Example* on the next page to find the one that is closest to your topic.
3. Yes, the **Topic Categories for Things** is the section best suited for your topic *Poison Ivy*.
4. Now, choose two to four categories from this section that you would like to include in your research of this topic.
5. Yes, **identification, location, and important characteristics** are good categories to start with. (You can change, modify, or add categories as you find out more about your topic.)
6. You will now make your own *Outline Guide* that lists the topic categories that you have chosen from the *Main Point Outline Guide Example*. Put the title *Outline Guide* on the top line of your paper. Next, list the three categories chosen with four or five lines between them.

CHAPTER 17 LESSON 1

Main Point Outline Guide Example

Topic Categories for People

Automatic main points: Introduction / Conclusion
Choose 3 main points for the body of the report:

1. Childhood
2. Adult life
3. People or events that influenced his/her life
4. Accomplishments (may use up to three)
5. Characteristics (may describe up to three)
6. Unusual and interesting facts
7. Add another main point to fit your topic.

Topic Categories for Animals

Automatic main points: Introduction / Conclusion
Choose 3 main points for the body of the report:

1. Habitat (where it lives)
2. Physical characteristics (what it looks like)
3. What it eats and how it gets its food
4. Enemies
5. Unusual and interesting facts
6. Single animal or part of a group of animals?
7. Add another main point to fit your topic.

Topic Categories for Things

Automatic main points: Introduction / Conclusion
Choose 3 main points for the body of the report:

1. Location
2. Physical appearance, makeup, or identification (size, shape, looks, feel, weight, liquid, etc.)
3. Can it be classified into different groups?
4. Important behavior, characteristics, or use?
5. Unusual and interesting facts
6. Does it change with time?
7. Add another main point to fit your topic.

Topic Categories for Places

Automatic main points: Introduction / Conclusion
Choose 3 main points for the body of the report:

1. Location
2. Is it real or imaginary?
3. Famous landmarks or physical characteristics (may use up to three)
4. Why is this place important or interesting?
5. What people and animals live there?
6. Major industries, products, and services
7. Add another main point to fit your topic.

Topic Categories for a Process

Automatic main points: Introduction / Conclusion
Choose 3 main points for the body of the report:

1. A process is how something is done or made.
2. Identify what the process is.
3. Identify why the process is necessary.
4. List the steps you must take in order to complete the project or process in the most logical order.
5. Add another main point to fit your topic.

Topic Categories for an Event

Automatic main points: Introduction / Conclusion
Choose 3 main points for the body of the report:

1. What was the event?
2. When and where did the event occur?
3. Reasons why the event occurred
4. Who or what was involved in the event?
5. What was the effect of the event?
6. Widespread importance of the event.
7. Add another main point to fit your topic.

Topic Categories for Opinion, etc.

Automatic main points: Introduction / Conclusion
Main Points

1. First point and supporting sentences
2. Second point and supporting sentences
3. Third point and supporting sentences
4. Add another main point to fit your topic.

Topic Categories for Ideas, etc.

Automatic main points: Introduction / Conclusion
Main Points

1. Facts
2. Reasons
3. Examples
4. Add another main point to fit your topic.

CHAPTER 17 LESSON 2

Step 3. Select sources by skimming.

Skimming

1. Skimming is reading only the key parts of a source to quickly determine if that source has information that will fit into the topic categories you have selected from the outline guide.

2. The key parts to skim are titles, topic headings in boldface type, first sentences of paragraphs, underlining, captions under pictures, text outlined by boxes, questions, and summaries.

3. The best way to skim several paragraphs in a longer article is to read all of the first paragraph because it usually contains a brief summary of the article. Then read only the first sentence of each paragraph in the body of the article. This reading will give you a brief summary of each paragraph. Finally, read all of the last paragraph because it restates the most important points.

4. As you skim an article, consider these things: Does this information give enough facts about your topic categories? Is the information interesting enough to use in your report? Is the information presented clearly, and is it easy to understand?

5. Skimming a source will quickly help you decide if the source can be used, if the source cannot be used, or if new topic categories need to be chosen. If the source has enough information about your topic categories, then it **can be used**. If the source does not have enough information about your topic categories, then it **cannot be used**. If, after skimming several sources, you cannot find enough information about the original topic categories, you need to **choose new topic** categories.

An Encyclopedia Source

Encyclopedias are always good sources for reports because they give you ideas for different categories, along with a general introduction to your topic Encyclopedia articles on your narrowed topic are usually easy to find because they are listed alphabetically. However, if you cannot find your narrowed topic in an encyclopedia, you may need to look under a broader topic. (Example: Narrowed topic: Woodpeckers; Broader topic: Birds)

Before you leave your first encyclopedia article, go to the end of that article. There will usually be a list of related encyclopedia articles that also fit your topic. This list will be helpful whether you use the first article or not. (Always check the publication date of the encyclopedia. Depending on the nature of the topic, material in an older encyclopedia could be outdated.)

A Book Source

Books give you details about your topic. Use the card catalog to find books related to your topic. Then use the book's index and table of contents to find the information you need. Look in the table of contents to get an overall picture of what the book is about. If you see any chapter titles that relate to your topic, skim the pages in those chapters. Also, look in the index for information related to your topic. Then look on the specific pages the index lists to see if the information can be used.

A Magazine Source or Computerized Information

Magazine articles also give you more details about your topic. Use the *Readers' Guide to Periodical Literature* to find magazine articles related to your topic. Magazine articles are listed alphabetically by topic and by author. Some entries have cross-references (marked *See* or *See also*) that will help you find related articles. Some libraries also have information that can be accessed through computers. Computers provide an excellent way for you to search for different types of information. Always ask the librarian to assist you with computerized information or periodical materials because they cannot be checked out.

CHAPTER 17 LESSON 2

Guided Assignment: Select sources by skimming.

1. Look at the encyclopedia article on poison ivy below.
2. Skim the article. (Skim all boldface headings, and skim the first sentence of each paragraph in the article.)
3. After skimming the article, decide whether you will use the article from this source.

Poison Ivy

Poison ivy. Poison ivy is the common name of a well-known, poisonous woodland plant belonging to the Cashew family. The poison from this plant causes a red, extremely itchy rash in many people every year. Many times this rash is accompanied by tiny blisters and severe inflammation. In order to avoid the complications of this skin rash, it is important to know several basic facts about the poison ivy plant.

One very important fact to know about poison ivy is where it is found. Generally, it can be found in both the United States and Canada. Specifically, it can be found twining around trees as vines. Also, if it has nothing about which it can twine, it may be found growing as a ground creeper or as a small bush.

Another important fact to know is what poison ivy looks like. Both vining and bush plants have leaves that are shiny green in summer and red and orange in autumn. The leaves of the plant grow in clusters of three leaflets with each leaflet being notched at the edges. It also has clusters of tiny, white, textured berries that grow close to the stem. Many people confuse poison ivy with Virginia creeper, a vining plant with notched leaves, dark blue berries, and clusters of five leaflets.

Poison ivy rash. An equally important fact to know is how people can get a poison ivy rash. There are several ways a person can become infected by poison ivy. First, one may be infected by his skin's coming in contact with the poisonous oil contained in all parts of the plant. Also, a person may become infected by touching clothing, shoes, or pets that have come into contact with the oil from the plant. Finally, one may be infected simply from the smoke from a burning poison ivy plant.

There are many ways to avoid infection from the poison ivy plant. First, you must learn to recognize and avoid it. If you find the poison ivy plant in areas near your home and yard, you can kill it with a good weed killer. Poison ivy infection can also be prevented by the use of pills that provide immunity if taken before exposure.

Classification. Common poison ivy, *Toxicodendron, radicans*
See also Cashew; Poisonous Plants; Virginia creeper.

98

Article from *Coffman Encyclopedia*, 1994, Vol. 15, "Poison Ivy" by Jason T. Wells

---

CHAPTER 17 LESSON 2

Step 4. Make a bibliography card for each source selected.

As soon as you decide to use an article in an encyclopedia, book, or periodical (source) in your report, immediately make a bibliography note card that records specific, detailed information about that source in the order given below. You will later use your bibliography cards to make a bibliography page for your report. The bibliography page gives credit to the sources used in your report and tells others where they can find information on your subject.

1. To record a book source on your bibliography card, write the name of the author, the title of the book, the place, the publisher, and the date of publication.
   Brown, Sara. North American Plants. New York: Sunset Publishing, 1993.

2. To record an encyclopedia source on your bibliography card, write the name of the author, the title of the article, the title of the encyclopedia, and the edition (date) of the encyclopedia.
   Wells, Jason T. "Poison Ivy." Coffman Encyclopedia. 1994 ed.

3. To record a magazine source on your bibliography card, write the name of the author, the title of the article, the name of the magazine, the date and volume number of the magazine, and the page numbers of the entire article in a magazine, not just the page you used.
   Juarez, Ricardo. "The Basics About Poison Ivy." America's Favorite Campsites May 1994: 68-69.

4. For more information about your topic, check for lists of other suggested books and articles on your topic in the books and articles that you read.

Bibliography Card Examples

Bibliography Card (Book)	Bibliography Card (Encyclopedia)
Brown, Sara. North American Plants. New York: Sunset Publishing, 1993.	Long, John and Wayne Christen. "Poisonous Plants." The Educator's Encyclopedia. 1992 ed.

Bibliography Card (Encyclopedia)	Bibliography Card (Magazine)
Wells, Jason T. "Poison Ivy." Coffman Encyclopedia. 1994 ed.	Juarez, Ricardo. "The Basics About Poison Ivy." America's Favorite Campsites May 1994: 68-69.

Guided Assignment: Make a bibliography card for each source selected.

1. After you decide to use the encyclopedia article "Poison Ivy," you must make a bibliography card immediately.
2. First, write **Bibliography Card (Encyclopedia)** at the top of your note card.
3. Second, use the directions and examples above to help you correctly record the information about your encyclopedia source on your note card. (Make sure you follow the format exactly.)

CHAPTER 17 LESSON 2

Step 5. Take notes.

You must develop the ability to take notes on what you read in order to write a report. After you have found information that tells about the topic categories you have listed in your outline guide, summarize the information in your own words by using phrases and abbreviations. Write your notes on note cards that have been labeled with the topic categories.

Things to do before you begin taking notes.

1. Make sure you have completed a bibliography card for each source you select.

2. Since every report will have introductory and concluding note cards, write the words **Introduction** and **Conclusion** at the top of two note cards. (Make additional cards if you need them.)

3. Make several note cards for each topic category from your outline guide. Write the names of the topic categories at the top of the cards. (You may make up to eight cards for each category.)

4. The notes you take on each note card must support the topic category written on that note card. The topic categories will help you be selective in your reading and will organize your note-taking.

5. Keep in mind that you may want to revise your outline guide and change your topic categories as you see what information is available. Your outline guide must be flexible because it will usually go through changes as you determine the direction of your report.

Things to do after you begin taking notes.

6. Write your notes on note cards, and use a different note card for each set of facts you record. Then later, when you get to the outlining step of your report, it will be easier to shuffle and rearrange the order of your information just by shifting the order of the cards.

7. As you read, write notes that will give facts and details that support the topic categories at the top of each note card. You will probably make several note cards using the same topic categories in order to include the necessary facts and details that support each category.

8. Writing good notes requires good judgment and a clear idea of what you are trying to do. As with most things, the more you take notes, the better you will get at it. In the meantime, to make taking notes easier, follow these suggestions:

>   Summarize the information as you put it in your own words.
>   Write your notes in phrases, not complete sentences.
>   Put only one note or closely-related notes on each note card.
>   Make sure each note taken is important for your reader to know.
>   Each note should be a supporting fact or detail about the topic category at the top of each card.
>   If you use the exact words of a writer, put them in quotation marks.

9. At the bottom of every note card, write the title of the source and the page number you have used so you will know where to find that information quickly and easily if you need it again.

10. Your introduction note cards will be a little different from the note cards with topic categories. For the introduction, look for interesting general information, definitions, or questions that are necessary to the general understanding of your paper or that would give extra information to make an interesting introduction.

11. For the conclusion note cards, try to find several summarizing facts that support your introductory statements. Then, during your outlining stage, you will make your final note cards based on conclusions that you have drawn from your research.

CHAPTER 17 LESSON 2

Introduction
well-known, poisonous plant
produces rash in many people
<u>Coffman Encyclopedia</u>, 1994, Vol. 15, p. 98

Identification
poison ivy berries
grow in clusters close to stem
are tiny, white, textured berries
<u>Coffman Encyclopedia</u>, 1994, Vol. 15, p. 98

Introduction
red, itchy rash
tiny blisters, severe inflammation
<u>Coffman Encyclopedia</u>, 1994, Vol. 15, p. 98

Identification
confused with Virginia Creeper - grows on a vine with notched leaves, has dark blue berries, and has clusters of more than 5 leaflets
<u>Coffman Encyclopedia</u>, 1994, Vol. 15, p. 98

Location
found in U. S. and Canada
<u>Coffman Encyclopedia</u>, 1994, Vol. 15, p. 98

Important Characteristics
infected by skin touching poison oil in all parts of the plant
<u>Coffman Encyclopedia</u>, 1994, Vol. 15, p. 98

Location
grows as vine, ground creeper, or small bush
<u>Coffman Encyclopedia</u>, 1994, Vol. 15, p. 98

Important Characteristics
infected by touching clothes, shoes, or pets that have poison oil from plant on them
<u>Coffman Encyclopedia</u>, 1994, Vol. 15, p. 98

Identification
green and shiny leaves in summer
red and orange leaves in autumn
<u>Coffman Encyclopedia</u>, 1994, Vol. 15, p. 98

Important Characteristics
infected from contact with smoke from burning poison ivy
<u>Coffman Encyclopedia</u>, 1994, Vol. 15, p. 98

Identification
grows in clusters of 3 leaflets
leaflets notched at edges
<u>Coffman Encyclopedia</u>, 1994, Vol. 15, p. 98

Conclusion
avoid infection, recognize and avoid plant, kill plant around home with weed killer, take pills for summer immunity
<u>Coffman Encyclopedia</u>, 1994, Vol. 15, p. 98

Guided Assignment: Take notes on note cards.

1. Make note cards with the following titles:

   Introduction (Write this title at the top of 2 note cards.)
   Location   (Write this title at the top of 2 note cards.)
   Identification (Write this title at the top of 4 note cards.)
   Important Characteristics   (Write this title at the top of 3 note cards.)
   Conclusion   (Write this title at the top of 1 note card.)

2. You skimmed the article on poison ivy earlier to determine if it could be used as a source. Now, after you have made the decision to use it as a source, **you must read the complete article before you begin taking notes.** Read the article "Poison Ivy."

3. After you have read the article, begin taking notes on your note cards. As you take your notes, start at the beginning of the article and work to the end. As you work with each paragraph, select the note cards with the category titles that match the information for that paragraph. Write your notes in phrases on the appropriate note card.

4. At the bottom of every note card, write the title of the source and the page number you used.

CHAPTER 17 LESSON 3

Step 6. Organize note cards.

Once you have finished your reading and note-taking, the next step is to begin arranging or organizing all the information you have found.

1. Since you have used general topic categories at the top of each note card, most of your information is already organized into different categories.

2. Now sort your note cards into piles according to the titles of the categories at the top of the note cards. (You should have these piles: introduction, three or four topic categories, and conclusion.)

3. Next, arrange these categories in the order that you want to present them in your report.

4. Arrange the note cards within each category in a logical order for your report.

5. Finally, number all your note cards in the upper right-hand corner to prevent them from getting out of order. Put the bibliography cards at the end.

6. Put all cards in a Ziploc bag to be handed in with your final report.

Guided Assignment: Organize note cards.

1. Sort your note cards into these piles according to their titles:

   Introduction (2 note cards), **Location** (2 note cards), **Identification** (4 note cards), **Important Characteristics** (3 note cards), **Conclusion** (1 note card).

2. Next, arrange these categories in a logical order for your report. (Your categories are already in a logical order so that you do not need to rearrange them.)

3. Now, arrange the note cards within each category in a logical order for your report.

4. Finally, number all your note cards in the upper right-hand corner to prevent them from getting out of order. Put the bibliography cards at the end.

5. Put all cards in a ziploc bag to be handed in with your final report.

Learning about outlines.

In order to develop good report-writing techniques, you must learn to make and use an outline effectively. An **outline** is a concise, written list of the information on your note cards in the order it will appear in your report. This outline planning will give you a visual map of your report. The outline is your final organizational tool.

There are two kinds of outlines: the **topic outline** and the **sentence outline**. In a topic outline, information is written in single words or phrases. In a sentence outline, information is written in complete sentences. Because outlines have very rigid rules about how they are organized and formatted, outlines should never have a mixture of phrases and sentences. Since the topic outline is the easiest and most commonly-used outline, you will learn about outline format by studying the topic outline.

All outlines follow the same plan. Information in an outline is listed in order from general information to specific information. The most general information is listed as main topics. Specific information about each main topic is listed as subtopics. More specific information about each subtopic is listed as details. Study the guidelines on the next page for making a topic outline.

CHAPTER 17 LESSON 3

Learning about outlines (continued).

Outlines have a vocabulary and a set of rules that are unique to outlining. Study how to make an outline below. Then follow the procedures as you begin to make and use outlines on your own.

Outline Title

1. At first, your outline title should be the same or similar to your narrowed topic. This will help you stay focused on the main idea of your report. If you decide to change the title for your final paper, you must remember to change your outline title.
2. Capitalizing rules for titles are the same for outlines as for final papers: Capitalize the first word, the last word, and all the important words in your title. Conjunctions, articles, and prepositions with fewer than five letters are not usually capitalized unless they are the first or last word. Titles for reports are not underlined or placed in quotation marks unless the title is a quotation.

Main Topics

1. Main topics are the main categories of information about your topic. These are the general ideas.
2. There must always be two or more main topics.
3. Main topics are indicated by Roman numerals with a period after each Roman numeral. (I. II.)
4. The periods after the Roman numerals must be lined up under each other.
5. Every first word in a main topic is always capitalized.

Subtopics

1. Subtopics are specific ideas that support the main topics.
2. There must always be two or more subtopics. (If you only have one, do not put it in the outline.)
3. Subtopics are indicated by capital letters with a period after each capital letter. (A. B.)
4. Each capital letter is indented under the first word of the main topic.
5. The periods after the capital letters must be lined up under each other.
6. Every first word in a subtopic is always capitalized.

Details

1. Details are specific ideas about the subtopics.
2. There must always be two or more details. (If you only have one, do not put it in the outline.)
3. Details are indicated by Arabic numerals with a period after each numeral. (1. 2.)
4. Each Arabic numeral is indented under the first word of the subtopic.
5. The periods after the Arabic numerals must be lined up under each other.
6. Every first word in a detail is always capitalized.

Parallel Outline Form

1. All the main topics in an outline should be in parallel form. This means that all the main topics should begin the same way: all nouns, all verbs, all noun phrases, all verb phrases, all prepositional phrases, etc. If necessary, change or rearrange the words of your outline so they are parallel.
   (I. Location; II. Identification; III. Infection) (I. Where poison ivy is located; II. What poison ivy looks like; III. How infection from poison ivy occurs)
2. All the subtopics under Roman Numeral I must be in parallel form. The subtopics under Roman numeral II must be in parallel form. But Roman Numeral I subtopics do not have to be parallel with Roman Numeral II subtopics.
   (A. Is found in U. S. and Canada; B. Grows up trees) (A. Leaves; B. Berries; C. Virginia creeper)
3. All the details under Subtopic A must be parallel. The details under Subtopic B must be in parallel form. But Subtopic A details do not have to be parallel with Subtopic B details.
   (1. Grows in clusters; 2. Has tiny, white, textured berries); (1. Red, itchy rash; 2. Tiny blisters; 3. Severe inflammation)

CHAPTER 17 LESSON 3

Guided Assignment: Write a first draft outline. Follow the directions below.

Step 7. Write a first draft outline.

You will make three outlines for each report you write: a first draft outline, a second draft outline, and a final outline. The purpose of the **first draft** is to transfer your notes from note cards to correct outline form. Then, in the **second draft**, you will put your outline in parallel form and add details. Your **final outline** will show the organization of your final report. All three outlines will be handed in with your report.

First Draft Outline

To make the **first draft** of your outline, you must have your outline guide and the note cards (that you have already organized) ready to use. Remember, the purpose of the **first draft** is to transfer your notes from note cards to correct outline form.

1. **Title.** Write your outline title on the top line of your paper. It should be the same or similar to your narrowed topic.

2. **Main topics.** Look at the titles written at the top of each note card. They *are Introduction, Location, Identification, Important characteristics,* and *Conclusion.* These note card titles will be the main topics of your outline. To write the main topics on your paper, put a Roman Numeral beside each one, capitalize the first word, and skip several lines after each topic to give you room to write the rest of your outline.

3. **Subtopics for the first main topic.** Look at the notes on the note cards titled *Introduction.* There are four notes: (1.) *well-known poisonous plant* (2.) *produces rash in many people* (3.) *red, itchy rash* (4.) *tiny blisters and severe inflammation.* You will write them as subtopics A-D. Position your subtopic letters directly under the first letter of the main topic, put a period after each letter, and capitalize the first word of each subtopic.

4. **Subtopics for the second main topic.** Look at the notes under the second main topic titled *Location.* There are two notes: (1.) *found in U.S. and Canada* (2.) *grows as vine, ground creeper, or small bush.* You will write them as subtopics A and B. Position your subtopic letters directly under the first letter of the main topic, put a period after each letter, and capitalize the first word of each subtopic.

5. **Subtopics for the third main topic.** Look at the notes under the third main topic titled *Identification.* The notes *green and shiny leaves in summer* and *red and orange leaves in autumn* will be Subtopics A and B. The notes *grows in clusters of 3 leaflets* and *leaflets notched at edges* will be Subtopics C and D. The notes *poison ivy berries; grow in clusters close to stem; are tiny, white, textured berries* will be Subtopic E -G. Finally, the notes *confused with Virginia creeper; grows on a vine with notched leaves; has dark blue berries;* and *has clusters of more than 5 leaflets* will be Subtopics H- K.

6. **Subtopics for the fourth main topic.** Look at the notes under the fourth main topic titled *Important characteristics.* The notes on each of the note cards will be Subtopics A, B, and C.

7. **Subtopics for the fifth main topic.** Look at the notes under the fifth main topic titled *Conclusion.* The notes can be written as Subtopics A, B, C, and D.

CHAPTER 17 LESSON 3

Guided Assignment: Write a second draft outline. Follow the directions below.

Step 8. Write a second draft outline.

In this second draft, you will change some of the wording of your first draft as you add details and put your outline in parallel form.

1. **Title.** You will probably keep the same title unless you have decided on a better one. Write your outline title on the top line of the second draft.

Working with main topics

2. **Main topic criteria.** Look at the main topics on your first draft outline. They are *Introduction, Location, Identification, Important characteristics,* and *Conclusion.* Since these five main topics were originally topic categories you chose from the Outline Guide, you must now decide if you need to change the way they are worded or keep them the same. You have to consider two criteria (standards) for main topics before you make your choice. Your first criteria is that each topic is not vague. Each topic must be worded in the best way to give the reader an idea of the information that is covered in the subtopics listed under it. The second criteria is that all the main topics are in parallel form. (Do they all start the same way? For example: Do they all start with nouns? Do they all start with verbs? Do they all start with an adjective-noun combination?, etc.)

3. **Meeting main topic criteria.** Now, on your first draft outline sheet, go through each main topic, one by one, to see if each one meets the two criteria above. As you can see, the topics *Introduction, Location, Identification,* and *Conclusion* meet the first criteria. They are not vague. They are all worded so that the reader has an an idea of the information that is covered under them. These topics also meet the second criteria: they are parallel. However, the topic *Important characteristics* does not meet either of the criteria for main topics. First, the topic *Important characteristics* is very vague and is not worded so that the reader has an idea of the type of information that is covered in the subtopics. Second, it is not parallel with the other topics. It starts with an adjective, not a noun.

4. **Rewording main topics.** There are three reasons to reword main topics. They do not meet the first or second main topic criteria as listed above, or you do not like how a main topic is worded and want to change it. To reword the vague topic *Important characteristics,* look at all the subtopics under that topic.

   As you read through these subtopics, notice that all the information is about how people become infected from poison ivy. Although there are several ways to word this topic, you must decide which way you like the best. Possible choices: *Infection* or *How infection from poison ivy occurs.*

5. **Making main topics parallel.** If you completely change one or more main topics, you must now check to make sure all the topics are parallel with the ones you have reworded. Parallel means each main topic must start with the same grammatical form. They must all start with nouns, verbs, etc. If all your topics are not parallel, you must now change the other topics to parallel forms.

   If you chose *Infection* as your renamed topic, it is already parallel with the other main topics. If you chose *How infection from poison ivy occurs,* you must change the other main topics so that they are parallel. To do that, reword them so that they each begin the same way. Since the renamed topic starts with the question word ***How***, start the other topics with question words that fit their subtopics. For example: ***Where*** *poison ivy is located* and ***What*** *poison ivy looks like.*

CHAPTER 17 LESSON 3

Step 8. Write a second draft outline (continued).

You do not have to change the topics *Introduction* and *Conclusion*. They will always stay the same in every outline you make.

Working with subtopics and details

There are four steps you must take as you streamline your subtopics and change some subtopics into details.

1. Study the subtopics listed under each main topic.
2. As you study the subtopics, check to see if there are any subtopics that are related enough to group together under a new title. Write this new title as a subtopic.
3. Write the subtopics that were grouped as details under the new subtopic title.
4. If necessary, reword subtopics and details to put them in parallel form.

6. **Subtopics/Details for the first main topic.**
    1. Study the subtopics listed under the first topic *Introduction*.
    2. Subtopics A and B, *Well-known poisonous plant* and *Produces rash in many people,* are specific ideas that support the main topic, so you will keep them as subtopics.
    3. Subtopics C and D, *Red, itchy rash* and *Tiny blisters, severe inflammation,* are actually details that give specific information about Subtopic B. Therefore, write **Red**, *itchy rash,* **Tiny** *blisters,and* **Severe** *inflammation* as Details 1, 2, and 3 under Subtopic B, *Produces rash in many people.* Position the detail numbers directly under the first letter of the subtopic, put a period after each number, and capitalize the first word of each detail.
    4. To make Subtopics A and B parallel, start each one with a verb: **Is** *a well known poisonous plant* and **Produces** *rash in many people.* The details for Subtopic B are parallel since they start with adjectives: *1. Red, itchy rash; 2. Tiny blisters; 3. Severe inflammation.*

7. **Subtopics/Details for the second main topic.**
    1. Study the subtopics listed under the second topic *Where poison ivy is located.*
    2. Subtopics A and B *Found in U. S. and Canada* and *Grows as vine, ground creeper, or small bush* are specific ideas that support the main topic, so you will keep them as subtopics.
    3. There are no subtopics that need to be changed into details.
    4. To make Subtopics A and B parallel, start each one with a present tense verb: **Is found** *in U. S. and Canada* and **Grows** *as vine, ground creeper, or small bush.*

CHAPTER 17 LESSON 3

Step 8. Write a second draft outline (continued).

8. **Subtopics/Details for the third main topic.**

   1. Study the subtopics listed under the first topic *What poison ivy looks like*.

   2. Subtopics A-D are talking about poison ivy leaves. Subtopic E is talking about the poison ivy berries, and Subtopics F-I are talking about the Virginia creeper. You can easily group the related subtopics together and give them a new subtopic title. Write *Leaves*, *Berries*, and *Virginia creeper* as the new Subtopics A, B, and C.

   3. Since you have all new subtopic titles, write all the old subtopics as details under the appropriate subtopic. Example: Under the subtopic *Leaves*, write ***Green*** *and shiny leaves in summer,* ***Red*** *and orange leaves in autumn,* ***Grows*** *in clusters of 3 leaflets, and* ***Leaflets*** *notched at edges* as Details 1, 2, 3, and 4. Work through the subtopics *Berries* and *Virginia creeper* the same way. Be sure to position the detail numbers directly under the first letter of the subtopic, put a period after each number, and capitalize the first word of each detail.

   4. All three subtopics are parallel since they start with nouns. To make the details under Subtopic A parallel, start each one with an adjective: ***Green*** *shiny leaves in summyuer,* ***Red****, orange leaves in autumn,* ***Three*** *leaflets in a cluster, and* ***Notched*** *edges in leaflets.* Make two details under Subtopic B and start them with verbs: ***Grow*** *in clusters and* ***Have*** *tiny, white textured berries.* Finally, start the four details under Subtopic C with the same verbs listed on the note cards.

9. **Subtopics/Details for the fourth main topic.**

   1. Study the subtopics listed under the fourth topic, *How infection from poison ivy occurs*.

   2. Subtopics A, B, and C are specific ideas that support the main topic, so you will keep them as subtopics.

   3. There are no subtopics that need to be changed into details.

   4. All three subtopics are parallel since they start with verbs.

10. **Subtopics/Details for the last main topic.**

   1. Study the subtopics listed under the last topic *Conclusion*.

   2. Subtopics A, B, C, and D are specific ideas that support the main topic, so you will keep them as subtopics.

   3. There are no subtopics that need to be changed into details.

   4. All four subtopics are parallel since they start with verbs.

Even though it is not always possible, learning to take your notes in parallel form can save you time and effort as you put your notes in outline form.

CHAPTER 17 LESSON 3

First Draft Outline	Second Draft Outline

I. Introduction
  A. Well-known, poisonous plant
  B. Produces rash in many people
  C. Red, itchy rash
  D. Tiny blisters, severe inflammation
 	
II. Location
  A. Found in the U. S. and Canada
  B. Grows as vine, ground creeper, or small bush
 	
III. Identification
  A. Green and shiny leaves in summer
  B. Red and orange leaves in autumn
  C. Grows in clusters of three leaflets
  D. Leaflets notched at edges
  E. Poison ivy berries
  F. Grow in clusters close to stem
  G. Are tiny, white textured berries
  H. Confused with Virginia creeper
  I. Grows on a vine with notched leaves
  J. Has dark blue berries
  K. Has clusters of more than five leaflets
 	
IV. Important characteristics
  A. Infected by skin touching oil in all parts of plant
  B. Infected by skin touching clothes, shoes, or pets that have poison oil on them
  C. Infected from contact with smoke from burning poison ivy
 	
V. Conclusion
  A. Avoid Infection
  B. Recognize and avoid plant
  C. Kill plant around home with weed killer
  D. Take pills for summer immunity
	I. Introduction
	  A. Is a well-known, poisonous plant
	  B. Produces rash in many people
	    1. Red, itchy rash
	    2. Tiny blisters
	    3. Severe inflammation
	
	II. Where poison ivy is located
	  A. Is found in the U. S. and Canada
	  B. Grows as vine, ground creeper, or small bush
	
	III. What poison ivy looks like
	  A. Leaves
	    1. Green, shiny leaves in summer
	    2. Red, orange leaves in autumn
	    3. Three leaflets in a cluster
	    4. Notched edges in leaflets
	  B. Berries
	    1. Grow in clusters close to stem
	    2. Are tiny, white textured berries
	  C. Virginia creeper
	    1. Confused with poison ivy
	    2. Grows on a vine with notched leaves
	    3. Has dark blue berries
	    4. Has clusters of more than five leaflets
	
	IV. How infection from poison ivy occurs
	  A. Infected by skin touching oil in all parts of plant
	  B. Infected by skin touching clothes, shoes, or pets that have poison oil on them
	  C. Infected from contact with smoke from burning poison ivy
	
	V. Conclusion
	  A. Avoid Infection
	  B. Recognize and avoid plant
	  C. Kill plant around home with weed killer
	  D. Take pills for summer immunity

Note:

As you finish your report in the next two lessons, Lesson 4 and Lesson 5, make sure you follow the directions given for each step very carefully.

CHAPTER 17 LESSON 4

Step 9. Write a rough draft.

With your notes and outline before you, write your rough draft. Be sure to follow the order of your outline. If you decide to include another topic or eliminate a topic, stop and reorganize the outline. Remember, your outline is the visual "map" of your report. It will keep you going in the right direction. Keep it up-to-date. Always keep in mind that you should use your own words in your report as you present facts and give examples. This will make your paper special, because no one writes quite like you.

Guidelines for writing your rough draft

1. Use a pencil and skip every other line on your notebook paper.

2. Your report will be at least a five-paragraph report that will be similar in form to the five-paragraph essay. You will have an introductory paragraph, a three or four paragraph body, and a concluding paragraph.

3. **Introduction.** Look at your outline and write at least three sentences for the introductory paragraph. The **first sentence** is a topic sentence that tells what your report is about. The **second sentence** is an extra information or definition sentence that tells more about the topic. The **third sentence** is an enumeration sentence that tells how many main topics will be in the report.

4. **Body.** Look at your note cards and the first main topic on your outline (Roman numeral II.) Write a topic sentence that states your first point and tells what the second paragraph will be about. Remember to indent. Then, look at your note cards and the subtopics and details on your outline and write complete sentences that support the main idea of this paragraph. Be sure to write the subtopic sentences and detail sentences in the order of your outline.

   For the next two paragraphs, look at the main topics, the subtopics, and the details on your outline (Roman numerals III. and IV.) Write a topic sentence for each point that tells what each paragraph will be about. Write supporting sentences and detail sentences to develop each main topic.

5. **Conclusion.** Look at your outline to write a concluding paragraph. Write one or two sentences that include summarizing facts that support statements in your introduction. Write a final sentence for your report based on conclusions you have drawn from your research.

6. **Title Page.** Make a title page with the information that is shown in the example below. The title page will be the first page of your final paper.

7. **Bibliography Page.** At the end of your report, you will use your bibliography cards to list all the books and articles (sources) that you actually used in writing your paper. This bibliography page will be the last page of your report and will be turned in with your final paper. Use the example below to help you.

Title of Paper By (Your Name) Teacher's Name Date Period Class	Bibliography Wells, Jason T. "Poison Ivy." Coffman Encyclopedia. 1994 ed.

CHAPTER 17 LESSON 5

Step 10. Edit the rough draft.

Revision is part of writing. During your editing time, check the spelling, usage, capitalization, and punctuation of your report. You should also remember to check for good organization, for clear and logical development of ideas, and for your general statements to be supported by details and examples. After you edit your rough draft, have at least one more person edit it. The final responsibility for editing, however, is yours.

Guidelines for editing your rough draft

1. Is the first line of each paragraph indented?
2. Does your paper have an introduction, body, and conclusion?
3. Does each sentence support the main idea of each paragraph?
4. Do your main topics and supporting sentences follow the order of your outline?
5. Have you capitalized and punctuated your sentences correctly?
6. Have you spelled each word correctly?
7. Have you read your report orally to see how it sounds?
8. Have you checked for sentence fragments and run-on sentences?
9. Are your sentences varied to avoid monotony?
10. Have you completed a title page and a bibliography page and checked for correct form?

Step 11. Write the final outline.

Check over your second draft outline to see if there are any revisions necessary after writing and editing the rough draft for your report. Make any necessary changes. Then write your final outline neatly in ink. It will be handed in with your final report.

Step 12. Write the final report.

Before you recopy your edited rough draft for your final paper, reread the introductory and concluding paragraphs. Your introduction should get the reader's interest and should briefly tell the main idea of the report. Your conclusion should restate your most important points. Make any necessary changes. Also, decide if you want to include illustrations with your final report. If so, they must be completed at this point. Then write your final report neatly in ink. Finally, proofread your final paper again.

Step 13. Put the final report and all related research work in the correct order.

Title page - in ink
Final report - in ink
Illustrations (optional)
Bibliography page - in ink
Final Outline - in ink
Rough draft - in pencil
First draft outline - in pencil
Second draft outline - in pencil
Note cards and bibliography cards (Put all cards in a ziploc bag.)

Step 14. Hand in final report and all related papers.

Make sure all papers are in order and ready to be handed in. Then, hand in your research report and all related papers when your teacher calls for them.

CHAPTER 17 LESSON 5 APPLICATION TEST

Exercise 1: Classify each sentence.

1. _____ During the rescue the firefighters became heroes in the eyes of the frightened families.

2. _____ Our favorite vacation place is the beach along the eastern coast of Florida.

3. _____ Fifteen tons of wheat will be an unusually large shipment for our small freight company.

Directions: Complete the noun job table. Use Sentence 3.

List the Noun Used	List the Noun Job	Singular or Plural	Common or Proper
4.	5.	6.	7.
8.	9.	10.	11.
12.	13.	14.	15.
16.	17.	18.	19.

Exercise 2: On notebook paper, write the correct answer to each question below.

20. List the 14 steps for researching a topic and writing a report.
21. Name the two kinds of outlines.
22. Name three sources you can use for a report.
23. Write the 5 things an outline must have.
24. Write the order of the pages of your report when they are handed in.

Exercise 3: Match the definitions. Write the correct number from the second column beside each concept in the first column.

_____	25. a detailed list of the sources used in your report	1.	parallel form
_____	26. a card for each source used in your report	2.	subtopics
_____	27. reading the key parts to select a source	3.	note cards
_____	28. indicate the details in an outline	4.	bibliography
_____	29. give more information about a main topic	5.	capital letters
_____	30. file that lists all books in the library	6.	title of source and page number
_____	31. where to write notes	7.	periodical
_____	32. indicate main topics in an outline	8.	sentence and topic
_____	33. what to write at the top of each note card	9.	main topics, subtopics, details
_____	34. how notes are written	10.	bibliography card
_____	35. two kind of outlines	11.	skimming
_____	36. what to write at the bottom of a note card	12.	in phrases, in your own words
_____	37. parts of an outline	13.	card catalog
_____	38. outline parts should begin the same way	14.	Roman numerals
_____	39. indicate subtopics in an outline	15.	a topic category
_____	40. magazine	16.	Arabic numerals

CHAPTER 18 LESSON 1

Mixed Patterns 1-4

The sentences that you will classify with your teacher will be a mixture of Pattern 1: SN V P1, Pattern 2: SN V-t DO P2, Pattern 3: SN V-t IO DO P3, and Pattern 4: SN LV PrN. As you classify these sentences, look carefully at the main parts so you can identify the correct pattern for each sentence.

Point of View Chart

Point of View	Explanation	Singular Point of View Pronouns	Plural Point of View Pronouns
First person	the person speaking	I, me, my, mine	we, us, our, ours
Second person	the person spoken to	you, your, yours	you, your, yours
Third person	the person spoken about	he, him, his, she, her, hers, it, its	they, them, their, theirs

Guided Practice: Identify the point of view of each sentence by writing **1** for first, **2** for second, or **3** for third in each blank.

1. ____ I asked Mom a question.   3. ____ He asked Mom a question.   5. ____ You asked Mom a question.
2. ____ I asked her a question.   4. ____ He asked her a question.   6. ____ You asked her a question.

Guided Practice: Identify the point of view of each paragraph as 1st, 2nd, or 3rd by putting parentheses around the number.

Person:
1st 2nd 3rd   I stared in disbelief at the mummy before my eyes! The features had been perfectly preserved for thousands of years. This exhibit was certainly interesting to me.

Person:
1st 2nd 3rd   He stared in disbelief at the mummy before his eyes! The features had been perfectly preserved for thousands of years. This exhibit was certainly interesting to him.

Pronoun Cases of Personal Pronouns

Pronouns function in sentences in any of the jobs in which nouns function: as subjects, as objects (objects of the preposition, direct and indirect objects), as predicate nouns, and as possessive nouns. A *noun* may be used for all these jobs *without* changing its form (except for possessive nouns), but most of the personal *pronouns must change forms* to show whether they function as the subject ,the object, or a possessive. (*It* and *you* are exceptions.) When these pronouns change form, they are in different cases: the subjective case, the objective case, and the possessive case. Study the chart below to learn the forms of each of the personal pronouns for each case.

Pronoun Cases Chart

Pronoun Case	Explanation	Singular Pronoun Forms	Plural Pronoun Forms
Subjective case	used as a SP or a Pred Pronoun	I, you, he, she, it	we, you, they
Objective case	used as an DO, IO, OP	me, you, him, her, it	us, you, them
Possessive case	used to show ownership (PP)	my, your, his, her, its mine, yours, hers	our, your, their ours, yours, theirs

Guided Practice: Underline the correct pronoun choices. Then write the pronoun job (**SP, OP, IO, DO, PP**) in the blank.

1. (____) (We, Us) wanted programs for (____) (he and I, him and me).   2. (____) (He and I, Him and me) searched quickly for (____) (they, them).   3. Jim and (____) (us, we) boys didn't notice Casey and (____) (they, them).

Guided Practice: Using Sentences 1-3 below, write each underlined pronoun in the chart under **Pronoun**. Under **Job**, write **SP, OP,IO, DO,** or **PP** to tell its job in the sentence. Under **Case**, write **S** for the subjective case, **O** for the objective case, or **P** for the possessive case. Finally, write **S** for singular or **P** for plural.

1. <u>She</u> dedicated <u>her</u> song to <u>him</u>.   2. <u>They</u> gave Sam and <u>me</u> a birthday party.   3. <u>He</u> walked <u>her</u> to <u>her</u> car.

Pronoun	Job	Case (S, O, P)	S-P	Pronoun	Job	Case (S, O, P)	S-P
a.				e.			
b.				f.			
c.				g.			
d.				h.			

CHAPTER 18 LESSON 1 SKILL TEST

Exercise 1: Write each underlined pronoun in the chart under **Pronoun**. Under **Job**, write **SP, OP, IO, DO**, or **PP** to tell its job in the sentence. Under **Case**, write **S** for the subjective case, **O** for the objective case, or **P** for the possessive case. Finally, write **S** for singular or **P** for plural. (*Use the letter C to signify compound jobs:* **COP**)

1. You (a) talked quietly on the phone about him (b).
2. She (c) skipped happily along the path to her (d) house.
3. He (e) sang sweetly for us (f) at the concert.
4. My (g) mom searched desperately for any information about him (h) and me (i).
5. We (j) boys gave Frank and him (k) a rod and reel set for their (l) birthday.

Pronoun	Job	Case (S, O, P)	S-P	Pronoun	Job	Case (S, O, P)	S-P
a.				g.			
b.				h.			
c.				i.			
d.				j.			
e.				k.			
f.				l.			

Exercise 2: Underline the correct pronoun choices. Then write each pronoun job (**SP, OP, IO, DO, PP**) in the blank.

6. (She, Her) walked through the crowd with (he and I, him and me).	a.	b.
7. (He and I, Him and me) read loudly to (they, them).	c.	d
8. (He, Him) cried sadly for (she and I, her and me).	e.	f.
9. (They, Them) worked quietly in the library with (us, we).	g.	h.
10. Paul and (her, she) invited (us, we) boys to the movies.	i.	j.

Exercise 3: Identify the point of view of each sentence by writing **1** for first, **2** for second, or **3** for third in each blank.

11. _____ I listened as the teacher spoke.
12. _____ Finish spreading the fertilizer.
13. _____ We are working in our yard.
14. _____ Jay and Mitch worked in their yard.
15. _____ They picked up rocks and planted grass.
16. _____ You need to check this paper carefully.

Exercise 4: Identify the point of view of each paragraph as 1st, 2nd, or 3rd by putting parentheses around the number.

17.	Person: 1st 2nd 3rd	This is how you find the stadium. First, you travel north on Maple Street. Then, turn left on Oak Street and go 5 blocks. You will see the stadium on the right.
18.	Person: 1st 2nd 3rd	Patti and Jan like to sing songs with their children. They are always thinking of silly dances to go with the songs. They entertain the neighborhood with their funny songs and dances.
19.	Person: 1st 2nd 3rd	I often baby-sit for Sandy and Bill. I like to take their little girls to the park. We have fun on the swings and slides. Sometimes I pack my ice chest with a picnic lunch for us.

Exercise 5: Write personal pronouns in the blanks to make each paragraph the appropriate point-of-view.

20. 1st Person	(a) _____ enjoy watching old movies at (b) _____ house. (c) _____ like to eat popcorn while (d) _____ watch. (e) _____ favorite movies are the old Westerns that were popular when (f) _____ parents were young.
21. 3rd Person	John likes to play (a) _____ trombone loudly. (b) _____ family is proud of (c) _____; therefore, (d) _____ don't mind when (e) _____ practices loudly for long hours. (f) _____ just wear earplugs and keep smiling.

CHAPTER 18 LESSON 2

Independent Research Writing Assignment # 30, Part 1

For your first independent research writing assignment, you will only be required to use an encyclopedia source, which is provided below. All steps that you will use for researching a topic and writing a report will be listed at the beginning of your assignment so that you can follow them. In this assignment, you will do Steps 1-6. (Remember to keep your note cards in a ziplock bag so that you will not lose them.) Always refer back to Chapter 17 for examples and detailed explanations of each step.

Research Steps for Independent Writing Assignment # 30, Part 1

Step 1: Narrow the topic. **Cave Dwellers** (This is your narrowed topic.)
Step 2: Make an outline guide.
Step 3: Select sources by skimming.
Step 4: Make a bibliography card for each source selected.
Step 5: Take notes.
Step 6: Organize note cards.

ENCYCLOPEDIA SOURCE

Cave Dwellers

Speleology is the science of caves. Therefore, a speleologist is a "cave-scientist." Cave scientists spend much of their time researching the world's caves. Part of this research includes a look into the life forms that inhabit caves. Speleologists have identified three types of creatures that live in caves. They call them troglobites, troglophiles, and trogloxenes.

Troglobites are permanent cave dwellers that live constantly inside caves. They inhabit the cave's deepest recesses. Some of these include the blindfish, found in caves throughout the world. Blindfish usually have translucent, or transparent, bodies, but no eyes. The blindfish locates its victim by sensors on its head and side. A less common but spectacular troglobite is the glowworm, which is actually the larvae of the cave gnat. Found in New Zealand, the glowworm is the only cave creature that has its own light source. Glowworms cluster on cave ceilings and give off a greenish-blue light. Another troglobite is the blind salamander. One variety is called Proteus because it is born with real, but sightless, eyes which it loses as it grows older. This pinkish-white, transparent cave creature can survive for long periods without food. One of the most common American cave varieties is the Ozark blind salamander.

Next are the troglophiles. These are creatures that live inside the cave but leave to feed, usually at night. Two of these nocturnal creatures are the bat and the cave cricket. Bats of all varieties inhabit caves. They usually sleep during the daytime, hanging upside down from the ceilings or walls. At dusk they exit the cave to feed, sometimes in whole colonies. The exit of a whole colony, such as the nightly bat flight at Carlsbad Caverns, is quite spectacular. Like the bat, the cave cricket generally remains inside the cave during the day and exits to feed at night. However, its exit is usually in cycles or "shifts," with one-third of the cricket population leaving one night, the second third the next, and so on.

Last are the trogloxenes. These are actually visitors to the cave that do not live far inside year-round as the troglobites do. Some birds may be included in this category. Such is the oilbird of South America (so named for the blubber taken from its young for oil used by local inhabitants). The oilbird is a brown owl-like bird that nests and breeds near the surface of the cave (but far enough in to qualify the bird as a trogloxene). These birds feed on seed and fruit outside the cave and are basically nocturnal in their feeding habits. Another trogloxene is the "Daddy-Long-Legs," which hibernates inside caves in winter in clusters of thousands on the walls, but in summer lives outside. Actually, man can be considered a trogloxene. He does enter caves at times, but his actual use of caves for living is infrequent.

Article from *Coffman Encyclopedia*, 1994, Vol. 3, "Cave Dwellers" by Teddie Faye Raines   38

Note to the student: The bibliographical information provided at the bottom of this article is **not** in the correct order. Part of your assignment is to record it correctly on your bibliography card. Any time you see bibliographical information in any of the articles provided in future chapters, remember to record it correctly on your bibliography cards.

CHAPTER 18 LESSON 3 APPLICATION TEST

Exercise 1: Mixed Patterns 1-4. Classify each sentence.

1. _____ Clothes, jewelry, and scarves were the items in her dresser drawer.

2. _____ Coach Hawkins is giving Tony and me lessons in wrestling after school.

3. _____ A flock of bewildered pigeons circled overhead during the electrical storm.

Exercise 2: Write each underlined pronoun in the chart under **Pronoun**. Under **Job**, write **SP, OP, IO, DO**, or **PP** to tell its job in the sentence. Under **Case**, write **S** for the subjective case, **O** for the objective case, or **P** for the possessive case. Finally, write **S** for singular or **P** for plural.

4. Our (a) new dog waits eagerly for us (b) in the afternoon.
5. He (c) barks at us (d) playfully in front of our (e) house.
6. We (f) play with him (g) every day after school in their (h) backyard.

Pronoun	Job	Case (S, O, P)	S-P	Pronoun	Job	Case (S, O, P)	S-P
a.				e.			
b.				f.			
c.				g.			
d.				h.			

Exercise 3: Underline the correct pronoun choices. Then write each pronoun job (**SP, OP, IO, DO, PP**) in the blank.

7. (They, Them) waved at (him and me, he and I) from the window.	a.	b.
8. (She and I, Her and me) have spoken to the principal about (they, them).	c.	d.
9. (We, Us) girls baked (you, your) a cake yesterday.	e.	f.
10. (He and I, Him and Me) gave (they, them) tickets to the NCAA basketball tournament.	g.	h.

Exercise 4: Identify the point of view of each paragraph as 1st, 2nd, or 3rd by putting parentheses around the number.

11.	Person: 1st 2nd 3rd	You learn how to be an effective speaker by following certain steps. First, you need to know your topic. Next, you organize your notes and practice. Finally, you look at your audience, smile, and begin.
12.	Person: 1st 2nd 3rd	Jim and I love early morning walks along the beach. We enjoy feeling the sand between our toes, and we enjoy watching the gentle morning waves sweep along the beach.
13.	Person: 1st 2nd 3rd	Toni and Jack looked at each other and laughed. They couldn't believe their luck! They had found their tickets to the game in Grumpy's doghouse!

Exercise 5:   **Editing Paragraph**

Find each error and write the correction. Use the Editing Guide to help you. **Editing Guide: Capitals: 23 Commas: 6 Apostrophes: 5 A/An: 1 Misspelled Words: 2 Subject-Verb Agreement: 6 Quotations: 4 End Marks: 11**

the whole famile watch gleefully as dad turns on the tv to watch the basketball trounment

soon dad leaps out of his easy chair and shout no that wasnt an foul get some glasses ref so

that you can see the fouls then dad grab the remote control and switch the channel off the

basketball game the quiet golf tournament doesnt help dads mood finally, he cant stand it any

longer anxiously, dad switch back just as his favorite team the arkansas razorbacks shoots the

winning basket oh no i cant believe i missed the whole thing dad moan

Note: The commas provided after the transition words *finally* and *anxiously* are not included in the total commas on the Editing Guide.

CHAPTER 18 LESSON 3

Independent Research Writing Assignment #30, Part 2
For the second part of your independent research writing assignment, you will do Steps 7-8. These steps will guide you as you continue your assignment. Always refer back to Chapter 17 for examples and detailed explanations of each step.

Research Steps for Independent Writing Assignment #30, Part 2
Step 7: Make a first draft outline.
Step 8: Make a second draft outline.

CHAPTER 18 LESSON 4

Word Analogy Exercise: Choose the correct missing word and put the letter in the blank.

1. motive:reason::pledge _____   a. promise   b. lie   c. help   d. pretend
2. serious:funny:: _____ :anxious   a. talking   b. frantic   c. peaceful   d. disgusted
3. baseball:home run::football: _____   a. soccer   b. touchdown   c. goal   d. basket

Independent Research Writing Assignment #30, Part 3
For the third part of your independent research writing assignment, you will do Steps 9-10. These steps will guide you as you continue your assignment. Always refer back to Chapter 17 for examples and detailed explanations of each step.

Research Steps for Independent Writing Assignment #30, Part 3
Step 9: Write a rough draft.

Step 10: Edit your rough draft.

CHAPTER 18 LESSON 5

Independent Research Writing Assignment #30, Part 4
For the fourth part of your independent research writing assignment, you will do Steps 11-14. These steps will guide you as you finish your assignment. Always refer back to Chapter 17 for examples and detailed explanations of each step.

Research Steps for Independent Writing Assignment #30, Part 4
Step 11: Write your final outline.
Step 12: Write your final report.
Step 13: Put final report and all related research work in the correct order.
Step 14: Hand in final report and all related papers.

CHAPTER 19 LESSON 1

Sentence Pattern 5 and Predicate Adjective

A **Pattern 5** sentence has this word order: subject noun / linking verb / predicate adjective (**SN LV PA**). Pattern 5 is the same as Pattern 4 in that they both have linking verbs. Pattern 5 is different from Pattern 4 because it has an adjective (instead of a noun) in the predicate that modifies only the subject noun. This adjective is called a **predicate adjective**.

To find a predicate adjective, always ask the adjective question *what kind* of subject after the verb. A predicate adjective comes after a linking verb that links or connects it to the subject. A predicate adjective is labeled **PA**.

Sample Sentence for the exact words to say to find the linking verb and predicate adjective.

1. Her new dress is magnificent!
2. What is magnificent? dress - SN
3. What is being said about dress? dress is - V
4. Dress is what? magnificent - verify the adjective
5. What kind of dress? magnificent - PA
    (Say: magnificent - predicate adjective.)
6. Is - LV
7. What kind of dress? new - adj
8. Whose dress? her - PPA

9. SN LV PA P5 Check *(Say: Subject noun, linking verb, predicate adjective, Pattern 5, check.)*
10. Check the verb: linking verb.
11. Check again for prepositional phrases.
12. No prepositional phrases.
13. Exclamation point, strong feeling, exclamatory sentence.
14. Go back to the verb - divide the complete subject from the complete predicate.
15. Is there an adverb exception? No.
16. Is this sentence in a natural or inverted order?
    Natural - no change.

A question and answer example of Sentence 5 from the Introductory Sentences is written out for you below.

Question and Answer Flow Example

Question and Answer Flow for Sentence 5: Our dinner portions at the banquet were quite modest.

1. What were quite modest? portions - SN
2. What is being said about portions? portions were - V
3. Portions were what? modest - verify the adjective
4. What kind of portions? modest - PA
5. Were - LV
6. How modest? quite - Adv
7. At - P
8. At what? banquet - OP
9. The - A
10. What kind of portions? dinner - Adj

11. Whose portions? Our - PPA
12. SN LV PA P5 Check
13. Check the verb: linking verb.
14. Check again for prepositional phrases.
15. (At the banquet) - Prepositional phrase
16. Period, statement, Declarative sentence
17. Go back to the verb - divide the complete subject from the complete predicate.
18. Is there an adverb exception? No.
19. Is this sentence in a natural or inverted order?
    Natural - no change.

Classified Sentence:

```
                          PPA  Adj    SN    P   A   OP      LV  Adv  PA
            SN  LV         Our dinner portions (at the banquet) / were quite modest.  D
            PA  P5
```

Assignment

1. Write one **Practice Sentence** following these labels:
    PPA   Adj   SN   LV   PA   P   A   OP

2. Write an **Improved Sentence** from the Practice Sentence. Make at least two synonym changes, one antonym change, and your choice of complete word changes.

CHAPTER 19 LESSON 1

Pronouns and Their Antecedents

An **antecedent** is the noun that a pronoun replaces. The antecedent can be in the same sentence as the pronoun, or it can be in a different sentence.
Example 1: The *girl* loved *her* new shoes.
Example 2: The *girl* smiled. *She* loved *her* new shoes.

The pronoun *her* takes the place of the noun *girl*. Therefore, *girl* is the antecedent of the pronoun *her*. *Shoes* is not an antecedent because the pronoun *her* does not take the place of the noun *shoes*. Every personal pronoun must have an antecedent that it replaces.

The antecedent for every pronoun should be clear, and the pronoun should agree with its antecedent in both gender (male or female) and number (singular or plural).

1. If the antecedent **(girl)** is singular, then the antecedent's pronoun **(she, her, etc.)** must be singular.
2. If the antecedent **(girls)** is plural, then the antecedent's pronoun **(they, their, etc.)** must be plural.
3. If the antecedent **(girl, boy)** is a particular gender, then the antecedent's pronoun must be the same gender **(she, her or he, him, his, etc.).**

Guided Practice: Underline the correct personal pronoun. Put parentheses around its antecedent.
1. The bird squawked angrily at (its, their) owners.
2. The birds squawked angrily at (its, their) owners.
3. Jane's bird squawked angrily at (her, him) last night.

Guided Practice: Write the correct personal pronoun in the blank. Put parentheses around its antecedent.
1. Several prisoners escaped from the jail. _____ were captured today.
2. My dad goes fishing every day. _____ always takes _____ favorite fishing rod.

Other Types of Pronouns

In addition to the commonly-used personal pronouns, there are several other types of pronouns. In this chapter, you will study demonstrative and interrogative pronouns, demonstrative and interrogative adjectives, and the difference between demonstrative and interrogative pronouns and demonstrative and interrogative adjectives.

Demonstrative Pronouns

1. The demonstrative pronouns are *this, these, that, those*.
2. *This* and *that* are singular. *These* and *those* are plural.
3. Demonstrative pronouns point out which persons or things are referred to: **This** is my book.
4. *This* and *these* often point to persons or things that are near.
5. *That* and *those* point to persons or things farther away.
6. Demonstrative pronouns are usually found in a Pattern 4 sentence.
7. A demonstrative pronoun used as the subject means the same thing as the predicate noun.
   (**This** is my **book**. **These** are my **rings**. **That** was a good **meal**. **Those** are his **notes**.)
8. A demonstrative pronoun clearly points out its antecedent. (**This** is my **book**. **These** are my **books**.)

CHAPTER 19 LESSON 1

Demonstrative Adjectives

1. The demonstrative adjectives are *this, these, that, those.*
2. *This* and *that* are singular. *These* and *those* are plural.
3. Demonstrative adjectives modify nouns and are located in front of the nouns they modify. They always answer the **which** question. **This book** belongs to my dad. **Which** book? **This** book.
4. Use *this* and *these* to point out someone or something near.
5. Use *that* and *those* to point out something farther away.
6. The demonstrative adjective must agree in number with the noun it modifies:
   Singular noun - Singular adjective (**This** book)   Plural noun - plural adjective (**These** books)
7. A demonstrative pronoun has an antecedent. A demonstrative adjective never has an antecedent.
   Pronoun: **This** is a new **book**.   Adjective: **This book** is new.

Guided Practice: Write the four demonstrative pronouns in the correct column in the chart below.

Singular, near	Plural, near	Singular, far	Plural, far
1.	2.	3.	4.

Guided Practice: Identify the underlined word as a demonstrative pronoun or adjective and as singular or plural by underlining the correct choices. If the underlined word is a pronoun, write its antecedent in the blank.

1. This is my mom's new car.   (Dem Pro, Dem Adj) (Singular, Plural) (Antecedent _____)

2. This car belongs to my mother. (Dem Pro, Dem Adj) (Singular, Plural) (Antecedent _____)

Guided Practice: In the first blank, write the demonstrative pronoun that agrees in number with its antecedent. In the second blank write the antecedent. Underline the correct verb that agrees in number with the subject.

3. _____ (is, are) your muddy shoes by the back door! (Antecedent _____)

4. _____ (is, are) his jacket on the chair. (Antecedent _____)

Interrogative Pronouns

1. The interrogative pronouns are *who, what, which, whose, whom.*
2. An interrogative pronoun always begins with *wh: who, what, which, whose, whom.*
3. An interrogative pronoun asks a question, and it is usually used as the subject of a sentence.
   Who ate the pie? *What* are you doing? *Which* is the correct answer? *Whose* are these keys?
4. Sometimes the interrogative pronoun is a direct object. *Whom* do you like? (You do like *whom*?)
5. It is often difficult to choose between *who* or *whom* in a question. The pronoun **who** is used as a **subject** in a sentence: **(Who, Whom) is at the door?**
6. To check yourself, write an answer to the question using *he* for the pronoun *who*. **He is at the door.** (You will use the pronoun **Who** as the subject of this question.)
7. The pronoun **whom** is used as an **object** in a sentence: **(Who, Whom) did the students select?**
8. To check yourself, write an answer to the question using *him* for the pronoun *whom*. **The students selected him.** (You will use the pronoun **Whom** as the direct object of this question.)

Remember, the parts of a sentence can be rearranged in a subject-verb-object order to help you decide whether to use *who* or *whom*.

CHAPTER 19 LESSON 1

Interrogative Adjectives

1. The interrogative adjectives are *what, which,* and *whose.*

2. Interrogative adjectives modify nouns and ask a question:
   What book is used for science? **Which** book belongs to my sister? **Whose** books are on the table?

3. An interrogative pronoun is used alone. An interrogative adjective is used in front of the noun it modifies. Pronoun: **Which** is the newest car?   Adjective: **Which** car is newest?

Guided Practice: Tell whether the underlined word is an interrogative pronoun or adjective by underlining the (**Int Pro, Int Adj**) in parentheses.

1. <u>What</u> were the solutions to our problem? (Int Pro, Int Adj)

2. <u>What</u> book will you read for your report? (Int Pro, Int Adj)

Guided Practice: Underline the correct interrogative pronoun for the practice sentences below.

3. (Who, Whom) ordered the flowers?

4. The flowers were ordered by (who, whom)?

5. (Who, Whom) will you call for flowers?

CHAPTER 19 LESSON 2

Guidelines for Taking Notes from Two Sources

1. Go back to Chapter 17 and follow the examples given under note-taking.

2. Make sure you have chosen and listed the topic categories in your outline guide. You are only going to take notes that fit under the topic categories listed in your outline guide.

3. Take notes from one source at a time and put the notes on your note cards under the correct topic categories. You will not repeat notes from the second source that you have already taken from the first source.

4. The only difference between taking notes from one source and two sources is that you have more information, more bibliography cards, and more note cards. All the information you gather from the two sources should be different.

CHAPTER 19 LESSON 2

Independent Research Writing Assignment #31, Part 1

For your second independent research writing assignment, you will be required to use two sources, which are provided below. In this assignment, you will do Steps 1-5. Always refer back to Chapter 17 for examples and detailed explanations of each step.

Research Steps for Independent Writing Assignment #31, Part 1

Step 1: Narrow the topic. **Storms**
Step 2: Make an outline guide.
Step 3: Select sources by skimming.
Step 4: Make a bibliography card for each source selected.
Step 5: Take notes.

ENCYCLOPEDIA SOURCE	BOOK SOURCE
Tornadoes	**Tornado Safety**
Tornadoes are powerful storms with destructive winds that rotate at speeds of more than 200 miles per hour. Tornadoes are usually accompanied by heavy rain, thunder, lightning, and a loud, roaring sound. These violent windstorms are also called twisters, funnel clouds, or cyclones. Tornadoes usually occur along a weather front where a cool, dry mass of air meets a warm, moist mass of air. When these two air masses collide, a line of violent thunderstorms called a squall line occurs. Extremely rapid movement of warm air pushing upward, followed by more warm air rushing in and also pushing upward, sometimes causes the air to rotate. The rotating air then forms a tornado. When one of these spinning funnel clouds drops down to earth from a mass of dark thunderclouds, it can cause extensive property damage and death to anything or anyone in its path. The path of a tornado can vary in size from several hundred yards wide to 1 1/2 miles wide. Tornadoes can occur anywhere in the world, but most occur in the midwestern United States between the Mississippi River and the Rocky Mountains and in the southern United States along the states that border the Gulf of Mexico. In the United States, tornadoes tend to move across the land in a southwest to northeast direction at speeds of 10-60 miles per hour. Most tornadoes last less than an hour, but some have been reported to last several hours and travel a distance of 200 miles.	For a large portion of the United States, especially the South and Midwest, tornado safety is an important subject. If a tornado is approaching, there are things a person can do to protect himself from these life-threatening windstorms. If time permits, the safest thing to do is to seek shelter in a storm shelter, basement, or other underground structure. If you are unable to get to an underground shelter, seek safety inside a sturdy building, preferably one made of brick, concrete, or stone. Unsafe buildings include mobile homes, metal buildings, and buildings with wide-span roofs, such as gymnasiums, churches, and auditoriums. These structures tend to collapse under the violent 100-200 mile per hour winds of a tornado. Once inside a sturdy building, protect yourself by hiding under heavy furniture, in closets, or under stairwells. Stay away from windows and mirrors, and cover your body with a mattress or heavy blanket to protect against the flying debris carried by violent tornado winds. If you are driving in a car when a tornado approaches, you may be able to outrun the tornado if you are not in traffic. Tornadoes usually move in a southwest to northeast direction at varying rates of thirty to sixty miles per hour. Escape is possible if you can drive faster than the tornado and in a southwest to northeast direction. However, a vehicle is no match for a twister. Unless you are sure you can outrun the tornado, you should stop your car and seek shelter in a ditch or ravine. Lie flat on the ground and cover your face and head with your arms. Avoid trees and utility lines.
Coffman Encyclopedia, 1994, Vol. 19, "Tornado" by J. Blue, p. 111.	Book: *Violent Storms* by Jill Levin, Solo Press, Chicago, 1993. p. 9.

CHAPTER 19 LESSON 2 SKILL TEST A

Exercise 1: Write the four demonstrative pronouns in the correct column in the chart below. Identify the underlined word as a demonstrative pronoun or adjective and as singular or plural by underlining the correct choices. If the underlined word is a pronoun, write its antecedent in the blank.

Singular, near	Plural, near	Singular, far	Plural, far
1.	2.	3.	4.

5. <u>These</u> new cars are on sale. (Pro, Adj) (Singular, Plural) _____
6. <u>That</u> is my first grade teacher in the blue dress. (Pro, Adj) (Singular, Plural) _____
7. <u>This</u> record player does not work properly. (Pro, Adj) (Singular, Plural) _____
8. <u>Those</u> are our lawn chairs there on the beach. (Pro, Adj) (Singular, Plural) _____
9. <u>This</u> is your science experiment on the table here. (Pro, Adj) (Singular, Plural) _____
10. <u>That</u> storm destroyed my garden last night. (Pro, Adj) (Singular, Plural) _____
11. <u>These</u> are the best paintings in the art show. (Pro, Adj) (Singular, Plural) _____
12. <u>Those</u> buildings are protected with fire insurance. (Pro, Adj) (Singular, Plural) _____

Exercise 2: In the first blank, write a demonstrative pronoun that agrees in number with its antecedent. In the second blank write the antecedent. Underline the correct verb that agrees in number with the subject.

13. _____ (is, are) the ladies in your club by the far door. _____

14. _____ (is, are) our classroom in here. _____

15. _____ (was, were) my sister's picture in the newspaper. _____

16. _____ (was, were) my favorite flowers in this entire garden! _____

Exercise 3: Tell whether the underlined word is an interrogative pronoun or adjective by underlining the **Int Pro** or the **Int Adj** in parentheses.

17. <u>Which</u> is the smallest piece of candy? (Int Pro, Int Adj)
18. <u>Which</u> programs are listed in the television magazine? (Int Pro, Int Adj)
19. <u>Whose</u> are those tickets on the table? (Int Pro, Int Adj)
20. <u>Whose</u> car keys are on the shelf by the door? (Int Pro, Int Adj)
21. <u>What</u> are your answers to my questions? (Int Pro, Int Adj)
22. <u>What</u> papers are lying all over the floor? (Int Pro, Int Adj)
23. <u>Who</u> has been invited to your party? (Int Pro, Int Adj)
24. <u>Whom</u> does the teacher help every day? (Int Pro, Int Adj)

Exercise 4: Underline the correct interrogative pronoun in the sentences below.

25. (Who, Whom) gave the order to advance?
26. The team was coached by (who, whom)?
27. (Who, Whom) did you see at the game?

28. To (who, whom) did you wish to speak?
39. Yesterday (who, whom) heard the shot?
30. (Who, Whom) did they select?

CHAPTER 19 LESSON 3 APPLICATION TEST

Exercise 1: Classify each sentence.

1. _____ The adhesive tape was too sticky for the children.

2. _____ After the ceremony Sandra will be too tired for a shopping trip.

3. _____ My new boss was very tactful about the new rules and regulations on the job.

Directions: Complete the noun job table. Use Sentence 2.

List the Noun Used	List the Noun Job	Singular or Plural	Common or Proper
4.	5.	6.	7.
8.	9.	10.	11.
12.	13.	14.	15.

Exercise 2: Underline the demonstrative and interrogative words and then identify them by writing their abbreviations in the blank. (Use these abbreviations: **Dem Pro, Dem Adj, Int Pro, Int Adj**)

_____ 16. This is a fantastic view of the ocean!
_____ 17. That house burned to the ground on Christmas Eve.
_____ 18. What is the name of your school?
_____ 19. Which teams are picked for the exhibition game?
_____ 20. These file cabinets are full of tax records.
_____ 21. Who is the man in the white suit?
_____ 22. Whose sweater was left in the back of the room?
_____ 23. Those are the most colorful flowers in this show.
_____ 24. Whom did the judges name as the winner?
_____ 25. That is the science building over there.
_____ 26. These are the only books about Eisenhower in the library.
_____ 27. What time is the championship game on television?

Exercise 3: Underline the correct interrogative pronoun in the sentences below.

28. (Who, Whom) will you ask to the dance?
29. The plane was piloted by (who, whom)?
30. The chocolate pie was for (who, whom)?
31. Jim, (who, whom) was at the door?

Exercise 4:   **Editing Paragraph**

Find each error and write the correction. Use the Editing Guide to help you. **Editing Guide: Capitals: 10 Commas: 7 Apostrophes: 4 Misspelled Words: 4 Quotations: 10 End Marks: 6**

rick rolled over and groaned sleepily as his sister came bouncing in his room early one spring morning time to get up for school she anounced cheerfully as she fliped on the lights and opened the blinds

janet moaned rick as he cautosly opened one eye would you please tiptoe out the door after you turn the lights out and shut the blinds im so tired and its too early to get up

late night movies and early mornings dont mix chuckled janet then she added mischeivously lifes tough in the big city rick

CHAPTER 19 LESSON 3

Independent Research Writing Assignment #31, Part 2
For the second part of your independent research writing assignment, you will do Steps 6-8. These steps will guide you as you continue your assignment. Always refer back to Chapter 17 for examples and detailed explanations of each step.

Research Steps for Independent Writing Assignment #31, Part 2
Step 6: Organize note cards.
Step 7: Make a first draft outline.
Step 8: Make a second draft outline.

CHAPTER 19 LESSON 4

Word Analogy Exercise: Choose the correct missing word and put the letter in the blank.

1. Dalmation:dog::Siamese: _____   a. cat   b. eat   c. poodle   d. breed
2. dusk:dawn::summer: _____   a. winter   b. autumn   c. night   d. morning
3. assemble:construct::brave: _____   a. scared   b. build   c. astonish d. courageous

Independent Research Writing Assignment #31, Part 3
For the third part of your independent research writing assignment, you will do Steps 9-10. These steps will guide you as you continue your assignment. Always refer back to Chapter 17 for examples and detailed explanations of each step.

Research Steps for Independent Writing Assignment #31, Part 3
Step 9: Write a rough draft.
Step 10: Edit your rough draft.

CHAPTER 19 LESSON 5

Independent Research Writing Assignment #31, Part 4
For the fourth part of your independent research writing assignment, you will do Steps 11-14. These steps will guide you as you finish your assignment. Always refer back to Chapter 17 for examples and detailed explanations of each step.

Research Steps for Independent Writing Assignment #31, Part 4
Step 11: Write your final outline.
Step 12: Write your final report.
Step 13: Put final report and all related research work in the correct order.
Step 14: Hand in final report and all related papers.

CHAPTER 19 LESSON 5 SKILL TEST B

Exercise 1: Write the four demonstrative pronouns in the correct column in the chart below. Identify the underlined word as a demonstrative pronoun or adjective and as singular or plural by underlining the correct choices. If the underlined word is a pronoun, write its antecedent in the blank.

Singular, near	Plural, near	Singular, far	Plural, far
1.	2.	3.	4.

5. <u>These</u> props are for our play. (Pro, Adj) (Singular, Plural) _____
6. <u>These</u> are the props for the play. (Pro, Adj) (Singular, Plural) _____
7. <u>That</u> was my favorite song on the radio. (Pro, Adj) (Singular, Plural) _____
8. <u>That</u> girl helps my aunt with her garden. (Pro, Adj) (Singular, Plural) _____
9. <u>Those</u> were Aunt Sophie's photographs. (Pro, Adj) (Singular, Plural) _____
10. <u>Those</u> pies tasted delicious yesterday. (Pro, Adj) (Singular, Plural) _____
11. <u>This</u> is the finest goldfish in the pond. (Pro, Adj) (Singular, Plural) _____
12. <u>This</u> watch is not keeping accurate time. (Pro, Adj) (Singular, Plural) _____

Exercise 2: In the first blank, write a demonstrative pronoun that agrees in number with its antecedent. In the second blank write the antecedent. Underline the correct verb that agrees in number with the subject.

13. _____ (is, are) Dad's muddy shoes on the porch. _____

14. _____ (is, are) our basketball team on the court. _____

15. _____ (was, were) Jenny's books over there. _____

16. _____ (was, were) an enjoyable evening. _____

Exercise 3: Tell whether the underlined word is an interrogative pronoun or adjective by underlining the **Int Pro** or the **Int Adj** in parentheses.

17. <u>Which</u> is the best costume for the contest? (Int Pro, Int Adj)
18. <u>Which</u> movie did you see at the theater? (Int Pro, Int Adj)
19. <u>Whose</u> coat is still hanging on the coat hook? (Int Pro, Int Adj)
20. <u>Whose</u> are those shoes? (Int Pro, Int Adj)
21. <u>What</u> subjects are offered at the community college? (Int Pro, Int Adj)
22. <u>What</u> is the name of the longest street in town? (Int Pro, Int Adj)
23. <u>Which</u> are the fish from the Gulf of Mexico?   (Int Pro, Int Adj)
24. <u>Whose</u> are these computer discs? (Int Pro, Int Adj)

Exercise 4: Underline the correct interrogative pronoun in the sentences below.

25. (Who, Whom) did the announcer call ?
26. The contest was won by (who, whom)?
27. (Who, Whom) does the crowd like best?
28. To (who, whom) does this mess belong?
29. (Who, Whom) solved the puzzle the fastest?
30. (Who, Whom) answered the doorbell just now?

CHAPTER 20 LESSON 1

Pattern 5 Review

You will review Pattern 5 by classifying a set of Practice Sentences with your teacher. As you classify these sentences, look carefully at the main parts so you can identify Pattern 5 easily and accurately.

Indefinite Pronouns

In this chapter, you will study another type of pronoun. This is the indefinite pronoun. *Indefinite* means not definite or not specific. A pronoun that does not refer to a definite person, place, or thing is called an **indefinite pronoun.** The list below will tell you which indefinite pronouns are singular, which ones are plural, and which ones can be either singular or plural.

Indefinite Pronoun Chart

1. These indefinite pronouns are considered singular and take a singular verb:
   another, anybody, anyone, anything, each, either, everybody, everyone, everything, much, neither, nobody, no one, nothing, one, somebody, someone, something.

2. These indefinite pronouns are always plural and take a plural verb: **both, few, many, several, others.**

3. These indefinite pronouns are either singular or plural, depending on how they are used in the sentence: **all, any, half, most, none, some.**

There are four general rules you should know about indefinite pronouns that will help you use them correctly. Understanding each of these rules will make working with indefinite pronouns easier. Study each rule and the examples below.

Rule 1. Indefinite pronouns can be used as subjects or objects, but if an indefinite word is used as an adjective, then it is not an indefinite pronoun.

Subject: **Several** voted for the amendment. Object: The coach praised **several** of the players. Adjective: **Several** men were in line.

Guided Practice: In the first column write *IP* or *Adj* to show if the underlined word is an indefinite pronoun or an adjective. In the second column write *SP, OP, DO, IO* to show the job of the indefinite pronoun. If the word is an adjective, write *Adj* in the second column.

IP or Adj		Pronoun Job/Adj
	1. <u>Each</u> of you can drive around the practice course.	
	2. <u>Each</u> person can drive around the practice course.	
	3. The school gave <u>many</u> of the students an award.	
	4 My mother shopped for <u>anything</u> on sale.	
	5. The President wrote <u>several</u> of his own speeches.	

CHAPTER 20 LESSON 1

Rule 2: Indefinite pronouns must have subject-verb agreement if they are used as subjects.
    Singular subject: **No one** *likes* this movie.   Plural subject: **Many** *like* this movie.

Rule 3: Indefinite pronouns must also agree in number and gender with any possessive pronouns that refer to them. If there is no way to determine gender from the context of the sentence, the male gender is assumed.
    Singular indefinite pronoun: **Everybody** chooses *his* own seat.   Plural indefinite pronoun: **Others** choose *their* seats.

Guided Practice: Underline each indefinite pronoun and write **S** or **P** for singular or plural in the blank. Underline the correct verb and the correct possessive pronoun to agree with the subject. Use the Indefinite Pronoun Chart to help you.

6. _____ Nobody (finish, finishes) (his, their) chores before noon!

7. _____ Few (has, have) completed (his, their) science projects.

8. _____ One of the students (walk, walks) a long distance to (his, their) bus stop.

9. _____ Everyone (is, are) making (her, their) mother a present.

Rule 4: If a singular/plural indefinite pronoun (*all, any, half, most, none, some*) is followed by a prepositional phrase, the object of the preposition determines whether the indefinite pronoun is singular or plural.
    Singular indefinite pronoun: **None** of the *bread* is on the table.   Plural indefinite pronoun: **All** of the *children* are sleeping.

Guided Practice: Underline each indefinite pronoun and write **S** or **P** for singular or plural in the blank. Underline the correct verb and the correct possessive pronoun to agree with the subject. Use the Indefinite Pronoun Chart to help you.

10. _____ Most of the old books (was, were) in (its, their) original covers.

11. _____ Most of this old car (is, are) in (its, their) original condition.

12. _____ Some of the students (ride, rides) (his, their) bicycles to school every day.

13. _____ Some of the silver (has, have) lost (its, their) shine.

14. _____ All of the flour (was, were) in (its, their) container.

15. _____ All of the eggs (was, were) sitting in (its, their) containers.

Guided Practice: Write an indefinite pronoun in the blank. Make sure it agrees with the verb and possessive pronoun in number. (*Answers may vary.*)

16. _____ listens for her name on the loud-speaker. (*must be singular*)

17. _____ listen for their names on the loud-speaker. (*must be plural*)

18. _____ in my class studies quietly for his test. (*must be singular*)

19. _____ understand fully about our new grading system. (*must be plural*)

20. _____ of the new students were introduced to their classes. (*must be plural*)

CHAPTER 20 LESSON 1 SKILL TEST

Exercise 1: Underline the correct personal pronoun once and its antecedent twice.

1. My cow had (her, their) calves in March.
2. Andrea made chicken for our guests. (She, They) enjoys cooking.
3. My ring fell through the boards on the deck. (It, They) were only two inches apart.
4. Linda found flower seeds for the garden. Jan helped her plant (it, them) in the ground.
5. Music and movies are very entertaining. (It, They) are my favorites!

Exercise 2: In the first column write **IP** or **Adj** to show if the underlined word is an indefinite pronoun or an adjective. In the second column write **SP, OP, DO, IO** to show the job of the indefinite pronoun. If the word is an adjective, write **Adj** in the second column.

IP or Adj		Pronoun Job/Adj
	6. <u>Both</u> of my parents enjoy mystery books.	
	7. <u>Both</u> shoes were covered with mud from the creek bed.	
	8. The telephone rang repeatedly for <u>someone</u> down the hall.	
	9. <u>Everything</u> was perfectly arranged in the display case.	
	10. Susan left <u>everything</u> on the table in the kitchen.	
	11. <u>Several</u> magazines were donated to the school library.	
	12. The company gave <u>several</u> of the employees a raise.	
	13. I did not hear from <u>any</u> of you over summer vacation.	
	14. <u>Another</u> child asked for permission first.	
	15. <u>Everybody</u> at the concert was singing with the choir.	

Exercise 3: For blanks 16-20, write five indefinite pronouns that are always plural. Then for blanks 21-25, write five indefinite pronouns that are either singular or plural, depending on how they are used in the sentence.

16.	17.	18.	19.	20.
21.	22.	23.	24.	25.

Exercise 4: Underline each indefinite pronoun and write **S** or **P** for singular or plural in the blank. Then underline the correct verb. Use the indefinite pronoun chart to help you.

26. ___ All of the cake (is, are) gone.
27. ___ None of the flowers (was, were) wilted.
28. ___ All of the students (is, are) here.
29. ___ Most of the bread (has, have) mold on it.
30. ___ Most of the people (has, have) a job.
31. ___ Everyone with tickets (were, was) admitted.
32. ___ Several of my dogs (is, are) hungry.
33. ___ One of the tables (is, are) broken.
34. ___ Few of the guests (has, have) a bobsled.
35. ___ Several in this box (is, are) torn.
36. ___ Each of the cars (has, have) a big price tag.
37. ___ Few in our class (has, have) failed.
38. ___ Neither of the dresses (interest, interests) me.
39. ___ Some of the milk (is, are) sour.
40. ___ None of the material (was, were) wasted.
41. ___ Some of the grapes (is, are) sour.
42. ___ All of my work (is, are) finished.
43. ___ Some of the glare (has, have) disappeared.
44. ___ Everyone in the audience (is, are) clapping.
45. ___ Both of the pies (is, are) apple.
46. ___ Somebody (know, knows) the answer.
47. ___ Everything on the tables (is, are) delicious.
48. ___ Someone in the stands (is, are) waving at us.
49. ___ Nobody (know, knows) our phone number.
50. ___ Both of the trees (is, are) old.
51. ___ No one in the crowd (look, looks) familiar.

CHAPTER 20 LESSON 2

Independent Research Writing Assignment #32, Part 1

For your next independent research writing assignment, you will be required to use three sources, which are provided on the next two pages. In this assignment, you will do Steps 1-5. (Remember to keep your note cards in a Ziploc bag so that you will not lose them.) Always refer back to Chapter 17 for examples and detailed explanations of each step.

Research Steps for Independent Writing Assignment #32, Part 1

Step 1: Narrow the topic.

Step 2: Make an outline guide.

Step 3: Select sources by skimming.

Step 4: Make a bibliography card for each source selected.

Step 5: Take notes.

Guidelines for Taking Notes from Three Sources:

1. Go back to Chapter 17 and follow the examples given under note-taking.
2. Make sure you have chosen and listed the topic categories in your outline guide. You are only going to take notes that fit under the topic categories listed in your outline guide.
3. Take notes from one source at a time and put the notes on your note cards under the correct topic categories. You will not repeat notes from the second or third source that you have already taken from the first source.
4. The only difference between taking notes from one or two sources and three sources is that you have more information, more bibliography cards, more note cards, etc. All the information you gather from all three sources will be different.

CHAPTER 20 LESSON 2

ENCYCLOPEDIA SOURCE

Ancient Maya

The ancient Maya civilization existed in what is presently southern Mexico and Central America from 800 B.C. to the early 1500's A.D. This highly-advanced Indian culture was noted for developing an accurate 365-day calendar based on the study of astronomy and mathematics and for developing an advanced system of mathematics based on the number 20 which included dots and dashes for numbers and a special symbol for the number zero. The Maya produced brightly-colored paintings, pottery, and sculpture, an advanced form of writing, and exceptional architecture that included pyramids made from limestone. These advancements are amazing considering the fact that Mayans did not have the wheel, horses, or oxen to carry stones.

Most of the Mayan people lived in thatched huts on individual family farms where they grew corn, beans, squash, tomatoes, chili peppers, and avocados. The men and boys cleared the land and farmed. The women and girls cooked, made clothing, cared for younger children, and gathered firewood and water. Mayan children were taught language, mathematics, and job skills by their families. Because of the hot tropical climate, Mayan clothing was made from woven cotton. Men wore loin cloths, and women wore loose fitting dresses down to their ankles. Jewelry was made from shells, feathers, and carved jade.

Mayan cities were centers for religious festivals and marketing. Religion played a very important role in the daily life of the Maya. They fasted, prayed, and sacrificed to many gods and goddesses. Dancing and feasts were favorite activities at their many religious festivals. During these festivals, the Maya played a game on a specially-designed court in which they tried to hit a rubber ball through a stone ring with their hips or elbows.

For reasons unknown to scientists, the Mayan people began to abandon their cities and leave the southern regions in 800 A. D. Then their territory was invaded by the Toltec Indians of Mexico in 950 A. D., and the cultures of the Mayan and Toltec were mixed. About 1440, the Mayan rulers were overthrown by the Mayan people. When the Spanish conquerors invaded in the early 1500's, what was left of Mayan control was easily overcome.

Author: Jamie J. Causey Source: *Coffman Encyclopedia*, 1995, Vol. 13, page 205.

CHAPTER 20 LESSON 2

BOOK SOURCE	MAGAZINE SOURCE
Ancient Persia	**Ancient Scandinavia**

Ancient Persia

The ancient Persian Empire stretched from the Mediterranean Sea to what is now Pakistan and from the southern part of Russia to the Gulf of Oman. Its center was in Persia in what is presently a part of Iran and Afghanistan. Early Persians were nomads who moved to that area in 900 B. C. from what is now southern Russia. Persia was conquered by Alexander the Great in 331 B. C. and later by Arabs in 641 A. D.

The Persians made lasting contributions to religion, government, and economic practices in the known world. The Persian people believed in gods of nature. They worshipped these gods on mountains instead of building temples for their religious ceremonies. Being truthful and honorable in business matters was important to the Persian people.

In addition, Persians were responsible for developing a highly-effective system of government in which sections of the empire were ruled by *satraps*, who answered to the king. The satraps developed a system of laws that were consistent throughout the empire and instituted a "secret service" to enforce it. Persian leaders also developed a postal system based on a series of couriers or messengers who relayed information between government officials.

Early Persians lived in mud huts and were farmers of grain and livestock. These farmers developed an efficient underground irrigation system to water the desert regions in the lowlands. Later, as cities developed and the need for farm tools decreased, making pottery, weaving cloth and rugs, and making pots and pans out of copper became important occupations. Because of its location near the Mediterranean Sea, Persia became an important connection to trade routes to the Far East.

Author: Carl Covington Source: *Ancient Cultures* Publisher: Lafferty Books, New York Copyright: 1991 Pages: 96-101.

Ancient Scandinavia

Scandinavia is a region of Europe that includes what are now Denmark, Sweden, and Norway. The people of this region during the time from 2000 B. C. were called Vikings. This name came from Vik, a pirate center in southern Norway. During this time, pirates and warriors from this Scandinavian region looted and terrorized Europe, and others from this region sailed and explored the North Atlantic Ocean.

Instead of pirating, most of the people in Scandinavia spent their time as farmers. Other occupations included fishing, metalworking, shipbuilding, and woodcarving. Vikings are especially noted for their shipbuilding and navigating. Viking shipbuilders were responsible for inventing the *keel*, an attachment of wood that extended the entire length of a ship and improved the ship's speed and traveling distance. Viking navigators developed a system of determining the latitude, using a table of figures and a measuring stick. Viking navigators also used ravens to help them find land.

Viking warriors were bold and fierce. When they invaded an area, they came in swiftly in their warships and took the people by surprise. Using axes, bows, spears, and swords, they overtook their victims quickly, often killing women and children and plundering and burning villages.

The Vikings spoke a Germanic language and used an alphabet made up of characters called runes. They lived in villages that were ruled by a king or chief. The people were divided into three classes: nobles, freeman, and slaves. Religion played an important part in the life of the Vikings. They worshipped a variety of gods, the most memorable being Thor, the ruler of the sky. Our weekday, Thursday, was named after this god.

Author: Vonda C. Clark Source: *Explorer's World*, March 1994 Pages 39-41.

CHAPTER 20 LESSON 3 APPLICATION TEST A

Exercise 1: Classify each sentence.

1. _____ Mrs. Gruff was exceedingly angry with the four boys and their obnoxious dogs.

2. _____ Mark and Dewayne are extremely intelligent.

3. _____ The dogs in the fenced yard seemed unusually happy and playful at the approach of the boys.

Directions: Complete the noun job table. Use Sentence 3.

List the Noun Used	List the Noun Job	Singular or Plural	Common or Proper
4.	5.	6.	7.
8.	9.	10.	11.
12.	13.	14.	15.
16.	17.	18.	19.

Exercise 2: Draw one line under the subject and write **S** or **P** for singular or plural in the blank. Then underline the correct verb and the correct possessive pronoun to agree with the subject. Use the Indefinite Pronoun Chart to help you.

20. _____ The flowers (loses, lose) (its, their) petals in the strong wind.
21. _____ Many of the boys (competes, compete) in (his, their) division.
22. _____ Neither of the women (like, likes) (her, their) dessert.
23. _____ Tom and Sally (goes, go) to town in (his, her, their) convertible.
24. _____ Each member of the girls' team (earn, earns) (her, their) own letter.
25. _____ Each of the girls in the contest (try, tries) (her, their) best.
26. _____ Did every member (pays, pay) (their, his) dues?
27. _____ The crowd (wave, waves) (their, its) flags and (yells, yell).
28. _____ Everyone in the club (supports, support) (his, their) team.
29. _____ (Don't, Doesn't) all of the animals in the zoo have (its, their) good points?
30. _____ Everyone (clap, claps) (his, their) hands at the pep rally.
31. _____ Few in the audience (want, wants) (his, their) names announced.
32. _____ Each of the soldiers (run, runs) twenty miles a day in (his, their) unit.

Exercise 3: In the first column write **IP** or **Adj** to show if the underlined word is an indefinite pronoun or an adjective. In the second column write **SP, OP, DO, IO** to show the job of the indefinite pronoun. If the word is an adjective, write **Adj** in the second column.

IP or Adj		Pronoun Job/Adj
	33. <u>Many</u> waited patiently in line for their tickets.	
	34. He wanted a <u>few</u> of the seashells on the beach.	
	35. <u>Several</u> packages arrived in the mail.	
	36. Dad gave <u>somebody</u> a call on the phone.	
	37. Susan left hurriedly with <u>everything</u> in her hands.	

Exercise 4: Underline each indefinite pronoun and write **S** or **P** for singular or plural in the blank. Underline the correct verb and the correct possessive pronoun to agree with the subject. Use the Indefinite Pronoun Chart to help you.

38. _____ Nobody (take, takes) (his, their) break at this time.

39. _____ Few (has, have) computers in (her, their) homes.

40. _____ Either of the answers (is, are) correct.

41. _____ Any of these books (is, are) available to the public.

CHAPTER 20 LESSON 3 APPLICATION TEST B

Exercise 5: Review! Underline the correct pronoun choice in each sentence.

1. Between you and (I, me), there's nothing to do.
2. The money was divided between Mr. Jones and (he, him).
3. (We, Us) designers have interesting work.
4. Sam asked (we, us) boys to be present.
5. (We, Us) programmers deserve a raise.
6. Linda and (her, she) will bring dessert.
7. Are you going with Anna and (her, she)?
8. (Him and me)(He and I) are radio hams.
9. That solution seems beyond Charlie and (him, he).
10. Larry, Jason, and (me, I) are studying for our chemistry test.
11. The scoutmaster saw that everyone had (his, their) shoes on.
12. Everybody expected to hear (his, their) name called.
13. It was (us, we).
14. This is (him, he).
15. This is (her, she).
16. Have you any news for (us, we) girls?
17. (We, Us) members are going to have a meeting.

Exercise 6: Write an indefinite pronoun in the blank. Make sure it agrees with the verb and possessive pronoun in number.

18. _____ of the money sits in a vault in the bank. (*must be singular*)

19. _____ concentrates on her own project. (*must be singular*)

20. _____ of the students were painting murals. (*must be plural*)

21. _____ from the school has joined the debate team. (*must be singular*)

Exercise 7:   **Editing Paragraph**
Find each error and write the correction. Replace each word underlined once with a synonym. Use the Editing Guide to help you. **Editing Guide: Synonyms: 1 Capitals: 22 Commas: 3 Periods: 3 Apostrophes: 3 Misspelled Words: 5 Subject-Verb Agreement: 2 Pronoun Usage: 4 End Marks: 9**

my friends and me love to make hard candy for our christmas carnivel hard candy is easy to make and fun to eat us girls get together on the first saturday of december at lindas house on oak street in canton ohio to make our carnivel candy we makes hard candy by boiling suger and corn syup until it forms a <u>heavy</u> syrup us girls then add flavors and coloring to the syrup then we make the syrup into shapes while it is still worm when its cool it is hard candy everyone tell we girls what a good job we do after last years carnivel mr j c simpson said that we girls should also make cream candy to sell next year

Exercise 8: Identify each complete sentence below by putting a slash between each sentence. Then rewrite the paragraph on your notebook paper. Correct fragments and improve sentences by using a combination of simple, compound, and complex sentences. Underline simple sentences once, compound sentences twice, and put parentheses around the complex sentences.

Larry is going to camp this summer and Joe is going too and I am going with them and we are going with Boy Scout Troop 14 and we are going on a Greyhound bus and our camp is called Camp Evergreen and Camp Evergreen is located north of Bird Lake and Bird Lake is located near Benson, Minnesota and lots of swimming and fishing and are excited about our trip

CHAPTER 20 LESSON 3

Independent Research Writing Assignment #32, Part 2

For the second part of your independent research writing assignment, you will do Steps 6-7. These steps will guide you as you continue your assignment. Always refer back to Chapter 17 for examples and detailed explanations of each step.

Research Steps for Independent Writing Assignment #32, Part 2

Step 6: Organize note cards.
Step 7: Make a first draft outline.

CHAPTER 20 LESSON 4

Independent Research Writing Assignment #32, Part 3

For the third part of your independent research writing assignment, you will do Steps 8-10. These steps will be listed at the beginning of your assignment so that you can follow them. Always refer back to Chapter 17 for examples and detailed explanations of each step.

Research Steps for Independent Writing Assignment #32, Part 3

Step 8: Make a second draft outline.
Step 9: Write a rough draft.
Step 10: Edit your rough draft.

CHAPTER 20 LESSON 5

Independent Research Writing Assignment #32, Part 4

For the fourth part of your independent research writing assignment, you will do Steps 11-14. These steps will guide you as you finish your assignment. Always refer back to Chapter 17 for examples and detailed explanations of each step.

Research Steps for Independent Writing Assignment #32, Part 4

Step 11: Write your final outline.
Step 12: Write your final report.
Step 13: Put final report and all related research work in the correct order.
Step 14: Hand in final report and all related papers.

CHAPTER 21 LESSON 1

Mixed Patterns 1-5

The sentences that you will classify with your teacher will be a mixture of Pattern 1: SN V P1, Pattern 2: SN V-t DO P2, Pattern 3: SN V-t IO DO P3, Pattern 4: SN LV PrN P4, and Pattern 5: SN LV PA P5. As you classify these sentences, look carefully at the main parts so you can identify the correct pattern for each sentence.

Identify and Categorize Kinds of Pronouns

You have already studied several kinds of pronouns. In this chapter, you will identify the pronouns you have studied and then categorize them according to name, singular or plural, case (subjective, possessive, or objective), and person (first, second, or third person).

Study the charts below on identifying and categorizing pronouns. Then use the chart as you work through the practice exercises.

Pronoun Charts

Demonstrative Pronouns		Indefinite Pronouns			Interrogative Pronouns
Singular	Plural	Singular Only	Plural Only	Singular or Plural	
This That	These Those	another, anybody, anyone, each anything, either, everybody, one everyone, everything, much, something, someone, somebody, nothing, no one, nobody, neither	both, few many, others several	all, any half, most none, some	who, what whom, which whose

Personal Pronoun Point of View (Person)		
Point of View	Singular	Plural
First person	I, me, my, mine	we, us, our, ours
Second person	you, your, yours	you, your, yours
Third person	he, him, his, she, her, hers, it, its	they, them, their, theirs

Personal Pronoun Case		
Pronoun Case	Singular	Plural
Subjective case	I, you, he, she, it	we, you, they
Objective case	me, you, him, her, it	us, you, them
Possessive case	my, his, her, your, its mine, yours, hers	our, your, their, yours

CHAPTER 21 LESSON 1

Guided Practice on Identifying and Categorizing Kinds of Pronouns

Identify each set of pronouns in the box below by writing these abbreviations in the column labeled *Pro Name:* **D** for demonstrative pronouns, **I** for indefinite pronouns, **Int** for interrogative pronouns, and **P** for personal pronouns.

Write **S** or **P** for singular or plural in the *S or P* column. If the pronouns can be either singular or plural, write **S, P** in the blank.

Also, identify *personal pronouns* in the last two columns according to person (1st, 2nd, or 3rd) or case (S-subjective, P-possessive, or O-objective). Remember, you must also identify either the person or the case of each set of personal pronouns listed on a line.

	Pro Name			For personal pronouns only	
	D, I, Int, P	S or P		Person: 1, 2, 3	Case: S, P, O
1.			you, your, yours		
2.			she, her, hers		
3.			anybody, anyone, anything		
4.			we, us, our, ours		
5.			these, those		
6.			another, each, either		
7.			he, him, his		
8.			both, few, many, several, others		
9.			I, you, he, she, it		
10.			this, that		
11.			everything, everybody, everyone		
12.			our, your, their		
13.			neither, no one, one		
14.			me, you, him, her, it		
15.			nothing, nobody		
16.			it, its		
17.			you, we, they		
18.			my, his, her, your, its		
19.			I, me, my, mine		
20.			all, some, none		
21.			you, your, yours		
22.			they, them, their, theirs		
23.			most, any		
24.			us, you, them		

Table title: Guided Practice: Pronoun Identification Box

Write the five interrogative pronouns.

1.	2.	3.	4.	5.

CHAPTER 21 LESSON 1

Independent Research Writing Assignment #33, Part 1

In this independent research writing assignment, you will be required to go to the library to select your sources. But there are several things to do before you go to the library. First, you must select a topic from the list below, narrow the topic, and then have it approved by your teacher. You will do only the first research step today. Possible writing topics:

Insects	Famous First Ladies/Presidents	American Inventions
Foreign Countries	Animals	Famous Athletes
Snakes	Plants	History

Research Steps for Independent Writing Assignment #33, Part 1

Step 1: Narrow the topic.

CHAPTER 21 LESSON 2

Independent Research Writing Assignment #33, Part 2

In this independent research writing assignment, you will be required to go to the library to select your sources. But there are several things to do before you go to the library. You should have already selected, narrowed and gotten teacher approval of your topic. (*If not, go back to Step 1 in Lesson 1 and do that step.*) After your narrowed topic has been approved, go to Step 2 and make an outline guide. You should go to the outline guide in Chapter 17 to help you. After you have completed your outline guide, go to the library to select the sources you will use in your report. (Follow your teacher's directions for library time.) Remember to make a bibliography card for each source selected. You will do only Research Steps 2-4 today.

Research Steps for Independent Writing Assignment #33, Part 2

Step 2: Make an outline guide.
Step 3: Select sources by skimming.
Step 4: Make a bibliography card for each source selected.

CHAPTER 21 LESSON 3

Independent Research Writing Assignment #33, Part 3

In this independent research writing assignment, you will be required to go to the library again to take notes from your selected sources. (Follow your teacher's directions for library time.) Remember to take notes on note cards. You will do only Research Step 5 today.

Research Steps for Independent Writing Assignment #33, Part 3

Step 5: Take notes.

CHAPTER 21 LESSON 1 SKILL TEST

Exercise 1: Identify each set of pronouns in the box below by writing these abbreviations in the column labeled *Pro Name:* **D** for demonstrative pronouns, **I** for indefinite pronouns, **Int** for interrogative pronouns, and **P** for personal pronouns. Write **S** or **P** for singular or plural in the *S or P* column. If the pronouns can be either singular or plural, write **S,P** in the blank. Also, identify *personal pronouns* in the last two columns according to person (1st, 2nd, or 3rd) and case (S-subjective, P-possessive, or O-objective).

| | Pro Name | | | For personal pronouns only | |
	D, I, Int, P	S or P		Person: 1, 2, 3	Case: S, P, O
1.			us, you, them		
2.			neither, no one, one		
3.			anybody, anyone, anything		
4.			me, you, him, her, it		
5.			nothing, nobody		
6.			it, its		
7.			he, him, his		
8.			everything, everybody, everyone		
9.			my, his, her, your, its		
10.			this, that		
11.			she, her, hers		
12.			both, few, many, several, others		
13.			we, us, our, ours		
14.			these, those		
15.			another, each, either		
16.			they, them, their, theirs		
17.			I, you, he, she, it		
18.			I, me, my, mine		
19.			you, your, yours		
20.			all, some, none		
21.			you, your, yours		
22.			you, we, they		
23.			our, your, their		
24.			most, any		

Write the five interrogative pronouns.

1.	2.	3.	4.	5.

CHAPTER 21 LESSON 3 APPLICATION TEST A

Exercise 1: Mixed Patterns 1-5. Classify each sentence.

1. _____ Will the pleasant professor finally proceed with the history lesson?

2. _____ The governor and his secretary had a thorough knowledge of the government

of Great Britain and the United States.

3. _____ Read Sally and me a bedtime story tonight.

4. _____ That old Ford is an antique car.

Directions: Complete the noun job table. Use Sentence 4.

List the Noun Used	List the Noun Job	Singular or Plural	Common or Proper
5.	6.	7.	8.
9.	10.	11.	12.

Exercise 2: Complete the chart below by writing these eight pronouns in the correct column: *they, him, her, who, this, everyone, both, these.*

Demonstrative Pronouns		Indefinite Pronouns		Interrogative Pronoun	Personal Pronouns		
Singular	Plural	Singular	Plural		Subjective	Possessive	Objective

Exercise 3:   **Editing Paragraph**
Find each error and write the correction. Use the Editing Guide to help you. **Editing Guide: Homonyms: 1   Capitals: 14   Commas: 1   Periods: 4   Apostrophes: 2   Misspelled Words: 7   Colons: 3   End Marks: 8**

dave turned sixteen at 8 05 a m on tuesday morning and he walked eagerly into the texas state

revenue office at 8 10 to take his driving test he passed the written test with flying colors and waited

confidently for his turn to test-drive with the state trooper the sober-faced policeman gave him a

passing certifiate and sent him inside the revenue office to get his license

dave walked slowly out of the revene office at 5 10 p m on tuesday afternoon without his license

he liked sadly at all the papers in his hand and remebered the long waiting lines and all the clerks

behind eight diferent windows he still couldnt beleive how many times he had stood in line at the wrong

window he hoped he could get in line early enough tomorrow morning too finally get his drivers license

he sighed again as he put a quater in the pay phone and called his mom to come drive him home

CHAPTER 21 LESSON 3 APPLICATION TEST B

Exercise 4: Identify each set of pronouns in the box below by writing these abbreviations in the column labeled *Pro Name:* **D** for Demonstrative pronouns, **I** for Indefinite pronouns, **Int** for Interrogative pronouns, and **P** for Personal pronouns. Write **S** or **P** for singular or plural in the *S or P* column. If the pronouns can be either singular or plural, write **S,P** in the blank. Also, identify *personal pronouns* in the last two columns according to person (1st, 2nd, or 3rd) and case (S-subjective, P-possessive, or O-objective). **Personal pronouns must have answers for both person and case.**

	Pro Name			For personal pronouns only	
	D, I, Int, P	**S or P**		**Person: 1, 2, 3**	**Case: S, P, O**
1.			anybody		
2.			we		
3.			these		
4.			each		
5.			him		
6.			both		
7.			I		
8.			this		
9.			anything		
10.			our		
11.			me		
12.			neither		
13.			it		
14.			you		
15.			my		
16.			some		
17.			your		
18.			they		
19.			any		
20.			us		
21.			her		
22.			either		
23.			his		
24.			hers		
25.			that		
26.			their		
27.			everybody		
28.			mine		
29.			none		
30.			those		
31.			few		

Table title: **Pronoun Identification Box**

Write the five interrogative pronouns.

32.	33.	34.	35.	36.

Exercise 5: Underline the correct pronoun for the sentences below.

37. Larry showed (she, her) and Ted his car.

38. (Who, Whom) did Sue visit?

39. The coach gave Bob and (I, me) an award.

40. This is (he, him).

CHAPTER 21 LESSON 4

Independent Research Writing Assignment #33, Part 4

In this independent research writing assignment, you will be required to go to the library again to continue taking notes from your selected sources. (Follow your teacher's directions for library time.) Remember to take notes on note cards. You will do only Research Step 5 today.

Research Steps for Independent Writing Assignment #33, Part 4

Step 5: Take notes.

CHAPTER 21 LESSON 5

Independent Research Writing Assignment #33, Part 5

In this independent research writing assignment, you will be required to go to the library again to finish Step 5 (taking notes from your selected sources). You will also do Research Step 6 and begin Step 7 if you have time. (Follow your teacher's directions for library time.)

Research Steps for Independent Writing Assignment #33, Part 5

Step 5: Take notes.
Step 6: Organize note cards.
Step 7: Make a first draft outline.

CHAPTER 22 LESSON 1

Pattern 6, Object Complement Noun

A **Pattern 6** has a noun **after** the direct object. This noun, called the object complement, re-names the direct object, but it does more than this. The object complement names what the direct object has become as a result of the action of the verb. In the sentence "We elected him president," we say, "elected him what? president - object complement." As you can see, he *(him)* becomes president (the object complement) as a result of the action of the verb *elected*.

To find an object complement noun, always ask *what* after the direct object. A Pattern 6 object complement noun is labeled **OCN**, and you say **object complement noun**. To learn how to identify an object complement noun, read the Question and Answer Flow below for this sentence: They elected **him president**.

Sample Sentence for the exact words to say to find the object complement noun.

1. They elected him president.
2. Who elected him president? They - SP
3. What is being said about they? they elected - V
4. They elected whom? him - verify the pronoun
5. Does the pronoun *him* mean the same thing as *they*? No.
6. Him - DO
7. Elected - V-t
8. They elected him what? president
9. Does president mean the same thing as him? Yes.
10. President - OCN
11. SN V-t DO OCN P6 Check
12. Check the verb: verb-transitive.
13. Check again for prepositional phrases.
14. No prepositional phrases.
15. Period, statement, declarative sentence.
16. Go back to the verb - divide the complete subject from the complete predicate.
17. Is there an adverb exception? No.
18. Is this sentence in a natural or inverted order? Natural - no change.

Pattern 7, Object Complement Adjective

A **Pattern 7** has an adjective **after** the direct object that tells what kind of direct object. To find an objective complement adjective, always ask *what* after the direct object. A Pattern 7 object complement adjective is labeled **OCA**, and you say **object complement adjective**. To learn how to identify an object complement adjective, read the Question and Answer Flow below for this sentence: We painted the **barn red**.

Sample Sentence for the exact words to say to find the object complement adjective.

1. We painted the barn red.
2. Who painted the barn red? we - SP
3. What is being said about we? we painted - V
4. We painted what? barn - verify the noun
5. Does barn mean the same thing as we? No.
6. Barn - DO
7. Painted - V-t
8. We painted the barn what? red
9. Does red tell what kind of barn? Yes.
10. Red - OCA
11. The - A
12. SN V-t DO OCA P7 Check
13. Check the verb: verb-transitive.
14. Check again for prepositional phrases.
15. No prepositional phrases.
16. Period, statement, declarative sentence
17. Go back to the verb - divide the complete subject from the complete predicate.
18. Is there an adverb exception? No.
19. Is this sentence in a natural or inverted order? Natural - no change.

Assignment

1. Write one **Practice Sentence** following these labels:

   A SN P A Adj OP V-t DO A OCN

2. Write a second **Practice Sentence** following these labels:

   A Adj SN V-t DO OCA

CHAPTER 22 LESSON 1

More Pronouns

In this chapter, you will study reflexive and intensive pronouns. These pronouns are the easiest to identify because both types end with *-self or -selves*. Study the definitions and examples below to find out how the reflexive and intensive pronouns are different.

Reflexive Pronouns

1. The reflexive pronouns end with -self or -selves.
2. Singular reflexive pronouns are *myself, yourself, himself, herself*, and *itself*.
3. Plural reflexive pronouns are *ourselves, yourselves*, and *themselves*.
4. Reflexive pronouns usually refer back to the subject.
5. Reflexive pronouns can be direct objects, indirect objects, or objects of prepositions.
6. Examples: Direct object - **Jamie** found **himself** in a lot of trouble. Indirect object - **She** bought **herself** a car. Object of the preposition - Our **babies** never worried about **themselves**.
7. Reflexive pronouns cannot be left out; they are necessary to the meaning of the sentence.
8. A reflexive pronoun must always have an antecedent in the same sentence.
9. Reflexive pronouns should not be used in place of personal pronouns; they are used in addition to personal pronouns.
10. The pronouns *hisself, ourself*, and *theirselves* are not correct. Always use the correct forms: *himself, ourselves,* and *themselves*.

Intensive Pronouns

1. The intensive pronouns also end with *-self* or *-selves*.
2. Singular intensive pronouns are *myself, yourself, himself, herself*, and *itself*.
3. Plural intensive pronouns are *ourselves, yourselves*, and *themselves*.
4. Intensive pronouns can be used right after another noun or pronoun to **intensify**, or emphasize, that noun or pronoun, or they can come at the end of the sentence to emphasize the same noun or pronoun.
   Examples: **I myself** collect valuable stamps.   The **boss himself** checked the machine.
   Examples: **I** collect valuable stamps **myself**.   The **boss** checked the machine **himself**.

5. Intensive pronouns can be left out; they are not necessary to the meaning of the sentence.
6. An intensive pronoun must always have an antecedent in the same sentence.
7. Intensive pronouns should not be used in place of personal pronouns; they are used in addition to personal pronouns.
8. The pronouns *hisself, ourself*, and *theirselves* are not correct. Always use the correct forms: *himself, ourselves,* and *themselves*.

Guided Practice: Write a reflexive or intensive pronoun in the first blank and write **R** or **I** in the second blank to identify the pronoun as reflexive or intensive.

1. They _____ are to blame. ____

2. The car _____ was in good shape. _____

3. He wanted the painting for _____. ____

4. She never gave _____ a chance. _____

CHAPTER 22 LESSON 1

Contractions and Confusing Pronouns

A contraction is two words shortened into one word. This new word always has an apostrophe that takes the place of the letters that have been left out. Some contractions and possessive pronouns are often confused because they sound the same. Knowing how to use possessive pronouns and contractions correctly is essential in writing. A contraction chart and a list of confusing pronouns and contractions are listed below. Contractions and their meanings have been listed according to their verb families.

Contraction Chart				Pronoun	Contraction
AM		**HAS**			
I am	– I'm	has not	– hasn't	**its**	**it's**
		he has	– he's	(owns)	(it is)
IS		she has	– she's	*its coat*	*It's cute.*
is not	– isn't				
he is	– he's	**HAVE**			
she is	– she's	have not	– haven't	**your**	**you're**
it is	– it's	I have	– I've	(owns)	(you are)
who is	– who's	you have	– you've	*your car*	*You're right!*
that is	– that's	we have	– we've		
what is	– what's	they have	– they've		
there is	– there's			**their**	**they're**
		HAD		(owns)	(they are)
ARE		had not	– hadn't	*their house*	*They're gone.*
are not	– aren't	I had	– I'd		
you are	– you're	he had	– he'd		
we are	– we're	she had	– she'd	**whose**	**who's**
they are	– they're	you had	– you'd	(owns)	(who is)
		we had	– we'd	*whose cat*	*Who's going?*
WAS, WERE		they had	– they'd		
was not	– wasn't				
were not	– weren't	**WILL /SHALL**			
		will not	– won't		
DO, DOES, DID		I will	– I'll		
do not	– don't	he will	– he'll		
does not	– doesn't	she will	– she'll		
did not	– didn't	you will	– you'll		
		we will	– we'll		
CAN		they will	– they'll		
cannot	– can't				
		WOULD			
LET		would not	– wouldn't		
let us	– let's	I would	– I'd		
		he would	– he'd		
		she would	– she'd		
		you would	– you'd		
		we would	– we'd		
		they would	– they'd		
		SHOULD, COULD			
		should not	– shouldn't		
		could not	– couldn't		

CHAPTER 22 LESSON 1

Guided Practice:
Write the correct contraction beside each word.

Guided Practice:
Write the correct word beside each contraction.

1. I am	6. he's
2. she is	7. you've
3. was not	8. we're
4. they would	9. let's
5. we will	10. she'd

Guided Practice: Underline the correct contraction or possessive pronoun for each sentence.

1. (Their, They're) working hard in the garden with (their, they're) tomatoes.

2. (Its, It's) a disaster that (its, it's) raining. The river overflowed (its, it's) banks.

3. (Your, You're) new dress is very becoming.

4. (Whose, Who's) are these folders on this desk?

Guided Practice: Underline the correct contraction or possessive pronoun for each sentence.

Ann and María like to shop on (their, they're) days off. (Their, They're) favorite place to shop is

J.C. Penny's at the mall. (Its, It's) fun to catch all the great sales. (They're, Their) mom can't believe

(they're, their) buying more clothes. She's worried about (who's, whose) going to keep up with all of them.

Ann and María don't know (who's, whose) clothes belong to whom!

CHAPTER 22 LESSON 1 SKILL TEST

Exercise 1: Write the correct contraction beside these words.

1. is not _____	6. I am _____	11. has not _____
2. you have _____	7. does not _____	12. she has _____
3. there is _____	8. they had _____	13. you will _____
4. they will _____	9. we have _____	14. were not _____
5. we would _____	10. let us _____	15. cannot _____

Exercise 2: Write the correct words beside each contraction.

16. he'll _____	21. we've _____	26. aren't _____
17. don't _____	22. they're _____	27. it's _____
18. hasn't _____	23. you're _____	28. I'll _____
19. I've _____	24. who's _____	29. I'd _____
20. they'd _____	25. it's _____	30. she'd _____

Exercise 3: Underline the correct contraction or possessive pronoun for each sentence.

31. (Your, You're) going to the mall in (your, you're) car today.

32. (Whose, Who's) the guest speaker tonight?

33. (Their, They're) sure (their, they're) books were stolen?

34. (Whose, Who's) is the best apple pie in the baking contest?

35. (Its, It's) finally time to celebrate because the class receives (its, it's) award.

36. (Your, You're) sure that (their, they're) still here?

Exercise 4: Write a reflexive or intensive pronoun in the first blank and write **R** or **I** in the second blank to identify the pronoun as reflexive or intensive.

1. The instructors _____ missed their early class. _____

2. Dad chuckled to _____ during the play. _____

3. The old rifle _____ was in excellent condition. _____

4. The young army cook gave _____ an extra helping. _____

Exercise 5: Underline the correct contraction or possessive pronoun in each sentence.

Larry and Jerry are the best players on (your, you're) football team. (They're, Their) talent and hard work are admired by everyone in town. (Its, It's) fun to watch them play ball. (They're, Their) always running touchdowns. (Its, It's) no secret (whose, who's) team will win the conference.

Exercise 6: Write a paragraph on your notebook paper using and underlining contractions and possessive pronouns.

CHAPTER 22 LESSON 2

Independent Research Writing Assignment #33, Part 6

If you have not finished your library research by this time, check with your teacher for a library schedule. In this independent research writing assignment, you will finish your first draft outline and make your second draft outline. You will do Research Steps 7-8 today. Always remember to check Chapter 17 for examples of what to do for each step assigned.

Research Steps for Independent Writing Assignment #33, Part 6

Step 7: Make a first draft outline.
Step 8: Make a second draft outline.

CHAPTER 22 LESSON 3

Independent Research Writing Assignment #33, Part 7

In this independent research writing assignment, you will finish your second draft outline and write a rough draft. Remember to add illustrations if they are needed to explain certain points in your report. You can work on the illustrations at home if you do not have enough time in class to do them. Always check back to Chapter 17 for examples of what to do for each step assigned.

Research Steps for Independent Writing Assignment #33, Part 7

Step 9: Write a rough draft.

CHAPTER 22 LESSON 3 APPLICATION TEST A

Exercise 1: Mixed Patterns 6-7. Classify each sentence.

1. _____ Bad TV habits can make a person lazy.

2. _____ The committee named Elizabeth head of the litter campaign.

3. _____ The judges declared Polly the winner of the skating competition.

4. _____ No one in the kindergarten class colored his pumpkin orange!

Directions: Complete the noun job table. Use Sentence 2.

List the Noun Used	List the Noun Job	Singular or Plural	Common or Proper
5.	6.	7.	8.
9.	10.	11.	12.
13.	14.	15.	16.
17.	18.	19.	20.

Exercise 2: Complete the chart below by writing these seven pronouns in the correct column: *anybody, that, we, us, few ours, what.*

Demonstrative Pronouns		Indefinite Pronouns		Interrogative Pronoun	Personal Pronouns		
Singular	Plural	Singular	Plural		Subjective	Possessive	Objective

Exercise 3: Underline the correct contraction or possessive pronoun for each sentence.

1. (You're, Your) parents said that (you're, your) leaving for Utah on Sunday.
2. (They're, Their) working outside in (they're, their) back yard on the pool.
3. (Who's, Whose) watching the house while (you're, your) in Europe on (you're, your) vacation?
4. (It's, Its) too bad (they're, their) late for the concert.

Exercise 4: Punctuate the quotations and capitalize words as needed.

5. yummy exclaimed harold that chocolate cake looks delicious

6. jerry arent your parents picking you up after the game asked amanda

Exercise 5:   **Editing Paragraph**

Find each error and write the correction. Use the Editing Guide to help you. **Editing Guide: Homonyms: 1 Capitals: 18 Commas: 5 Periods: 2 Misspelled Words: 4 End Marks: 6**

the small boy eyed his mom in dispair ms smith his latin teacher had been talking to his mom

for ten minutes he knew his grades in biology I and calculus II were excellant his grades in latin class

had droped just a little but they were still good sudenly his mom winked at him said good bye to

ms smith and motioned for him to sit beside her she lovingly reminded her son that he was only ten

years old and had to more years before he entered the venus technical college for advanced aerodynamics

CHAPTER 22 LESSON 3 APPLICATION TEST B

Exercise 6: Write the correct contraction beside these words.

1. it is _____
2. there is _____
3. is not _____
4. you have _____
5. they will _____
6. will not _____
7. you have _____
8. let us _____
9. he will _____

10. I am _____
11. I will _____
12. you will _____
13. was not _____
14. do not _____
15. they have _____
16. we would _____
17. have not _____
18. does not _____

Exercise 7: Write the correct words beside each contraction.

19. you're _____
20. they're _____
21. he's _____
22. they'd _____
23. he'll _____
24. we'd _____
25. I've _____
26. don't _____

27. we've _____
28. hasn't _____
29. who's _____
30. I'm _____
31. they're _____
32. you'd _____
33. it's _____
34. wasn't _____

Exercise 8: Write a reflexive or intensive pronoun in the first blank and write **R** or **I** in the second blank to identify the pronoun as reflexive or intensive.

35. The phone _____ was working perfectly. _____

36. My older sister looked at _____ in the mirror. _____

37. My friends built _____ a sand castle on the beach. _____

38. I _____ enjoyed the banquet very much. _____

39. Randy painted the car _____. _____

Exercise 9: Underline the correct pronoun choice.

40. Sandy and (I, me) were packing for our trip to the mountains.
41. You and (he, him) have eaten too much.
42. Mother frowned at Linda and (I, me).
43. (Us, we) boys are going camping this weekend.
44. Adam and (he, him) are the class clowns.
45. Lindsay talked to Mom and (I, me) about the trip.
46. The storm caught Dad and (I, me) inside the store.

CHAPTER 22 LESSON 4

Independent Research Writing Assignment #33, Part 8

In this independent research writing assignment, you will finish your rough draft. Then you will edit your rough draft according to your teacher's editing schedule. Always check back to Chapter 17 for examples of what to do for each step assigned.

Research Steps for Independent Writing Assignment #33, Part 8

Step 10: Edit your rough draft.

CHAPTER 22 LESSON 5

Independent Research Writing Assignment #33, Part 9

In this independent research writing assignment, you will do a final personal edit of your rough draft. Then you will make final corrections to your outline and write your final outline according to the guidelines learned in Chapter 17.

Research Steps for Independent Writing Assignment #33, Part 9

Step 11: Write your final outline.

CHAPTER 23 LESSON 1

Pattern 6 and Pattern 7 Review

You will review Pattern 6 and Pattern 7 by classifying a set of practice sentences with your teacher. As you classify these sentences, look carefully at the main parts so you can identify Pattern 6 and Pattern 7 easily and accurately.

Assignment

1. Write a **Practice Sentence** for Pattern 6 and make up your own labels.
2. Write a second **Practice Sentence** for Pattern 7 and make up your own labels.

Appositives

1. A noun directly following another noun or pronoun to identify, or rename, it is an **appositive**, or a **noun in apposition**.

2. An appositive is in the same case as the noun which it renames. (If it renames the subject, it is in the subjective case. If it renames an object, it is in the objective case.)

3. At this level, you will just be concerned with learning how to identify appositives. Therefore, at this time, you are to set off all appositives (with their modifiers) with commas. Later, you will study differences in punctuation rules for appositives.

4. An appositive may occur in any of the seven patterns which you have learned. Since an appositive is extra information, it can also be used to combine choppy sentences.
   Example: Biographies appeal to many people. They are stories of persons' lives.
   Biographies, stories of persons' lives, appeal to many people.

5. An appositive is different from an object complement noun (OCN). An object complement always follows a direct object and names what the direct object **has become** as a result of the action of the verb. For example, in the sentence "We elected him president," *president*, the OCN, names what the direct object (*him*) has become (*president*) as a result of the action of the verb (*elected*).

   A direct object, on the other hand, can have an appositive. For example, in the sentence "We chose Brad, my brother," *my brother* is not an OCN. We did not choose *Brad* to be my brother. *My brother* simply follows Brad and re-names him. *My brother* in this sentence is an appositive.

   Examples of appositives being used in different ways are given below.

Examples of Appositives Used in Patterns 1-7

Pattern 1: Anthony, **my friend**, is here.

Pattern 2: I hugged Sara, **my sister**.

Pattern 3: I gave Bill, **the postman**, a letter.

Pattern 4: Sue, **the girl next door**, is my friend.

Pattern 5: The clown, **a circus performer**, is funny.

Pattern 6: They, **the people**, elected him President.

Pattern 7: The old man, **my grandfather**, painted the barn red.

CHAPTER 23 LESSON 1

Guided Practice: Underline the appositives in each sentence and put the commas where they belong.

1. John our lawyer told us the bad news.
2. Samuel proudly drove his new truck a Ford to school.
3. In the evenings Gail Hames my sister-in-law walks with me around the track.
4. We invited the Richardsons our friends to lunch.
5. Mark Twain the great humorist was an American.

Guided Practice: Combine the two choppy sentences by means of appositives.

6. Many books were written about Daniel Boone. Daniel Boone was a great frontiersman.

Student Note for Independent Research Writing Assignment #33
After you finish your Skill Test, use the rest of the period to get all research steps up-to-date. You should be able to finish your research paper in Lesson 2. Remember to add illustrations if they are needed to explain certain points in your report. You will share your reports in Lessons 3-5.

CHAPTER 23 LESSON 2

Independent Research Writing Assignment #33, Part 10
In this independent research writing assignment, you will write your final report and do another personal edit of your final paper. Then you will put all your related research work in the correct order. You will do Research Steps 12-13 today. Always remember to check Chapter 17 for examples of what to do in these final steps.

Research Steps for Independent Writing Assignment #33, Part 10

Step 12: Write your final report.
Step 13: Put final report and all related research work in the correct order.

CHAPTER 23 LESSON 1 SKILL TEST

Exercise 1: Write the correct contraction beside these words.

1.	he is	_____	6.	I am	_____	11.	I had	_____
2.	you have	_____	7.	was not	_____	12.	does not	_____
3.	you had	_____	8.	do not	_____	13.	they had	_____
4.	you will	_____	9.	had not	_____	14.	we have	_____
5.	you would	_____	10.	let us	_____	15.	I have	_____

Exercise 2: Write the correct words beside each contraction.

16.	didn't	_____	21.	he'd	_____	26.	I'm	_____
17.	they'd	_____	22.	they're	_____	27.	aren't	_____
18.	hasn't	_____	23.	you're	_____	28.	you'd	_____
19.	I've	_____	24.	who's	_____	29.	you've	_____
20.	he's	_____	25.	it's	_____	30.	let's	_____

Exercise 3: Underline the appositive in each sentence and put the commas where they belong.

31. Fred hid in the shack an old deserted beach bungalow.

32. The crew of the shuttle saw the lights bright stars in the sky.

33. John the lawyer on the case presented the winning argument.

34. Mary dug a hole a tiny cavity in the front lawn.

35. Bethany proudly drove the red car a Lexus to the bank for a loan.

36. The koala a lover of eucalyptus leaves is a native of Australia.

37. The naturalist gave the birds two orioles plenty of birdseed during the winter months.

38. The monk walked to the monastery door a massive wooden frame and entered the long hall.

39. Will Henry our leader be open to that suggestion?

40. Take your lunch two sandwiches and an orange and go to the park.

Exercise 4: Write a reflexive or intensive pronoun in the first blank and write **R** or **I** in the second blank to identify the pronoun as reflexive or intensive.

41. My brother laughed at _____ when his trick backfired. _____

42. The students _____ supervised the halls. _____

43. The funny circus clown gave _____ a round of applause. _____

44. My father said that the motorcycle _____ was a piece of junk. _____

CHAPTER 23 LESSON 3

Independent Research Writing Assignment #33, Part 11

In this independent research writing assignment, you will have all your research papers ready to hand in to your teacher. Your teacher will start Share Time, and you will hand in your report after you have read it to the class. Be sure to keep response sheets on each report during Share Time. Your teacher will give you any additional instructions, if needed.

Research Steps for Independent Writing Assignment #33, Part 11

Step 13: Put final report and all related research work in the correct order.
Step 14: Hand in final report and all related papers.
Step 15: Share Time.

Share Time for a Report

You will now prepare to share your report with the class. Look over the Share Time Guidelines below to make sure you understand what you are to do for reader preparation and audience response. Your teacher will tell you what to do with your audience response sheet after the reports have been read. Remember to be courteous to other students as you listen to their reports.

Share Time Guidelines	
Reader Preparation	**Audience Response**
1. Have your paper ready to read when called upon.	1. Pay attention and listen attentively.
2. Write the title of your story on the board.	2. After each reader finishes reading his/her report, the audience (students) will write a brief response to the report read using the guidelines below.
3. Stand with your feet flat on the floor and your shoulders straight. Do not shift your weight as you stand.	1. Title of the report.
4. Hold your paper about chin high to help you project your voice to your audience.	2. Main idea
5. Make sure you do not read too fast.	3. List 3 main topics covered.
6. Read in a clear voice that can be heard so that your audience does not have to strain to hear you.	4. Tell what you liked best about the report.

CHAPTER 23 LESSON 3 APPLICATION TEST

Exercise 1: Classify each sentence.

1. _____ My sister gleefully painted the wall orange.

2. _____ The cheerleaders named little Amy their cheerleading mascot.

3. _____ Did the teacher believe Julius Caesar a villain?

Directions: Complete the noun job table. Use Sentence 1.

List the Noun Used	List the Noun Job	Singular or Plural	Common or Proper
4.	5.	6.	7.
8.	9.	10.	11.

Exercise 2: Complete the chart below by writing these seven pronouns in the correct column: *another, those, whom, I, her, its, others.*

Demonstrative Pronouns		Indefinite Pronouns		Interrogative Pronoun	Personal Pronouns		
Singular	Plural	Singular	Plural		Subjective	Possessive	Objective

Exercise 3: Underline the correct contraction or possessive pronoun for each sentence.

1. "(You're, Your) a lucky boy," she said. "I am happy to present (you're, your) award!"
2. (They're, Their) yelling and waving (they're, their) arms at the bus driver!
3. (Who's, Whose) umbrella is on the kitchen table?
4. (It's, Its) feet are too big for (it's, its) body.

Exercise 4: Underline the appositive in each sentence and put the commas where they belong.

5. After the storm last night Julia found two damaged trees a pine and a cedar.
6. The lamp an antique oil model hung on Uncle Bertram's den wall.
7. Jerome yelled for his soccer team an exciting group of players.
8. Above the clouds thick cumulous billows the dark birds flew.
9. Hazel a rabbit in *Watership Down* becomes the chief rabbit.

Exercise 5:   **Editing Paragraph**

Find each error and write the correction. Use the Editing Guide to help you. **Editing Guide: Homonyms: 2 Capitals: 15 Commas: 6 A/An: 1 Misspelled Words: 4 End Marks: 7**

everyone began gathering at dawn in the parking lot of northside jounior high school excited seventh graders greeted friends and carried dufel bags and pillows to there buses anxious parents gave last minute instructions to chaprones busy teachers worked hard too keep children parents chaperones and belongings organized finally everything was ready for departur as the buses pulled away happy students waved at sleepy parents already dreaming of their beds at home the seventh graders and an few brave adults were going to space camp in huntsville alabama

CHAPTER 23 LESSON 4

Independent Research Writing Assignment #33, Part 12

In this independent research writing assignment, you will have all your research papers ready to hand in to your teacher. Your teacher will start Share Time again, and you will hand in your report after you have read it to the class. Be sure to keep response sheets on each report during Share Time. Your teacher will give you any additional instructions if needed.

Research Steps for Independent Writing Assignment #33, Part 12

Step 13: Put final report and all related research work in the correct order.
Step 14: Hand in final report and all related papers.
Step 15: Share Time.

CHAPTER 23 LESSON 5

Independent Research Writing Assignment #33, Part 13

In this independent research writing assignment, you will have all your research papers ready to hand in to your teacher. Your teacher will start Share Time again, and you will hand in your report after you have read it to the class. Be sure to keep response sheets on each report during Share Time. Your teacher will give you any additional instructions if needed.

Research Steps for Independent Writing Assignment #33, Part 13

Step 13: Put final report and all related research work in the correct order.
Step 14: Hand in final report and all related papers.
Step 15: Share Time.

CHAPTER 24 LESSON 1

Regular and Irregular Verbs

Most verbs are **regular verbs**. This means that they form the past tense merely by adding -**ed**, -**d**, or -**t** to the main verb: *climb, climbed*. This simple procedure makes regular verbs easy to identify. Some verbs, however, do not form their past tense in this regular way. For this reason, they are called **irregular verbs**. Most irregular verbs form their past tense by having a **vowel spelling change** in the word: *s<u>i</u>ng, s<u>a</u>ng, s<u>u</u>ng* or <u>*eat, ate, eaten*</u>.

To decide if a verb is regular or irregular, remember to do these five things:

1. Avoid using helping verbs because they do not determine whether a verb is regular or irregular.
2. Look only at the main verb because the main verb determines whether a verb is regular or irregular.
3. Decide how the main verb is made past tense: (*-ed, -d, or -t ending*) or (*vowel spelling change*).
4. If the main verb is made past tense with an *-ed*, *-d*, or *-t* ending, it is a regular verb. (climb, climbed)
5. If the main verb is made past tense with a vowel spelling change, it is an irregular verb. (sing, sang, sung)

There are about seventy irregular verbs. A partial listing of the most common irregular verbs is contained in the irregular verb chart located in the Reference pages. Refer to this chart whenever necessary.

Guided Practice: Identify each verb as regular or irregular and put **R** or **I** in the blank. Then write the past tense form.

need _____ _____   ring _____ _____   drive _____ _____

grow _____ _____   hurry _____ _____   rain _____ _____

Verb Tenses

When you are writing paragraphs, you must use verbs that are in the same tense. Tense means time. The tense of a verb shows the time of the action. Verbs change from one tense to another tense (depending on when the action takes place) so that you can tell whether something is happening now, has happened in the past, or will happen in the future. There are six tenses that you use every day in your speaking and writing. **These six tenses are present tense, past tense, future tense, present perfect tense, past perfect tense, and future perfect tense.**

Simple Tenses

The present, past, and future tenses are called the **simple tenses**.

1. The **simple present tense** tells what happens now.
   (**Examples:** We <u>climb</u> over the rocks. We <u>eat</u> dinner.)

   A. Identify simple present tense verbs by their singular form **-s or -es endings** (climbs, eats) or by their plural form, **no -s or -es ending** (climb, eat).
   B. Simple present tense verbs have a singular form and a plural form.
   C. No helping verbs are used with the simple present tense verbs.

2. The **simple past tense** tells what happened before now.
   (**Examples:** We <u>climbed</u> over the rocks. We <u>ate</u> dinner.)

   A. Identify past tense verbs by their **-ed, -d, -t endings** (climbed) or by their irregular past tense spelling (ate).
   B. Past tense verbs do not have a singular or plural form.
   C. No helping verbs are used with the simple past tense verbs.

3. The **simple future tense** tells what will happen later.
   (**Examples:** I <u>will climb</u> over the rocks. We <u>will eat</u> dinner.)

   A. Identify future tense verbs by the helping verbs **will** or **shall** (will/shall climb, will/shall eat).
   B. Future tense verbs do not have a singular or plural form.
   C. Only the helping verbs **will** or **shall** can be used with the simple future tense.

CHAPTER 24 LESSON 1

Perfect Tenses

The **perfect tenses** include the present perfect, the past perfect, and the future perfect. You can identify the perfect tenses easily by following the guidelines below.

1. **Present perfect tense** verbs are identified only by the helping verbs **has** or **have**.
   A. The helping verb **has** is singular, and the helping verb **have** is plural.
   B. Use *has* or *have* with a main verb.
   (has finished, have finished - has eaten, have eaten)

2. **Past perfect tense** verbs are identified only by the helping verb **had**.
   A. The helping verb **had** does not have a singular or plural form because it is past tense.
   B. Use *had* with a main verb.
   (had finished - had eaten).

3. **Future perfect tense** verbs are identified only by the helping verbs **will have** or **shall have**.
   A. Future perfect tense verbs do not have a singular or plural form.
   B. Use **will/shall have** with a main verb,
   (will have finished, shall have finished - will have eaten, shall have eaten)

When you tell about something that is happening in two time periods, one earlier than the other, you will use the perfect tenses. The word *perfect* means **something which is completed.** Therefore, all *perfect tenses* tell about something that began at an earlier time and that **is completed** in a present, past, or future time.

4. The **present perfect tense** tells about an action that has begun in the past but is completed in the present. (**Examples:** He has finished his homework. We have eaten our dinner.)

5. The **past perfect tense** tells about an action that was completed before another event, which was also in the past. (**Examples:** He had finished his homework before Mom came home. We had eaten our dinner before company arrived.)

6. The **future perfect tense** tells about an action that will be completed at a certain time in the future. (**Examples:** By Friday, he will have finished his homework. We will have eaten our dinner by game time.)

Guided Practice: Underline each verb or verb phrase. In the first column, identify the verb tense by writing its corresponding number in the blank from the following list: (1) Present Tense (2) Past Tense (3) Future Tense (4) Present Perfect Tense (5) Past Perfect Tense   (6) Future Perfect Tense. Then, in the second column, write **R** or **I** for Regular or Irregular.

Verb Tense	R or I

1. The graduates have already received their diplomas.

2. Dixie chased the raccoon off the porch and up a tree.

3. I will have earned fifty bonus points by Friday.

4. Aaron studies his Latin for two hours every day.

5. Mitchell will swim tomorrow at the city pool.

6. Andrea had written several letters to her parents.

CHAPTER 24 LESSON 1

Guidelines for Finding the Simple and Perfect Tenses

When you are writing paragraphs, it is best to keep your writing in the same tense. Simple and perfect tenses are used together to keep writing in the same tense. You are allowed to make a reference to another time frame by using other tenses to make that reference. Therefore, it is important to know how to recognize what determines the tense of each sentence you write. You have learned about the six tenses: the three simple tenses and the three perfect tenses. To keep from becoming confused about what tense you are in, just train yourself to quickly recognize four things:

1. If there is only **one verb** in a sentence, the tense will be either **simple present** or **simple past**.
2. If there is a **will or shall** helping verb with a main verb, the tense will be **simple future**.
3. If there is a **has, have** or **had** helping verb with a main verb, the tense will be either **present perfect** or **past perfect**.
4. If there is a **will** or **shall** plus the helping verb **have** with a main verb, the tense will be **future perfect tense**.

If you have a verb phrase, it is the **helping verb, not the main verb, that determines the tense**. If you have a present perfect tense helping verb, your writing will be in present perfect tense even though a main verb has an *-ed* ending. Use the regular verb examples below and the helping verb chart at the bottom of the page to help you learn the simple and perfect tenses. (*Present tense and past tense are not included in the helping verb chart because there are no helping verbs with the simple present and past tenses.*)

Simple Present Tense	**Simple Past Tense**	**Simple Future Tense**
What to look for: **one verb** with s, es, or plain ending.	What to look for: **one verb** with -ed ending.	What to look for: **will** or **shall** with a main verb.
1. He <u>walks</u> to the park.	3. He <u>walked</u> to the park.	5. He <u>will walk</u> to the park.
2. They <u>walk</u> to the park.	4. They <u>walked</u> to the park.	6. They <u>shall walk</u> to the park.

Present Perfect Tense	**Past Perfect Tense**	**Future Perfect Tense**
What to look for: **has or have** with a main verb.	What to look for: **had** with a main verb.	What to look for: **will / shall have** with a main verb.
1. He <u>has walked</u> to the park.	3. He <u>had walked</u> to the park.	5. He <u>will have walked</u> to the park.
2. They <u>have walked</u> to the park.	4. They <u>had walked</u> to the park.	6. They <u>shall have walked</u> to the park.

Helping Verb Chart Example

Future Tense	Present Perfect Tense		Past Perfect Tense	Future Perfect Tense
2 verbs	Singular-1	Plural-1	1 verb	3 verbs
will/ shall	has	have	had	will/shall + have

Guided Practice: Fill in the helping verb chart.

Future Tense	Present Perfect Tense		Past Perfect Tense	Future Perfect Tense
2 verbs	Singular-1	Plural-1	1 verb	3 verbs

CHAPTER 24 LESSON 1

Verb Conjugation Using the Six Tenses

A list of all the forms of a verb in a specific order, usually by the six tenses, is called a **verb conjugation**. All verb conjugations will be done in third person. Just follow the example of the verb conjugation that is given below.

Study the conjugation of the verb **climb** below. Use it as an example as you conjugate other verbs.

Example of the Conjugation of the Verb *Climb*

Present		Past	Future	Present Perfect	Past Perfect	Future Perfect
(No helping verbs)		(No helping verbs)	(will or shall)	(has or have)	(had)	(will/shall) + have
Singular climbs	Plural climb	climbed	will climb shall climb	has climbed have climbed	had climbed	will have climbed shall have climbed

Guided Practice: Conjugate the verb *walk*. Use the verb conjugation chart above to help you.

Conjugation of the Verb *Walk*						
Present		Past	Future	Present Perfect	Past Perfect	Future Perfect
(No helping verbs)		(No helping verbs)	(will or shall)	(has or have)	(had)	(will/shall) + have
Singular	Plural					

Guided Practice: Conjugate the verb *go.* Use the verb conjugation chart above to help you.

Conjugation of the Verb *Go*						
Present		Past	Future	Present Perfect	Past Perfect	Future Perfect
(No helping verbs)		(No helping verbs)	(will or shall)	(has or have)	(had)	(will/shall) + have
Singular	Plural					

CHAPTER 24 LESSON 1 SKILL TEST A

Exercise 1: Fill in the helping verb chart.

Future Tense	Present Perfect Tense		Past Perfect Tense	Future Perfect Tense
2 verbs	Singular-1	Plural-1	1 verb	3 verbs

Exercise 2: Underline each verb or verb phrase. In the first column, identify the verb tense by writing its corresponding number in the blank from the following list: (1) Present Tense (2) Past Tense (3) Future Tense (4) Present Perfect Tense (5) Past Perfect Tense (6) Future Perfect Tense. Then, in the second column, write **R** or **I** for Regular or Irregular.

Verb Tense	R or I

1. They frequently talk about current events in that class.

2. Raymond talked on the phone for several minutes.

3. My parents will talk to your parents about our trip.

4. These office machines run all day on a small amount of electricity.

5. My Uncle Ray ran for mayor last November.

6. Our men's club will run in the Boston Marathon next month.

7. Joanne has talked to the salesperson for over an hour.

8. The contestants had answered every question within the time limit.

9. By tonight the children will have opened their presents.

10. Aunt Pat always imitates Aunt Sue at our family reunions.

Exercise 3: Conjugate the verb *begin* in the chart below.

Conjugation of the Verb *Begin*					
Present		**Past**	**Future**	**Present Perfect**	**Past Perfect**	**Future Perfect**
(No helping verbs)		(No helping verbs)	(will or shall)	(has or have)	(had)	(will/shall) + have
Singular	Plural					

Exercise 4: Conjugate the verb *work* in the chart below.

Conjugation of the Verb *Work*					
Present		**Past**	**Future**	**Present Perfect**	**Past Perfect**	**Future Perfect**
(No helping verbs)		(No helping verbs)	(will or shall)	(has or have)	(had)	(will/shall) + have
Singular	Plural					

CHAPTER 24 LESSON 2

Principal Parts of Verbs

Every verb has four principal parts, or basic forms, that are used to make the six different tenses of verbs. In order to speak and write correctly, you must learn how to use the principal parts to form the different verb tenses with ease and confidence. The four principal parts are called **present, past, past participle, and present participle**. Study the principal parts and examples below.

Principal Parts	Regular Verbs	How they are made	Irregular Verbs	How they are made	Helping Verb Needed
Present	climb	climb (climbs)	sing	sing (sings)	none
Past	climbed	climb + ed	sang	sang (vowel change)	none
Past participle	climbed	climb + ed	sung	sung (vowel change)	has, have, had
Present participle	climbing	climb + ing	singing	sing + ing	am, is, are, was, were, be, been

Principal Parts Used to Make the Simple Tenses

1. Simple present tense is made from the **present principal** part (*see the chart above*). (climb, sing)
2. Simple past tense is made from the **past principal** part (*see the chart above*). (climbed, sing)
3. Simple future tense is made with the helping verb **will** and the **present principal** part (*see the chart above*). (will/shall climb, will/shall sing)

Principal Parts Used to Make the Perfect Tenses

1. Present perfect tense is made with the helping verbs **has** or **have** and the **past participle** part (*see the chart above*). (has/have climbed, has/have sung)
2. Past perfect tense is made with the helping verbs **had** and the **past participle** (*see the chart above*). (had climbed, had sung)
3. Future perfect tense is made with the helping verbs **will** and **have** and the **past participle** part (*see the chart above*). (will/shall have climbed, will/shall have sung)

Progressive and Emphatic Forms of Verbs

Progressive form. Some principal parts are also used to make other verb forms of the six tenses. Progressive verbs are made by using the *present participle (-ing verb)* and one of the *be* helping verbs: *am, is, are, was, were, be, been*. Progressive verbs are used to show continuous action by using *-ing* verbs. Progressive verbs can be made with all six tenses.

1. **Present progressive** verbs are made with the helping verbs **am, is,** or **are** and the present participle (*-ing verb*). (am/is/are climbing, am/is/are singing)
2. **Past progressive** verbs are made with the helping verbs **was** or **were** and the present participle (*-ing verb*). (was/were climbing, was/were singing)
3. **Future progressive** verbs are made with the helping verbs **will/shall** and **be** and the present participle (*-ing verb).* (will/shall be climbing, will/shall be singing)
4. **Present perfect progressive** verbs are made with the helping verbs **has, have** and **been** and the present participle (-ing verb). (has/have been climbing, has/have been singing)
5. **Past perfect progressive** verbs are made with the helping verbs **had** and **been** and the present participle (-ing verb). (had been climbing, had been singing)
6. **Future perfect progressive** verbs are made with the helping verbs **will/shall** and **have** and **been** and the present participle (-ing verb). (will/shall have been climbing, will/shall have been singing)

Emphatic form. Emphatic verbs are made by using the *present principal part* and one of the *do, does, did* helping verbs. *Emphatic verbs* are used to give special emphasis to the action of a verb. Emphatic verbs can be made in only two tenses: present and past.

7. **Present emphatic** verbs are made with the helping verbs **do** or **does** and the present principal part. (do/does climb, do/does sing)
8. **Past emphatic** verbs are made with the helping verb **did** and the present principal part. (did climb, did sing).

CHAPTER 24 LESSON 2

Guidelines for Finding the Tense of the Progressive and Emphatic Verb Forms

Remember, it is important to know how to recognize which verb to use to keep your writing in the same tense. In Lesson 1, you learned about the six tenses. In this lesson, you have just learned about the progressive and emphatic forms and how they depend heavily on helping verbs; therefore, it is important that you expand your knowledge of helping verbs.

Since the helping verb determines the tense of a verb phrase, you must be able to quickly recognize the tense of a helping verb as soon as you see it. When you look at the verb phrase to tell what tense it is, look at the helping verb, **not** the main verb. The progressive verb form can be made in all six tenses. The emphatic verb form can be made in only two tenses: present and past. Use the Helping Verb Chart below to help you learn the helping verbs which form the progressive and emphatic verb forms. (*Present and past tense are not included in the chart because they have no helping verbs.*)

Present Progressive		Past Progressive		Future Progressive
Singular: *am, is* I am eating. He is eating.	Plural: *are* They are eating.	Singular: *was* He was eating.	Plural: *were* They were eating.	Singular or Plural: *will / shall + be* He will/shall be eating. They will/shall be eating.
Present Perfect Progressive		**Past Perfect Progressive**		**Future Perfect Progressive**
Singular: *has + been* He has been eating.	Plural: *have + been* They have been eating.	Singular: *had + been* He had been eating.	Plural: *had + been* They had been eating.	Singular or Plural: *will / shall + have been* He will/shall have been eating. They will/shall have been eating.
Present Emphatic		**Past Emphatic**		
Singular: *does* He does eat.	Plural: *do* They do eat.	Singular: *did* He did eat.	Plural: *did* They did eat.	

Sample Helping Verb Chart							
Future Tense	**Present Perfect**		**Past Perfect**	**Future Perfect**	**Progressive Form**		**Emphatic Form**	
2 verbs	Singular-1	Plural-1	1 verb	3 verbs	Singular-5	Plural - 4	Singular-2	Plural-2
will, shall	has	have	had	will/shall + have	am, is, was, be, been	are, were, be, been	does, did	do, did

Guided Practice: Fill in the helping verb chart.

Future Tense	Present Perfect		Past Perfect	Future Perfect	Progressive Form		Emphatic Form	
2 verbs	Singular-1	Plural-1	1 verb	3 verbs	Singular -5	Plural - 4	Singular-2	Plural-2

CHAPTER 24 LESSON 2

Guided Practice: Underline the verb or verb phrase in each sentence. Then identify the verb tense or verb form by writing its corresponding number in the blank from the following list: (1) Present Tense (2) Past Tense (3) Future Tense (4) Present Perfect Tense (5) Past Perfect Tense (6) Future Perfect Tense (7) Progressive Form (8) Emphatic Form

_____ 1. Rebecca will have exercised already.

_____ 2. Joshua mows lawns for extra money.

_____ 3. Those sailors will depart from New York.

_____ 4. Mother had waxed the floor before the party.

_____ 5. The fans are shouting for a touchdown.

_____ 6. The children have been eating candy.

_____ 7. The cow has grazed in our pasture this week.

_____ 8. Daniel typed on the computer until midnight.

_____ 9. The puppies have opened their eyes.

_____10. He will have talked for an hour on the phone.

_____11. Ruth did explain the directions clearly.

_____12. Dad will have been lighting the charcoal.

Verb Conjugation Using the Six Tenses and the Progressive and Emphatic Forms

Remember, a list of all the forms of a verb in a specific order, usually by the six tenses, is called a **verb conjugation**. The progressive and emphatic forms have also been added to the bottom of your regular verb conjugation chart. All verb conjugations will still be done in third person. Just follow the example of the verb conjugation that is given below.

Study the conjugation of the verb **throw** below. Use it as an example as you conjugate other verbs.

Example of the Conjugation of the Verb *Throw*					
Write the names of the four principal parts: **present, past, past participle, and present participle**					
Present	**Past**	**Future**	**Present Perfect**	**Past Perfect**	**Future Perfect**
(No helping verbs)	(No helping verbs)	(will or shall)	(has or have)	(had)	(will/shall) + have
Singular **throws** / Plural **throw**	**threw**	**will throw** **shall throw**	**has thrown** **have thrown**	**had thrown**	**will have thrown** **shall have thrown**

Simple Progressive Forms			**Perfect Progressive Forms**			**Simple Emphatic**	
am, is, are	was, were	will, shall + be	has, have + been	had + been	will, shall + have been	do, does	did
am throwing is throwing are throwing	was throwing were throwing	will be throwing shall be throwing	has been throwing have been throwing	had been throwing	will have been throwing shall have been throwing	do throw does throw	did throw

Guided Practice: Conjugate the verb *Go*. Use the verb conjugation chart above to help you.

Conjugation of the Verb *Go*					
Write the names of the four principal parts:					
Present	**Past**	**Future**	**Present Perfect**	**Past Perfect**	**Future Perfect**
(No helping verbs)	(No helping verbs)	(will or shall)	(has or have)	(had)	(will/shall) + have
Singular / Plural					

Simple Progressive Forms			**Perfect Progressive Forms**			**Simple Emphatic**	
am, is, are	was, were	will, shall + be	has, have + been	had + been	will, shall + have been	do, does	did

CHAPTER 24 LESSON 2 SKILL TEST B

Test Exercise 1: Conjugation of the Verb *Look*					
Write the names of the four principal parts:					
Present	**Past**	**Future**	**Present Perfect**	**Past Perfect**	**Future Perfect**
(No helping verbs)	(No helping verbs)	(will or shall)	(has or have)	(had)	(will/shall) + have
Singular	Plural				

Simple Progressive Forms			Perfect Progressive Forms			Simple Emphatic	
am, is, are	was, were	will, shall + be	has, have + been	had + been	will, shall + have been	do, does	did

Test Exercise 2: Conjugation of the Verb *Talk*					
Present	**Past**	**Future**	**Present Perfect**	**Past Perfect**	**Future Perfect**
(No helping verbs)	(No helping verbs)	(will or shall)	(has or have)	(had)	(will/shall) + have
Singular	Plural				

Simple Progressive Forms			Perfect Progressive Forms			Simple Emphatic	
am, is, are	was, were	will, shall + be	has, have + been	had + been	will, shall + have been	do, does	did

Test Exercise 3: Conjugation of the Verb *Sink*					
Present	**Past**	**Future**	**Present Perfect**	**Past Perfect**	**Future Perfect**
(No helping verbs)	(No helping verbs)	(will or shall)	(has or have)	(had)	(will/shall) + have
Singular	Plural				

Simple Progressive Forms			Perfect Progressive Forms			Simple Emphatic	
am, is, are	was, were	will, shall + be	has, have + been	had + been	will, shall + have been	do, does	did

Test Exercise 4: Conjugate the verb *Fly* on your paper.

CHAPTER 24 LESSON 2 SKILL TEST C

Exercise 1: Fill in the helping verb chart.

Future Tense	Present Perfect		Past Perfect	Future Perfect	Progressive Form		Emphatic Form	
2 verbs	Singular-1	Plural-1	1 verb	3 verbs	Singular - 5	Plural - 4	Singular-2	Plural-2

Exercise 2: Underline each verb or verb phrase. In the first column, identify the verb tense by writing its corresponding number in the blank from the following list: (1) Present Tense (2) Past Tense (3) Future Tense (4) Present Perfect Tense (5) Past Perfect Tense (6) Future Perfect Tense (7) Progressive Form (8) Emphatic Form. Then, in the second column, write **R** or **I** for Regular or Irregular. (*Progressive and emphatic verbs are identified by form without noting the tense.*)

Verb Tense	R or I

1. The army helicopter had landed safely on the landing pad.

2. A flock of geese is landing on the lake behind our house.

3. The successful actor's chauffeur will drive him to the awards ceremony.

4. The eager children watch expectantly for signs of the first snow.

5. The excited second grader did find a quarter on the playground.

6. Dad and Grandpa will have slept for eight hours by now.

7. Three happy toddlers were splashing in the wading pool.

8. Our committee had been deciding the best theme for the dance.

9. You did an excellent job on your science project this year.

10. A freight company will have moved our furniture to Utah by next week.

11. The grouchy woman grumbled under her breath about the weather.

12. The young doctor is an expert on diseases of the skin.

13. The company boss will raise your salary at the end of the year.

14. Mrs. Sanders has been driving our school bus for fifteen years.

15. The door to the baby's room does creak loudly on its hinges.

Exercise 3: Conjugate the verb *see* in the chart below.

Conjugation of the Verb *See*					
Write the names of the four principal parts:					
Present		**Past**	**Future**	**Present Perfect**	**Past Perfect**	**Future Perfect**
(No helping verbs)		(No helping verbs)	(will or shall)	(has or have)	(had)	(will/shall) + have
Singular	Plural					

Simple Progressive Forms			Perfect Progressive Forms			Simple Emphatic	
am, is, are	was, were	will, shall + be	has, have + been	had + been	will, shall + have been	do, does	did

CHAPTER 24 LESSON 3 SKILL TEST D

Exercise 1: Fill in the helping verb chart.

Future Tense	Present Perfect		Past Perfect	Future Perfect	Progressive Form		Emphatic Form	
2 verbs	Singular-1	Plural-1	1 verb	3 verbs	Singular - 5	Plural - 4	Singular-2	Plural-2

Exercise 2: Underline each verb or verb phrase. In the first column, identify the verb tense by writing its corresponding number in the blank from the following list: (1) Present Tense (2) Past Tense (3) Future Tense (4) Present Perfect Tense (5) Past Perfect Tense (6) Future Perfect Tense (7) Progressive Form (8) Emphatic Form. Then, in the second column, write **R** or **I** for Regular or Irregular. *(Progressive and emphatic verbs are identified by form without noting the tense.)*

Verb Tense	R or I

1. My Aunt Molly bakes her lasagna for one hour.

2. The girls had eaten at the Chinese restaurant for lunch.

3. The judges did choose a beautiful girl as the winner.

4. The skilled surgeons will operate on several heart patients this morning.

5. The small child's balloon had burst into tiny pieces.

6. The drama club will be performing this afternoon for our class.

7. The campaign workers have been telling everyone about their candidate.

8. Those trained soldiers do shoot accurately under pressure.

9. Our neighbors planted flowers and bushes in their front yard.

10. By this time tomorrow morning, we will have driven 500 miles on our trip.

11. That old truck has pulled many disabled vehicles in the last ten years.

12. The children in the hospital will have been laughing at the silly clown.

13. My grandmother does a good job at the bakery.

14. My grandfather was a pilot during the Korean War.

15. Government officials are considering a compromise of their trade policies.

Exercise 3: Conjugate the verb *hop* in the chart below.

Conjugation of the Verb *Hop*					
Write the names of the four principal parts:					
Present	**Past**	**Future**	**Present Perfect**	**Past Perfect**	**Future Perfect**
(No helping verbs)	(No helping verbs)	(will or shall)	(has or have)	(had)	(will/shall) + have
Singular / Plural					

Simple Progressive Forms			Perfect Progressive Forms			Simple Emphatic	
am, is, are	was, were	will, shall + be	has, have + been	had + been	will, shall + have been	do, does	did

CHAPTER 24 LESSON 4 SKILL TEST E

Exercise 1: Fill in the helping verb chart.

Future Tense	Present Perfect		Past Perfect	Future Perfect	Progressive Form		Emphatic Form	
2 verbs	Singular-1	Plural-1	1 verb	3 verbs	Singular -5	Plural - 4	Singular-2	Plural-2

Exercise 2: Underline each verb or verb phrase. In the first column, identify the verb tense by writing its corresponding number in the blank from the following list: (1) Present Tense (2) Past Tense (3) Future Tense (4) Present Perfect Tense (5) Past Perfect Tense (6) Future Perfect Tense (7) Progressive Form (8) Emphatic Form. Then, in the second column, write **R** or **I** for Regular or Irregular. *(Progressive and emphatic verbs are identified by form without noting the tense.)*

Verb Tense	R or I

1. This medicine will prevent minor ailments during your trip.

2. After tonight, the tiny infant will have slept in her crib only twice.

3. I open the mail every day with a letter opener.

4. All students will be using this textbook for the coming year.

5. The caterpillar had become a butterfly through metamorphosis.

6. We will have walked five miles at the end of the course.

7. The innocent rabbit didn't see the fox behind the bushes.

8. The players finished the game after three extra innings.

9. The golf team had been playing at the country club last week.

10. That row of children will move at the proper time after the play.

11. My math teacher erased the answers from the board!

12. Our dog Bozo does like our cat Bingo most of the time.

13. The electric company will be sending a refund check soon.

14. The security guards have closed these doors for a reason.

15. Mom drinks coffee with cream every morning at breakfast.

Exercise 3: Conjugate the verb *drive* in the chart below.

Conjugation of the Verb *Drive*							
Write the names of the four principal parts:							
Present		Past	Future	Present Perfect	Past Perfect	Future Perfect	
(No helping verbs)		(No helping verbs)	(will or shall)	(has or have)	(had)	(will/shall) + have	
Singular	Plural						

Simple Progressive Forms			Perfect Progressive Forms			Simple Emphatic	
am, is, are	was, were	will, shall + be	has, have + been	had + been	will, shall + have been	do, does	did

CHAPTER 24 LESSON 5 POSTTEST

Exercise 1: Identify the part of speech or the sentence job of each word. Write the abbreviation above the word.

1. _____ Several plump robins searched diligently for juicy worms in my back yard.

2. _____ For my birthday my generous parents gave me the most important item on my list.

3. _____ Quickly, Jocelyn and her little brother led the five horses into the barn.

4. _____ Four very excited fans were irate after the referee's call!

5. _____ Can that history teacher make this class interesting to his students?

6. _____ My two cousins in El Paso are students at Coronado High School.

7. _____ After an exciting election John Conner named Sarah Warren chairman of the committee.

Exercise 2: Identify each pronoun as indefinite or personal (**I, P**) and as singular or plural (**S, P**). Underline your choices.

8. we   **(I or P) (S or P)**   10. everybody **(I or P) (S or P)**   12. she   **(I or P) (S or P)**   14. both **(I or P) (S or P)**
9. each **(I or P) (S or P)**   11. they   **(I or P) (S or P)**   13. either **(I or P) (S or P)**   15. it   **(I or P) (S or P)**

Exercise 3: Identify each verb as regular or irregular and put **R** or **I** in the blank. Then write the past tense form.

16. cook _____ _____   17. swim _____ _____   18. break _____ _____

Exercise 4: Fill in the helping verb chart and name the four principal parts of a verb.

19. Write the names of the four principal parts:

Future Tense	Present Perfect		Past Perfect	Future Perfect	Progressive Form		Emphatic Form	
2 verbs	Singular-1	Plural-1	1 verb	3 verbs	Singular -5	Plural - 4	Singular-2	Plural-2

Exercise 5: Correct the errors in the following paragraph. Replace words underlined once with a synonym and words underlined twice with an antonym. Use the editing guide: **Capitals: 27 Homonyms: 6 End Marks: 7 Commas: 4 Semicolons: 1 Subject-Verb Agreement: 4 Apostrophes: 2 Synonym: 3 Antonym: 1 Spelling: 2**

during march my whole family enjoy watching the n c a a division 1 national mens basketball

tournament we each <u>choose</u> the too teams we think will make the finals susan and dad <u>always</u>

picks u c l a as one of there teams last year some of the games was in kansas city kansas which

is near our home sense the games was so close we went two one session and saw for <u>excellent</u>

games my <u>dream</u> is to play collage basketball however i am to short i guess ill just have to

consintrate on growing

CHAPTER 25 LESSON 1

Changing Verb Tenses

Remember, verb tenses in sentences are used to tell the reader what time an event takes place. In writing, one of the most common mistakes students make is to mixing present tense and past tense verbs. Mixing verb tenses can make your writing awkward and confusing to your reader.

The door opened, and my nephew comes into the kitchen and grinned.

In this sentence *opened* and *grinned* are past tense, and *comes* is present tense. The shift from past to present and back to past leaves your reader wondering about the time these actions take place. To make your writing clear and effective, choose a verb tense, or time, of your writing and stick to it.

Guided Practice:

Paragraph 1: Change these present tense verbs to past tense verbs in Paragraph 2.

    My uncle <u>is</u> a clown, and he <u>loves</u> his job. He and his fellow clowns <u>make</u> people happy. Audiences <u>laugh</u> in hearty anticipation of the clowns' next antics. People of all ages <u>forget</u> their troubles while they <u>are</u> <u>entertained</u> by these master entertainers. The clown act <u>is</u> truly astounding!

Paragraph 2: Past Tense

    My uncle _____ a clown, and he _____ his job. He and his fellow clowns _____ people happy. Audiences _____ in hearty anticipation of the clowns' next antics. People of all ages _____ their troubles while they _____ _____ by these master entertainers. The clown act _____ truly astounding!

Paragraph 3: Change these mixed verb tenses to past tense verbs in Paragraph 4 and present tense verbs in Paragraph 5.

    My brother <u>is</u> a champion swimmer. His strokes <u>were</u> smooth and perfect as he <u>slices</u> through the water with ease. Whenever he <u>swims</u>, my brother always <u>reminded</u> me of an otter; he <u>loves</u> to play in the water.

Paragraph 4: Past Tense

    My brother _____ a champion swimmer. His strokes _____ smooth and perfect as he _____ through the water with ease. Whenever he _____, my brother always _____ me of an otter; he _____ to play in the water.

Paragraph 5: Present Tense

    My brother _____ a champion swimmer. His strokes _____ smooth and perfect as he _____ through the water with ease. Whenever he _____, my brother always _____ me of an otter; he _____ to play in the water.

CHAPTER 25 LESSON 1 SKILL TEST A

Paragraph 1: Change the past tense verbs to present tense verbs in Paragraph 2.

I <u>looked</u> at Butch and <u>shook</u> my head. Butch <u>was</u> my guard dog. He <u>looked</u> ferocious, he <u>sounded</u> ferocious, and he <u>had</u> the pedigree for being a ferocious dog since he <u>was</u> a Doberman. But Butch <u>was</u> a wimp! He <u>was</u> afraid of the dark, and he <u>ran</u> and <u>hid</u> if someone <u>yelled</u> at him. Butch also <u>loved</u> strangers and <u>tagged</u> happily along after he <u>greeted</u> them. As I <u>continued</u> to shake my head, Butch <u>walked</u> over and <u>laid</u> his head in my lap. As he <u>looked</u> at me with those loving, trusting eyes, my heart <u>melted</u>. I <u>loved</u> my big wimp.

Paragraph 2: Present Tense

I _____ at Butch and _____ my head. Butch _____ my guard dog. He _____ ferocious, he _____ ferocious, and he _____ the pedigree for being a ferocious dog since he _____ a Doberman. But Butch _____ a wimp! He _____ afraid of the dark, and he _____ and _____ if someone _____ at him. Butch also _____ strangers and _____ happily along after he _____ them. As I _____ to shake my head, Butch _____ over and _____ his head in my lap. As he _____ at me with those loving, trusting eyes, my heart _____. I _____ my big wimp.

Paragraph 3: Change the mixed verb tenses to past tense verbs in Paragraph 4 and present tense verbs in Paragraph 5.

Cody <u>practices</u> his trumpet solo every afternoon after school. His sisters <u>complained</u> that the noise <u>interfered</u> with their television viewing. Cody <u>informs</u> his sisters that he <u>made</u> music, not noise. When Cody's dog <u>begins</u> howling, his sisters <u>giggled</u> and <u>run</u> from the room. Soon they <u>reappear</u> with three pairs of ear muffs, one pair for each of them and one pair for the dog.

Paragraph 4: Past Tense

Cody _____ his trumpet solo every afternoon after school. His sisters _____ that the noise _____ with their television viewing. Cody _____ his sisters that he _____ music, not noise. When Cody's dog _____ howling, his sisters _____ and _____ from the room. Soon they _____ with three pairs of ear muffs, one pair for each of them and one pair for the dog.

Paragraph 5: Present Tense

Cody _____ his trumpet solo every afternoon after school. His sisters _____ that the noise _____ with their television viewing. Cody _____ his sisters that he _____ music, not noise. When Cody's dog _____ howling, his sisters _____ and _____ from the room. Soon they _____ with three pairs of ear muffs, one pair for each of them and one pair for the dog.

CHAPTER 25 LESSON 2

Active and Passive Voice

The voice of a verb tells you whether the subject is doing the action or is receiving the action.

Active Voice. In most sentences, the subject is doing the action. When the subject is doing the action in a sentence, the verb is in the active voice. **(Dave threw the ball.)** To find the voice of the verb, ask this question: **"Is Dave (the subject) doing something?" Yes, Dave threw the ball.** Therefore, the verb *threw* is in the active voice.

Passive Voice. In some sentences, the subject receives the action. When the subject is receiving the action or having something done to it, the verb is in the passive voice. A passive verb is always a verb phrase (a helping verb and a main verb). **(The ball was thrown by Dave.)** To find the voice of the verb, ask this question: *"Was the ball (subject) doing something?" No, the ball was receiving the action or having something done to it (the ball was being thrown).* Therefore, the verb *was thrown* is in the passive voice.

Any time you use verbs in the active voice, you make your writing more forceful, more direct, and more effective. Therefore, try to choose the active voice whenever possible. You need to use the passive voice only when the person or thing performing an action is unknown or fairly unimportant.

Guided Practice: Underline the verb or verb phrase in each sentence. Then identify the voice of the verb by writing **A** or **P** for Active or Passive in the blank.

_____ 1. The spider crawled across the sidewalk.

_____ 2. The student with the problem was sent to the principal's office.

Guided Practice: Write an active and a passive sentence for each pair of words: **taxi / stop** and **ant / attack**. You choose the tense of the verb.

3.

4.

5.

6.

CHAPTER 25 LESSON 2 SKILL TEST B

Exercise 1: Underline the verb or verb phrase in each sentence. Then identify the voice of the verb by writing **A** or **P** for Active or Passive in the blank.

_____ 1. The aardvark shuffled off in search of ants.

_____ 2. I trust you completely.

_____ 3. The trees along West Main have been cut down.

_____ 4. Did you drive the car?

_____ 5. The birdseed was left on the ground.

_____ 6. The leaf floated on the water.

_____ 7. Your name is being called.

_____ 8. All the bears will be fighting over that honey.

_____ 9. Ann and Donna were selected as cheerleaders.

_____ 10. The squirrel carried the pecans to his nest in the oak tree.

_____ 11. Mrs. Rickard was thinking of a tough assignment for Friday.

Directions: Write an active sentence and a passive sentence using the words **wolf** and **stalk**. You choose the tense of the verb.

12.

13.

Exercise 2: Underline each verb or verb phrase. In the first column, identify the verb tense by writing its corresponding number in the blank from the following list: (1) Present Tense (2) Past Tense (3) Future Tense (4) Present Perfect Tense (5) Past Perfect Tense (6) Future Perfect Tense (7) Progressive Form (8) Emphatic Form. Then, in the second column, write **R** or **I** for Regular or Irregular. (*Progressive and emphatic verbs are identified by form without noting the tense.*)

Verb Tense	R or I

14. The uneasy passenger did change his seat several times on the plane.

15. Both girls have mailed their letters.

16. All the tourists were waving from the deck of the ship.

17. Every day we sit at the same table in the cafeteria.

Exercise 3: Conjugate the verb *give* in the chart below.

Conjugation of the Verb *Give*					
Write the names of the four principal parts:					
Present	**Past**	**Future**	**Present Perfect**	**Past Perfect**	**Future Perfect**
(No helping verbs)	(No helping verbs)	(will or shall)	(has or have)	(had)	(will/shall) + have
Singular / Plural					

Simple Progressive Forms			**Perfect Progressive Forms**			**Simple Emphatic**	
am, is, are	was, were	will, shall + be	has, have + been	had + been	will, shall + have been	do, does	did

CHAPTER 25 LESSON 2 SKILL TEST C

Paragraph 1: Change the present tense verbs to past tense verbs in Paragraph 2.

Not too far from where I <u>live</u>, a young couple <u>make</u> their home in a little brown house. They <u>do</u> not <u>have</u> any children. What they <u>do have are</u> two brightly colored macaws that they <u>bring</u> out into their front yard on nice days. It <u>is</u> always fun to walk past their house when the macaws <u>are</u> <u>sitting</u> on their perches on the porch of the brown house. As I <u>approach</u>, the birds <u>become</u> talkative, and they often <u>call</u> out hilarious remarks as I <u>walk</u> past.

Paragraph 2: Past Tense

Not too far from where I _____, a young couple _____ their home in a little brown house.

They _____ not _____ any children. What they _____ _____ _____ two brightly colored

macaws that they _____ out into their front yard on nice days. It _____ always fun to walk past

their house when the macaws _____ _____ on their perches on the porch of the brown house. As I

_____, the birds _____ talkative, and they often _____ out hilarious remarks as I _____

past.

Paragraph 3: Change the mixed verb tenses to past tense verbs in Paragraph 4 and present tense verbs in Paragraph 5.

My little sister Stephanie <u>has</u> a very unusual pastime. She <u>catches</u> bees. She <u>owned</u> what we <u>call</u> a "bug box." It <u>was</u> a little framed box with screen walls. A little door <u>opens</u> at one end. First, Stephanie <u>trapped</u> the bee in a glass jar. Then she <u>places</u> the mouth of the jar over the open "bug box" door. Finally, she <u>shakes</u> the bee into the box and <u>slammed</u> the door.

Paragraph 4: Past Tense

My little sister Stephanie _____ a very unusual pastime. She _____ bees. She _____

what we _____ a "bug box." It _____ a little framed box with screen walls. A little door

_____ at one end. First, Stephanie _____ the bee in a glass jar. Then she _____ the

mouth of the jar over the open "bug box" door. Finally, she _____ the bee into the box and ___

_____ the door.

Paragraph 5: Present Tense

My little sister Stephanie _____ a very unusual pastime. She _____ bees. She _____

what we _____ a "bug box." It _____ a little framed box with screen walls. A little door

_____ at one end. First, Stephanie _____ the bee in a glass jar. Then she _____ the

mouth of the jar over the open "bug box" door. Finally, she _____ the bee into the box and ___

_____ the door.

CHAPTER 25 LESSON 3 SKILL TEST D

Exercise 1: Underline the verb or verb phrase in each sentence. Then identify the voice of the verb by writing **A** or **P** for Active or Passive in the blank.

_____ 1. Clear the deck!

_____ 2. A large storm was brewing over the lake.

_____ 3. The bridge to the castle was guarded by two alligators in armor.

_____ 4. We were almost shocked by the faulty electrical outlet.

_____ 5. Does your dog Hector have fleas?

_____ 6. All the hazelnuts had been picked by noon.

_____ 7. Could you send Mrs. Graham a card?

_____ 8. The artist painted a beautiful picture of Cagle's Mill.

_____ 9. By midnight, the refrigerator had already been raided.

_____10. The evidence was collected by Investigator Hubbard.

Exercise 2: Write an active sentence and a passive sentence using the words **pizza** and **cook**. You choose the tense of the verb.

11.

12.

Exercise 3: Underline each verb or verb phrase. In the first column, identify the verb tense by writing its corresponding number in the blank from the following list: (1) Present Tense (2) Past Tense (3) Future Tense (4) Present Perfect Tense (5) Past Perfect Tense (6) Future Perfect Tense (7) Progressive Form (8) Emphatic Form. Then, in the second column, write **R** or **I** for Regular or Irregular. (*Progressive and emphatic verbs are identified by form without noting the tense.*)

Verb Tense	R or I

13. The nurses will be needing more supplies for their clinic.

14. Our gymnastics instructor has taught us a new floor exercise every day.

15. These suit pants fit perfectly at the waist.

16. Our parents had planned carefully for our hiking trip into the canyon.

17. Yesterday my horse hurt his leg on a barbed-wire fence.

Exercise 4: Conjugate the verb *cheer* in the chart below.

Conjugation of the Verb *Cheer*					
Write the names of the four principal parts:					
Present	**Past**	**Future**	**Present Perfect**	**Past Perfect**	**Future Perfect**
(No helping verbs)	(No helping verbs)	(will or shall)	(has or have)	(had)	(will/shall) + have

Singular	Plural				

Simple Progressive Forms			Perfect Progressive Forms			Simple Emphatic	
am, is, are	was, were	will, shall + be	has, have + been	had + been	will, shall + have been	do, does	did

CHAPTER 25 LESSON 3 SKILL TEST E

Paragraph 1: Change the past tense verbs to present tense verbs in Paragraph 2.

    One night Marti, her brother Seth, and I <u>went</u> to Costa Rico's for dinner. Our waitress evidently <u>was</u> new on the job. We all <u>ordered</u> the Enchilada Special. When our order <u>came</u>, it <u>was</u> tamales and guacamole. We all <u>liked</u> tamales as well as guacamole, but we <u>hadn't</u> <u>ordered</u> it tonight. We also <u>ordered</u> punch to drink, but what <u>did</u> we <u>get</u>? Iced tea. The final blow <u>came</u> when Marti <u>told</u> the waitress we <u>had</u> not <u>ordered</u> all this. The waitress <u>said</u> to Marti, "I'm so sorry, sir." At that point, we all <u>gave</u> up.

Paragraph 2: Present Tense

    One night Marti, her brother Seth, and I _____ to Costa Rico's for dinner. Our waitress evidently _____ new on the job. We all _____ the Enchilada Special. When our order _____, it _____ tamales and guacamole. We all _____ tamales as well as guacamole, but we _____ _____ it tonight. We also _____ punch to drink, but what_____ we ____? Iced tea. The final blow _____ when Marti _____ the waitress we _____ not _____ all this. The waitress _____ to Marti, "I'm so sorry, sir." At that point, we all _____ up.

Paragraph 3: Change the mixed verb tenses to past tense verbs in Paragraph 4 and present tense verbs in Paragraph 5.

    At 10 A.M. on a muggy June morning, I <u>am</u> <u>jogging</u> along when I <u>noticed</u> a very dark cloud moving in from the southwest. I <u>stop</u> for a minute at my mailbox, and I <u>heard</u> an ominous growl of thunder. As I <u>headed</u> up the driveway, I <u>freeze</u> in my steps as a blinding flash of air-to-ground lightning <u>hit</u> a tree about one hundred and fifty feet to my right. I <u>shot</u> into my house, <u>sailed</u> to the basement, and <u>bury</u> my head in a pile of freshly-laundered clothes.

Paragraph 4: Past Tense

    At 10 A.M. on a muggy June morning, I _____ _____ along when I _____ a very dark cloud moving in from the southwest. I _____ for a minute at my mailbox, and I _____ an ominous growl of thunder. As I _____ up the driveway, I _____ in my steps as a blinding flash of air-to-ground lightning _____ a tree about one hundred and fifty feet to my right. I _____ into my house, _____ to the basement, and _____ my head in a pile of freshly-laundered clothes.

Paragraph 5: Present Tense

    At 10 A.M. on a muggy June morning, I _____ _____ along when I _____ a very dark cloud moving in from the southwest. I _____ for a minute at my mailbox, and I _____ an ominous growl of thunder. As I _____ up the driveway, I _____ in my steps as a blinding flash of air-to-ground lightning _____ a tree about one hundred and fifty feet to my right. I _____ into my house, _____ to the basement, and _____ my head in a pile of freshly-laundered clothes.

CHAPTER 25 LESSON 4

Taking Notes in Outline Form from an Oral Lecture

Listening is the most frequently-used way for students to gain information. However, listening is not an easy skill to master, and many students have trouble remembering what they hear.

Hearing is not the same thing as listening. **Listening is using your ears and your mind**. Listening is learning to write things down. When you write things down, you are actually doing and seeing what is being said. Therefore, when you really know how to listen, you not only hear the information, but you also see it and think it as you write it.

Writing things down, or taking notes, prevents you from forgetting 80 percent of what you hear. Therefore, it is extremely important to have a system of taking notes that is quick and easy for you, but also effective and productive for your time and effort.

The note-taking skills that you learn now can also be used in other subject areas that require sorting and organizing large amounts of detailed information. This is especially true of history, literature, and science courses. Whether you are listening to an oral lecture from a teacher or reading written information on your own, note-taking skills will give you an easier way to study material that you need to learn.

As you perfect your note-taking skills, you will be developing a lifetime learning tool that will greatly benefit you in the future.

Study the guidelines below on how to take notes in outline form from an oral lecture. These guidelines will help you learn what to listen for and how to record important facts. They will help you develop the ability to take notes that are organized and easy to study later.

Guidelines for Taking Notes in Outline Form from an Oral Lecture

Things you need to do BEFORE the lecture begins:

1. Have several sheets of paper ready to use (whether you need them or not).

2. Have several pencils or pens ready to use (whether you need them or not).

3. Always have your name and date written on your paper. This should already be a habit.

4. Write down the topic of the lecture (if you know it).

5. Make a skeleton outline on your paper. (Use the front and back of your paper if necessary.)

   Set up at least four Roman numerals for main topics with lots of spacing for subtopics and details.

6. Relax, because when the lecture begins, you will begin taking notes immediately.

7. And, remember, taking good notes does not mean trying to write down everything that is said.

8. Be ready to listen for main points and details to fill out your skeleton outline.

CHAPTER 25 LESSON 4

Guidelines for Taking Notes in Outline Form from an Oral Lecture, Continued

Things you need to do AFTER the lecture begins:

1. Know what you are listening for and know how to record the information you hear in an easy-to-understand format.

2. Listen for the main topics, or main ideas, of what will be discussed in the lecture. These main ideas will usually be presented at the beginning of the lecture and expanded and repeated as the lecture continues. As you hear each main idea, list it as a main topic beside one of your Roman numerals.

3. Usually, each main topic will have important details that support it. As you hear and identify each detail that supports a main topic, list it as a subtopic beside a capital letter.

4. Just remember your outline form, and it will be easy to sort the ideas you hear in the lecture and put them in their proper places.

5. Of course, if you can clearly identify details about the subtopics, list them beside "numerical" or Arabic numerals under the specific subtopic they support.

6. Remember, you are taking notes. Write in phrases, summarize or condense what is said when necessary, use abbreviations (as long as you can read them later), and draw simple illustrations in your notes if they help clarify a point.

7. Use the space at the right-hand side of your paper and the margin for revising or adding things you have forgotten to write in your notes.

8. Read over your outline, make additions or corrections as needed, highlight the notes that are especially important, and look up vocabulary you do not understand. Hand in your note outline when your teacher calls for it.

Oral Lecture Exercise: Follow the guidelines above as your teacher reads your first oral lecture. Your first oral lecture will be titled *Bonsai*.

CHAPTER 25 LESSON 4 SKILL TEST F

Exercise 1: Underline the verb or verb phrase in each sentence. Then identify the voice of the verb by writing **A** or **P** for Active or Passive in the blank.

_____ 1. The house was wired by an experienced electrician.

_____ 2. Bill tripped over the bottle and fell into the basement.

_____ 3. The old lady body-slammed the mugger.

_____ 4. In the hurricane, the houses were removed from their foundations.

_____ 5. At the bookstore, Sir Robbley was surrounded by autograph-seekers.

_____ 6. With a grip of steel, Mrs. Briggs grabbed the thief and ejected him from her office.

_____ 7. On the lily pads, the four frogs croaked a symphony.

_____ 8. Mr. White approached the intercom with three pages of announcements.

_____ 9. Among the branches of the large magnolia tree, the blossoms were opening.

Exercise 2: Write an active sentence and a passive sentence using the words **man** and **drive**. You choose the tense of the verb.

10.

11.

Exercise 3: Underline each verb or verb phrase. In the first column, identify the verb tense by writing its corresponding number in the blank from the following list: (1) Present Tense (2) Past Tense (3) Future Tense (4) Present Perfect Tense (5) Past Perfect Tense (6) Future Perfect Tense (7) Progressive Form (8) Emphatic Form. Then, in the second column, write **R** or **I** for Regular or Irregular. (*Progressive and emphatic verbs are identified by form without noting the tense.*)

Verb Tense	R or I

12. The intermediate class will swim twice the length of the pool.

13. Planes from the nearby military base fly overhead regularly.

14. Jack does appreciate everyone's hard work on the project.

15. The attentive class had listened carefully to the flight instructor.

16. The earthquake victims have taken the supplies to their shelter.

Exercise 4: Conjugate the verb *grow* in the chart below.

Conjugation of the Verb *Grow*					
Write the names of the four principal parts:					
Present	**Past**	**Future**	**Present Perfect**	**Past Perfect**	**Future Perfect**
(No helping verbs)	(No helping verbs)	(will or shall)	(has or have)	(had)	(will/shall) + have
Singular Plural					

Simple Progressive Forms			**Perfect Progressive Forms**			**Simple Emphatic**	
am, is, are	was, were	will, shall + be	has, have + been	had + been	will, shall + have been	do, does	did

CHAPTER 25 LESSON 4 SKILL TEST G

Paragraph 1: Change the present tense verbs to past tense verbs in Paragraph 2.

Mrs. Noddley from Pleasant Springs <u>loves</u> to ride a mo-ped. She <u>has</u> one that she <u>uses</u> frequently. Everyone in the neighborhood <u>knows</u> Mrs. Noddley, and they <u>smile</u> when they <u>see</u> her. Mrs. Noddley <u>waves</u> at everyone as she <u>rides</u> along on her vehicle. She often <u>wears</u> cut-off overalls and a red T-shirt with a straw hat as she <u>cruises</u> along. Strangers who <u>visit</u> Pleasant Springs <u>are</u> often <u>surprised</u> to see an eighty-five-year-old woman riding a mo-ped.

Paragraph 2: Past Tense

Mrs. Noddley from Pleasant Springs _____ to ride a mo-ped. She _____ one that she _____ frequently. Everyone in the neighborhood _____ Mrs. Noddley, and they _____ when they _____ her. Mrs. Noddley _____ at everyone as she _____ along on her vehicle. She often _____ cut-off overalls and a red T-shirt with a straw hat as she _____ along. Strangers who _____ Pleasant Springs _____ often _____ to see an eighty-five-year-old woman riding a mo-ped.

Paragraph 3: Change the mixed verb tenses to past tense verbs in Paragraph 4 and present tense verbs in Paragraph 5.

Jeff <u>stayed</u> home while his parents <u>are</u> <u>visiting</u> relatives for the evening. Since it <u>looked</u> like rain, he <u>went</u> outside and <u>parks</u> his bike under the patio cover. Then he <u>rushed</u> back to the house before it <u>rains</u>. Jeff <u>moaned</u> as he <u>realized</u> the front door <u>was</u> <u>locked</u>. He <u>looks</u> at the rain, and he <u>looked</u> at the locked door. Then he <u>grins</u>. He <u>knew</u> just what to do. He <u>crawls</u> through the "emergency" window.

Paragraph 4: Past Tense

Jeff _____ home while his parents _____ _____ relatives for the evening. Since it _____ like rain, he _____ outside and _____ his bike under the patio cover. Then he _____ back to the house before it _____. Jeff _____ as he _____ the front door _____ _____. He _____ at the rain, and he _____ at the locked door. Then he _____. He _____ just what to do. He _____ through the "emergency" window.

Paragraph 5: Present Tense

Jeff _____ home while his parents _____ _____ relatives for the evening. Since it _____ like rain, he _____ outside and _____ his bike under the patio cover. Then he _____ back to the house before it _____. Jeff _____ as he _____ the front door _____ _____. He _____ at the rain, and he _____ at the locked door. Then he _____. He _____ just what to do. He _____ through the "emergency" window.

CHAPTER 25 LESSON 5 SKILL TEST H

Student Writing Assignment #34: Essay from the outline of the oral lecture on *Bonsai*.

Exercise 1: Underline the verb or verb phrase in each sentence. Then identify the voice of the verb by writing **A** or **P** for Active or Passive in the blank.

_____ 1. A barn owl could be seen in the field behind our farmhouse.

_____ 2. The elderly gentleman carefully selected vegetables from the bins at the market.

_____ 3. The elderly gentleman was selected as the town's outstanding citizen.

_____ 4. The yellow daisies bloomed by the side of the old country road.

_____ 5. Mrs. Rogers was driven to the hospital by her husband.

_____ 6. Coffee brewed in the pot over the open campfire.

_____ 7. The sleeping child was carried upstairs to her bedroom after dark.

_____ 8. Each child's picture was taped to the wall outside the classroom.

_____ 9. Rachel was tripped by the extension cord.

Exercise 2: Write an active sentence and a passive sentence using the words **raccoon** and **frighten**. You choose the tense of the verb.

10.

11.

Exercise 3: Underline each verb or verb phrase. In the first column, identify the verb tense by writing its corresponding number in the blank from the following list: (1) Present Tense (2) Past Tense (3) Future Tense (4) Present Perfect Tense (5) Past Perfect Tense (6) Future Perfect Tense (7) Progressive Form (8) Emphatic Form. Then, in the second column, write **R** or **I** for Regular or Irregular. (*Progressive and emphatic verbs are identified by form without noting the tense.*)

Verb Tense	R or I

12. The ice in the glass on the table melted quickly.

13. The frightened child had awakened suddenly from nightmares.

14. This heavy anchor does sink quickly to the bottom of the ocean.

15. The storyteller is telling an interesting tale about an old farmer.

16. Our group will be standing near the entrance to the park.

Exercise 4: Conjugate the verb *cry* in the chart below.

Conjugation of the Verb *Cry*					
Write the names of the four principal parts:					
Present	**Past**	**Future**	**Present Perfect**	**Past Perfect**	**Future Perfect**
(No helping verbs)	(No helping verbs)	(will or shall)	(has or have)	(had)	(will/shall) + have
Singular Plural					

Simple Progressive Forms			Perfect Progressive Forms			Simple Emphatic	
am, is, are	was, were	will, shall + be	has, have + been	had + been	will, shall + have been	do, does	did

CHAPTER 25 LESSON 5 SKILL TEST I

Paragraph 1: Change the mixed tense verbs to past tense verbs in Paragraph 2.

Mindy <u>reads</u> Richard Adams' book *Watership Down* and <u>likes</u> it so much that she <u>bought</u> a hardcover edition. She <u>says</u> it <u>was</u> a story about a number of rabbits who <u>leave</u> their warren to seek safety. It <u>seems</u> that their warren <u>is</u> endangered. The rabbits <u>faced</u> many dangers as they <u>travel</u> to their new home. Mindy <u>urges</u> me to read the book because she <u>thinks</u> it <u>was</u> very good.

Paragraph 2: Past Tense

Mindy _____ Richard Adams' book *Watership Down* and _____ it so much that she _____ a hardcover edition. She _____ it _____ a story about a number of rabbits who _____ their warren to seek safety. It _____ that their warren _____ endangered. The rabbits _____ many dangers as they _____ to their new home. Mindy _____ me to read the book because she _____ it _____ very good.

Paragraph 3: Change the mixed verb tenses to present tense verbs in Paragraph 4.

I <u>had</u> <u>visited</u> three national parks this summer and <u>have</u> <u>studied</u> the different kinds of wildlife in each park. The first park <u>is</u> Yosemite National Park. In this park, it <u>was</u> very common for bears to raid campsites at night. Also, in the high country, a traveler <u>saw</u> elk or moose if he <u>is</u> lucky. The second national park <u>was</u> the Grand Canyon. On the rim of the Grand Canyon, squirrels, chipmunks, and canyon jays <u>beg</u> for food from tourists. Down in the canyon itself, rattlesnakes, cougars, and even coati mundis <u>roamed</u>. The third national park <u>was</u> the Everglades. Since this park <u>is</u> a great marsh, it <u>had</u> many types of waterfowl as well as fish. Probably its most popular animal with tourists <u>is</u> the alligator. Many different types of animals <u>lived</u> in the parks of the United States, and travelers <u>had</u> a chance to see many of them in such parks as Yosemite National Park in California, the Grand Canyon in Arizona, and the Everglades in Florida.

Paragraph 4: Present Tense

I _____ _____ three national parks this summer and _____ _____ the different kinds of wildlife in each park. The first park _____ Yosemite National Park. In this park, it _____ very common for bears to raid campsites at night. Also, in the high country, a traveler _____ elk or moose if he _____ lucky. The second national park _____ the Grand Canyon. On the rim of the Grand Canyon, squirrels, chipmunks, and canyon jays _____ for food from tourists. Down in the canyon itself, rattlesnakes, cougars, and even coati mundis _____. The third national park _____ the Everglades. Since this park _____ a great marsh, it _____ many types of waterfowl as well as fish. Probably its most popular animal with tourists _____ the alligator. Many different types of animals _____ in the parks of the United States, and travelers _____ a chance to see many of them in such parks as Yosemite National Park in California, the Grand Canyon in Arizona, and the Everglades in Florida.

CHAPTER 26 LESSON 1

A prepositional phrase is a group of words made up of a preposition and a noun or pronoun object. Whole prepositional phrases function either as adjectives by modifying nouns and pronouns or as adverbs by modifying verbs, adjectives, and adverbs. Like one-word adjectives and adverbs, prepositional phrases functioning as adjectives and adverbs add important details to sentences. The location of a prepositional phrase will help you identify it as either an adjective or adverb phrase.

Prepositional Adjective Phrases

If a prepositional phrase modifies a noun or pronoun it is called an **adjective phrase**. A prepositional phrase functioning as an adjective modifies like a one-word adjective by telling *what kind* or *which one*.

Location. An adjective phrase almost always comes directly after the noun or pronoun it modifies.

After the **subject noun:** The pretty **girl** *in the red convertible* waved. (*in the red convertible* tells **which** girl.)
After a **predicate noun:** Excessive speed is one **cause** *of motor accidents*. (*of motor accidents* tells **which** cause.)
After a **direct object:** We saw the **jackrabbit** *with long ears*. (*with long ears* tells **which** jackrabbit.)
After an **indirect object:** The judges gave the **poodle** *with the pink bow* first prize. (*with the pink bow* tells **which** poodle.)

If two prepositional phrases are located together, with one right after the next, most of the time, the second phrase will modify the object of the first phrase: We built a house on the **side** *of the hill*. (*of the hill* tells which side)

More than one adjective phrase may be used to modify the **same** noun:
The **pumpkin** *on the porch by the door* is scary. (*on the porch* and *by the door* tell **which** pumpkin.)

Note: Sometimes the prepositional phrase that comes directly after a direct object will not modify the direct object, but will modify the verb. *(See example below.)*

We **saw** the jackrabbit *with our binoculars*. (*with our binoculars* does not tell which jackrabbit.)

In this sentence, the prepositional phrase *with our binoculars* tells **how we saw** the jackrabbit: *with our binoculars*. (Always check to see if the prepositional phrase describes the noun it follows by answering an adjective question. If it does not make sense, then it could modify another noun or a verb.)

Prepositional Adverb Phrases

If a prepositional phrase modifies a verb, adjective, or adverb, it is called an **adverb phrase** or **adverbial phrase**. A prepositional phrase functioning as an adverb modifies like a one-word adverb by telling *how, when, where,* or *why*.

Location. A prepositional adverb phrase can be located at the beginning of the sentence, directly after the verb, or it can be separated from the word it modifies by being located somewhere else in the sentence. It can also follow another prepositional phrase.

Our team **plays** *in the tournament*. (*In the tournament* tells **where** our team played.)

Sam **broke** his bat *during the game*. (*During the game* tells **when** Sam broke his bat.)

At the game Joe **hit** a home run. (*At the game* tells **where** Joe hit a home run.)

The car **headed** *down the street toward the bridge*. (*Toward the bridge* tells **where** the car headed.)

Guided Practice: Put parentheses around each prepositional phrase and write *Adj* or *Adv* above each phrase to tell whether it is an adjective or adverb. Then write the word each phrase modifies beside the *Adj* or *Adv* label.

1. The children on the back row clapped loudly after the performance.

2. Eric finished his homework for English and math during study hall.

3. During the tour we will visit the homes of the stars.

4. During art class Jeremy easily sketched a dog with a huge hat on its head.

CHAPTER 26 LESSON 1 SKILL TEST A

Exercise 1: Put parentheses around the prepositional phrases in each sentence. Write *Adj* or *Adv* above each phrase to tell whether it is an adjective or adverb phrase. Then write the word each phrase modifies beside the *Adj* or *Adv* label.

1. The best skiers in the group headed for the ski jump.

2. The illustrator in the museum drew with charcoal.

3. Above us the fireworks exploded brilliantly in the sky.

4. Jack London wrote many stories about Alaska.

5. We hid behind the tree.

6. Anna is the one in the pretty red suit.

7. My brother drove Dad's car down Main Street during the rush hour.

8. The lady with the funny purse walked along the street.

9. Bring me the book on the desk by the window.

10. The man in the gas station found a puppy under his hood.

11. All of us eyed the cake hungrily.

12. Everyone in the room laughed at the funny joke.

13. Our house is a cottage with white trim.

14. One of the longest rivers in America is the Columbia.

15. The club members are planning an overnight hike after school.

Exercise 2: Underline the verb or verb phrase in each sentence. Then identify the voice of the verb by writing **A** or **P** for Active or Passive in the blank.

_____ 16. The smelly cans of garbage in the alley were collected every Tuesday morning.

_____ 17. Mr. Keys, the museum director, removed several exquisite art pieces from the display.

_____ 18. Mr. Keys was removed from the art museum on Friday.

_____ 19. My uncle's prized antique car was polished for the local antique car show.

_____ 20. My uncle polished his prized antique car for the local antique car show.

Exercise 3: Write an active sentence and a passive sentence using the words **parents** and **call**. You choose the tense of the verb.

21.

22.

CHAPTER 26 LESSON 1 SKILL TEST B

Exercise 4: Underline each verb or verb phrase. In the first column, identify the verb tense by writing its corresponding number in the blank from the following list: (1) Present Tense (2) Past Tense (3) Future Tense (4) Present Perfect Tense (5) Past Perfect Tense (6) Future Perfect Tense (7) Progressive Form (8) Emphatic Form. Then, in the second column, write **R** or **I** for Regular or Irregular. (*Progressive and emphatic verbs are identified by form without noting the tense.*)

Verb Tense	R or I

23. The pageant contestant has already sung her song for the judges.

24. The hunters had not looked for squirrels in those woods.

25. These two boys do understand their math homework.

26. My neighbor will have already heard about the new garbage collection days.

27. Rhonda will read the whole book this weekend.

Exercise 5: Conjugate the verb *write* in the chart below.

Conjugation of the Verb *Write*					
Write the names of the four principal parts:					
Present	**Past**	**Future**	**Present Perfect**	**Past Perfect**	**Future Perfect**
(No helping verbs)	(No helping verbs)	(will or shall)	(has or have)	(had)	(will/shall) + have

Singular	Plural				

Progressive form			Emphatic form	
present (am,is,are)	past (was, were)	future (will+be)	present (do, does)	past (did)

Paragraph 1: Change the present tense verbs to past tense verbs in Paragraph 2.

I am sitting in front of the fireplace, and the flames are laughing at me as they lick at the large oak log. I am thinking that I need a good movie to watch, but I do not want to travel to a video store. Also, the potato chips I am munching and the hot chocolate I am drinking convince me that I do not want to leave my comfortable spot on the couch. Suddenly I spy an old, dusty book in the corner of my shelf. As I stare at the book, I slowly realize that I have not read a book in years. My hands tremble in excitement as I open the book and begin to read.

Paragraph 2: Past Tense

I _____ _____ in front of the fireplace, and the flames _____ _____ at me as they _____ at the large oak log. I _____ _____ that I _____ a good movie to watch, but I _____ not _____ to travel to a video store. Also, the potato chips I _____ _____ and the hot chocolate I _____ _____ _____ me that I _____ not _____ to leave my comfortable spot on the couch. Suddenly I _____ an old, dusty book in the corner of my shelf. As I _____ at the book, I slowly _____ that I _____ not __ _____ a book in years. My hands _____ in excitement as I _____ the book and _____ to read.

CHAPTER 26 LESSON 2 SKILL TEST C

Exercise 1: Put parentheses around the prepositional phrases in each sentence. Write *Adj* or *Adv* above each phrase to tell whether it is an adjective or adverb phrase. Then write the word each phrase modifies beside the *Adj* or *Adv* label.

1. The boats on the water raced everywhere.

2. They will start early in the morning.

3. During library time I am reading a book about oceanography.

4. The adult snake curled around its eggs in its cage.

5. The mosquitoes in the park by the lake swarmed the unsuspecting campers.

6. The computer in Dad's office was extremely powerful.

7. The jazz band will play in the pavilion by the river.

8. The flowers from Gill were placed on the table in the study.

9. On the plane I usually read several magazines.

10. The colorful kite with the long tail fluttered gaily in the air above the houses and trees.

11. At the Mexican restaurant our family ate enchiladas and cheese dip for an hour.

12. My friend from school is coming to my house after dinner.

13. On Saturday my father took us to the ball game.

14. A few of the animals in the national park are found on the endangered species list.

15. Our neighbors across the street work in their yard in the evenings.

Exercise 2: Underline the verb or verb phrase in each sentence. Then identify the voice of the verb by writing **A** or **P** for Active or Passive in the blank.

_____ 16. An expert tailor was consulted about the latest designs for our fashion show.

_____ 17. The coach of our football team was dunked in the dunking booth at our school carnival.

_____ 18. The cans of tuna were opened and distributed quickly to the hungry cats.

_____ 19. A crop duster sprayed chemicals on the field of soybeans.

_____ 20. The two small girls happily picked daffodils on Round Mountain.

Exercise 3: Write an active sentence and a passive sentence using the words **lion** and **hunt**. You choose the tense of the verb.

21.

22.

CHAPTER 26 LESSON 2 SKILL TEST D

Exercise 4: Underline each verb or verb phrase. In the first column, identify the verb tense by writing its corresponding number in the blank from the following list: (1) Present Tense (2) Past Tense (3) Future Tense (4) Present Perfect Tense (5) Past Perfect Tense (6) Future Perfect Tense (7) Progressive Form (8) Emphatic Form. Then, in the second column, write **R** or **I** for Regular or Irregular. (*Progressive and emphatic verbs are identified by form without noting the tense.*)

Verb Tense	R or I

23. David will have sung his song on the radio by now.

24. Several men painted the gym last weekend.

25. My older brother had fixed the flat tire already.

26. Our new puppy always barks at the cat.

27. The customer representative has listened very carefully to your complaint.

Exercise 5: Conjugate the verb *carry* in the chart below

Conjugation of the Verb *Carry*					
Write the names of the four principal parts:					
Present		**Past**	**Future**	**Present Perfect**	**Past Perfect**	**Future Perfect**

Present		**Past**	**Future**	**Present Perfect**	**Past Perfect**	**Future Perfect**
(No helping verbs)		(No helping verbs)	(will or shall)	(has or have)	(had)	(will/shall) + have
Singular	Plural					

Paragraph 1: Change the present tense verbs to past tense verbs in Paragraph 2.

    Larry's mom <u>stops</u> Larry in the hallway and <u>asks</u> him to describe a messy kitchen. Larry <u>scratches</u> his head as he <u>thinks</u> how to describe a messy kitchen to his mother. It <u>is</u> hard for him to imagine a messy kitchen because his mom <u>keeps</u> such a clean kitchen. He <u>eyes</u> his mom with suspicion as he <u>begins</u> to describe a messy kitchen. He <u>describes</u> a sink with lots of dirty dishes. Then he <u>describes</u> messy countertops, messy floors, and a messy kitchen table in such vivid detail that he <u>talks</u> for a full ten minutes. As Larry <u>stops</u> and <u>gasps</u> for breath, he <u>gives</u> his mother a victory grin and <u>waits</u> for her approval of his messy kitchen description. (*Continued in Lesson 4.*)

Paragraph 2: Past Tense

    Larry's mom _____ Larry in the hallway and _____ him to describe a messy kitchen. Larry _____ his head as he _____ how to describe a messy kitchen to his mother. It _____ hard for him to imagine a messy kitchen because his mom _____ such a clean kitchen. He _____ his mom with suspicion as he _____ to describe a messy kitchen. He _____ a sink with lots of dirty dishes. Then he _____ messy countertops, messy floors, and a messy kitchen table in such vivid detail that he _____ for a full ten minutes. As Larry _____ and _____ for breath, he _____ his mother a victory grin and _____ for her approval of his messy kitchen description.

CHAPTER 26 LESSON 3 SKILL TEST E

Second Oral Lecture: *Piranha.*

Exercise 1: Put parentheses around the prepositional phrases in each sentence. Write **Adj** or **Adv** above each phrase to tell whether it is an adjective or adverb phrase. Then write the word each phrase modifies beside the **Adj** or **Adv** label.

1. The shelves in the kitchen need two coats of paint.

2. In the early morning the news carrier left the newspaper in our box.

3. Before the concert my uncle tuned his violin in the orchestra pit.

4. The hands on the clock moved silently toward the deadline.

5. Beyond the gate, we could hear hungry coyotes on the prowl.

6. During the day the doctors in the emergency room handled several crisis situations.

7. The diamond jewelry was locked in the case at night.

8. A special consultant from the company advised us in a meeting about our insurance.

9. By noon my sister will have finished her interview for museum director.

10. Everyone at the theater enjoyed the movie premier.

11. Keith drove the speed boat down the river to the next dock.

12. He ran up the hill and into the house.

13. After work I stopped at the donut shop.

14. Show us the painting of the old church in our town.

15. After supper, the small children in our house go to bed.

Exercise 2: Underline the verb or verb phrase in each sentence. Then identify the voice of the verb by writing **A** or **P** for Active or Passive in the blank.

_____ 16. At the castle, a heavy wooden door was slammed in my face.

_____ 17. Five buckets of blueberries were considered a good haul for an hour's work.

_____ 18. The black and white skunk poked curiously around the trash in the city dump.

_____ 19. Billy's new hat was found under the wood pile behind his store.

_____ 20. Billy found his new hat under the wood pile behind his store.

Exercise 3: Write an active sentence and a passive sentence using the words **elephants** and **alarm**. You choose the tense of the verb.

21.

22.

CHAPTER 26 LESSON 4 SKILL TEST F

Student Writing Assignment #35: Lecture essay on *Piranha*.

Exercise 4: Underline each verb or verb phrase. In the first column, identify the verb tense by writing its corresponding number in the blank from the following list: (1) Present Tense (2) Past Tense (3) Future Tense (4) Present Perfect Tense (5) Past Perfect Tense (6) Future Perfect Tense (7) Progressive Form (8) Emphatic Form. Then, in the second column, write **R** or **I** for Regular or Irregular. (*Progressive and emphatic verbs are identified by form without noting the tense.*)

Verb Tense	R or I

1. My sister will be beginning her computer training tomorrow.
2. My parents have gone to Mexico this week for a sales meeting.
3. I will have completed all my assignments before the date of the final exam.
4. You do arrive promptly every day at dinner time.
5. The entire class had read a total of 500 books for the contest.

Exercise 5: Conjugate the verb *take* in the chart below.

Conjugation of the Verb *Take*					
Write the names of the four principal parts:					
Present	**Past**	**Future**	**Present Perfect**	**Past Perfect**	**Future Perfect**
(No helping verbs)	(No helping verbs)	(will or shall)	(has or have)	(had)	(will/shall) + have
Singular Plural					

Paragraph 1: Change the past tense verbs to present tense verbs in Paragraph 2.

    Larry's mother <u>looked</u> at him with a big smile on her face as she <u>commented</u> on his vivid imagination. She <u>patted</u> his back and <u>told</u> him how accurate his description <u>was</u> of a messy kitchen. Then she <u>held</u> his hand as she <u>led</u> him to her kitchen. As she <u>opened</u> the door, she <u>told</u> Larry that she now <u>wanted</u> him to describe how he <u>was going</u> to clean up the mess from his bunking party last night.

    Larry <u>stared</u> at the messiest kitchen he <u>had</u> ever <u>seen.</u> His mother totally <u>ignored</u> his desperation. She <u>waved</u> good-bye to him as she <u>left</u> him to his cleaning.

Paragraph 2: Present Tense

    Larry's mother _____ at him with a big smile on her face as she _____ on his vivid imagination. She _____ his back and _____ him how accurate his description _____ of a messy kitchen. Then she _____ his hand as she _____ him to her kitchen. As she _____ the door, she _____ Larry that she now _____ him to describe how he _____ _____ to clean up the mess from his bunking party last night.

    Larry _____ at the messiest kitchen he _____ ever _____. His mother totally _____ his desperation. She _____ good-bye to him as she _____ him to his cleaning.

CHAPTER 26 LESSON 5 SKILL TEST G

Exercise 1: Underline each verb or verb phrase. In the first column, identify the verb tense by writing its corresponding number in the blank from the following list: (1) Present Tense (2) Past Tense (3) Future Tense (4) Present Perfect Tense (5) Past Perfect Tense (6) Future Perfect Tense (7) Progressive Form (8) Emphatic Form. Then, in the second column, write **R** or **I** for Regular or Irregular. (*Progressive and emphatic verbs are identified by form without noting the tense.*)

Verb Tense	R or I

1. Mrs. Blue's class did not understand all the concepts on the semester test.
2. After today the athlete will have jogged one hundred miles for his training.
3. That lucky girl found several old coins in her collection.
4. The yellow sunflowers have stood in a tall row by the fence all summer.
5. The cows and calves will eat hay in the field across the road.

Paragraph 1: Change the past tense verbs to present tense verbs in Paragraph 2.

Samantha <u>felt</u> sorry for herself. She <u>didn't</u> <u>have</u> any friends, and she <u>wasn't</u> <u>doing</u> well in school. She <u>decided</u> she <u>was</u> a failure at an early age. As she <u>walked</u> around in the park with her head down, she <u>felt</u> a pair of eyes on her. As Samantha <u>raised</u> her head, she <u>looked</u> directly into a pair of alert, blue eyes. The blue eyes <u>belonged</u> to a boy about her age in a bright orange cap. He <u>walked</u> quickly to her side and <u>enlisted</u> her help to supervise a tag game for kids from the shelter down the street. Later, as Samantha <u>walked</u> home, her head <u>was</u> <u>held</u> high, and her eyes <u>were</u> bright with the prospect of helping the shelter kids again tomorrow. With a spring in her step, Samantha <u>decided</u> she <u>wasn't</u> a failure after all. She <u>liked</u> her new friends at the shelter who <u>volunteered</u> their time after school and on weekends. She even <u>decided</u> that she <u>had</u> to do better in school since she <u>wanted</u> to become a counselor.

Paragraph 2: Present Tense

Samantha _____ sorry for herself. She _____ _____ any friends, and she _____ _____ well in school. She _____ she _____ a failure at an early age. As she _____ around in the park with her head down, she _____ a pair of eyes on her. As Samantha _____ her head, she _____ directly into a pair of alert, blue eyes. The blue eyes _____ to a boy about her age in a bright orange cap. He _____ quickly to her side and _____ her help to supervise a tag game for kids from the shelter down the street. Later, as Samantha _____ home, her head _____ _____ high, and her eyes _____ bright with the prospect of helping the shelter kids again tomorrow. With a spring in her step, Samantha _____ she _____ a failure after all. She _____ her new friends at the shelter who _____ their time after school and on weekends. She even _____ that she _____ to do better in school since she _____ to become a counselor.

CHAPTER 27 LESSON 1

Verbals

You have learned that some words do two jobs at the same time. For example, the possessive noun and the possessive pronoun both perform a noun job and, at the same time, modify like an adjective. These two functions are clearly illustrated in the following sentence: *My younger sister's room is a disaster.* The word *sister's* modifies *room* like an adjective (tells which room) but is modified by *younger* like a noun. The word *sister's* can perform both the noun job and the adjective job at the same time.

Now you will study three more groups of words that perform different jobs at the same time. These groups of words are participles, gerunds, and infinitives. Participles, gerunds, and infinitives are called **verbals**. The word *verbal* means "like a verb." A **verbal** is a word made from a verb and used as an adjective, noun, or adverb in a sentence.

First Verbal: Participle

A **participle** is a word that is made from a verb and **used as an adjective** in a sentence. Because participles are made from verbs, they look like verbs and have verb endings *-ed*, *-en*, *-t*, or *-ing,* but they modify nouns and pronouns because they function as adjectives.

    Examples: I watched the *laughing* hyenas. (*What kind of hyenas? laughing - Adj*)
                 The *collapsed* bridge was dangerous. (*What kind of bridge? collapsed - Adj*)
                 The *stolen* car was returned to its owner. (*What kind of car? stolen - Adj*)
                 He ate the *burnt* toast. (*What kind of toast? burnt - Adj*)

Like adjectives, participles are usually found *in front of* the nouns they modify. Sometimes, though, a participle can be found *after* the noun it modifies.

    Example: The children smelled the cookies *baking*. (*What kind of cookies? baking - Adj*)

After a sentence has been classified, add a verbal check for a participle:

        SP   **V-t**   **A**   **PAdj**   **DO**
    Example: I watched the *laughing* hyenas. (Say: *Verbal check for a participle: Is there an adjective*
                                    made from a verb that ends in -ed, -en,-t, or -ing? Yes. Laughing -
                                      Participle-Adjective.) (Write *P* in front of the *Adj* label: *PAdj.*)

Guided Practice: Classify each sentence. Then write the participle in the first blank and the word it modifies in the second blank.

1. We watched the rippling stream. _____ modifies _____

2. The cleaned room passed mother's inspection. _____ modifies _____

3. This is her chosen occupation. _____ modifies _____

4. We heard the bells ringing. _____ modifies _____

Guided Practice: Underline each participle once and each verb twice, and write *P* or *V* above each participle or verb.

  1. The mother soothed her crying infant.

  2. The infant was crying for his mother.

  3. The buzzing insects drove Mother crazy!

  4. Those insects are buzzing in Mother's ear.

  5. The polished furniture sparkled brightly.

  6. Please oil that squeaking door!

  7. Larry's combed hair looked neat and clean.

  8. We bought a woven basket at the craft fair.

CHAPTER 27 LESSON 1 SKILL TEST A

Exercise 1: Classify each sentence. Then write the participle in the first blank and the word it modifies in the second blank.

1. The cleaning lady mopped the floor. _____ modifies _____

2. The talking birds entertained us. _____ modifies _____

3. A chosen group of students attended the concert. _____ modifies _____

4. Grandmother could hear the water dripping. _____ modifies _____

5. Aunt Sue found the ripped curtain! _____ modifies _____

6. Six sliced peaches filled the bowl. _____ modifies _____

7. We saw the blossoming cherry trees. _____ modifies _____

8. The disturbed ants crawled away hurriedly. _____ modifies _____

9. Our frozen hands could not open the door. _____ modifies _____

10. The raging fire burned forty acres. _____ modifies _____

11. Station KWOT is proud of its large listening audience. _____ modifies _____

12. We were assigned a written report. _____ modifies _____

13. The honking geese landed on the marsh. _____ modifies _____

14. Allison found her broken necklace. _____ modifies _____

15. Jason could see the icicles melting outside. _____ modifies _____

Exercise 2: Underline each participle once and each verb twice, and write *P* or *V* above each participle or verb.

16. The torn pages of the old book were fragile.

17. I smelled bread baking.

18. Those barking dogs were annoying my sister.

19. That home run resulted in a broken window!

20. The window was broken during the game.

21. Juanita could hear the cows mooing.

22. The cows were mooing.

23. The slithering snakes frightened my kids!

24. A lighted pathway helped us after dark.

25. Two snakes slithered at the bottom of a cage.

26. A relaxing vacation is in my future.

27. Jan and Joe relaxed on their vacation.

28. My teacher lost her reading glasses.

29. Our class was reading a poem by Longfellow.

CHAPTER 27 LESSON 1 SKILL TEST B

Exercise 3: Put parentheses around each prepositional phrase, and write *Adj* or *Adv* above each phrase to tell whether it is an adjective or adverb phrase. Then write the word each phrase modifies beside the *Adj* and *Adv* label.

1. I borrowed the book on the desk from Jonathan.

2. The bird's nest in the cedar tree was built by sparrows.

3. Hungry children from the city sat silently beside the busy road.

4. By this evening every thank-you letter to the presenters should be written.

5. Under the couch I found a pair of mittens and five pennies.

Exercise 4: Complete the chart below by writing these eight pronouns in the correct column: *another, others, whose, these, that, their, him, he.*

Demonstrative Pronouns		Indefinite Pronouns		Interrogative Pronoun	Personal Pronouns		
Singular	Plural	Singular	Plural		Subjective	Possessive	Objective
6.	7.	8.	9.	10.	11.	12.	13.

Exercise 5: Underline the correct pronoun choice.

14. (We, Us) ladies enjoyed the visit to the gallery.

15. (Who, Whom) is your favorite fiction author?

16. The friendly dog gave Sam and (I, me) a shake.

17. This is (she, her).

18. The cake was given to (he and I, him and me).

19. Please visit (we, us) players after the game.

20. For (who, whom) is this music being played?

21. Paul and (me, I) were discussing tennis.

22. This is (her, she) day to do the laundry.

23. (He and I, Him and me) gave everyone cake.

Exercise 6: Underline each indefinite pronoun, and write *S* or *P* for singular or plural above it. Then underline the correct verb.

24. Many of the exotic birds (is, are) available.

25. Few of the buildings (has, have) elevators.

26. Some (study, studies) in their rooms.

27. Everyone (park, parks) his car in this lot.

28. Most of the pencils (has, have) erasers.

29. Most of the candy (has, have) coconut in it.

30. None of the telephones (was, were) antiques.

31. Nothing (upset, upsets) Mother like fighting.

32. Both (send, sends) their regards.

33. All of my socks (has, have) holes in them.

Exercise 7: Draw one line under the subject, and write *S* or *P* for singular or plural. Then underline the correct verb and the correct possessive pronoun to agree with the subject.

34. Each of the gentlemen (ride, rides) (his, their) horse to the stable.

35. Some of the turtles (lay, lays) (its, their) eggs in the water.

36. Some of the coffee (has, have) lost (its, their) flavor.

37. Few in the crowd (like, likes) to see (his, their) team lose.

CHAPTER 27 LESSON 2 SKILL TEST C

Exercise 1: Classify each sentence. Then write the participle in the first blank and the word it modifies in the second blank.

1. Matt pulled his laughing brother out of the mud. _____ modifies _____

2. Randy handed Anna the damaged vase. _____ modifies _____

3. The scolded puppy crept under the bed. _____ modifies _____

4. The swimming team won first place. _____ modifies _____

5. Leah located the missing key. _____ modifies _____

6. The fallen tree stretched across the road. _____ modifies _____

7. The chimney was covered with creeping ivy. _____ modifies _____

8. Shannon carried the sign to the painted bench. _____ modifies _____

9. The smiling candidate greeted his supporters victoriously. _____ modifies _____

10. The elected officials met with the committee. _____ modifies _____

11. Everyone heard the girls singing. _____ modifies _____

12. Soldiers arrived at the deserted village. _____ modifies _____

13. Whispering pine trees swayed in the wind. _____ modifies _____

14. The cracked vase was damaged during the earthquake. _____ modifies _____

15. The freezing temperature killed the plants. _____ modifies _____

Exercise 2: Underline each participle once and each verb twice, and write *P* or *V* above each participle or verb.

16. The snoring man kept his wife up all night.

17. The man snored all night.

18. Broken dishes lay everywhere on the floor.

19. Dishes were broken by the running children.

20. Bells chimed in the distance.

21. We could hear bells chiming in the distance.

22. Covered wagons carried pioneers westward.

23. Wagons were covered with canvas cloth.

24. A drizzling rain dampened our high spirits.

25. Rain drizzled all during the day of our picnic.

26. Daisy cleaned her sleeping puppies.

27. Daisy's puppies were sleeping in the barn.

28. Buzzing bees surrounded the beekeeper.

29. The bees were buzzing around their hive.

30. Those boys were laughing at their own jokes!

31. Those laughing boys were telling jokes.

CHAPTER 27 LESSON 2 SKILL TEST D

Exercise 3: Put parentheses around each prepositional phrase, and write **Adj** or **Adv** above each phrase to tell whether it is an adjective or adverb phrase. Then write the word each phrase modifies beside the **Adj** or **Adv** label.

1. During the night the wind whipped at the shutters of my windows.
2. Someone at the game will win a free ticket to the tournament.
3. Everyone in our class will have finished his test in time.
4. The small brown bat clung to the brick wall outside the building.
5. Behind the shed Dad painted a wooden chair for Mother's birthday.

Exercise 4: Complete the chart below by writing these eight pronouns in the correct column: *somebody, both, which, this, those, we, mine, her.*

Demonstrative Pronouns		Indefinite Pronouns		Interrogative Pronoun	Personal Pronouns		
Singular	Plural	Singular	Plural		Subjective	Possessive	Objective
6.	7.	8.	9.	10.	11.	12.	13.

Exercise 5: Underline the correct pronoun choice.

14. The door was unlocked for Rick and (him, he).
15. Please help (her and me, she and I) to the car.
16. (Who, Whom) is the speaker at our meeting?
17. The doctor will give (we, us) sisters a call later.
18. To (who, whom) was this order given?
19. You and (I, me) will arrive at six o'clock.
20. (We, Us) citizens demand a recount of votes.
21. Those flowers were bought for (we, us) girls.
22. (He and I, Him and her) will wait in line.
23. Dan and (I, me) talked on the phone to Dad.

Exercise 6: Underline each indefinite pronoun, and write **S** or **P** for singular or plural above it. Then underline the correct verb.

24. Nobody in the cave (has, have) his own light.
25. None of the pigs (like, likes) bread for food.
26. Both of the shoes (fit, fits) my swollen feet.
27. All of the meat (was, were) on the table.
28. Anything (is, are) capable of happening today.
29. Most of the eggs (is, are) in the basket.
30. Many (has, have) their reports published.
31. Some of the coins (is, are) not on the shelf.
32. Few (want, wants) brownies for dessert.
33. Any of the trucks (ride, rides) smoothly.

Exercise 7: Draw one line under the subject and write **S** or **P** for singular or plural. Then underline the correct verb and the correct possessive pronoun to agree with the subject.

34. No one in the room (enjoy, enjoys) (his, their) meal.
35. Both of the children (write, writes) (her, their) assignments on graph paper.
36. Everybody (talk, talks) to (himself, themselves) during the morning break.
37. One of the alligators (eat, eats) fish every day for (his, their) meal.

CHAPTER 27 LESSON 3

Second Verbal: Gerund

Remember that a verbal is made from a verb but is used as another part of speech in a sentence. The second verbal you will study is a called a gerund. **A gerund is a word that is made from a verb and used as a noun**. Because gerunds are made from verbs, they look like verbs and usually have the *-ing* verb ending, but they are used as nouns. This means that a gerund can perform any of the noun jobs. A gerund can be the subject, object of a preposition, direct object, predicate noun, indirect object, or object complement of a sentence. The examples below show some of the ways gerunds can be used as nouns.

Subject: *Swimming* is fun. (What is fun? swimming - SN)

Object of the proposition: By *studying,* he passed the test. (By what? studying - OP)

Direct object: We like *hiking.* (We like what? hiking - DO)

Indirect object: The judges gave her *skating* high marks. (Judges gave marks to what? skating - IO)

Object complement (noun): The teacher called his behavior *cheating.*

Predicate noun: Her favorite pastime is *skating.* (Pastime is what? skating - PrN)

(Don't be fooled by sentences like this one: *He is skating.* In this sentence, *is* is the helping verb, and *skating* is the main verb. *Skating* is not a gerund because it is not functioning as a predicate noun that renames the subject.)

After a sentence has been classified, add a verbal check for a gerund:

        GSN   LV PA

Example: Swimming is fun. (Say: *Verbal check for a gerund: Is there a noun made from a verb that ends in -ing? Yes. Swimming - Gerund-Subject Noun.*)

        (Write *G* in front of the *SN* label: *GSN*)

Guided Practice: Classify each sentence. Then label each gerund with a *G* in front of the noun job.

1. Jogging was Dad's favorite morning activity.

2. By diving, Carl found the pennies.

3. My brother enjoys diving.

4. The editor gave her writing a fair chance.

5. Her idea of fun was skiing.

6. The referee called their actions fighting.

Verbal Checklist for Participles and Gerunds

1. Verbal check for a participle: Is there an adjective made from a verb that ends in *-ed, -en, -t,* or *-ing*?

2. Verbal check for a gerund: Is there a noun made from a verb that ends in *-ing*? (*Possible gerund nouns include: SN, OP, IO, DO, PrN, or OCN.*)

Guided Practice: Underline each participle or gerund once and each verb twice. Write *P, G*, or *V* above each participle, gerund, or verb.

1. My son dislikes flying.

2. My son is flying to Arizona next week.

3. Mom bought flying insect spray at the store.

4. Sailing is one of my favorite summer activities.

5. The sailing fleet left from their port Tuesday.

6. We will be sailing for the islands next month.

7. By jumping, we escaped the burning building.

8. We jumped on the trampoline for an hour.

CHAPTER 27 LESSON 3 SKILL TEST E

Exercise 1: Classify each sentence. Then label each gerund with a **G** in front of the noun job.

1. We heard the sound of whistling.

2. Winning makes him happy.

3. Mowing has been a worthwhile project.

4. You can forget fighting.

5. His favorite sport will be swimming.

6. Delaying will make the boss angry.

7. She uses a mop for cleaning.

8. Cleaning can be a difficult job.

9. Some people enjoy cleaning.

10. For gardening, you need an open, sunny area.

11. The younger children disliked waiting.

12. The man's occupation is painting.

13. We liked your singing and dancing.

14. Kelly used an extra long pole for vaulting.

15. Reading is Lindsay's favorite hobby.

Exercise 2: Underline each participle and gerund once and each verb twice. Write **P**, **G**, or **V** above each participle, gerund, or verb.

16. Modeling is a glamorous occupation.

17. Beth modeled winter coats at the mall.

18. The kids used modeling clay for their animals.

19. For traveling, we need several small bags.

20. We need several small traveling bags.

21. We will travel with several small bags.

22. Our teacher made writing a fun subject.

23. Two teachers helped with our writing class.

24. The teacher writes examples on the board.

25. I need typing paper for my class.

26. Sue is typing her letter on special paper.

27. Sue bought special paper for typing.

28. Jon was running in the hall of the school.

29. Jon was punished for running.

30. I could hear running water upstairs.

31. Yelling makes my elderly aunt nervous.

32. Yelling children were heard in the street.

33. That lady always yells at her children!

CHAPTER 27 LESSON 3 SKILL TEST F

Exercise 3: Put parentheses around each prepositional phrase and write **Adj** or **Adv** above each phrase to tell whether it is an adjective or adverb phrase. Then write the word each phrase modifies beside the **Adj** or **Adv** label.

1. The stone bowls from the museum were originally painted in bright colors.

2. The men in the army listened silently to their leader's instructions.

3. Nobody in our music class brought his (or her) band instrument to class.

4. A flock of bewildered geese flew north for the winter.

5. During the storm, lightning hit the barn with all the hay.

Exercise 4: Complete the chart below by writing these eight pronouns in the correct column: *hers, it, those, others, everything, this, who, him.*

Demonstrative Pronouns		Indefinite Pronouns		Interrogative Pronoun	Personal Pronouns		
Singular	Plural	Singular	Plural		Subjective	Possessive	Objective
6.	7.	8.	9.	10.	11.	12.	13.

Exercise 5: Underline the correct pronoun choice.

14. (She, Her) and Dad went to the game.

15. The winners were Louise and (I, me).

16. (We, Us) students need a leader.

17. The wolf frightened Jerry and (I, me).

18. Sam saw Sara and (I, me) at the dance.

19. Todd invited only (we, us) boys to the game.

20. These books are for Dan and (I, me).

21. (She, Her) and I are going shopping.

22. This is (he, him).

23. You and (he, him) have been selected.

Exercise 6: Underline each indefinite pronoun, and write **S** or **P** for singular or plural above it. Underline the correct verb.

24. All of the water (was, were) spilled.

25. Most of the water (was, were) spilled.

26. Some of the water (was, were) spilled.

27. All of the students (was, were) present.

28. Most of the students (was, were) present.

29. Neither of the cars (is, are) red.

30. Everyone (has, have) a duty to vote.

31. Most (is, are) willing to try.

32. Everyone (expect, expects) an answer.

33. None of the horses (trot, trots) smoothly.

Exercise 7: For each numbered word, write the singular possessive form in the first blank and the plural possessive form in the second blank.

Word	Singular Possessive	Plural Possessive	Word	Singular Possessive	Plural Possessive
34. teacher			37. house		
35. baby			38. man		
36. woman			39. city		

CHAPTER 27 LESSON 4 SKILL TEST G

Exercise 1: Classify each sentence. Then label each participle with a **P** and each gerund with a **G** in front of its job in the sentence.

1. His favorite water sport is skiing.

2. After the craft fair, Dorothy's hobby will be tole painting.

3. The chopped onions made a delicious onion salad.

4. With his driving, we desperately needed nerves of steel.

5. The blowing curtains scared my little sister.

6. The stolen pie was found by my dad.

7. The man's occupation is painting.

8. The stranger found my broken camera.

9. At the contest the spectators loudly cheered the band's superb marching.

10. Swarming bees stung the hungry bears.

11. The senate voted on the renewed health plan.

12. Today we happily celebrated his wedding.

13. Printing can be a big headache.

14. The constant coughing made me miserable.

Exercise 2: Underline each participle and gerund once and each verb twice, and write **P**, **G**, or **V** above each one.

15. Dad planted the wheat.

16. Planting is Dad's job.

17. The planted wheat grows after a big rain.

18. Planting is done in the spring.

19. Blowing leaves tumbled across the yard.

20. The leaves were blowing across the yard.

21. The fallen leaves were a sign of autumn.

22. The leaves were removed by raking.

23. My uncle yelled loudly at the ball game.

24. The crowd supported the team by yelling.

25. The yelling crowd supported the team.

26. Yelling was encouraged by the cheerleaders.

27. The cheerleaders continued yelling.

28. Writing comes easily to some.

29. My writing assignment is due tomorrow.

30. I am writing my term paper.

CHAPTER 27 LESSON 4 SKILL TEST H

Exercise 3: Write only the <u>pattern number</u> in the blank beside each sentence. Classify only the pattern core in each sentence. Use these pattern core examples to guide you: P1-SN V,   P2-SN V-t DO,   P3-SN V-t IO DO, P4-SN LV PrN,   P5-SN LV PA,   P6-SN V-t DO OCN,   P7-SN V-t DO OCA

P_____ 1. The seals in the first ring are playing ball with their keeper.

P_____ 2. The angry fat man yelled loudly at the very noisy boys in his doughnut shop.

P_____ 3. Exercise can make a person energetic.

P_____ 4. During the blinding rainstorm, Artie mistakenly made a wrong turn.

P_____ 5. We considered him a hero.

P_____ 6. Yesterday Jay gave Leroy three new tires for his old Ford truck.

P_____ 7. Across the long, swinging bridge, Anne casually walked to her aunt's house above the river.

P_____ 8. Soon Louise will become the richest woman in the South.

P_____ 9. In the middle of the night he left George a secret message on the steps outside his house.

P_____ 10. The troops had a late breakfast and an early supper today.

P_____ 11. The children from the elementary schools painted the posts blue and white.

P_____ 12. Those chickens on Mrs. Brown's farm became potluck for the hungry people of the village.

P_____ 13. The athletes seemed nervous before the final meet.

P_____ 14. Helga crept down the stairs in a suit of red thermal underwear with a baseball bat in her hand.

P_____ 15. Donnie gave Ray a bundle of sticks for his new wood stove.

P_____ 16. The expert student mechanic crawled under the frame of the old abandoned school bus.

P_____ 17. Soon the lazy water buffalo at the edge of the water sluggishly walked away in search of food.

P_____ 18. The queen has become a basket case.

P_____ 19. After the storm the desert sun left the desert dry.

P_____ 20. The tail of an opossum is long and scaly.

P_____ 21. At the sound of the horn, the long tan lizard rapidly leaped to the side of the dusty road.

P_____ 22. In the dark basement Sam suddenly saw a gray rat with a curled tail.

P_____ 23. The long, green fuzzy worm with the strange purple horns on its head slowly crept along beneath the brilliantly green leaves of the luscious strawberry plants in the back rows of the country garden.

Exercise 4: For each numbered word, write the singular possessive form in the first blank and the plural possessive form in the second blank.

Word	Singular Possessive	Plural Possessive	Word	Singular Possessive	Plural Possessive
24. Smith			27. mouse		
25. berry			28. glass		
26. goose			29. ox		

CHAPTER 27 LESSON 5

Third Verbal: Infinitive

Before you study the third verbal, it would be helpful to review what you have learned about verbals thus far. You already know several things about verbals.

1. **Verbals** are words made from verbs but used as other parts of speech. There are three verbals: the participle, the gerund, and the infinitive.
2. A **participle** is a verbal that is used as an adjective and that ends in -*ed, -en, -t,* or -*ing.*
3. A **gerund** is a verbal that is used as a noun and that ends in -*ing.*

The third verbal is the **infinitive.** An infinitive is a word made from a verb that has the word *to* directly before it (*to run, to laugh, to see, etc.*). **The infinitive is made from a verb and used as an adjective, an adverb, or a noun.**

Even though infinitives can be used as three different parts of speech, they are the easiest of the verbals to find because of the word *to* in front of them. The *to* in front of the infinitive is often called the "sign" of the infinitive. Even though the infinitive can be used as an adjective or noun, you will not confuse it with a participle or a gerund because the infinitive has a *to* in front of it, and the participle and gerund do not. The examples below show some of the ways infinitives can be used as nouns, adjectives, and adverbs.

> **Subject:** *To study* is important. (What is important? to study - SN)
> **Direct Object:** She likes *to travel*. (She likes what? to travel - DO)
> **Predicate Noun:** His job is *to paint*. (Does to paint mean the same thing as job? Yes - PrN)
> **Adjective:** The person *to call* is Jim. (Which person? the one to call - Adj modifying the SN)
> **Adverbs:** The children went outside *to play*. (Went why? to play - Adv)

Even though infinitives are easy to find with the word *to* in front of them, you must take care not to confuse a prepositional phrase beginning with *to* with an infinitive beginning with *to*. **You must always remember that the preposition "to" always has an object (noun or pronoun) that follows it, and the "sign" of the infinitive "to" always has a verb that follows it.**

> *noun*
> They have gone **to the library**. Prepositional phrase

> *verb*
> I wanted **to order** a sandwich. Infinitive

Before you begin the Question and Answer Flow, do a verbal check for an infinitive. Identify any "to" followed by a verb as an infinitive. Put an *I* above it, and later you will determine its job in the sentence as you classify the sentence.

>   **ISN LV   PA**
> Example: To read is educational. (Before you classify say: *"Verbal check for an infinitive: Is there a 'to' with a verb after it? Yes. The infinitive is "to read."* Write *I* above "to read.")

Guided Practice: Write *I* above the infinitive in each sentence. Then classify each sentence and label the function of each word in the sentence.

1. Jana loves to dance.

2. His favorite pastime is to read.

3. To skydive is adventurous.

4. Carla went to the mall to shop.

5. He knew the candidate to select.

CHAPTER 27 LESSON 5 CONTINUED

Guided Practice: Underline the infinitive or prepositional phrase in each sentence. Then write *I* for Infinitive or *PP* for prepositional phrase above it.

1. The athletes listened carefully to their coach.

2. To coach requires much patience.

3. Every morning, I like to write.

4. Mom writes to my sister in Spain every week.

5. To play is the children's greatest joy.

6. We looked to our supervisor for advice.

Verbal Checklist for Participles, Gerunds, and Infinitives

1. Verbal check for a participle: Is there an adjective made from a verb that ends in *-ed, -en, -t,* or *-ing?*

2. Verbal check for a gerund: Is there a noun made from a verb that ends in *-ing?* (*Possible gerund nouns include: SN, OP, IO, DO, PrN,* or *OCN.*)

3. Verbal check for an infinitive: Is there a "to" with a verb after it? Yes. The infinitive is (name the infinitive.)

Use the Verbal Checklist to work the guided practice below.

Guided Practice: Underline each participle, gerund, or infinitive once, and underline each verb twice. Write *P, G, I,* or *V* above each participle, gerund, infinitive, or verb.

1. To hike is my dream.

2. My friend is hiking to the next town tomorrow.

3. Missy borrowed hiking boots from her cousin.

4. My friends love hiking.

5. The first graders can't wait to read.

6. Grandmother has lost her reading glasses.

7. By reading, we improved our test scores.

8. We are reading *The Diary of Anne Frank.*

CHAPTER 27 LESSON 5 SKILL TEST I

Exercise 1: Write *I* above the infinitive in each sentence. Then classify each sentence and label the function of each word in the sentence.

1. The horse to ride is Chester.

2. To vote, he stepped into the booth.

3. I want to win.

4. I know the place to park.

5. Maria bribed the judges to win.

6. To exercise is healthy.

7. To call, you must press the button.

8. The family's choice was to fly.

9. Houses to buy are plentiful.

10. We need to laugh.

11. The lady bowed her head to cry.

12. His objective is to win.

Exercise 2: Underline the infinitive or prepositional phrase in each sentence. Then write *I* for Infinitive or **PP** for prepositional phrase above it.

13. His whole family came to our country.

14. They worked hard to survive.

15. All the students had to study.

16. To walk was his only desire.

17. We traveled to Europe.

18. My brother likes to ski.

19. He reported to headquarters.

20. He wanted to read.

21. My sister returned to college.

22. Our grandmother came to visit yesterday.

23. He likes to travel.

24. The player to watch is Jim.

25. Phil walked quickly to the store.

26. Sally and Linda had to apologize.

27. He gave his help to needy families.

28. Rhonda wanted to help.

29. We hurried to the garden.

30. The water rushed to our steps.

Exercise 3: Underline each participle, gerund, or infinitive once, and underline each verb twice. Write *P*, *G*, *I*, or *V* above each participle, gerund, infinitive, or verb.

31. To help is the only answer.

32. Our church is helping in the rescue effort.

33. David lent a helping hand to the homeless.

34. Helping made me feel good inside.

35. The music director asked everyone to listen.

36. Listen to the flutes during this next selection.

37. Listening was difficult for the small children.

38. It was music to our listening ears.

Exercise 4: Write three sentences using an infinitive as a noun, an adjective, and an adverb. Label each sentence.

CHAPTER 27 LESSON 5 SKILL TEST J

Exercise 5: Write only the <u>pattern number</u> in the blank beside each sentence. Classify only the pattern core in each sentence. Use these pattern core examples to guide you: P1-SN V, P2-SN V-t DO, P3-SN V-t IO DO, P4-SN LV PrN, P5-SN LV PA, P6-SN V-t DO OCN, P7-SN V-t DO OCA

P_____ 1. The bird on the dogwood limb is a yellow flycatcher.

P_____ 2. The registered voters in Pope County elected Mr. Hydro county judge.

P_____ 3. Immediately the barber handed Clyde a mirror for a quick look at his chopped haircut.

P_____ 4. William is very excited and happy at the idea of a visit from a real movie star.

P_____ 5. The tall giant broke the limb over the head of the ugly monster.

P_____ 6. Around the frantic settlers, the hostile Indians moved in a widening circle.

P_____ 7. Mrs. Dustin delightfully named her new baby girl Angelica.

P_____ 8. That pizza from the refrigerator tastes somewhat moldy.

P_____ 9. Did Anthony walk quietly through the hall on the way to the Math Department?

P_____ 10. Bring me the contributions and gifts to the shelter for the homeless.

P_____ 11. In the winter the fur of an ermine becomes white.

P_____ 12. The stage managers will be you and Terry.

P_____ 13. The businessmen considered him a success.

P_____ 14. The best cooks in cooking class are Beth and Lynn.

P_____ 15. Do you believe the commander of the army competent?

P_____ 16. The haughty girl gave Sylvia a scornful look.

P_____ 17. After a thrilling finish the crowd enthusiastically applauded the actors.

P_____ 18. The insensitive students labeled him careless after his unnerving accident.

P_____ 19. The sign over the gas pumps swayed in the wind with a creaking noise.

P_____ 20. The company in Washington sent Harry and Linda a crate of pens.

P_____ 21. In a moment of temptation, the weasel at the chicken house was thinking about a delicate taste of some tender fowl.

P_____ 22. Into the middle of the crowd, the three skinny little bullfighters walked with the attitude of men in charge.

Exercise 6: For each numbered word, write the singular possessive form in the first blank and the plural possessive form in the second blank.

Word	Singular Possessive	Plural Possessive	Word	Singular Possessive	Plural Possessive
23. Miller			26. fish		
24. company			27. deer		
25. butterfly			28. wife		

CHAPTER 28 LESSON 1 SKILL TEST A

Exercise 1: Write *I* above the infinitive in each sentence. Then classify each sentence and label the function of each word in the sentence.

1. To believe is to see.

2. This is the picture to take.

3. The librarian prefers to read.

4. Sherry loves to paint.

5. The teacher to have is Mrs. Dewitt.

6. The dog obviously wants to eat.

7. To boast is poor taste.

8. The rooster likes to crow.

9. To reduce, she went to a fitness center.

10. This is the team to beat.

11. They went to the beach to swim.

12. Our plan was to leave.

13. To cooperate produces good relationships.

14. You will have to work.

15. We wanted to sing.

16. Dave learned to sing.

17. They tried to run.

18. To swim is my favorite pastime.

Exercise 2: Underline the infinitive or prepositional phrase in each sentence. Then write *I* for Infinitive or *PP* for prepositional phrase above it.

19. Mr. Smith came to the office.

20. We went to the park.

21. We wanted to swim.

22. We stayed to the end.

23. We tried to dive.

24. The boys are going to win.

25. The boys are going to the game.

26. My younger brother wanted to drive.

27. We all drove to the beach.

28. The students were told to study.

29. He ran to the house.

30. All the students plan to go.

31. The children want to leave.

32. He walked to the door.

33. He had always wanted to travel.

34. Dad sent roses to Mom.

35. Hand the mail to Chris.

36. To work is a necessity.

CHAPTER 28 LESSON 1 SKILL TEST B

Exercise 3: Underline the verbals and identify each one with an abbreviation and function. Gerunds: **GSN, GDO, GOP, GPrN,** or **GOCN.** Participles: **PAdj.** Infinitives: **IAdj, IAdv, ISN, IDO,** or **IPrN.**

Infinitives

1. To act is Claudia's greatest ambition.

2. The house to buy is on the corner.

3. The little children at the park loved to play.

4. My neighbor's dog loves to bite.

Gerunds

5. Today we happily celebrated his arriving.

6. By studying he passed the test.

7. Dreaming is an interesting occupation.

8. The student enjoyed outlining.

Participles

9. We watched the rippling stream.

10. The talking birds entertained us.

11. The fire department rescued the stranded kitten.

12. This is her chosen occupation.

Exercise 4: Underline the verbals and identify each one with an abbreviation and function. Gerunds: **GSN, GDO, GOP, GPrN,** or **GOCN.** Participles: **PAdj.** Infinitives: **IAdj, IAdv, ISN, IDO,** or **IPrN.**

13. The children wanted to help.

14. The smashed car lay in the ditch.

15. Writing is my favorite pastime.

16. The breaking glass made a loud sound.

17. Swimming is Julie's favorite sport.

18. This is the song to sing.

19. That pipe needs draining.

20. Jody relaxed by reading.

21. The reading teacher is very good.

22. My family loves to ski.

23. The ringing bells were loud.

24. Tanning can cause skin problems.

25. The growling dog walked toward Andrew.

26. To knit is difficult for some people.

CHAPTER 28 LESSON 2 SKILL TEST C

Exercise 1: Underline the verbals and identify each one with an abbreviation and function. Gerunds: *GSN, GDO, GOP, GPrN,* or *GOCN*. Participles: *PAdj*. Infinitives: *IAdj, IAdv, ISN, IDO,* or *IPrN*.

Infinitives

1. Ed chose to cooperate.

2. James is the person to help.

3. She only came to watch.

4. To perform had always been his dream.

Gerunds

5. Playing is a child's way of life.

6. At the contest the spectators cheered the band's marching.

7. A good mental exercise is writing.

8. My brother is always tired of studying.

Participles

9. The stolen jewelry could not be found.

10. A scrubbing brush was used for the filthy floor.

11. The cooked apples tasted delicious.

12. The little girl was charmed by the talking doll.

Exercise 2: Underline the verbals and identify each one with an abbreviation and function. Gerunds: *GSN, GDO, GOP, GPrN,* or *GOCN*. Participles: *PAdj*. Infinitives: *IAdj, IAdv, ISN, IDO,* or *IPrN*.

13. The difficulty of moving bothered us.

14. To compete takes practice.

15. The spinning wheel whirled around.

16. His hobby is cooking.

17. We saw the lady fanning.

18. The students in my class like to talk.

19. The watching dog sprang forward.

20. The committee chose to adjourn.

21. Complaining will only cause trouble.

22. We left after paying.

23. We must learn to wait.

24. He earns money by painting.

25. The broken dish lay in pieces.

26. Kathleen studies to learn.

CHAPTER 28 LESSON 2 SKILL TEST D

Exercise 3: Underline the verbal in each sentence. Write **P** for Participle, **G** for Gerund, and **I** for Infinitive in the blank at the end of each sentence.

1. The man to call is Sam J. Jones. _____

2. Entire villages failed to survive. _____

3. The cows were kept in a holding pen. _____

4. Building is a carpenter's occupation. _____

5. They were called the losing team. _____

6. To farm was his life's goal. _____

7. Building blocks are good toys for toddlers. _____

8. The determined boy finished the race. _____

9. By squinting, I could see the sign. _____

10. We wanted to travel. _____

11. Harvested grain was stored in the warehouse. _____

12. We were told to listen. _____

13. The sleeping baby spent his day in a cradle. _____

14. The librarian promoted reading. _____

15. The men will enjoy golfing. _____

16. We heard the wind blowing. _____

17. To leave would be a mistake. _____

18. The excited scientist had discovered a cure. _____

19. My uncle always liked to whistle. _____

20. My uncle destroyed his health by smoking. _____

21. The frightened mother snatched her child and ran. _____

22. After our vacation, we needed to rest. _____

23. The x-ray showed a broken bone. _____

24. My laundry needs washing. _____

CHAPTER 28 LESSON 3

Participial, Gerund, and Infinitive Phrases

Before you study verbal phrases, it would be helpful to review what phrases are.

1. **A phrase** is a group of words that does not have a subject and verb.
2. **A phrase** is used as another part of speech in a sentence.

You have already seen how participles, gerunds, and infinitives function as different parts of speech. You have also seen how a prepositional phrase can function as an adjective or adverb phrase in a sentence.

Just as there are prepositional phrases, there are also verbal phrases. One way to make a verbal phrase is to add a prepositional phrase directly after the verbal it modifies. See the examples below of verbal phrases containing prepositional phrases.

Participle:	The man *working* is Wayne. (Which man? working - Adj)
Participial phrase:	The man *working* **in his garden** is Wayne. (Which man? man working in his garden - Adj)
Gerund:	*Working* is good for you. (What is good for you? working - SN)
Gerund phrase:	*Working* **in the yard** is good for you. (What is good for you? working in the yard - SN)
Infinitive:	*To sail* is great. (What is great? to sail - SN)
Infinitive phrase:	*To sail* **on the lake** is great. (What is great? to sail on the lake - SN)

The verbal phrases that contain a verbal followed by a prepositional phrase are easy to identify. However, there are times when you can also have verbal phrases that contain objects (nouns and pronouns) that follow the verbal. Objects used after verbals are often necessary to complete the verbal phrase. See the examples below of verbal phrases containing objects.

Participle:	The child *watching* is Ted. (Which child? watching - Adj)
Participial phrase:	The child *watching* **TV** is Ted (Which child? watching TV - Adj)
Gerund:	*Collecting* is my grandfather's hobby. (What is my grandfather's hobby? collecting - SN)
Gerund phrase:	*Collecting* **stamps** is my grandfather's hobby. (What is my grandfather's hobby? collecting stamps - SN)
Infinitive:	My sister went *to see*. (Sister went why? to see - Adv)
Infinitive phrase:	My sister went *to see* **the lawyer**. (Sister went why? to see the lawyer - Adv)

CHAPTER 28 LESSON 3

Participial, Gerund, and Infinitive Phrases, Continued

To find verbal phrases, use the verbal checklist to find a participle, gerund, or infinitive. Then look to see if the participle, gerund, or infinitive is followed by a prepositional phrase or an object (noun or pronoun). The verbal phrase is the verbal plus the related prepositional phrase or the related object (noun or pronoun) that follows it.

Example: I heard the phone **ringing in the office**.

Verbal check for a participle: Is there an adjective made from a verb that ends in -ed, -en, -t, or -ing? Yes. Ringing - Participle Adjective.
Verbal check for a participial phrase: Is the participle followed by a prepositional phrase or an object? Yes - prepositional phrase - in the office. Participial phrase - ringing in the office.

Example: Jan's job is **leading the music**.

Verbal check for a gerund: Is there a noun made from a verb that ends in -ing? Yes. Leading - Gerund - Predicate noun.
Verbal check for a gerund phrase: Is the gerund followed by a prepositional phrase or an object? Yes - object - music. Gerund phrase - leading the music.

Example: Our choir was asked **to sing in the contest**.

Verbal check for an infinitive: Is there a "to" with a verb after it? Yes. The infinitive is "to sing."
Verbal check for an infinitive phrase: Is the infinitive followed by a prepositional phrase or an object? Yes - prepositional phrase - in the contest. Infinitive phrase - to sing in the contest.

Verbal Checklist for Participles, Gerunds, Infinitives and Verbal Phrases

1. Verbal check for a **participle:** Is there an adjective made from a verb that ends in **-ed, -en, -t,** or **-ing**?
2. Verbal check for a **participial phrase:** Is the participle followed by a prepositional phrase or an object (noun or pronoun) that relates to the participle?
3. Verbal check for a **gerund:** Is there a noun made from a verb that ends in *-ing*? (*Possible gerund nouns include:* **SN, OP, IO, DO, PrN,** or **OCN**.)
4. Verbal check for a **gerund phrase:** Is the gerund followed by a prepositional phrase or an object (noun or pronoun) that relates to the gerund?
5. Verbal check for an infinitive; Is there a "to" with a verb after it? Yes. The infinitive is (name the infinitive.)
6. Verbal check for a **infinitive phrase:** Is the infinitive followed by a prepositional phrase or an object (noun or pronoun) that relates to the infinitive?

Guided Practice: Underline the verbal phrase in each sentence. Write *P* for a Participial Phrase, *G* for a Gerund Phrase, and *I* for an Infinitive Phrase in the blank at the end of each sentence.

1. Holding his poster, Jeff explained his project. _____

2. The tree fallen into the stream was dead. _____

3. Riding the ferris wheel makes me ill. _____

4. She enjoys singing in the choir. _____

5. Margaret decided to call for a pizza. _____

6. She wanted to help the lost kitten. _____

Guided Practice: Underline the verbal phrases and identify each one with an abbreviation and function. Gerund Phrase: *GSN, GDO, GOP, GPrN, or GOCN*. Participial Phrase: *PAdj*. Infinitive Phrase: *IAdj, IAdv, ISN, IDO or IPrN*.

PAdj
1. <u>Singing her song</u>, Jan won the talent show.

IDO
2. Lyn wanted <u>to listen to the music</u>.

GSN
3. <u>Looking at the bright sun</u> hurt my eyes.

GDO
4. The puppies feared <u>getting their shots</u>.

CHAPTER 28 LESSON 3 SKILL TEST E

Exercise 1: Underline the verbal phrases and identify each one with an abbreviation and function. Gerunds: **GSN, GDO, GOP, GPrN,** or **GOCN.** Participles: **PAdj.** Infinitives: **IAdj, IAdv, ISN, IDO,** or **IPrN.**

Infinitive Phrases

1. Every effort to save the puppy succeeded.

2. Juan and Maria offered to help their father.

3. Our plan was to make a sand castle.

4. Everyone came to see the last game.

5. Mother was anxious to have a new house.

6. We came to encourage the Quiz Bowl candidates.

7. Our decision to buy a boat was a foolish one.

8. To meet the President was a great privilege.

Gerund Phrases

9. Hearing sleigh bells brought back memories.

10. I remember singing in the play.

11. Dan's job is running the company.

12. The time for asking questions is at the end of the meeting.

13. My brothers enjoy working with their hands.

14. My greatest goal was getting an education.

15. The younger children disliked waiting for their food.

16. Sipping hot cider through a straw was a fun idea on a cold day.

Participial Phrases

17. The football team wearing red jerseys stumbled off the field in defeat.

18. The man holding the large box walked through the curious crowd.

19. The teacher opening her door is the club advisor.

20. The girl getting in the car found her purse.

21. They spilled the water steaming in the pot.

CHAPTER 28 LESSON 3 SKILL TEST F

Exercise 2: Underline the verbal phrase in each sentence. Write **P** for a Participial Phrase, **G** for a Gerund Phrase, and **I** for an Infinitive Phrase in the blank at the end of each sentence.

1. His assignment was to go to the store. _____

2. By winning at table tennis, he won $100. _____

3. The pies cooling in the window smelled good. _____

4. To leap off a cliff became the job of the stunt man. _____

5. The couple enjoyed walking in the park. _____

6. The time to call at my house is not midnight. _____

7. Campaigning for office is costly. _____

8. Rachel does not like painting in acrylics. _____

9. The tourist standing near the falls almost fell in. _____

10. We stood before the gate guarded by twenty men. _____

11. He flew to Chicago to visit with his cousin. _____

12. To write with ease, one must practice. _____

13. The athlete running at top speed won the marathon. _____

14. To hide the bone delighted Snoopy. _____

15. I couldn't remember learning that dance. _____

16. The tourists climbing up the ladder peered into the Indian ruin. _____

17. Working on the railroad provided a good income for our family. _____

18. He was told to listen for their return. _____

19. We watched Mr. Harris washing his car. _____

20. Jan always wants to win at card games. _____

21. My mother encouraged playing in the band. _____

22. We came to hear the music. _____

23. Thinking of everything is a requirement for this job! _____

CHAPTER 28 LESSON 4 SKILL TEST G

Exercise 1: Underline the verbal phrases and identify each one with an abbreviation and function. Gerund Phrases: **GSN, GDO, GOP, GPrN**, or **GOCN**. Participial Phrases: **PAdj**. Infinitive Phrases: **IAdj, IAdv, ISN, IDO**, or **IPrN.**

Infinitive Phrases

1. That was an event to erase from your memory.

2. Alexis forgot to signal with the turnlight.

3. To sit by the fire is a pleasant experience.

4. The congressman's purpose was to win in the big election.

5. You only came to my house to visit with my uncle.

6. One of Aladdin's three wishes was to be a prince.

7. To be the winner is an honor.

Gerund Phrases

8. Awakening before daybreak can be a problem.

9. The mechanic just finished working on my car.

10. Standing in line for a ticket was necessary.

11. Great-grandmother remembers traveling in a hand-cranked car.

12. Janet's job was helping in the kitchen.

13. The children passed the time by watching the seals.

14. Walking at the mall became a daily routine.

Participial Phrases

15. Leaning with his ear to the keyhole, Eric tried to hear the conversation.

16. The duck swimming near the bank glided past our boat.

17. We saw the man shopping for a car.

18. The man answering our knock slammed the door in our faces.

19. The worker digging in the trench did not hear me.

CHAPTER 28 LESSON 4 SKILL TEST H

Exercise 2: Underline the verbal phrase in each sentence. Write **P** for a Participial Phrase, **G** for a Gerund Phrase, and **I** for an Infinitive Phrase in the blank at the end of each sentence.

1. The lasagna cooked in the microwave was unusual. _____

2. By sneaking past the guard, the spy entered the castle. _____

3. The team trailing by ten points came from behind and won. _____

4. To sing like a nightingale is not easy for everyone. _____

5. The little boy remembered to wash behind his ears. _____

6. The director observed the whispering in the choir. _____

7. The author speaking at the podium talked about space travel. _____

8. Rebecca went to the museum to look at the paintings. _____

9. To pay by check is best. _____

10. To study with Seth is helpful. _____

11. We loved the cookies baked by Evelyn. _____

12. Aunt Sandy remembered to write a note. _____

13. They wanted to evacuate the building. _____

14. Sneezing on my paper was messing up my work. _____

15. The secretary wearing the blue suit is getting a raise. _____

16. All the children had a chance to vote in the election. _____

17. My brother hated shaving his beard. _____

18. The doctor wanted to operate on my toe. _____

19. Working with her roses made the elderly lady happy. _____

20. The elderly lady working with her roses was happy. _____

21. The committee asked to see the final reports. _____

22. Sailing to the Bahamas sounds like a great vacation. _____

23. To be an astronaut was his greatest ambition. _____

CHAPTER 28 LESSON 5 SKILL TEST I

Exercise 1: Underline the verbal phrases and identify each one with an abbreviation and function. Gerund Phrases: **GSN, GDO, GOP, GPrN**, or **GOCN**. Participial Phrases: **PAdj**. Infinitive Phrases: **IAdj, IAdv, ISN, IDO,** or **IPrN.**

Infinitive Phrases

1. He preferred to watch from the stands.

2. To lead at the half encouraged them.

3. The game to play at the fire station is checkers.

4. The teenagers wanted to hurry to the concert.

5. A good exercise for one's heart is to walk at a fast pace.

6. To hide the Easter eggs for the children was a delightful activity.

7. We wanted to dance in the hotel's ballroom.

Gerund Phrases

8. To Lynn, swimming in the lake was scary.

9. Vaulting at the track meet was Priscilla's strongest event.

10. The girls' midnight recreation at the sleepover was fighting with pillows.

11. Becoming a member gave Gladys a sense of satisfaction.

12. I actually enjoy singing in the shower.

13. Tumbling down the hill is a new experience.

14. All campers must avoid stepping in poison ivy.

Participial Phrases

15. The twins swimming in the lake found a large mussel shell.

16. Lisa located the key missing from her purse.

17. The ivy creeping over the chimney housed several birds' nests.

18. The chef carrying the wedding cake fell down the steps.

19. The students clapping in the stands shouted for their team.

20. She waited for the next flight going to Finland.

21. The donkey carried the supplies ordered by the doctor.

CHAPTER 28 LESSON 5 SKILL TEST J

Exercise 2: Underline the verbal phrase in each sentence. Write **P** for a Participial Phrase, **G** for a Gerund Phrase, and **I** for an Infinitive Phrase in the blank at the end of each sentence.

1. Jeff decided to go to New York. _____

2. The horse tied to the fence belonged to Uncle Jack. _____

3. The cake bought at the store was fresh. _____

4. During our vacation, we discovered snorkeling on the reefs. _____

5. My older sister wanted to plan for her wedding. _____

6. The merchandise stolen from the store was recovered by the police. _____

7. I had to deliver the pizza. _____

8. Overeating during meals caused my weight gain. _____

9. We need to change the flat tire. _____

10. Dancing in the school play was embarrassing for me. _____

11. My new hobby is spelunking in northern Arkansas. _____

12. Everyone at the party liked the bread baked by Aunt Jewell. _____

13. Cutting with scissors is always a challenge for small children. _____

14. Typing on the computer was Mom's least favorite job at work. _____

15. The cookies eaten before lunch gave everyone a stomachache. _____

16. To dine at Ritzi's was a special birthday treat. _____

17. For the soldiers, to surrender to the enemy was unthinkable. _____

18. The trees downed by the storm were piled by the side of the road. _____

19. Last Saturday our group's job was raking leaves. _____

20. The money earned by Sally was spent for her family's food. _____

21. Our family bought a new tent for camping in the park. _____

22. Sandra enjoyed driving across the state. _____

23. The political candidate was congratulated for winning the election. _____

24. The present arriving from Ireland was for me. _____

CHAPTER 29 LESSON 1

Clauses

You have studied phrases. A phrase is a group of words that does not have a subject and main verb (that is, a verb that would be used in one of the SN V patterns you have studied.) Also, a phrase is used as a single part of speech.

You have studied prepositional phrases which are used as adjectives and adverbs. You have also studied verbal phrases using participles, gerunds, and infinitives. The participial phrases are used as adjectives, the gerund phrases are used as nouns, and the infinitive phrases are used as adjectives, adverbs, and nouns.

Now, you are going to study clauses. The picture at the end of the reference section will help you remember the big difference between a clause and a phrase. As you can see, this picture shows that a clause has a subject and a main verb. A clause is different from a phrase because it is the **clause**, not the phrase, that has a subject and main verb. Remember, the picture shows Santa Clause, not Santa Phrase.

Therefore, every time you see a subject with its main verb in a sentence, you know that you have a clause.

Two Kinds of Clauses

Independent Clause. In the Shurley Method you have studied about independent sentences and subordinate sentences. Another term for an independent sentence is an independent clause. The independent sentence, or independent clause, has a SN and V and can stand alone. It makes complete sense when it stands alone.

Dependent Clause. Another name for a subordinate sentence is a subordinate clause. Subordinate sentences, or clauses, are also called *dependent*, so you will call this type of clause a *dependent clause*. Even though a dependent clause has a subject and verb, it cannot stand alone the way an independent clause can. The dependent clause must be connected to an independent clause in order to be correct.

Later, you will learn the different kinds of clauses and how they are used. In this lesson, you will learn to find how many clauses you have in each sentence. To find how many clauses are in each sentence, just follow a simple set of guidelines.

CHAPTER 29 LESSON 1

Guidelines for Finding How Many Clauses Are in a Sentence

Sample sentence: _____ **The cat that I saw is a Siamese.**

1. What is the first main verb in the sentence. (saw)
2. Ask the subject question: Who saw? I - SP
3. What is being said about I? I saw - V
4. Put a number 1 above the first subject-verb combination.

1   1

Sample sentence: _____ **The cat that I saw is a Siamese.**

5. Is there another verb? Yes - is
6. What is? cat - SN
7. What is being said about cat? cat is - V
8. Put a number 2 above the second subject-verb combination.

2   1 1 2

Sample sentence: __2__ **The cat that I saw is a Siamese.**

9. Number of clauses? 2
   You find this number by counting the number of subject-verb combinations in the sentence. Write the number in the blank to the left of the sentence.

How to find clauses when the SUBJECT is compound

Sample sentence: _____ **Brad and Herman have their own comedy routine.**

1. What is the first main verb in the sentence? have
2. Who have? Brad and Herman - CSN, CSN
3. What is being said about Brad and Herman? Brad and Herman have - V
4. Put a number 1 above the first subject-verb combination.

1   1   1

Sample sentence: __1__ **Brad and Herman have their own comedy routine.**

5. Is there another verb? No.
6. Number of clauses? 1 (_Two CSN's with one V equals only one S-V combination, therefore, only one clause._)

How to find clauses when the VERB is compound

Sample sentence: _____ **Brad plays the trumpet and has his own comedy routine.**

1. What is the first main verb in the sentence? plays and has
2. Who plays and has? Brad - SN
3. What is being said about Brad? Brad plays and has - CV, CV
4. Put a number 1 above the first subject-verb combination.

1   1   1

Sample sentence: __1__ **Brad plays and has his own comedy routine.**

5. Is there another verb? No.
6. Number of clauses? 1 (_One **SN** with two **CV's** equals only one **S-V** combination, therefore, only one clause._)

CHAPTER 29 LESSON 1

Guided Practice: Number each **S-V** combination and write the number of clauses for each sentence in the blank.

_____ 1. I have an interesting story about my dog, Winky.

_____ 2. Winky, who is a black cocker spaniel, begs for food at the table.

_____ 3. When we have corn-on the-cob, he whines for a piece.

_____ 4. After he gets it, he takes it to my bedroom.

_____ 5. I have a white stuffed kitten that sits beside my bed.

_____ 6. Winky will beg for the kitten, and I usually set it on the rug beside the bed and leave it there.

_____ 7. I return later and find that Winky has given the ear of corn to the cat and that he is satisfied.

CHAPTER 29 LESSON 1 SKILL TEST A

Exercise 1: Number each **S-V** combination and write the number of clauses for each sentence in the blank.

_____ 1. Angelica owned a parakeet named Vigorous and kept him in a large, roomy cage.

_____ 2. Apparently Vigorous did not think that his cage was "roomy" enough.

_____ 3. One day when Angelica shut the cage door, she did not snap it.

_____ 4. Vigorous found that he could get out.

_____ 5. As Angelica entered the room, a flurry of feathers sailed toward her.

_____ 6. Vigorous perched on her head, and his owner was quite surprised.

_____ 7. Because my brother Carl's band instrument is drums, our home has become noisy.

_____ 8. Yesterday, as he came in the front door, he only mentioned drums, and I got a headache.

_____ 9. My dreams are turning into nightmares that are filled with giant drums.

_____10. Before the nightmare is over, the drums sprout legs and chase me through a gigantic

percussion section.

_____11. I have told my brother that he must make his room soundproof.

_____12. The person who invented the drum is in trouble with me.

_____13. When Brian left his cap in the fork of the apple tree, it was "no big thing."

_____14. Three days later, he returned and found a robin with a half-built nest in his cap.

_____15. Since he had two other caps, he left it there.

_____16. As time passed, Brian watched his cap, and soon four eggs lay in the nest.

_____17. Before long, he saw four tiny brown heads over the edge of the nest because the four eggs had

hatched.

CHAPTER 29 LESSON 2

Differences in the Two Types of Clauses: Independent Clauses and Dependent Clauses

Independent Clause. An independent clause can stand alone because it has a subject and main verb and expresses a complete thought.

SN   V

Independent Clause A: The plumber repaired the leaky faucet.

Dependent Clause. A dependent clause cannot stand alone even though it has a subject and a verb because it does not express a complete thought.

SN   V

Dependent Clause B: When the plumber repaired the leaky faucet.

Every clause has a subject and a main verb. Therefore, both Sentence A and Sentence B are clauses because they both contain subjects and main verbs. However, Sentence A is an independent clause because it expresses a complete thought and can stand alone. Sentence B, on the other hand, is a dependent clause because it does not express a complete thought and cannot stand alone.

Clause B does not express a complete thought because of the word that has been added at the beginning of the clause - *when*. The word *when* is a subordinate conjunction. Whenever a subordinate conjunction is added to a clause, that clause becomes dependent. Many dependent clauses are introduced by subordinate conjunctions.

There Are Some Subordinate Conjunctions in the Town

After, Although, As, As much as, Because,
Before, How, If, In order that, Inasmuch as,
Provided, Since, Than, That, Though, Unless, Until,
When, Where, Whether, (Pause) While.

Guidelines for Finding Independent Clauses and Dependent Clauses That Are Introduced by Subordinate Conjunctions

1. Read the sentence.
2. Number each S-V combination.
3. Write the total number of clauses for each sentence in the blank provided.
4. If there is only one S-V combination, you have only one independent clause.
5. A compound sentence will have two S-V combinations, and each combination will be the core of an independent clause.
6. Put parentheses around any subordinate conjunctions that are "introducers" of dependent clauses.
7. Underline all independent clauses once and all dependent clauses twice.

CHAPTER 29 LESSON 2

Guided Practice: Number each **S-V** combination and write the number of clauses for each sentence in the blank. Put parentheses around any subordinate conjunctions and underline the independent clauses once and the dependent clauses twice.

_____ 1. As I find time for writing, I will send you an account of my trip to Montana.

_____ 2. We left on Monday, inasmuch as we had planned to spend one day at Mount Rushmore.

_____ 3. Because we visited with friends in Omaha, we did not arrive in Butte until Thursday.

_____ 4. Kay and her family were excited, and they gave us a tremendous welcome.

CHAPTER 29 LESSON 2 SKILL TEST B

Exercise 1: Number each **S-V** combination and write the number of clauses for each sentence in the blank. Put parentheses around any subordinate conjunctions and underline the independent clauses once and the dependent clauses twice.

_____ 1. We do not know how the bumblebee got into the van.

_____ 2. It could have happened while we were at the curio shop with the lawn decorations.

_____ 3. Fred cannot remember whether the bee had been with us before the stop.

_____ 4. Before we had driven one-half mile, Molly screamed.

_____ 5. As Derrick and James started swatting, the bee shot to the front of the vehicle.

_____ 6. Sarah hit at the little pest, and Fred swerved.

_____ 7. He slammed on the brakes, and the car behind our van rear-ended us.

_____ 8. As another car avoided the accident, it ran a semi-rig off the road and into a ditch.

_____ 9. We were thankful that no one was hurt.

_____ 10. Unfortunately, the bee escaped before we could give him his punishment.

_____ 11. Travis baked three dozen sugar cookies, but he ate twenty-four of them after lunch.

_____ 12. After the members discussed plans for the next meeting, they drew for a door prize.

_____ 13. Fortunately, Dewayne bought his plane ticket before the ticket prices went up.

_____ 14. Because I enjoy hiking, Dan and I walked the two miles into town.

_____ 15. Since I have so little time, I will write you a longer letter later.

_____ 16. We visited the Berkley Pit and learned facts about copper mining after we ate lunch.

_____ 17. While we were there, we learned the history of the stately buildings.

_____ 18. You may fish here provided you have a fishing license.

CHAPTER 29 LESSON 3

Other Words That Introduce Dependent Clauses

There is one **H** word: **How**

There is one **TH** word: **That**

There are 14 **WH** words:

Who, Whom, Which, and What;

Whoever, Whomever, Whichever, and Whatever;

Whose, When, Where, and Why;

Whenever and Wherever.

Although some of these words appear to be subordinate conjunctions, they are not used as conjunctions. Do not be worried about their uses as conjunctions or other parts of speech. Just be aware that these words, like subordinate conjunctions, are "introducers" of dependent clauses.

Your next exercises will contain sentences with both independent clauses and also dependent clauses that are introduced by the H, TH, and WH words.

In these exercises coming up, be alerted! The words *Who, Which*, and *That* are "introducers" of dependent clauses, but they can also be the subject pronouns of the dependent clauses.

```
        SP  V           SP    V
Example:  I like people (who) work hard.
```

CHAPTER 29 LESSON 3

Guidelines for Finding Independent Clauses and Dependent Clauses That Are Introduced by Other Words

1. Read the sentence.
2. Number each S-V combination.
3. Write the total number of clauses for each sentence in the blank provided.
4. If there is only one S-V combination, you have only one independent clause.
5. A compound sentence will have two S-V combinations, and each combination will be the core of an independent clause.
6. Put parentheses around any *H, Th,* or *Wh* words that are "introducers" of dependent clauses.
7. Underline all independent clauses once and all dependent clauses twice.

Guided Practice: Number each **S-V** combination and write the number of clauses for each sentence in the blank. Put parentheses around any *H, TH,* or *WH* words that introduce a dependent clause. Underline the independent clauses once and the dependent clauses twice.

_____ 1. I knew exactly what I was serving.

_____ 2. My sister told me that she is going to the library.

_____ 3. They were uncertain who was coming.

_____ 4. The pilot whom the commander chose was very young.

_____ 5. The Youth Club, which meets once a month, scheduled its last meeting at my house.

CHAPTER 29 LESSON 3 SKILL TEST C

Exercise 1: Number each **S-V** combination and write the number of clauses for each sentence in the blank. Put parentheses around any **H**, **TH**, or **WH** words that introduce a dependent clause. Underline the independent clauses once and the dependent clauses twice.

_____ 1. You can always find ants wherever people are having picnics.

_____ 2. They are little creatures whose "noses" can sniff out food from miles away.

_____ 3. It does not matter where you securely set your food.

_____ 4. I have heard of few people who know of a plan to avoid ants.

_____ 5. A friend, whom I will not name, assured me of a foolproof method.

_____ 6. His idea, which was simple, was spraying the legs of the picnic table with insect repellant.

_____ 7. I do not know why I bothered with his suggestion.

_____ 8. Something that no one expects always happens.

_____ 9. The table whose legs I sprayed had an ant's nest under the tabletop.

_____ 10. Ants will join my picnic, whatever I do.

_____ 11. The boys ate whatever was in the refrigerator.

_____ 12. Mr. Murphy understood who the leader was.

_____ 13. The milk which you bought is spoiled.

_____ 14. We own the house where you once lived.

_____ 15. The girl whom he invited is Cassandra.

_____ 16. Did you tell Marcus that we are coming?

CHAPTER 29 LESSON 4

Review Section

1. You have now seen that all clauses have two main ingredients: a subject and a main verb. (Note: A main verb is a verb found in a S-V in a sentence. A verbal is not a main verb.)
2. You have learned to identify clauses.
3. You have studied the two types of clauses: independent and dependent.
4. You have found that dependent clauses are introduced by the "Introducers" called subordinate conjunctions and the *H, TH*, and *WH* words.
5. You have practiced identifying independent and dependent clauses.

Up to this point, you have done some exercises with dependent clauses introduced by subordinate conjunctions and some exercises with dependent clauses introduced by the *H, TH*, and *WH* words. Next, you will do exercises with mixed introducers. These sentences will include dependent clauses introduced by all the introducers you have studied.

Guidelines for Finding Independent Clauses, Dependent Clauses, and All Introducers of Dependent Clauses

1. Read the sentence.
2. Number each S-V combination.
3. Write the total number of clauses for each sentence in the blank provided.
4. If there is only one S-V combination, you have only one independent clause.
5. A compound sentence will have two S-V combinations, and each combination will be the core of an independent clause.
6. Put parentheses around any introducers of dependent clauses.
7. Underline all independent clauses once and all dependent clauses twice.

CHAPTER 29 LESSON 4 SKILL TEST D

Exercise 1: Number each **S-V** combination and write the number of clauses for each sentence in the blank. Put parentheses around any introducers of dependent clauses. Underline the independent clauses once and the dependent clauses twice.

_____ 1. In the 1960's, my grandfather owned about two dozen chickens, which he kept in a "hen house."

_____ 2. While these fowls were not very impressive to others, to my grandparents they were eggs and fried chicken.

_____ 3. One night some creature invaded the hen house, and a great disorder broke out about 11 p.m.

_____ 4. My grandfather, thinking that a weasel had come for his eggs and fried chicken, grabbed his shotgun and hurried to the hen house.

_____ 5. Although he took his flashlight with him, the chickens were so frantic that he only saw a shadow across the floor.

_____ 6. Before the invader could escape, Granddaddy fired a shot.

_____ 7. The invader that he shot was not a weasel, but a skunk!

_____ 8. If he had hurried to the hen house before, he now "flew" in the opposite direction.

_____ 9. My grandmother took one sniff and knew what had happened.

_____ 10. After Granddaddy had burned his clothes and had taken three hot, soapy baths, the smell of the skunk was only faint.

_____ 11. Since my little sister and her friends had been in the pool all afternoon, they were starved!

_____ 12. That pickle and mustard sandwich that you made is great!

_____ 13. If the snow stops, we can build a six-foot snowman.

CHAPTER 29 LESSON 4 SKILL TEST E

Exercise 1: Number each **S-V** combination and write the number of clauses for each sentence in the blank. Put parentheses around any introducers of dependent clauses. Underline the independent clauses once and the dependent clauses twice.

_____ 1. When Dan came home from school, he announced that he and his friends were going swimming

at Bayou Bluff.

_____ 2. Bayou Bluff, which was a swimmer's paradise, offered all sorts of fun in the water.

_____ 3. It was a broad stream that flowed over huge boulders past towering bluffs.

_____ 4. A series of rapids eventually widened out into slow, deep water where diving and

swimming were popular.

_____ 5. Dan and his buddies carried several inner tubes on which they would float the rapids.

_____ 6. Because the sun was so hot, Dan wore his new expensive sunglasses.

_____ 7. When he made his first trip down the rapids, he forgot that he was wearing his favorite

"shades."

_____ 8. As he reached the second set of rapids, Dan was laughing and did not see a large extended rock.

_____ 9. Before he could change course, the tube hit the rock and flipped, and Dan was dumped.

_____ 10. His glasses flew off, and, although he and his friends dived for them for an hour,

he never saw them again.

_____ 11. The dog will not attack you if you keep calm.

_____ 12. Chandra, whom the faculty selected, will represent the school at the convention.

_____ 13. Delia hid the candy whenever she left her room.

_____ 14. As the children watched, they saw where Mitchell put the box.

CHAPTER 29 LESSON 5

The Dependent Adjective Clause

1. The adjective clause and the regular adjective are different in two ways. The first difference is that a regular adjective is usually one word, and an adjective clause is made up of a subject and main verb, plus other words that go along with the subject and main verb. You ask the adjective questions to find adjective clauses.

2. The second difference is that most regular one-word adjectives come before the noun or pronoun they modify, but an adjective clause comes after it. Usually, the noun in front of an adjective clause is the word the adjective clause modifies. The word that an adjective clause modifies can be a subject, an object of the preposition, an indirect object, a direct object, a predicate noun, or an object complement.

How to Identify an Adjective Clause

```
          2      1     1      2
          SN    SP     V      V
```
Example: The student **who** laughed was Joey.

Who laughed is a clause because it has a SP V combination.
Who laughed describes or tells which *student*.
Student is a noun, and adjectives describe or modify nouns.
Therefore, *who laughed* is an adjective clause that modifies *student*.
Also notice that an adjective clause can interrupt the independent clause.

3. Some adjective clauses are introduced by the subordinate conjunctions **where** or **when** if they come directly after the noun they modify. **Where** or **when** words in an adjective clause will always tell **which noun**. These are exceptions and will not be used often.

```
        1       1                              2      2
        SN      V                              SN     V
```
Example: The teacher entered at the moment **when** the students were misbehaving.

When the students were misbehaving is a clause because it has a SN V combination.
When the students were misbehaving describes or tells which *moment*.
Since *moment* is a noun (object of the preposition), *when the students were misbehaving* is an adjective clause that modifies *moment*.
Also, notice that this adjective clause is introduced by the word *when* and comes directly after *moment*, the noun it modifies.

Relative Pronouns

A **relative pronoun** is both a pronoun and an "introducer" of dependent clauses. The relative pronouns are *who, whom, which,* or *that*. A relative pronoun also acts as a subject, an object, a predicate pronoun, or a possessive modifier in its own clause, but it does not ask a question as an interrogative pronoun does.

A relative pronoun is used to introduce adjective clauses. Although not all *WH* words will introduce adjective clauses, all *WH* words and the *TH* (*that*) word that function as relative pronouns will introduce adjective clauses.

How to use relative pronouns:
1. **Who** or **whom** always refers to a person.
   Example: *The student **who** laughed was Joey.*
2. **Which** refers to animals or inanimate objects.
   Example: *The cloth **which** covers the table is plaid.*
3. **That** refers to persons, animals, or things.
   Example: *The lens **that** he bought is a telephoto.*

CHAPTER 29 LESSON 5

Guided Practice: Number each **S-V** combination and write the number of clauses for each sentence in the blank. Put parentheses around any introducers of dependent clauses. Underline the independent clauses once and the dependent clauses twice. Identify the type of dependent clause by writing **Adj** and the word it modifies in the two blanks at the end of the sentence.

_____ 1. I met the man who discovered the cave. _____ _____

_____ 2. The city where he lives is Chicago. _____ _____

_____ 3. We could see the light through a hole that the miner had chiseled out. _____ _____

_____ 4. This is the same lady whom I saw. _____ _____

5. Write a sentence containing an adjective clause introduced by _who_. (_Who_ must be the SP of the adjective clause.)

CHAPTER 29 LESSON 5 SKILL TEST F

Exercise 1: Number each **S-V** combination and write the number of clauses for each sentence in the blank. Put parentheses around any introducers of dependent clauses. Underline the independent clauses once and the dependent clauses twice. Identify the type of dependent clause by writing **Adj** and the word it modifies in the two blanks at the end of the sentence.

_____ 1. The frosting which was all over his face was chocolate. _____ _____

_____ 2. The man whose tie was green polka-dotted performed a series of magic tricks. _____ _____

_____ 3. The stewardess whom you stopped is my cousin. _____ _____

_____ 4. He hired the two young men who worked hardest. _____ _____

_____ 5. He had been imprisoned in a dungeon where no light could enter. _____ _____

_____ 6. At the hour when most people were asleep, he left the house. _____ _____

_____ 7. I could not explain the mess in which we found in the room. _____ _____

_____ 8. The first runner who reaches the oak tree wins. _____ _____

_____ 9. There goes the man who owns the jeep. _____ _____

_____ 10. Beside the candle which was burning we found an old map. _____ _____

_____ 11. The umbrella that we noticed belongs to Jill. _____ _____

_____ 12. This is a time when you must listen. _____ _____

_____ 13. I know the girl whom you chose. _____ _____

On your notebook paper:

14. Write a sentence containing an adjective clause.

CHAPTER 30 LESSON 1

The Dependent Adverb Clause

1. The adverb clause and the regular adverb are different in two ways. The first difference is that a regular adverb is usually one word, and an adverb clause is made up of a subject and main verb, plus other words that go along with the subject and main verb.

2. The second difference is that the adverb clauses you will be working with at this level will ALL modify the verb, while the regular one-word adverbs you have used have modified verbs, adjectives, and other adverbs. You ask adverb questions to find adverb clauses.
   Example: <u>Before Anthony closed the door</u>, Amanda waltzed in.
   Waltzed when? Before Anthony closed the door.

3. ALL adverb clauses are introduced by subordinate conjunctions.
   Example: (Before) Anthony closed the door, Amanda waltzed in.
   The introducer of the adverb clause is the subordinate conjunction *Before*.

4. An adverb clause at the beginning of a sentence has to be set off by a comma.
   Example: <u>Before Anthony closed the door</u>, Amanda waltzed in.
   Notice the comma setting off the introductory adverb clause "Before Anthony closed the door."

How to Identify an Adverb Clause

```
1   1              2   2
SP  V             SP  V
```
Example: I saw the dog's teeth when it growled at me.

When it growled at me is a clause because it has a SP V combination.
Go to the verb and ask "saw when? *When it growled at me* **tells when**.
Adverbs tell *when*, and adverb clauses tell *when*.
Therefore, *when it growled at me* is an adverb clause.
Also notice that the adverb clause is introduced by the subordinate conjunction *when*.

There Are Some Subordinate Conjunctions in the Town
After, Although, As, As much as, Because,
Before, How, If, In order that, Inasmuchas,
Provided, Since, Than, That, Though, Unless, Until,
When, Where, Whether, (Pause) While.

Guided Practice: Number each **S-V** combination and write the number of clauses for each sentence in the blank. Put parentheses around the subordinating conjunction that introduces a dependent clause used as an adverb clause. Underline each independent clause once and each dependent clause twice. Identify the type of dependent clause by writing **Adv** and the verb it modifies in the two blanks at the end of the sentence.

_____ 1. Since you have been working all morning, I will do the rest of the digging. _____ _____

_____ 2. He bought a new book after he lost his first one. _____ _____

_____ 3. I eat kiwi fruit because I love it. _____ _____

_____ 4. I am climbing up before you get off the roof. _____ _____

5. Write a sentence containing an adverb clause and tell what adverb question it answers.

CHAPTER 30 LESSON 1 SKILL TEST A

Exercise 1: Number each **S-V** combination and write the number of clauses for each sentence in the blank. Put parentheses around the subordinating conjunction that introduces a dependent clause used as an adverb. Underline each independent clause once and each dependent clause twice. Identify the type of dependent clause by writing **Adv** and the verb it modifies in the two blanks at the end of the sentence.

_____ 1. We will be with the team until we finish our practice. _____ _____

_____ 2. The little man lived where the stream flows blue. _____ _____

_____ 3. Our picnic will be perfect provided it does not rain. _____ _____

_____ 4. I have been working on my serve since you saw my last tennis game. _____ _____

_____ 5. Before the whistle blew, he had scored two more points. _____ _____

_____ 6. As he left the plane, he took the strange attache case with him. _____ _____

_____ 7. When a bluebird flew in the window, Janelle was surprised. _____ _____

_____ 8. The postman enjoyed a cup of hot tea because it was a cold day. _____ _____

_____ 9. I hit a tree because my bike had no brakes. _____ _____

_____ 10. While I pop the popcorn, you bring in more wood. _____ _____

_____ 11. Since I have a new chessboard, we must have a game. _____ _____

_____ 12. The crowd yelled loudly as the cheerleaders came onto the court. _____ _____

_____ 13. Although I enjoy fruit yogurt, I love cappuccino better. _____ _____

_____ 14. When you are crossing the lawn, walk around the flowerbed. _____ _____

_____ 15. He will lend you his binoculars, provided you return them. _____ _____

On your notebook paper:

16. Write a sentence with an adverb clause in it. Tell what adverb question it answers.

CHAPTER 30 LESSON 2 SKILL TEST B

Exercise 1: Number each **S-V** combination and write the number of clauses for each sentence in the blank. Put parentheses around any introducers of dependent clauses. Underline each independent clause once and each dependent clause twice. Identify the type of dependent clause by writing **Adj** or **Adv** and the word it modifies in the two blanks at the end of the sentence.

_____ 1. The girl who is on the balance beam is Anna. _____ _____

_____ 2. After she has finished her performance, we will be leaving. _____ _____

_____ 3. We congratulated the team that won. _____ _____

_____ 4. I saw an old friend of mine as we walked across the parking lot. _____ _____

_____ 5. This is the school where I once attended. _____ _____

_____ 6. Mr. Franklin was a teacher whose class I loved. _____ _____

_____ 7. I enjoyed the gymnastic meet since my friend won several awards. _____ _____

_____ 8. Before my little sister could swim, she had a terrible fear of water. _____ _____

_____ 9. She was even afraid of her wading pool which was only six inches deep. _____ _____

_____ 10. The time that she dreaded most was her evening bath. _____ _____

_____ 11. When she cried loudly, I gave up! _____ _____

_____ 12. I took her down to the pool for lessons because I could not teach swimming. _____ _____

_____ 13. Now she has turned into a kid who is a regular "fish." _____ _____

_____ 14. If she stays in water any more, her skin will go into a permanent shrivel. _____ _____

On your notebook paper:

15. Write a sentence with adverb clause in it. Label it correctly.

16. Write a sentence with adjective clause in it. Label it correctly.

CHAPTER 30 LESSON 3

The Dependent Noun Clause used as a Direct Object (DO)

```
          SP  V        SP HV   V
```
Example: I know how you can write.

There are two clauses in this sentence because there are two subject-verb combinations. The first clause reads **I know**. Next, ask and verify the question for a direct object.

1. **I know** what? *how you can write*
2. Does *how you can write* mean the same thing as I? No.
3. *How you can write* - DO

Since **how you can write** is a clause used as a direct object, it is a noun clause.
This noun clause is introduced by the One **H** word, **how**.

The Dependent Noun Clause used as an Object of the Preposition (OP)

```
          SP    V              SP    V
```
Example: They gave the trophy to whoever won.

There are two clauses in this sentence because there are two subject-verb combinations. The first clause reads **They gave**. Next ask and verify the direct object question.

1. **They gave** what? *trophy*
2. Does *trophy* mean the same thing as they? No.
3. *Trophy* - DO

Notice that *trophy* is not a clause. It is a one-word direct object, not a part of a clause; so, you must check the rest of the sentence for a prepositional phrase that could be used as a clause.

4. To - P
5. To whom? **whoever won** - OP

Since **whoever won** is a clause used as an object of the preposition, it is a noun clause. This noun clause is introduced by a **wh** word, **whoever**.

Also notice that the preposition **to** is **not** part of the noun clause because only the noun clause is the object of the preposition. As you identify the noun clause that is the object of the preposition, do not include the preposition word as part of the noun clause. **Do not** underline the preposition word at all.

CHAPTER 30 LESSON 3

The Dependent Noun Clause used as a Subject Noun (SN)

It is impossible to separate a SN noun clause from its independent clause because the SN noun clause is the subject of the independent clause.

SP   V   HV   V
Example A: [Whoever wants this piece of cake] can have it.

1. The sentence for Example A has two main verbs. They are *wants* and *can have*.
2. Find the subject of *wants*: Who *wants*? **whoever - SP**
3. What is being said about *whoever*? **whoever wants - V**
4. Find the subject of *can have*: Who *can have*? **whoever wants this piece of cake - SN**

Notice, **whoever wants this piece of cake** has a subject and main verb; therefore, it is a clause. This noun clause is introduced by a **wh** word, **whoever**. A clause used as a subject is a noun clause because nouns are subjects. We put the SN noun clause in brackets.

SP   V   HV   HV   V
Example B: [That you won] should be recorded.

That you won is a dependent clause, but *should be recorded* is all that is left. The group of words *should be recorded* cannot be an independent clause. But look back at its subject.

1. What *should be recorded*? **That you won** - SN
2. What is being said about **That you won**? **That you won** *should be recorded* - V
3. *Should* - HV
4. *Be* - HV

That you won has a subject and main verb. Therefore, it is a clause. Since its job is SN, it must be a noun clause. **That you won** is a noun clause that is the subject of the independent clause. This noun clause is introduced by the word **that**, a subordinate conjunction. We put the SN noun clause in brackets.

Guided Practice: Number each **S-V** combination and write the number of clauses for each sentence in the blank. Put parentheses around the introducer of the dependent clause used as a noun. Underline each independent clause once and each dependent clause twice. Exception: When the noun clause is the SN, do not underline any clause in the sentence. Instead, put the noun clause used as a SN in Brackets. Also notice that each noun clause's function has been identified for you at the end of each sentence.

1. I know where you are. _DO_

2. Crystal will talk to whoever listens. _OP_

   For Bonus Practice

3. Whoever wins will eat lunch first. _SN_

4. That he is an artist is evident. _SN_

CHAPTER 30 LESSON 3 SKILL TEST C

Exercise 1: Number each **S-V** combination and write the number of clauses for each sentence in the blank. Put parentheses around the introducer of the dependent clause used as a noun. Underline each independent clause once and each dependent clause twice. Exception: When the noun clause is the SN, do not underline any clause in the sentence. Instead, put the noun clause used as a SN in Brackets. Also notice that each noun clause's function has been identified for you at the end of each sentence.

_____ 1. I believe that it is raining. **DO**

_____ 2. Joyce recognized whom you drew. **DO**

_____ 3. Chris sent the letter to whoever wanted it. **OP**

_____ 4. The principal knew why the student was dishonest. **DO**

_____ 5. He could not see where he was driving. **DO**

_____ 6. I can tutor whomever you send. **DO**

_____ 7. I remember whose mother bakes fantastic cookies. **DO**

_____ 8. He handed out invitations to whoever was there. **OP**

For Bonus Points: Using the Noun Clause as a Subject

_____ Bonus 1. That the radio is loud is obvious. **SN**

_____ Bonus 2. What he is doing helps. **SN**

CHAPTER 30 LESSON 4 SKILL TEST D

Number each **S-V** combination and write the number of clauses for each sentence in the blank. Put parentheses around the introducer of each dependent clause. Underline each independent clause once and each dependent clause twice. Exception: When the noun clause is the SN, do not underline any clause in the sentence. Instead, put the noun clause used as a SN in Brackets. Also write the name of each dependent clause (**Adj, Adv,** or **N**) at the end of each sentence. Use the following guides to help you. **Guided Practice: Adv: 2 Adj: 1 N: 2 Exercise 1: Adv: 4 Adj: 3 N: 2**

Guided Practice:

_____ 1. When the flea slipped, he fell off the dog's ear. _____

_____ 2. I know whose car will win the race. ____

_____ 3. The cliff diver never told us that he was afraid of heights. ____

_____ 4. The snail that defeated the inchworm amazed everyone. _____

_____ 5. Before you go to lunch, give Beth the report. ____

Exercise 1:

_____ 1. He gets mega-omelets because his father owns an ostrich farm. ____

_____ 2. Ricky sold the saddle to whoever offered him the most money. _____

_____ 3. The music that they love is classical. _____

_____ 4. She was a scuba diver who taught scuba lessons. ___

_____ 5. Since the inventor blew up his workshop, he was moved to the barn. _____

_____ 6. Rebecca told us how she found her way out of the jungle. ____

_____ 7. Lee, who was babysitting, found her three charges on the roof. _____

_____ 8. He told the story as I had hoped. ___

_____ 9. When the fish tugged on his line, Howard yanked. ____

For Bonus Points: Using the Noun Clause as a Subject

_____ 10. How you balance on that tightrope seems unbelievable. _____

CHAPTER 30 LESSON 5

Assignment Box for Troublesome Words That Give Special Problems in Usage

1. Look up your assigned words in the dictionary.
2. Write the correct pronunciation for your words.
3. Write the correct part of speech for your words.
4. Write all definitions for your words.
5. Tell the common usage problem for this pair of words.
6. Write a sentence for each of your words to demonstrate how each should be used.
7. Give an oral presentation of your words to the class.

Chart for Troublesome Words That Give Special Problems in Usage

1. accept, except	11. bring, take	20. like, as
2. adapt, adopt	12. complected, complexioned	21. principal, principle
3. advice, advise	13. farther, further	22. raise, rise
4. affect, effect	14. fewer, less	23. set, sit
5. all ready, already	15. himself, hisself	24. than, then
6. all right, alright	16. in, into	25. their, there, they're
7. all together, altogether	17. lay, lie	26. themselves, theirselves
8. among, between	18. learn, teach	27. to, too, two
9. awhile, a while	19. leave, let	28. when, where
10. beside, besides		29. whether, weather

CHAPTER 31 LESSON 1

Problems in Usage for Adjectives and Adverbs

The adjectives and adverbs **good** and **well**, **bad** and **badly**, **real** and **really**, and **sure** and **surely** are often confused. To avoid using these words incorrectly, remember two simple things:

1. **Adjectives** modify nouns and pronouns. **Good, bad, real**, and **sure** are adjectives that modify nouns and pronouns. (Sometimes, **well** is an adjective if it means "in good health.") (Sometimes **bad** can be a predicate adjective when it means "sorrowful.")

    Examples: I read a *good book*. (What kind of book? good - Adj)
    Alice had a *bad cold* in January. (What kind of cold? bad - Adj)
    Alice felt *bad* about her grade. (What kind of Alice? bad (sorrowful) - PA)
    Janet quietly whispered her *real name*. (What kind of name? real - Adj)
    The *doctor* was *sure* of his decision. (What kind of doctor? sure - PA)
    Grandmother is *well* this morning. (What kind of Grandmother? well - PA)

2. **Adverbs** modify verbs, adjectives, or other adverbs. **Well, badly, really**, and **surely** are adverbs that modify verbs, adjectives, or adverbs.

    Examples: Mother *spoke well* of Uncle Lewis. (Spoke how? well - Adv)
    The unwilling musicians *played* their instruments *badly*. (Played how? badly - Adv)
    We watched a *really interesting* movie. (How interesting? really - Adv)
    The filthy puppy *had surely visited* every mud puddle. (Visited how? surely - Adv)

Problems in Usage for Special Words

The words **principal** and **principle** and the words **affect** and *effect* are often confused. To avoid using these words incorrectly, it is important to know two things: the meanings of the words and how the words are used in sentences. Look at the words and examples below:

Principal. When **principal** is used as a **noun**, it means a person who is in a leading position or a thing that is important.
    Examples: 1. The *principal* met with parents of the students.
               2. He paid the *principal* on his loan.

Principal. When **principal** is used as an **adjective**, it *describes* a person or thing as the most important or the most influential.
    Examples: 1. The *principal* stockholder voted for our project.
               2. A *principal* reason was lack of funds.

Principle. The word **principle** is used as an **noun only**, and it means a basic rule, law, or fact.
    Examples: 1. The *principles* of algebra were taught well.
               2. Honesty is an important *principle* in life.

Effect. When **effect** is used as a **noun**, it means the result of an action or the personal property of someone.
    Examples: 1. The *effects* of crime are evident.
               2. His family kept his personal *effects* after he died.

Effect. When **effect** is used as a **verb**, it means to accomplish a result, or to bring about.
    Example: 1. The city council *effected* many positive changes for city parks.

Affect. The word **affect** is used as a **verb only**, and it means to influence someone or something.
    Example: 1. The beautiful music *affected* everyone in the audience.

CHAPTER 31 LESSON 1

Problems in Usage for Special Verbs

The verbs **sit** and **set, lie** and **lay,** and **rise** and **raise** are often confused. To avoid using these words incorrectly, it is important to know two things: the meanings of the verbs and whether or not the verbs are followed by direct objects. Look at the verbs and examples below. (*P-Parts stand for principal parts.*)

The verb **sit** means to rest in a seated position. *Sit* has **no direct object**. (P-Parts: sit, sat, sat, sitting)
    Example: 1. The exhausted shoppers *sit* on the mall bench. 2. The vase of roses *sits* on the piano.

The verb **set** means to put something down. *Set* has **a direct object**. (P-Parts: set, set, set, setting)
    Example: 1. Mother *set* a vase of roses on the piano. 2. The server *was setting* our food on the table.

The verb **lie** means to rest in a reclining position. *Lie* has **no direct object**. (P-Parts: lie, lay, lain, lying)
    Example: 1. The cows *lie* in the pasture every day. 2. An old hat *has lain* on the porch for weeks.

The verb **lay** means to put something down. *Lay* has **a direct object**. (P-Parts: lay, laid, laid, laying)
    Example: 1. Please *lay* your pencils on your desk. 2. The workers *laid* the asphalt in one afternoon.

The verb **rise** means to get up or go higher. *Rise* has **no direct object**. (P-Parts: rise, rose, risen, rising)
    Example: 1. We *rise* early every day at camp. 2. Smoke *was rising* from the demolished building.

The verb **raise** means to lift something up. *Raise* has **a direct object**. (P-Parts: raise, raised, raised, raising)
    Example: 1. The boys *raise* the flag each morning. 2. Students *were* politely *raising* their hands.

Common Verb Problems When Speaking

The verbs **went** and **gone, was** and **were, done** and **did,** and **come** and **came** are often used incorrectly. In the chart below, pay special attention to the correct and incorrect use of subject/verb agreement and helping verbs.

Correct	Incorrect
I *have gone*.	I *have went*.
I *have done* my work.	I *done* my work.
I *did* my work.	I *have did* my work.
We *were watching* television.	We *was watching* television.
You *were* our favorite teacher.	You *was* our favorite teacher.
I *came* early for this meeting.	I *have came* early for this meeting.

CHAPTER 31 LESSON 1 SKILL TEST A

Exercise 1: Underline the correct adjective or adverb choice in each sentence below. Write **Adj** or **Adv** and the word it modifies in the blanks at the end.

1. Our junior high wrestling team did (good, well) at the regional meet. _____ _____
2. Are you (sure, surely) about the correct departure time? _____ _____
3. A (real, really) inventor displayed his gadgets in a booth at the fair. _____ _____
4. Two of the pizzas tasted (real, really) delicious! _____ _____
5. Our pets were (sure, surely) the most unusual at the pet show. _____ _____
6. The student carpenters did a (good, well) job of framing the new house. _____ _____
7. The skiers will (sure, surely) stop for a rest at noon. _____ _____
8. Our teacher did not feel (good, well) after lunch. _____ _____
9. The results of the tests were (bad, badly). _____ _____
10. The girls sang their part of the song (bad, badly). _____ _____

Exercise 2: Underline the correct word choice in each sentence below. In the blank, write **N** for noun, **Adj** for adjective, and **V** for verb to tell how the word is used in the sentence.

11. The junior high (principal, principle) spoke with several students about their schedules. _____
12. The (affects, effects) of the earthquake have left the population in need of shelter and food. _____
13. The small children were most (affected, effected) by the frightening storm. _____
14. One scientific (principal, principle) that was emphasized was the law of gravity. _____
15. The (principal, principle) member of the committee visited our classroom to ask for our opinion. _____
16. The new governor has (affected, effected) better policies within the highway department. _____

Exercise 3: Underline the correct verb choice in each sentence below. In the blank, write **DO** if the verb has a direct object and **No DO** if it doesn't.

17. James is (sitting, setting) in the swing on the porch. _____
18. My uncle is (laying, lying) carpet on weekends for an extra job. _____
19. The dough for the homemade bread has (raised, risen) in the pan. _____
20. The artists have (set, sat) their supplies on the tables in the classroom. _____
21. Several dogs (lay, laid) in the doorway to the barn. _____
22. Three sleepy children (raised, rose) early before breakfast. _____
23. Grandpa has (raised, risen) the shelf for Grandma. _____
24. The beached whale had (laid, lain) on the shore for several days. _____
25. We are (setting, sitting) in our seats at the top of the stadium. _____

Exercise 4: Underline the correct verb choice in each sentence below.

26. We (was, were) helping my cousin feed his cows hay from the barn.
27. He (did, done) his chores every afternoon after school.
28. You (was, were) not on the list to get a refund.
29. I have (come, came) to pick up my father's paycheck.
30. Those youngsters had (gone, went) to the movies twice last week.

CHAPTER 31 LESSON 2

Guidelines for Writing Assignment #36: My Progress in English for the Year _____

1. Write an evaluation of your progress in English for this school year.
2. Reflect on your ability, knowledge level, and self-confidence at the beginning of the school year and compare it to what you are able to do now.
3. Think about the difference in your pretest and posttest scores.
4. Compare earlier writing pieces to recent writing pieces.
5. Compare earlier journal entries to later journal entries.
6. Include at least three things that have left a lasting impression on you in your study of English this year.
7. Conclude by telling two things:
   > How your progress in English has affected other subject areas.
   > What your parents think of your progress.

Guidelines for Writing Assignment #37: An Evaluation of My Goals

1. Look back at your long-term and short-term goals that you set at the beginning of the school year.
2. If your long-term and short-term goals are not available, your teacher will read to you the section on setting goals so you can write these goals now. (It is very important that you end the school year with a set of goals so you will know what things to do or not to do next year.)
3. Write an evaluation of whether or not you accomplished your goals during this school year.
4. Include in your evaluation the reasons why you did or did not accomplish your goals.
5. If your goals were not met, tell what you will do differently next year.
6. Include information about whether you made goals for your other subjects and what the results were.
7. Remember, goals are a part of your "cause and effect" situations as you go through life. Decide the direction you want your life to take and do the planning and work necessary to get there.

CHAPTER 31 LESSON 2 SKILL TEST B

Exercise 1: Underline the correct adjective or adverb choice in each sentence below. Write **Adj** or **Adv** and the word it modifies in the blanks at the end.

1. The kindergartners listened (good, well) during story time. _____ _____
2. My aunt felt (bad, badly) about running out of cake at the wedding. _____ _____
3. Several of the young authors wrote (good, well) stories for our collection. _____ _____
4. We did (bad, badly) on Mrs. Green's science test last week. _____ _____
5. Our mother looks (good, well) in her new hairstyle. _____ _____
6. I am (sure, surely) you will do a great job on your project. _____ _____
7. Those dogs have (sure, surely) eaten all their dog food by now. _____ _____
8. Most of the stolen jewelry contained (real, really) gems. _____ _____
9. I couldn't wait for some (real, really) spicy hot sauce from Taco Tom's. _____ _____
10. My baby brother had a (bad, badly) earache last night. _____ _____

Exercise 2: Underline the correct word choice in each sentence below. In the blank, write **N** for noun, **Adj** for adjective, and **V** for verb to tell how the word is used in the sentence.

11. A (principal, principle) part of the proposal includes a raise in taxes. _____
12. One (affect, effect) of the parent conference was improved study habits. _____
13. The voters were (affected, effected) by the candidate's speech. _____
14. The (principal, principle) of the new school has made a decision about new computer equipment. ____
15. The (principals, principles) of business law were discussed during the education conference. ____
16. Our present chairman (affected, effected) stricter rules for our committee. _____

Exercise 3: Underline the correct verb choice in each sentence below. In the blank, write **DO** if the verb has a direct object and **No DO** if it does not have a direct object.

17. Right now, several sacks of fertilizer (lay, lie) on the dock to be loaded. _____
18. Volunteers from the audience (raise, rise) their hands to play the games. _____
19. New sprouts are (raising, rising) from the ground in the garden. _____
20. Grandma's new chickens (lay, laid) colored eggs! _____
21. Please (set, sit) your painting equipment in the carport. _____
22. Our old parrot (sat, set) on his perch talking to our visitors. _____
23. Jason's wet clothes are (lying, laying) on the floor in the bathroom! _____
24. My little sister (lays, lies) her head on my pillow every night. _____
25. Two hundred soldiers (lay, laid) in the grave after the ground battle. _____

Exercise 4: Underline the correct verb choice in each sentence below.

26. The assembly workers have (did, done) a good job of meeting their quotas this month.
27. Charles has (came, come) to visit us every day this week.
28. You (was, were) able to hear the weather report on the radio.
29. I already (did, done) my report in the library.
30. Everyone has (gone, went) to the lake this weekend except me!

CHAPTER 31 LESSONS 3-4

Guidelines for Writing Assignment #38: My Autobiography

An **autobiography** is the story of a person's life that is written by that person.
A **biography** is the story of a person's life that is written by someone else.

You will write an autobiography by telling about your life. An outline is provided below to help guide you.

I. Family
   A. Birth
   B. Parents
   C. Brothers and sisters
   D. Grandparents
   E. Most influential family member

II. Family life
   A. Chores and responsibilities
   B. How we celebrate special holidays
   C. Family vacations
   D. Special things about my family
   E. My goals and ambitions

III. School days
   A. Friends
   B. Teachers
   C. Best and worst subjects
   D. Special things about school
   E. My goals and ambitions

IV. Special interests
   A. Hobbies
   B. My achievements
   C. My likes and dislikes
   D. Other
   E. My goals and ambitions
   F. The other most influential person in my life

CHAPTER 31 LESSON 5

About Fairy Tales

Fairy tales have been around for a long time. They are always fun to read or hear told. After reading or hearing several, we find that some of them are somewhat predictable because certain elements appear again and again in different stories.

Below are some predictable elements found in fairy tales. Certainly, there are some fairy tales that do not have all, or perhaps any, of these elements. But many of them do. Read these elements carefully.

Predictable Elements of Fairy Tales

1. The youngest, poorest, ugliest, or most mistreated (or even all four of these at once) person becomes the hero/heroine, usually by proving him/herself wisest or most honorable.

2. Something or someone has to be won, attained, solved, or retrieved. (This can be anything from a fair maiden to a cup of water.)

3. A series of ordeals or accomplishments is attempted by the hero to prove himself.

4. Sometimes talking beasts or supernatural aid helps or hinders the hero.

5. Warnings or cautions may be given to the hero. (He often ignores or forgets these, much to his dismay later.)

6. Repetition of words, phrases, clauses, or even whole sentences may be used for the effect this repetition creates.

7. A happy ending usually occurs, but it can include death to the villains.

CHAPTER 31 LESSON 5

The fairy tale to follow, "The Story of the Golden Bird," is an adaptation of a story by the Brothers Grimm. Shortly, you will read this story. First, read the worksheet below. You will write the answers to items on this worksheet on your notebook paper after you have read the story. You may look back at the story as you answer these questions.

Questions on *The Story of the Golden Bird*

1. What character in the story fulfills Element #1?

2. Name the three things (or persons) that have to be recovered or won by the hero.

3. Name the ordeal that the hero must go through (task he must perform) to win the hand of the Beautiful Princess.

4. Who (or what) fulfills Element #4?

5. A. What three warnings does the hero ignore when he must retrieve the three things or people?

   B. What two warnings does the hero ignore after he refuses to kill the fox?

6. Find an example of the use of repetition for effect in the story.

7. Explain:

   A. How the ending is happy.

   B. What villains die.

CHAPTER 31 LESSON 5

The Story of the Golden Bird
Adapted from Grimm's Fairy Tales

Once upon a time, in a great and majestic castle, lived a King who owned a Golden Apple Tree. Every morning the King sent his servant to count the golden apples on the tree as they were ripening. One morning the King's servant returned with the message that one of the golden apples was missing. It had apparently been stolen in the night.

The King was deeply grieved, and his eldest son, a favorite with his father, agreed to watch the tree the next night and see what was happening. At midnight, in spite of all he could do, he fell asleep, and the next morning another apple was missing.

The next night, the King's second son, also the pride of his father, took up his watch at the tree. Alas, he too fell asleep at midnight, and the next morning still another golden apple was gone.

Now the King had one other son, and he was the youngest, but the King had never considered him to be of much worth. The young man begged to keep watch also, but the King was reluctant, feeling he could do no better than the two eldest sons. Finally, he agreed to the youngest son's pleadings.

That night the youth found himself very sleepy just before midnight, but he did not let sleep overcome him, and at midnight he heard a noise in the golden apple tree. It was a Golden Bird, with beautiful golden feathers, and the bird had just taken another apple. The youngest son shot an arrow at him. The bird flew, but the arrow grazed its plumage, and one of its golden feathers dropped at the youngest son's feet.

He took the feather to his father, who was both delighted and amazed at this turn of events. The King was so entranced with the idea of a Golden Bird that he determined to have the whole bird. Accordingly, the eldest son was given the chance to recover the bird, and he left on his quest the next day, feeling confident that he would succeed in his assignment. As he came to the edge of a wood, he saw a fox sitting quietly, watching him. He drew his bow and was about to shoot him when, suddenly, the fox spoke.

"Do not shoot me, and I will give you good counsel. You are on your way to find the Golden Bird. Soon you will come to the Village of Two Inns. One of its two inns will be filled with song and merriment. The other will be somber and ill-looking. If you are wise, you will stay in the somber, ill-looking inn."

"What a foolish creature," thought the eldest son, and he raised his bow again and fired at the fox. But the fox spread his tail and darted into the woods.

Sure enough, the son came to the Village of Two Inns; and one looked fair with singing and dancing, and the other appeared somber and ill-looking. The son chose the merry inn and, soon forgetting his quest, remained at the inn.

When his brother did not return, the second son likewise set off to find the Golden Bird. He too met the fox who gave him the same counsel, which he, like his elder brother, did not follow. In fact, he soon joined his brother at the jolly inn.

When neither of the elder brothers returned, the youngest son petitioned his father to allow him to take up the quest for the Golden Bird.

CHAPTER 31 LESSON 5

The Story of the Golden Bird
Adapted from Grimm's Fairy Tales
Continued

"What can you do?" complained his father. "You are but my youngest son and not likely even to find your way back."

But the youngest son begged and pleaded, and, at last, his father sent him out, expecting never to see him again.

When he came to the woods, the same fox met him with his same wise counsel. However, the youngest son listened to the advice and assured the fox that he would never harm him, but would follow his instructions. At this assurance, the fox spread his tail wide and invited the youth to seat himself upon it, and he would make light his journey to the village. The youngest son hopped aboard and away over hill and dale they went, with the wind whistling past them.

At the village, the youngest son chose the somber, ill-looking inn and spent the night there, arising the next morning feeling refreshed and ready to continue his search.

At a good distance from the village, he met the fox again, who said, "You are indeed on the right path, and if you follow it straight ahead, you will come to a castle before which lies an entire company of armed men; but pay them no heed, for they are all sleeping soundly. Pass by them and enter the castle. Go down the great hall, and at its end, you will find a room in which two cages are hanging. One is an elaborate Golden Cage that is empty. The other is a plain wooden cage in which you will find the Golden Bird. No matter how much you desire it, do not take the Golden Bird out of the plain wooden cage and put it in the elaborate Golden Cage, or you will not fare so well."

The fox then stretched out his tail, the youth hopped aboard, and over hill and dale they went, with the wind whistling past them.

They arrived at the castle, and it was just as the fox had said. The company of armed men lay sleeping. The youth entered the castle, went down the great hall, and found the Golden Bird hanging in the plain wooden cage. As he started to take the wooden cage, he saw the elaborate Golden Cage. It was truly a spectacular device, and he found himself longing to put the creature in it and take both bird and cage. At length he succumbed to the temptation. He took the Golden Bird out of the plain wooden cage and put it into the elaborate Golden Cage. Just as he closed the cage door, the bird gave a sharp cry. The company of armed men awoke, stormed the great hall, and arrested the young son. He was taken to court and sentenced to die.

However, the King of the castle agreed to spare his life on one condition: He must bring to the King the Golden Horse that was faster than the wind. As a result, the King would reward him with the Golden Bird.

The youth was glad to still be alive, but where was he to find the Golden Horse? Just then he looked up, and there sat the fox again.

The fox said, "You did not heed my counsel, but I will still help you. Go straight down this path, and you will come to a palace. Go to the Royal Stables, and there you will find the Golden Horse. All the grooms will be sleeping nearby, but pay them no attention. Just do as I say. Saddle the horse with the saddle of wood and leather. Do not saddle him with the Golden Saddle nearby, or you will not fare so well."

CHAPTER 31 LESSON 5

The Story of the Golden Bird
Adapted from Grimm's Fairy Tales
Continued

At this, the fox stretched out his tail, the young man hopped aboard, and over hill and dale they went, with the wind whistling past them.

Everything was just as the fox had said. The young man walked past the sleeping grooms and was about to saddle the horse with the saddle of wood and leather, when he spied the Golden Saddle nearby. It was so beautiful that he felt compelled to saddle the horse with it. No sooner had he done so than the horse began to neigh loudly. The sleeping grooms awoke, and they carried him to the magistrate. He was taken to court where he was sentenced to die. However, the King of the palace agreed to spare his life if he would but bring back to him the Princess of the Golden Castle. He also promised to give the youth the Golden Horse as a reward.

The youngest son set out sadly, for where was he to find the Golden Castle? Fortunately, he soon happened upon the fox.

The fox said, "This road will take you to the Golden Castle, where you will find the Beautiful Princess. It will be evening when you reach the Golden Castle, and the Beautiful Princess will be on her way to bathe in the Royal Bathing House. Just before she enters it, rush up to her and kiss her. She will follow you anywhere, and you can take her away. But by no means must you allow her to bid her parents farewell or you will not fare so well."

The fox stretched out his tail, the youngest son hopped aboard, and over hill and dale they went, with the wind whistling past them.

At the Golden Castle it was just as the fox had said. As the beautiful princess came to the Royal Bathing House, the youngest son rushed out and kissed her, and she was willing to follow him anywhere. However, she begged to go and bid her parents farewell. At first, he refused her request, but as she began to weep profusely and fall down at his feet imploring him, he relented. No sooner had the Beautiful Princess entered the Golden Castle than he was thrown into a dungeon.

The king came to him the next day and agreed to spare his life under one condition: He must remove the giant hill nearby that blocked the king's view, and he must do it in eight days or he would die. His reward for performing this task was the hand of the king's daughter.

For seven long days the youngest son labored, attempting to dig and shovel the giant hill away. But at the end of the seventh day, he threw himself down in despair, knowing that he could not accomplish the task. At this the fox appeared.

The fox said, "I should do nothing for you, for you have completely disregarded my counsel on several occasions. In spite of the fact that you are undeserving, I desire to help you. Lie down and sleep; I will finish the task."

CHAPTER 31 LESSON 5

The Story of the Golden Bird
Adapted from Grimm's Fairy Tales
Continued

When the youngest son awoke on the eighth day, the giant hill was completely gone. He was filled with great joy and ran to tell the king. The king kept his promise and gave the youth his daughter, the Princess of the Golden Castle. With great happiness, the youngest son set out with her to return to his father's kingdom.

Before they had gone far, they met the fox. He told them that in order to obtain the Horse, they should go back to the king who had promised the Golden Horse to the youngest son, should he retrieve the Princess of the Golden Castle. The fox instructed the youth to appear to return the princess. Thereby, he would be given the Golden Horse. He was to mount the Horse and ride about the company, bidding them farewell with the shake of the hand of each. Last, he was to take the hand of the Princess, swing her up behind him, and ride away. No one could overtake them, because the Golden Horse was faster than the wind.

The youngest son followed the fox's instructions perfectly and carried off the Princess. Now he had both the Princess of the Golden Castle and the Golden Horse. The fox who was now accompanying them explained how the youngest son could gain possession of the Golden Bird. He said that he would take care of the Princess. The youth was to ride to the king who had promised him the Golden Bird in return for the Golden Horse. When the youth returned with the Golden Horse, there would be great joy, and the king would bring out the Golden Bird as his reward. The youth was to take the Golden Bird and again ride away on the Golden Horse. No one would be able to overtake him, because the Golden Horse was faster than the wind.

As usual, the fox's plan was a success. Then the fox said to the youngest son, "I have done much for you; now you must do much for me. You must kill me with your bow and arrow and then chop off my head and my feet."

The youngest son was horrified. He refused, for he said, "After all you have done for me, what kind of repayment would such an act be?"

At that, the fox said farewell, but he gave his two last warnings: "Buy no flesh from the hangman, and do not sit on the edge of a well."

The young man was touched by the fox's continued concern for him, but he could not understand such peculiar cautions and promptly forgot the advice. That afternoon he and the Princess arrived in the Village of the Two Inns. As they entered the town, all was astir, and they saw that there was about to be a hanging of two men in the village square. Now it so happened that these two men were the youngest son's two brothers. They had committed such evil acts that they were being executed. In love and pity for his own flesh, the youth offered to redeem their lives with money.

The people were willing to free them for money, but they could not understand why anyone should be willing to set such wicked men free. The youngest son paid the debt, and, taking his brothers and the Princess, set out for home, along with the Golden Horse and the Golden Bird.

CHAPTER 31 LESSON 5

The Story of the Golden Bird
Adapted from Grimm's Fairy Tales
Continued

It was a hot day as they traveled, and seeing a well, they decided to have a drink. Without a thought for the fox's advice, the youngest son sat on the edge of the well to rest. His wicked brothers, with one accord, pushed him headlong into the well and made off with the Princess, the Golden Horse, and the Golden Bird.

They threatened the Princess with death if she revealed their wickedness to their father, the King. When they arrived at home, they brought their ill-gotten treasures to him, and there was great rejoicing. However, for reasons the King could not understand, the Golden Horse would eat no hay, the Golden Bird would sing no song, and the Princess of the Golden Castle would only sit and weep.

But the youngest son was still alive! The well had been dry and moss-filled; therefore, he was unhurt, but he could not climb out, for the walls were damp and slick. Suddenly, he heard a stirring above him, and who should look down upon him but the fox. At once the creature leaped down to his friend and scolded him for not heeding the caution he had given the youth about buying no flesh from the hangman and sitting on the edge of a well. The youth was filled with grief and could but agree with the fox.

Then the fox said, "Yet again I shall help you; grasp my tail." With that, the youngest son grabbed the fox's tail, and the fox gave a great leap and landed both of them on solid ground outside the well.

Again the fox cautioned him, "Your brothers have even yet set armed watchers just outside this wood, lest you somehow escape. The watchers are assigned to kill any person fitting your description. So," he continued, "you must disguise yourself. Look to that peasant over there."

The youth saw an old beggar with ragged and torn clothes in a great, dusty gray hood. He soon exchanged clothes with the beggar and made his way to his father's castle.

Although no one recognized him, the Golden Horse at once began to eat his hay, the Golden Bird began to sing a glorious song, and the Princess leaped up in joy and said, "I feel as if my bridegroom has arrived!" Her courage restored, she took the King aside and told him the real story of his youngest son's bravery and the truth of what had befallen him.

The king commanded all the people in the castle to pass before him, and as the ragged beggar passed, the Princess went to him and kissed him. The King ordered the two wicked brothers to be put to death. The youngest son married the Princess of the Golden Castle immediately. His father, the King, saw his true worth and declared him the true heir to the throne.

One day as the youngest son was walking through the forest with his beautiful bride, the fox appeared again and said, "I have helped you to gain everything your heart has desired; will you not help me by doing what I have asked you to do? I beg of you to shoot me dead and cut off my head and feet."

The young man felt he must do the fox's bidding, even though it was against everything within him. No sooner had he done such a thing than the fox was changed into a handsome young man, none other than the brother of the Princess of the Golden Castle who had been enchanted by an evil magician. Now the youngest son and his bride and her beloved brother were free to live happily ever after.

CHAPTER 32 LESSON 1

Your Schedule for Writing a Fairy Tale in Lesson 1

Lesson 1
1. Read the predictable elements of fairy tales in Lesson 4 again.
2. Decide whether to write an original fairy tale or to write an adaptation of an existing fairy tale.
   (*If you choose to write an adaptation of an existing fairy tale, read several existing fairy tales to help you decide which fairy tale to use.*)
3. Brainstorm for ideas about your chosen fairy tale.
4. Organize your ideas into a rough draft outline to get an idea of the order in which you will write your fairy tale.
5. Brainstorm for a possible title for your fairy tale.

CHAPTER 32 LESSON 2-5

Your Schedule for Writing a Fairy Tale in Lessons 2-5

Lesson 2
Write the rough draft for your fairy tale.

Lesson 3
Edit your fairy tale with an editing partner.
(You are, of course, responsible for the final edit of your fairy tale.)
Write a final paper from the rough draft.
Illustrate your fairy tale.

Lesson 4
Begin oral presentations of fairy tales.

Lesson 5
Finish oral presentations of fairy tales.

CHAPTER 33 LESSON 1

THE EAGLE

He clasps the crag with crooked hands;
Close to the sun in lonely lands,
Ringed with the azure world, he stands.

The wrinkled sea beneath him crawls;
He watches from his mountain walls,
And like a thunderbolt he falls.

-Alfred, Lord Tennyson

The poem above, "The Eagle," was written by the famous British poet, Alfred, Lord Tennyson, who lived from 1809 to 1892. In 1850, he was named the official poet of England. (This title is called "Poet Laureate.")

Although "The Eagle" is a short work, it is a very popular poem, probably due to its sharp imagery that paints a powerful word picture of the majestic eagle, first as he sits high on his perch and then as he drops from the sky.

The poem is written in two three-line stanzas, or triplets, as they are called. It illustrates Tennyson's ability to say much in a few words. If you admire Tennyson's work, you may wonder if you would like writing poetry. Evidently Tennyson enjoyed writing poetry, since he began before he was ten years old. You can enjoy it, too. Poetry is "power in your pen" and gives you a chance to express what you feel deep inside. Such writing is important.

There are many different ways to organize the lines of a poem. A good form with which you can begin writing poetry is a three-line form somewhat like Tennyson's and yet different. It is called the *haiku*. Haiku is a Japanese verse form that is fun to write. Below is an example of haiku written by a seventh grade student.

THE SPOTTED FAWN

The spots on a fawn,
Dots of white on a brown back,
Snowflakes on a deer.

-Bethany Raines

Characteristics of Haiku

Notice the special features of haiku listed below. Most traditional haiku written today have these eight features.

1. Haiku has only three lines.
2. Haiku does not rhyme.
3. The subject of the poem is usually something in nature.
4. The whole haiku has a total of 17 syllables.
5. The first line has 5 syllables.
6. The second line has 7 syllables.
7. The third line has 5 syllables.
8. The haiku creates one clear image, or word picture.

CHAPTER 33 LESSON 1

Look at two more examples of haiku. Study them to see how many of the eight characteristics of haiku they contain.

HAIKU #1
Canadian geese, a long, ragged V, honking, in the sky above. *-Teddie Raines*

HAIKU #2
The angry storm tore The white shawl off the dogwood, Leaving its arms bare. *-Teddie Raines*

Notice that Haiku #1 is not a complete sentence. Haiku #2 is a complete sentence. Both are good haiku. Your haiku can be written either way. Also, notice that in Haiku #1, only the first word in the haiku is capitalized. In Haiku #2, the first word in each line is capitalized. It does not matter whether or not your haiku is a complete sentence. Also, you may capitalize whichever way you choose.

Before you write your haiku, compare Example A and Haiku #2 below. Which is the most effective as a poem? Haiku #2 is, of course. Example A has the form of a haiku, but it is not real poetry. In Example A, the three lines have a total of 17 syllables, and the lines contain 5-7-5 syllables. Also, even though the lines in Example A have the same meaning as Haiku #2, they simply report what has happened as if they were part of a newspaper account.

EXAMPLE A
A very strong storm blew the dogwood petals off and left the tree bare.

HAIKU #2
The angry storm tore The white shawl off the dogwood, Leaving its arms bare.

On the other hand, Haiku #2 uses personification and imagery to create a clear word picture of this event in nature. The storm is given human features such as the emotion of anger, the dogwood has "arms," and the white flowers of the dogwood are portrayed as a white shawl. Haiku #2 takes an ordinary event in nature and states it in a fresh, new way.

Whenever you write a haiku, you can use the *Steps for Writing Haiku* on the next page to guide you.

CHAPTER 33 LESSON 1

STEPS FOR WRITING HAIKU

1. Select something in nature that appeals to you. Narrow your subject down to a single specific idea about your subject.

   Example: Subject - inchworm   Specific idea: the way an inchworm moves

2. Write the subject down in noun form, possibly with an adjective or two. *
   Example: an inchworm

3. Count the syllables to see if you have enough to meet the five syllable requirement for your first line.
   Example: /an/ inch/worm/

           1   2   3   *(Since your first line needs to be five syllables, you are two syllables short.)*

4. If necessary, add another adjective or a verb that has the number of syllables you still need for the first line.
   Example: /a/ /lit/tle/ inch/worm/

           1   2 3   4   5   *(Now you have the five syllables for your first line.)*

5. For the second line, think of something special about your subject. You might want to use a verb or two to tell the action or a few words to describe what is special about the subject. Try to use imagery or personification to create a vivid mental picture. Remember, you need 7 syllables, and your end word should **not** rhyme with the end word in the first line. Add extra modifiers as needed to achieve the desired 7 syllables.
   Example: /arch/ing /and/ /stretch/ing a/long/
         1   2   3   4   5 6 7

6. For the last line, try to give your haiku an effective conclusion by adding an unusual ending to the specific idea you have developed. Remember, you need 5 syllables and your words should **not** rhyme.
   Example: /the/ /miles/ /of/ /my/ /arm/
         1   2   3   4   5

7. Check your completed haiku to be sure it has all 8 characteristics of a haiku.

   A little inchworm,
   Arching and stretching along
   The miles of my arm.

8. Decide how you want to capitalize the lines of your haiku. Put a period at the end of the last line and commas where they are needed.

9. If you wish, give your haiku a title.

*Remember this: Your haiku does not *always* have to start with a noun phrase. It can begin with a participle, an adjective, an adverb, or whatever YOU choose. Just make sure to choose words that tell about the single specific idea you are trying to portray. You can be as creative as you like.

Assignment

Use the *Characteristics of Haiku* and the *Steps for Writing Haiku* in this lesson to write your own haiku. Try writing your first haiku by beginning with a noun phrase like the example about the inchworm in the *Steps for Writing Haiku*. Illustrate your haiku.

Sharetime

Share your illustrated haiku with the class.

CHAPTER 33 LESSONS 2-5

Assignment

Use the *Characteristics of Haiku* and the *Steps for Writing Haiku* in this lesson to write two or three more haiku. Write one haiku by beginning with a noun phrase like the sample haiku about the inchworm in the *Steps for Writing Haiku*. Then write one or two more haiku by beginning them with participles, adjectives, adverbs, or verbs. Then select your best one to share with the class. Illustrate and display it in the classroom.

Look at the schedule below to guide your lessons for the rest of Chapter 33.

Your Schedule for Writing Haiku and Giving Oral Presentations in Chapter 33

Chapter 33 Lesson 2

Write one haiku following the example in the *Steps for Writing Haiku*. Write one or two haiku using a different beginning other than a noun phrase.
Edit your poems with an editing partner.
Do a final edit of your poems.
Choose one haiku to illustrate.

Chapter 33 Lesson 3

Give oral presentations of haiku.

Chapter 33 Lesson 4-5

Give oral presentations of autobiographies.

STUDENT REFERENCE
Definition Jingles for Chapter 1

Nyms Jingle
(Chapter I, Lesson 2)

Homonyms **sound** the same,
Like *to* and *too* and *two*.
Synonyms mean the **same,**
Like *small* and *little* do.
Antonyms are **opposites,**
Like *over* and *under* and *old* and *new.*
So, if you are in doubt, check it out;
Do what all good writers do.
Consult the dictionary and thesaurus
To help **your** writing, Dude!

Sentence Jingle
(Chapter 1, Lesson 5)

A sentence, sentence, sentence
Is complete, complete, complete
When 5 simple rules
It meets, meets, meets.

It has a subject, subject, subject
And a verb, verb, verb.
It makes sense, sense, sense
With every word, word, word.

Add a capital letter, letter,
And an end mark, mark.
Now our sentence has all its parts!

REMEMBER
Subject, Verb, Com-plete sense,
Capital letter, and an end mark, too.
Our sentence is complete,
And now we're through!

STUDENT REFERENCE
Definition Jingles for Chapter 2

Noun Jingle
(Chapter 2, Lesson 1)

It's a noun jingle, my friend.
Shake it to the left,
Shake it to the right,
Find a noun and then recite:
A noun names a person;
A noun names a thing;
A noun names a person,
Place, or thing.
And sometimes an idea.
Person, Place, / Thing, Idea,
Person, Place / Thing, Idea.
So, shake it to the left,
Shake it to the right,
Find those nouns
And feel just right!

Verb Jingle
(Chapter 2, Lesson 1)

A verb, a verb. What is a verb?
Haven't you heard?
There are two kinds of verbs:
The action verb and the linking verb.

The action verb shows a state of action,
Like **stand** and **sit** and **smile**.
The action verb is always doing
Because it tells what the subject does.
We **stand**! We **sit**! We **smile**!

The linking verb is a state of being,
Like **am, is, are, was**, and **were,**
Look, become, grows, and **feels.**
A linking verb shows no action
Because it tells what the subject is.
He **is** a *clown.* *He* **looks** *funny.*

Adverb Jingle
(Chapter 2, Lesson 1)

An adverb modifies a verb, adjective, or another adverb.
An adverb asks *How? When? Where? Why? Under what condition? and To what degree?*
To find an adverb: **Go, Ask, Get.**
Where do I **go**? To a verb, adjective, or another adverb.
What do I **ask**? How? When? Where? Why?
Under What Condition? and To What Degree?
What do I **get**? An ADVERB! (Clap) That's what!

Adjective Jingle
(Chapter 2, Lesson 1)

An adjective modifies a noun or pronoun.
An adjective asks *What kind? Which one? How many*?
To find an adjective: **Go, Ask, Get.**
Where do I **go**? To a noun or pronoun.
What do I **ask**? What kind? Which one? How many?
What do I **get**? An ADJECTIVE! (Clap)
That's what!

STUDENT REFERENCE
Definition Jingles for Chapter 3

Preposition Jingle (Chapter 3, Lesson 1)	**Object of the Prep Jingle** (Chapter 3, Lesson 1)	**Prepositional Phrase Jingle** (Chapter 3, Lesson 1)
A PREP PREP PREPOSITION Is a special group of words That connects a NOUN, NOUN, NOUN Or a PRO PRO PRONOUN To the rest of the sentence.	Dum De Dum Dum! An O-P is an N-O-U-N or a P-R-O After the P-R-E-P In an S-E-N-T-E-N-C-E. Dum De Dum Dum - DONE!!	I've been working with PREPOSITIONS 'Til I can work no more. They just keep connecting their OBJECTS To the rest of the sentence before. When I put them all together, The PREP and its NOUN or PRO, I get a PREPOSITIONAL PHRASE That could cause my mind to blow!

PREPOSITION FLOW JINGLE
(Chapter 3, Lesson 1)

1. **Preposition, Preposition Starting with an A.** (Fast) aboard, about, above, across, after, against, (Slow) along, among, around, at.	2. **Preposition, Preposition Starting with a B.** (Fast) before, behind, below, beneath, beside, between, (Slow) beyond, but, by.	3. **Preposition, Preposition Starting with a D.** down (slow & long), during (snappy),
4. **Preposition, Preposition Don't go away. Go to the middle And see what we say. E-F-I and L-N-O** except, for, from, in, inside, into, like, near, of, off, on, out, outside, over.	5. **Preposition, Preposition Almost through. Start with P and end with W.** past, since, through, throughout, to, toward, under, underneath, until, up, upon, with, within, without.	6. **Preposition, Preposition Easy as can be. We're all finished, And aren't you pleased? We've just recited All 49 of these.**

Noun Job Jingle
(Chapter 3, Lesson 2)

Nouns will give you a run for your money.
They do so many jobs
That it's not even funny.
A noun (person, place, or thing)
Is very appealing!
But it's the noun jobs
That make nouns so revealing.

To find the nouns in a sentence,
Go to their jobs, go to their jobs.
Nouns do the objective jobs:
They're the IO, DO, OC, and OP jobs;
And nouns do subjective jobs:
They're the SN, PN, and PrN jobs.
Jobs, Jobs, Noun Jobs! Yea!

STUDENT REFERENCE
Definition Jingles for Chapter 4

Pronoun Jingle
(Chapter 4, Lesson 1)

These little pronouns,
Hanging around,
Take the place of all the nouns.
With a smile and a nod and a
Twinkle of your eye,
Give those pronouns a big high
Five! Yea!

Subject Pronoun Jingle
(Chapter 4, Lesson 1)

There are seven subject pronouns
That are easy as can be:
I and we,   (clap twice)
He and she,   (clap twice)
It and they and you.   (clap three)

Object Pronoun Jingle
(Chapter 4, Lesson 1)

There are seven object pronouns
That are easy as can be:
Me and us,   (clap twice)
Him and her,   (clap twice)
It and them and you.   (clap three)

Definition Jingle for Chapter 5

Possessive Pronoun Jingle
(Chapter 5, Lesson 1)

There are seven possessive pronouns
That are easy as can be:
My and our,   (clap twice)
His and her,   (clap twice)
Its and their and your. (clap three times)

STUDENT REFERENCE
Definition Jingle for Chapter 5
(Chapter 5, Lesson 1)

VERB CHART FOR IRREGULAR VERBS

PRESENT	PAST	PAST PARTICIPLE		PRESENT PARTICIPLE	
become	became	(has)	become	(is)	becoming
begin	began	(has)	begun	(is)	beginning
blow	blew	(has)	blown	(is)	blowing
break	broke	(has)	broken	(is)	breaking
bring	brought	(has)	brought	(is)	bringing
burst	burst	(has)	burst	(is)	bursting
buy	bought	(has)	bought	(is)	buying
choose	chose	(has)	chosen	(is)	choosing
come	came	(has)	come	(is)	coming
do	did	(has)	done	(is)	doing
drink	drank	(has)	drunk	(is)	drinking
drive	drove	(has)	driven	(is)	driving
eat	ate	(has)	eaten	(is)	eating
fall	fell	(has)	fallen	(is)	falling
fly	flew	(has)	flown	(is)	flying
freeze	froze	(has)	frozen	(is)	freezing
give	gave	(has)	given	(is)	giving
go	went	(has)	gone	(is)	going
grow	grew	(has)	grown	(is)	growing
know	knew	(has)	known	(is)	knowing
lie	lay	(has)	lain	(is)	lying
lay	laid	(has)	laid	(is)	laying
make	made	(has)	made	(is)	making
ring	rang	(has)	rung	(is)	ringing
rise	rose	(has)	risen	(is)	rising
run	ran	(has)	run	(is)	running
see	saw	(has)	seen	(is)	seeing
sell	sold	(has)	sold	(is)	selling
sing	sang	(has)	sung	(is)	singing
sink	sank	(has)	sunk	(is)	sinking
set	set	(has)	set	(is)	setting
sit	sat	(has)	sat	(is)	sitting
shoot	shot	(has)	shot	(is)	shooting
swim	swam	(has)	swum	(is)	swimming
take	took	(has)	taken	(is)	taking
tell	told	(has)	told	(is)	telling
throw	threw	(has)	thrown	(is)	throwing
write	wrote	(has)	written	(is)	writing

VERB CHART FOR REGULAR VERBS

PRESENT	PAST	PAST PARTICIPLE	PRESENT PARTICIPLE
call	called	(has) called	(is) calling
play	played	(has) played	(is) playing
talk	talked	(has) talked	(is) talking
cry	cried	(has) cried	(is) crying
hop	hopped	(has) hopped	(is) hopping

STUDENT REFERENCE
Definition Jingle for Chapter 6

The 23 Helping Verbs Of the Mean, Lean Verb Machine Jingle
(Chapter 6, Lesson 1)

These 23 helping verbs will be on my test.
I gotta remember them, so I can do my best.
I'll start out with 8 and finish with 15;
Just call me the mean, lean, verb machine.

There are the 8 **be** verbs that are easy as can be:
    am, is, are --was and were,
    am, is, are --was and were,
    am, is, are --was and were,
    be, being, and been.
All together now, the 8 **be** verbs:
am, is are -- was and were -- be, being, and been,
am, is are -- was and were -- be, being, and been.

There're 23 helping verbs, and I've recited only 8.
That leaves fifteen more that I must relate:
    has, have, and had --do, does, and did,
    has, have, and had --do, does, and did,
    might, must, may --might, must, may.

Knowing these verbs will save my grade:
    can and could --would and should,
    can and could --would and should,
    shall and will,
    shall and will.
In record time I did this drill.
I'm the mean, lean verb machine - STILL!

Definition Jingle for Chapter 8

The Eight Parts of Speech Jingle
(Chapter 8, Lesson 1)

How do we learn the 8 parts of speech?
Well, you gotta have a rhythm, and you gotta have a plan.
Noun, verb, and pronoun are the leaders of the band!
Adjective and adverb are the next ones to land.
That only leaves the triplets for this music man:
Preposition, interjection, and conjunction.

Learn the NVP-AA-PIC,
And the 8 parts of speech you will receive.
NVP: noun, verb, pronoun.
AA: adjective and adverb.
PIC: preposition, interjection, and conjunction.
NVP-AA-PIC, NVP-AA-PIC.

Definition Jingle for Chapter 9

Subordinate Conjunction Jingle
(Chapter 9, Lesson 2)

There Are Some Subordinate Conjunctions in the Town

After, Although, As, As much as, Because,
Before, How, If, In order that, Inasmuch as,
Provided, Since, Than, That, Though, Unless,
Until,
When, Where, Whether, (Pause) While.

Definition Jingle for Chapter 10

Direct Object Jingle
(Chapter 10, Lesson 1)

1. A direct object is a noun or pronoun.

2. A direct object completes the meaning of the sentence.

3. A direct object is located after the verb-transitive.

4. To find the direct object, ask WHAT or WHOM after your verb.

STUDENT REFERENCE
Definition Jingle for Chapter 12

Transition Words Jingle
(Chapter 12 Lesson 1)

Listen, comrades, and you shall hear
About transition words
That make your writing smooth and clear.
Transition words are connecting words.
You add them to the beginning
Of sentences and paragraphs
To keep your ideas a-spinning.

These words can clarify, summarize, or emphasize,
Compare or contrast, inform or show time.
Learn them now, and your writing will shine!

Transition, Transition,
For words that SHOW TIME:
first, second, third, before, during and **after,
next, then,** and **finally.**

Transition, Transition,
For words that INFORM:
for example, for instance, in addition, and **as well;
next, another, also, besides,** and **along with.**

Transition, Transition,
For words that CONTRAST:
on the other hand, otherwise, and **however;
although, even though, but, yet, still.**

Transition, Transition,
For words that COMPARE:
as, also, like, and **likewise.**

Transition, Transition,
For words that CLARIFY:
for example, for instance, and **in other words.**

Transition, Transition,
For words that EMPHASIZE:
for this reason, truly, again, and **in fact.**

Transition, Transition
For words that SUMMARIZE:
as a result, therefore, in conclusion, and **last;
to sum it up, all in all, in summary,** and **finally.**

Definition Jingle for Chapter 13

Indirect Object Jingle
(Chapter 13, Lesson 1)

1. An indirect object is a noun or pronoun.

2. An indirect object receives what the direct object names.

3. An indirect object is located between the verb-transitive and the direct object.

4. To find the indirect object ask TO WHOM or FOR WHOM after the direct object.

Definition Jingles for Chapters 16 and 19

Predicate Noun Jingle
(Chapter 16, Lesson 1)

Listen, my comrades, and you shall hear
About predicate nouns from far and near.
No one knows the time or year
That the predicate nouns will appear.
Listen now to all the facts,
So you will know when the **Pred's** are back!
Dum De Dum Dum!
A predicate noun is a special noun in the predicate
That means the same thing as the subject word.
To find a predicate noun, ask *what* or *who*
After a linking verb.

Predicate Adjective Jingle
(Chapter 19, Lesson 1)

Listen, my comrades, and you shall hear
About predicate adjectives from far and near.
No one knows the time or year
That the predicate adjectives will appear.
Listen now to all the facts,
So you will know when the **Pred's** are back!
Dum De Dum Dum!
A predicate adjective is a special adjective in the
Predicate that modifies only the subject word.
To find a predicate adjective, ask *what kind of subject*
After a linking verb.

STUDENT REFERENCE
Definition Jingles for Chapters 22 and 23

Object Complement Jingle (Chapter 22, Lesson 1)
An object complement is also called an objective complement. An objective complement may be an adjective or a noun. An objective complement can easily be found. First, you find the direct object, And then you ask "What?" And an object complement Is what you've got!

Appositive Jingle (Chapter 23, Lesson 1)
Are you POSITIVE about APPOSITIVES? Yes, I'm POSITIVE about APPOSITIVES! I'm positive that an appositive Is a noun; I'm positive that an appositive Follows a noun or pronoun. I'm positive that an appositive Explains the noun or pronoun it follows. And I'm positive that appositives Are sometimes set off by commas; So, I'm POSITIVE about APPOSITIVES!

Definition Jingles for Chapter 24

Regular Verb Jingle (Chapter 24, Lesson 3)
A regular verb, regular verb, regular verb Is a main verb, main verb, main verb That forms the past tense, past tense, past tense With -ED, -D, -T on the end; I said with -ED, -D, -T on the end.

Irregular Verb Jingle (Chapter 24, Lesson 3)
An irregular verb, irregular verb, irregular verb Is a main verb, main verb, main verb That forms the past tense, past tense, past tense With a MIDDLE VOWEL CHANGE; I said - with a MIDDLE VOWEL CHANGE!

Note: Chapter 24, Mighty, Mighty Verb Tense Power Jingle is on the next page.

Definition Jingle for Chapter 29

Clause Jingle (Chapter 29, Lesson 2)		
The Dependent Clause	How the Dependent Clause is Used	The Independent Clause
The Dependent Clause is so wimpy; If left alone, it feels abused. Though it has a VERB and a SUBJECT, As a single part of speech it is used.	The parts of speech it may be used as Are A, A, N, it's plain to see. An Adjective, Adverb, and Noun clause, This wimpy dependent can be.	The Independent Clause is so macho. It flexes its muscles so grand. It has both a VERB and a SUBJECT; Alone it can superbly stand.
Chorus So, tie it on, tie it on, Tie it on to an Indepen. Tie it on, tie it on To an Independent Clause.	**Chorus** So, tie it on, tie it on, Tie it on to an Indepen. Tie it on, tie it on To an Independent Clause.	**Chorus** It can stand, it can stand, It can stand; it's an Indepen. It can stand, it can stand, It's an Independent Clause.

STUDENT REFERENCE
Definition Jingle for Chapter 24

The Mighty, Mighty Verb Tense Power Jingle
(Chapter 24, Lesson 3)

You've gotta have a rhythm, and you've gotta have a rhyme.
You've gotta know the tenses, or it isn't worth a dime.
You need the power-mighty, mighty verb tense power!

Basic Tenses, Basic Tenses, easy to define.
You've gotta know the verbs and how they all combine.
And that's power-mighty, mighty verb tense power!

Helping verbs are crucial since they determine the tense,
But you've gotta pay attention to the main verb ending hints.
And that's power-mighty, mighty verb tense power!

Simple tenses, Simple tenses, easy to make sense.
You know, there's not a helper, except for future tense.
It's just Present, Past, and Future,
Present, Past, and Future,
And the main verb ending hint is as easy as can be:
The past tense verb
Ends in -*ED*!

Perfect tenses, Perfect tenses, a little more advanced.
You've gotta know the helpers if you're gonna have a chance:
has, have, and had / will and shall,
has, have, and had / will and shall.
And the main verb ending hint is as easy as can be:
The main verb perfect tense
Ends in -*ED*!

Progressive form, Progressive form, long and woolly.
You've gotta listen closely to understand it fully:
am, is, are / was and were / be and been / will and shall,
am, is are / was and were / be and been / will and shall.
And the main verb ending hint is as easy as can be:
The main verb ends in an -ING.
No exceptions; it's guaranteed!

Emphatic Form, Emphatic Form, twist around the tongue.
You've gotta stay untangled - so keep it simple, Hon!
do, does, did / do, does, did,
And the main verb ending hint is as easy as can be:
There's no -ED ending or -ING
And there's no future form; it's guaranteed!

You've gotta have a rhythm, and you've gotta have a rhyme.
You've gotta know the tenses to walk the educated line!
Now, you've got the power, mighty, mighty verb tense power.

STUDENT INDEX

Due to the tremendous amount of review of concepts provided, this index lists only the page numbers on which the topic is introduced.

STUDENT INDEX

Due to the tremendous amount of review of concepts provided, this index lists only the page numbers on which the topic is introduced.